Human Resource Management: A Critical Text (3rd Edition)

Human Resource Management:
A Critical Text (3rd Edition)

John Storey

THOMSON

Australia • Canada • Mexico • Singapore • Spain • United Kingdom • United States

Human Resource Management: A Critical Text (3rd Edition)
John Storey

| **Publishing Director** | **Publisher** | **Editorial Assistant** |
| John Yates | Jennifer Pegg | James Clark |

| **Production Editor** | **Manufacturing Manager** | **Marketing Manager** |
| Lucy Mills | Helen Mason | Leo Stanley |

| **Typesetter** | **Production Controller** | **Cover Design** |
| KnowledgeWorks Global Ltd., India | Maeve Healy | Quarto Design |

| **Text Design** | **Printer** | |
| Design Deluxe Ltd., Bath, UK | C&C Offset, China | |

Contents

I Introduction 01

1 Human resource management today: an assessment 03

John Storey

2 The HR function: integration or fragmentation? 21

Raymond Caldwell and John Storey

3 Networked organizations and the negation of HRM? 39

Karen Legge

II Strategic issues 57

4 What is strategic HRM? 59

5 Facing up to the challenges of success: putting 'governance' at the heart of HRM 79

III Core practice areas 95

6 Employee resourcing and talent management 97

List of figures

List of tables

List of contributors

David Bevan—Lecturer, Royal Holloway, University of London, UK

Chris Brewster—Professor of International Human Resource Management, University of Reading Business School, UK

Raymond Caldwell—Reader in Organizational Change, Birkbeck College, London, UK

David Collings—Lecturer in HRM/OB, Management School, University of Sheffield, UK

Annette Cox—Lecturer in Employment Studies, Manchester Business School, University of Manchester, UK

Lee Dyer—Professor of Human Resource Studies, Chairperson of the Department of Human Resource Studies, ILR School, Cornell University, USA

Jeff Ericksen—Assistant Professor, Institute of Labor & Industrial Relations, University of Illinois, USA

Alan Felstead—Research Professor, Cardiff School of Social Sciences, Cardiff University, UK

Paul Iles—Professor of HRD, Leeds Business School, Leeds Metropolitan University, UK

Ian Kessler—University Reader in Employment Relations, Oxford Said Business School, Oxford University, UK

Karen Legge—Professor of Organizational Behaviour, Associate Dean (Academic Policy and Practice), Warwick Business School, University of Warwick, UK

Mick Marchington—Professor of Human Resource Management, Manchester Business School, University of Manchester, UK

Emma Parry—Research Fellow in the Human Resource Research Centre at Cranfield School of Management, UK

Graeme Salaman—Professor of Organization Studies, OU Business School, UK

Hugh Scullion—Professor of International Management, Strathclyde Business School, University of Strathclyde, Cranfield University, UK

Keith Sisson—Emeritus Professor of Industrial Relations, Warwick Business School, University of Warwick, UK

John Storey—Professor of Human Resource Management, OU Business School, UK

Shaun Tyson—Professor of Human Resource Management, Cranfield School of Management, Cranfield University, UK

Preface

This book is designed to meet the needs of advanced students but also to meet the needs of reflective practitioners and consultants. In order to fulfil this mission, the book retains certain fundamental features. When the first edition of this book was published there were few if any full-length treatments of human resource management. Now there are very many. But most of the available books offer standard, textbook-style treatment of the subject. This volume aims to stay true to the original ambition of providing fresh, reflective analysis, commentary and critique by drawing on the expertise of leading authorities in the field. Their original contributions set the agenda for debate rather than simply rehearse past debates.

The origins of this book go back to the publication in 1989 of *New Perspectives on Human Resource Management*. Since then, the volume has been updated through three further editions – in 1995, 2001 and now this current edition. The book has been rewritten in order to keep pace with the dynamic nature of its subject area. The book retains certain defining features: it seeks to provide coverage of the field in a fresh and exploratory way. Many of the chapter authors are not afraid to court controversy. The contributors have strong views and they make their case drawing on empirical research.

But, in addition to this continuity, there are also some new features. In recognition of the growing significance of the use of ICT in the contemporary management of the human resource, there is a new chapter on e-HR (Chapter 13, written by Emma Parry and Shaun Tyson). Another new topic is to be found in Chapter 15 on agility, creativity, innovation and 'dynamic organizations' written by Lee Dyer and Jeff Ericksen. In this latest edition, the regular chapter tracking changes to the HR profession itself is written by Raymond Caldwell (Chapter 2) while Keith Sisson (Chapter 5) switches his attention to a reassessment and reconceptualization of the whole notion of modern employment relations. He makes the case for putting 'governance' at the centre of the analysis. Also in this edition, Karen Legge (Chapter 3) undertakes a novel analysis of the employment implications of the networked organizational form.

Other chapter topics remain the same as in the previous edition – although each of them has been completely rewritten to take account of new developments. The core themes of HRM continue to be covered by the regulator expert contributors to this volume. Critical analysis and the careful scrutiny of received wisdom and popular nostrums remains a distinctive feature throughout the book. A new feature of this latest edition is the inclusion of many more illustrative examples in each chapter.

John Storey

Reviewer acknowledgements

Graham Hollinshead—University of West England
Peter Kidger—University of Salford
Gill Kirton—Queen Mary, University of London
Linda Trenberth—Birkbeck College, University of London

1 Introduction

The purpose of this first part of the book is to set the scene by introducing the idea of human resource management, identifying its origins, describing key developments in its trajectory and analysing the key developments in the function.

There are three chapters in this part. Chapter 1 'Human resource management today: an assessment', written by John Storey, has two main purposes. The first of these is to answer the question: 'What is human resource management?' The second is to identify and assess current issues as well as recent key trends and developments in employment management in its various modes. This assessment covers both theory and practice.

Chapter 2, 'The HR function: integration or fragmentation?' co-authored by Raymond Caldwell and the editor, focuses specifically on the HR/personnel function per se. Not all components of people management are handled solely by HR/personnel specialists. Some (mainly smaller organizations) may not even employ HR specialists at all. But the function merits some close attention because it has a presence in virtually all larger organizations and it employs large numbers of practitioners. This chapter examines what is happening to these specialists and the way their departments are structured and organized. This chapter also focuses on the challenges to the function including developments such as business partnering, the relative power and influence of the function, and trends in outsourcing.

Chapter 3, 'Networked organizations and the negation of HRM?' by Karen Legge focuses on one key aspect of the changes to the function. This aspect is the shift towards networked organizations and the consequent increased importance of interorganizational relations. Legge assesses the costs and benefits of these new organizational forms and the implications they carry for the human resource management function.

Human resource management today: an assessment

John Storey

This first chapter sets the scene for the book by undertaking two tasks. First it asks and seeks to answer the question: what is human resource management? Second, it comments on recent key trends and developments in the realms of theory and practice.

What is human resource management?

Human resource management (HRM) has two main forms of existence. One is in the form of academic discourse and activity – this finds expression in conferences, journals, books, courses in business schools and so on. The other is in the form of practice in organizations that employ people and thus have employment relationships. These two modes of existence at times intersect and trade off one another. At other times they exist relatively independently each fuelled by their own interests, priorities, prejudices and logics.

It is tempting to characterize this as the rhetoric versus reality split. But it is not as simple as that. HRM is both talked up and talked down – and examples can be found in either camp. The (positive spin) rhetoric is equally if not indeed even more present in the domain of 'practice' than it is in the halls of academe. Senior managers in HR are prone to rhetoricize to a degree that is often not matched in academic circles. Conversely, many academic observers are as prone to neglect the variety of practice in their commentaries. When there is an anxiety to point out the many instances where sophisticated people management practices are *not* in evidence, there can be a tendency to underestimate the amount of time and effort some organizations *do* expend in devising and maintaining such approaches.

The news item that follows, relating to a recent HR appointment, is one indication of the kind of attention given to, and resources committed to, HR in today's environment.

It is hard to imagine that it is scarcely much more than a decade and a half since the time when the term 'human resource management' (HRM) was rarely used – at least outside the USA. Yet nowadays the term is utterly familiar around the globe and

HRM in Action 1.1   Tesco offers king's ransom to fill top HR director role

Personnel Today, 19 September 2006

Supermarket giant Tesco is offering a massive £300,000 salary plus bonuses as it starts its search for a new group HR director, *Personnel Today* can reveal.

The HR job – the biggest in the private sector – is up for grabs after Clare Chapman accepted the role of director-general of workforce at the Department of Health.

The news confirms that Chapman took a serious cut in overall earnings to join the public sector in probably the most high-profile and challenging HR job in the UK. She will now earn between £200,000 and £220,000 for overseeing the people management of 1.3 million staff – a number that dwarfs Tesco's 270,000 employees.

Tesco has employed an executive headhunting firm to cold call a shortlist of potential candidates. They are told the salary details, but only find out the employer is Tesco if they say they are interested in the post. The HR director does not automatically get a seat on the board at Tesco, unlike other major functions. However, the role reports directly into chief executive Sir Terry Leahy.

hardly a week goes by without the publication of another book on the subject. When writing this chapter in the summer of 2006 I visited amazon.co.uk in order to see what range of books was available on this subject. Remembering that just 15 years or so ago there were scarcely any books at all with this title it is staggering to note the pace of growth at least as represented by publications. When I undertook this exercise in the year 2000 for the previous edition I found that there were 448 publications matching the title search 'human resources'. This in itself was a matter of surprise. But much more was to come. Just 6 years later there were 16,377 titles matching this search term. Moreover, there were 394 titles with the fuller term 'human resource management' in 2000 and this had grown to 1683 by Summer 2006 – an increase of 427%. By the autumn this had increased further to 1750.

There are now numerous textbooks, 'handbooks', encyclopaedias, encyclopaedic dictionaries, casebooks, research monographs and critiques. Moreover, the idea of HRM, according to the book titles available, seems to have colonized just about all industry and service sectors – most notably the 'hospitality industry', schools and further and higher education, health services, banks, the voluntary sector, government and the public sector, small and medium sized enterprises (SMEs) and even the military. There are also versioned books on HRM for many different occupational specialists: the ones that caught my eye were those directed towards sport and recreation managers and the one for golf course superintendents. Likewise, the territorial coverage is impressive: books can be found analysing HRM in China, Russia, Europe, Australia, the United States, India, and the Pacific Rim. There has also been a welter of publications on international HRM, HRM in multinational corporations and various cross-national comparisons in HRM practices.

In addition to the books there are, of course, the journals, the conferences, the academic subgroups, the practitioners and so on. And yet, as the phenomenon of HRM seems to flourish – at least at the conceptual level – it remains, and always has been from its earliest inception, highly controversial. There are numerous questions about its nature, its domain, its characteristics, its reach, its antecedents and its outcomes and impact. On each and all of these there is much disputation.

In the introduction to the 1995 edition of this book it was noted that when HRM emerged on the scene in the late 1980s it was 'a fragile plant' which many commentators predicted would not survive, it was often interpreted as a passing 'fad' and some academics of the time insisted that 'continuity rather than change' was the order of the day. But within a short period there were many signs that it had taken a fairly secure hold. The update above seems to confirm this assessment. Major American contributions have been eagerly received within the UK – not least by the HR practitioners' main professional body the Chartered Institute of Personnel and Development (CIPD). Thus, Ulrich (1997) and Pfeffer (1998) have both given a highly positive and uncritical fillip to the underlying propositions on HRM. Likewise, Mark Huselid of Rutgers University has been celebrated for providing statistical 'proof' of the performance outcomes of HRM policies and practices. The CIPD's own research is normally also cited as proof positive of the impact on performance of good human resource management.

Moreover, developments in the wider literature on management, strategy and organizations have produced theories markedly in tune and supportive of the HRM thesis: for example, the resource-based theory of the firm (RBV); the learning organization; human capital management; and knowledge management are all major strands of thinking and research that lend weight to the idea of HRM. For example, the critical importance of dynamic capabilities and a strategic mindset in an innovation-oriented economy heightens the need to attend to the management of human resources and other intangible assets (Davenport et al. 2006). And resource-based theories suggest that sustainable competitive advantage stems from unique bundles of resources that competitors cannot, or find extremely hard, to imitate (Barney 1991; Wernerfelt 1984). Ironically, it has tended to be economists and others who have argued the case that human assets in particular can fulfil this criterion (Davenport et al. 2006; Lippman and Rumelt 1982; Polanyi 1966; Teece et al. 1997).

Yet despite all these indicators, there persist deep uncertainties and controversies. Some of these relate to the potential manipulative nature of seeking to shape human behaviour at work. The 'willing slaves' element (Bunting 2000) of contemporary work environments involves extensive cooperation or complicity in living the 'brand values' consciously generated by senior executives and management consultants can naturally cause unease. Bunting's critique of modern management practices and culture at Asda and Orange includes, but extends beyond, HRM. But some of the debates are almost meaningless in the absence of an understanding of their origins. Those working in the field of employment management or the management of human resources (whether as academics or practitioners) ought to be able to make a special contribution to the furtherance of its understanding. As has been noted, while resource-based theory has 'extolled' the benefits of human assets, insights into the many difficult coping mechanisms required in order to realize this potential has to come from the 'organizational behaviour, organization theory and human resource management literature' (Coff 1997). So far at least, this contribution has arguably been lacking and insufficient.

But, in order to progress we need to be clear about the *different bases* of the continuing controversies. It can be suggested that these revolve largely around three different areas: first, the *meaning* of HRM, second, the *practice* of HRM and, third, the *ethical standing* of HRM. As there is a separate chapter in this volume devoted to the third item, we will focus here on just the first two controversies.

Controversies about meaning

Controversy in the area of meaning turns on the imprecision, variability, ambiguity and even contradictions that have been seen to imbue the construct. Noon (1992) asked whether HRM is 'a map, a model or a theory?' And there is indeed much to the point that there is a degree of evangelism about HRM and associated management movements.

Many critics have pointed to the contradictions and ambiguities inherent in the discourse about HRM. The troubled search for the essential unvarying meaning of HRM can become unnecessarily obsessive. Indeed, the postmodernist critique of 'management' has already made the point that all 'definitions' and conceptualizations of management/organizational approaches are socially constructed.

The constructionist and postmodern perspective aside, the simple fact is that much of the confusion arises and persists because people using the term (and nowadays that seems to be just about everyone – practitioners, academics, consultants and critics alike) frequently do so while ignoring a key distinction that was made at the very beginning of the debate (Guest 1987; Storey 1987). From the outset it was recognized that the term can be used in two different ways. On the one hand, HRM is used as a *generic term* simply denoting *any approach to employment management* while, on the other, HRM is used to refer to *one specific and arguably minority form* of approach to employment management. Both forms are defensible and both are in current use. Each form of use has its merits and each has its limitations.

In its generic broad and popular sense, it simply refers to any system of people management and naturally different types are therefore discernible. Within the generic usage it would not make sense to seek to measure the 'growth' or spread of human resource management anymore because one would then in effect simply be measuring 'employment relations happening'. But, when the term HRM first began to be adopted some 20 years ago into a climate where there was already a prevailing language (industrial relations, employment relations, personnel management, staff management and so on) to describe the processes of people management, it did denote a particular, and at that time, an innovative approach that marked a departure from prevailing norms.

In a historical setting (the mid-1980s) when the conventional wisdom was based on pluralism, custom and practice, mutuality, temporary truces and, perhaps most notably, the intermediation of specialist IR officers or personnel officers between line managers and workers represented by shop stewards, the disruptive potential of an interlocking set of beliefs and practices that challenged many of these norms was notable. During that time of significant change I was spending a 2-year period on a full-time basis (1986–88) visiting and working within organizations while Principal Research Fellow in the Industrial Relations Research Unit at the University of Warwick. It became evident that some significant and unusual innovations were in progress – tentative in some places but sure and confident in others. The vast majority of the organizations and the workplaces studied were unionized. But one notable initiative in these situations was that some of these companies had established new departments quite separate from the ongoing industrial relations/personnel departments that continued to deal with unions and negotiate productivity deals and which, on the surface, suggested business as usual. For example, in Lucas (at that time a multidivisional and multinational conglomerate with interests in aerospace, motor and industrial businesses) and Massey Ferguson (a tractor manufacturer) new 'human resource managers' began to work with the highest levels of general management to devise managed change initiatives outside the purview of the personnel/IR departments, which were far more strategic and business-related in their nature and scope of ambition. Similar, mould-breaking changes were taking place around the same time at British Airways. In these cases important changes were taking place alongside the ongoing employment management rituals. Dual systems were in operation. But, gradually, the last were to some considerable degree overtaken by the changes in the former. These changes were eventually to be copied by many other, but obviously not all, organizations.

Even today, the Workplace Employment Relations Survey seeks to track the extent and impact of this particular approach (Kersley et al. 2006). Specifying the distinctive elements has proved to be controversial. But it is possible to conceive of HRM as one 'recipe' among many others (Sisson and Storey 2000; Storey and Sisson 1993). The point to note is that there is a range of alternative ways to manage the employment relationship. Some of these ways are distinctive and some are indistinctive and piecemeal. One relatively distinctive approach among this range has been termed HRM. To describe an 'approach' or a 'recipe' one must be able to identify certain characteristic features. HRM as much as any managerial approach (arguably none of which is fully coherent, consistent and contradiction free) has proceeded from a fairly basic set of interlinked propositions. There are relatively few outright attempts to offer a formal 'definition' but the following indicates the essence of what most discussions about the distinctive form of HRM are talking about:

> Human resource management is a distinctive approach to employment management which seeks to achieve competitive advantage through the strategic deployment of a highly committed and capable workforce using an array of cultural, structural and personnel techniques.
>
> (Storey 1995: 5)

This can be seen as an encapsulation of a 'discursive formation'. Managers who seek to 'lead' and to 'change' do so to a large extent through the management of meaning. Exponents of HRM in its distinctive sense are usually alluding to this formulation to one degree or another. In other words it is a characterization of one line of thinking. It is perhaps necessary to spell out what our 'definition' does *not* mean. First, it does not mean that all management changes 'since 1979' are of this character (many initiatives over the past 25 to 30 years are patently diametrically opposite to this formulation – most notably those approaches relying on the casualization of labour). Second, it does not mean that workers exposed to HRM policies necessarily and unproblematically do become 'committed'. Third, it does not mean that all approaches to employment within the HRM mode necessarily in practice get every element in place. Even among the organizations broadly seeking to manage in this way there will typically be gaps and lapses. And, of course, there will be instances where the blatantly cynical use the language with little or no discernible reflection of this in their practice.

None of this should mean that it would be more helpful to simply stop talking about HRM. Some kind of label to indicate the set of characteristics we are going to describe would seem to be necessary. It might be, as Wood and deMenezes (1998) have suggested, that the term 'high commitment management' should be preferred – at least it has the advantage of distinguishing between the generic people management meaning and the more particular meaning. In recent years employers have begun to talk increasingly of 'employee engagement', a term that broadly equates with the notion of high commitment. A contemporary example of an approach that seems to broadly accord with HRM in this sense can be found in HRM in Action 1.2.

HRM in the particular sense emerged on the scene as historically situated phenomenon. It was a response to new levels and types of competition that had eroded confidence in traditional formulae. To some extent it can be regarded also as an attempted articulation of an alternative to the Fordist–IR model of labour management which aimed to secure compliance through temporary truces based on negotiated settlements. The key elements of the 'new' alternative approach are summarized in Figure 1.1. As can be seen from this figure, HRM is an amalgam of description, prescription, and

HRM in Action 1.2   Employee engagement at West Bromwich Building Society

This financial services organization loans money for house purchase. With more than 800 staff and 50 branches it has assets of £6 billion and had a pre-tax profit of £33.7 million in the year to April 2005. In recent years it has initiated an entirely new approach to people management and has treated this as a key part of its business strategy. In brief, it has sought to use a version of the employee–customer service–profit cycle which places employee engagement at the core of its management approach. The executive board treats people management seriously enough to establish a people board as a subgroup of its main board. It sets the direction and monitors the implementation of the new people strategy which has a total of 12 elements including a culture change programme and a coaching approach to people management for all line managers. Measurement of employee engagement is vital to its approach. It sees the concept of 'engagement' as people's willingness and ability to contribute discretionary effort. Since 2000 it has systematically measured the level of engagement in every department on a formal basis every year with an additional measure every six months. The results are benchmarked across other leading organizations and there is an active follow-up and intervention in each department when the results are known. The chief executive claims there is ownership of the process by line managers and a huge investment in interpreting the regular flow of data and in acting on it. Leadership is seen as critical: the chief executive was the first manager to be trained as a coach and this is now expected of all managers; no manager can earn a high performance bonus without having become an accredited coach. There are a number of other elements to this distinctive employment system but these aspects are sufficient to give the flavour. The organization claims the outcomes are evident in its high levels of customer satisfaction, its record-breaking financial results over successive years and its external recognition in the form of a UK Business Excellence Award for employee satisfaction and a best HR strategy award.

logical deduction. It describes the beliefs and assumptions of certain 'leading-edge' practitioners. The 'recipe' prescribes certain priorities. And it deduces certain consequent actions that seem to follow from the series of propositions. The first element shown in the figure concerns beliefs and assumptions. The most fundamental of these is the idea that, in the final analysis, it is the human resource among all the factors of production that really makes the difference. It is human capability and commitment that distinguish successful organizations from the rest. (Interestingly, with the predominance of the 'resourced-based view' in strategic management theory this kind of proposition has arguably become the new orthodoxy in modern management theory.) It follows logically from this premise that the human resource ought to be treated with great care. It is a special resource requiring and deserving managerial time and attention. Moreover, the human resource ought to be nurtured as a valued asset and not be regarded as an incidental cost. A further underlying belief is that the aim is not merely to seek compliance with rules and regulations from employees, but to strive for the much more ambitious objective of commitment and engagement.

The second main element in Figure 1.1 concerns *strategy*. The idea that HRM is a matter of strategic importance requiring the full attention of chief executives and

---

The HRM model   Figure 1.1

1 *Beliefs and assumptions*

- That it is the human resource which gives competitive edge.
- That the aim should be not mere compliance with rules, but employee commitment.
- That therefore employees should, for example, be very carefully selected and developed.

2 *Strategic qualities*

- Because of the above factors, HR decisions are of strategic importance.
- Top management involvement is necessary.
- HR policies should be integrated into the business strategy – stemming from it and even contributing to it.

3 *Critical role of managers*

- Because HR practice is critical to the core activities of the business, it is too important to be left to personnel specialists alone.
- Line managers are (or need to be) closely involved both as deliverers and drivers of the HR policies.
- Much greater attention is paid to the management of managers themselves.

4 *Key levers*

- Managing culture is more important than managing procedures and systems.
- Integrated action on selection, communication, training, reward and development.
- Restructuring and job redesign to allow devolved responsibility and empowerment.

senior management teams is seen as a further distinguishing characteristic. It stems, of course, from the first belief about sources of competitive advantage. This belief might lead, in turn, to the proposition that a HR director must have a place on the board in order to influence company policy formulation at the highest level. But, as long as the chief executive and other senior members are attending to the strategic aspects of HRM the precise functional composition of the board might be regarded as a secondary matter. An associated assumption is that decisions about human resources policies should not stem from a set of a priori notions about good professional personnel practice, but should take their cue from an explicit alignment of the competitive environment, business strategy and HRM strategy. Some exponents of strategic HRM would even suggest that HRM policies should not only derive from the corporate plan, but should constructively shape that plan.

The third element concerns the role of *line managers*. If human resources really are so critical for business success, the HRM is too important to be left to operational personnel specialists. Line managers are seen as crucial to the effective delivery of HRM policies: communicating with employees, holding performance appraisal interviews, target setting, encouraging involvement and engagement, managing performance-related pay, and so on. The moves to shared service centres and to repositioning personnel/HR as 'business partners' are the latest manifestations of this.

In practice, there is a further element to this. Much of the drive for HRM came, in fact, not from personnel specialists, but from line and general managers (see the evidence in Storey 1992). In some instances, HRM-type policies were pushed through despite the reluctance of personnel professions (this point has, in the meantime, frequently been overlooked or forgotten). In these cases, personnel were still clinging to the rationale that they were the privileged mediators between labour and management and that they alone could gauge the feasibility and practicability of new initiatives. Such protestations were cast aside by a newly resurgent managerialism in the 1980s. To this extent at least, the emergence of HRM can be seen as ultimately associated with an upsurge in managerial confidence. For example, initiatives such as the quality movement and more recently initiatives such as knowledge management (KM) have tended to arise from outside the HR/personnel specialist function. In the case of KM, the main drive has come from information and communication technology (ICT) specialists. So much is this the case that commentators have had to cajole personnel specialists to 'find their place' and role within this movement (e.g. Scarbrough et al. 1999).

There is a further strand to the idea of a critical role for managers. A great deal of HR activity and energy is directed at managers themselves, rather than shopfloor employees. A disproportionate amount of training and development activity and resources is consumed by management development. Where psychometric testing is used, this is more likely to be directed towards managers – both for selection and promotion purposes. Activity in the realms of attitudinal structuring, target setting, performance management and career planning is again typically geared mainly towards managers. In other words, the panoply of HRM technology is seen in its fullest form in the management of managers.

The fourth distinguishing feature of HRM relates to the *key levers* used in its implementation. A notable element, at least in the early years, was a shift of emphasis away from personnel procedures and rules as the basis of good practice, in favour of a new accent on the management of 'culture'. This trend was remarkable. Just a few years ago the idea of paying regard to something so intangible as 'organizational culture', still less spending senior management time in seeking to manage it, would have seemed implausible. Since then such an aspiration seems to have found a critical place in virtually every senior executive's agenda. So central is this that the twin ideas of 'managing culture change' and moving towards HRM has often appeared to coincide and become one and the same project.

Corporate culture management has generated much excitement because it is perceived to offer a key to the unlocking of consensus, flexibility and commitment. These are self-evidently prized objectives. 'Consensus' suggests the achievement of a common set of values and beliefs. It promises an alternative to industrial conflict. Few managers can imagine all disagreements would disappear (even if this were deemed desirable, which is questionable) but many aspire to the securing of consensus about fundamental objectives and priorities. 'Flexibility' and agility is the second prize. If the culture could be changed so as to remove restrictions on movement between erstwhile separate 'jobs', then productivity would be improved. (A new analysis of agility can be found in Chapter 15 written by Lee Dyer and Jeff Ericksen.) There is, of course, concern that the idea of 'flexibility' is merely a substitute term for greater managerial control. 'Commitment' (or employee engagement), the third prize in culture change programmes, is seen as potentially carrying labour performance on to an even higher plane. Beyond a simple willingness to work flexibly, there would be an apparent endeavour to succeed. Committed employees would 'go the extra mile' in pursuit of customer service and organizational goals.

These three prizes are obviously highly desirable from an employer's perspective. But how can they be attained? 'Managing' organizational culture is a complex venture. It means altering fundamentally the whole set of ways in which things are routinely done and possibly even seeking a shift in patterns of attitudes, beliefs and values. An array of organizational development (OD) techniques (or 'interventions', as consultants in the OD tradition prefer to term them) is on offer for this purpose. (Management of change is examined by Graeme Salaman in Chapter 8.)

Apart from the categories represented in the figure it is important to note also that human resource management has two characteristic qualities that extend across the categories. It has been noted that HRM has both 'hard' and 'soft' dimensions. The hard aspect relates to the business-focused and calculative aspects of managing 'headcounts' in as 'rational' a way as any other factor of production. It emphasises detached and coolly rational planning. It stresses the 'resource' aspect in the title and this aspect finds its reflection, for example, in the use of psychological tests as a way of sorting and selecting for entry, promotion or exit. (It would thus eschew for example industrial relations rules and procedures such as 'last in first out' or seniority arrangements or arguably any other form of 'custom and practice'.) The hard dimension finds its impetus and legitimation in a market-responsive mode of action. It reflects also the business strategy focus often found in HRM accounts. By contrast, the 'soft' face of HRM traces its roots to the human relations school and emphasizes communication, training and development, motivation, culture, values and involvement. It presages and echoes the resource-based model of the firm and suggests that competitive advantage can be gained by avoiding short-term cost cutting in favour of a longer term focus on building and sustaining capability and commitment.

In total, HRM whatever else it might or might not be, is an influential and in many quarters highly persuasive narrative that helps gives some shape, direction and meaning to an otherwise complex world. Given the controversies, some observers are tempted to dismiss the phenomenon as 'mere rhetoric' – rather than recognize its more serious status, at the very least, as important rhetoric. Two points can usefully be borne in mind here. The frequently made point that a few industrial relations academics have found new posts teaching HRM in business schools is true but relatively trivial. The power of the narrative goes well beyond that incidental. Take for example, the central conclusion of *Fortune* magazine's survey of the 'world's most admired companies'. Summarizing the expressed views of CEOs it states 'the ability to attract and hold on to talented employees is the single most reliable predictor of overall excellence'. Or take just one of the many major management consultancy groups specialising in HR. The Hay Group is a major US-based global consultancy. Its central 'pitch' to its corporate clients worldwide is classic HRM. Its strap line declaration is 'Hay Group – People Before Strategy'. It continues:

> Get the right people into your organisation, into the right roles, and they will not only create a better strategy – they will implement it more effectively. They will create the sustainable business models that drive most successful organisations. Global competition, customer focus and the need for speed and flexibility have transformed the business equation. But to get the results you want you must still depend on your people to carry the day. You must select talented individuals; develop, motivate and reward them; and provide them with the organizational cultures and work processes that will allow them to succeed.

> (Hay Group September 2006)

Corporate customers spend an awful lot of dollars as a result of such logic or narrative. Consultants aside, senior managers responsible in some way for making decisions affecting employment are expected to be able to articulate some coherent rationale for their stream of decisions. Some choose to adopt the HRM rhetoric. It becomes a question amenable to empirical testing whether the sense making and visioning is also accompanied by actual concrete organizational practices.

So much for the 'idealized' and narrated model. The question that may legitimately be asked next is how much of this has actually been put into practice. This brings us to the second area of controversy surrounding HR referred to earlier: the question of take-up and, where adopted, the question of impact. But before moving to the 'evidence' it is worth reiterating the point that HRM is an important phenomenon in its own right even at the conceptual rhetorical level. It has been an important and influential discourse among practitioners. Even when the precise label 'HRM' is not used, the underlying narrative is often quite clear.

Key trends and developments

The early debate about HRM was conducted largely in the absence of any data about actual practice. In recent years much more information both from large-scale surveys and from detailed case studies has become available. Here it is sufficient to note the broad thrust of the findings. The empirical data now available to us are of two kinds. The first relates to evidence about the extent of use of certain practices, the second concerns evidence about the impact and outcomes resulting from the implementation of these practices.

Evidence about practice

In general, empirical studies tend to find that there is more extensive use of the individual elements of HR practices (such as employee involvement, more careful attention to employee selection and to communication). The extent however to which these practices are linked together into a meaningful strategic whole is a more contentious matter.

The Workplace Employee Relations Survey (WERS) (Cully et al. 1999; Kersley et al. 2006) offers some recent and representative information about the extent of use of a number of HR practices and it contains some information about the strategic location of HR. This latest survey finds that a greater proportion of managers dealing with employment matters now have the HR label in their job title. In 1998 human resource managers were less common than personnel managers but by 2004 the situation had reversed: some 12% of respondents had the title of human resource manager whereas only 9% continued to use the title personnel manager (Kersley et al. 2006: 38). Bearing in mind that the WERS sample is of workplaces and not company-level management of employment, this probably understates the significance of HR in employment management.

But does the change in title signify anything of substance or is it a simple re-labelling as has long been suspected by many critics? The WERS analysts are adamant on this point: those managers using this title 'did exhibit a different professional profile to that of personnel managers – they spend more time on employment relations, are more qualified, and have been in post for less time – and are more likely to be responsible for pay and pensions entitlement than personnel managers' (Kersley et al. 2006: 70). The survey also found that:

> [The HR label] makes a difference in terms of the autonomy that local managers have when making decisions about employment relations matters. HR managers seem to have greater autonomy, especially with regard to pay, and line managers in workplaces with an HR manager also seem to have greater discretion on pay issues. These findings suggest that HR managers are a new breed of managers, and that the increase in their numbers is not the product of a re-labelling exercise.
>
> (Kersley et al. 2006: 70)

The final statement seems perhaps rather bold: there are certainly some cases where re-labelling best describes the situation. But the fact that even at workplace level the HR label appears to make such a statistical difference is especially noteworthy given that much of the differential impact of HRM occurs at corporate centres. A further point of note is that the latest workplace employment relations survey shows that at the workplace most managers of employment are non-specialists such as works managers, general managers and the like. What matters to employees in these organizations is what kinds of policy and practice are adopted and pursued by these kinds of manager. Thus, we can see that to simply study personnel/HR specialists in order to try to uncover the state of employment relations is rather too restricted an approach. But a surprising number of studies have been circumscribed in precisely this way.

The temptation to try to study the management of employment by focusing on samples of personnel specialists is understandable but it flies in the face of advice from the founding fathers of the field. It should be recalled that Beer et al. (1985) made clear that human resource management is a matter for senior general managers, they were not just commenting on possible changes or otherwise among personnel specialists. Their contention was that: 'Without either a central philosophy or strategic view – which can be provided *only by general managers* – HRM is likely to remain a set of independent activities, each guided by its own practice tradition' (1985: 2). Many subsequent discussions have neglected these caveats. For example, Gennard and Kelly (1995) and others have continued to focus on the specialist practitioners and have sought to assess the progress of HRM by whether the personnel specialists have changed or not.

Using an in-depth, qualitative research method for a study of 15 mainstream British employing organizations Storey (1992) found that the way in which managers were seeking to manage labour was indeed undergoing extensive and significant change at that time. This change was evident in a number of ways. Notably, the drive was coming from sources and along paths which were not conventionally regarded as part of industrial relations proper. There had been little sign of outright 'industrial relations reform' of the conventional kind (following, for example, the nostrums of Donovan (1968), Flanders (1970), or McCarthy and Ellis (1973)). Rather, the recasting had come about as a result of redesigns in production systems, organizational restructuring, quality initiatives and 'culture campaigns'. Moreover, many of the new initiatives (such as a stronger emphasis on direct communication) were occurring in workplaces with established trade unions. HR and IR were operating relatively separately, there was a 'dualism' in the unfolding pattern of employment management. This point was validated in the subsequent analyses of the Workplace Industrial Relations Survey, which confirmed that there was in fact greater likelihood of HR initiatives to be found in organizations with unions than in non-union settings. Notably, many of these initiatives had been devised, as well as driven and delivered, by non-personnel specialists.

Evidence about performance impact and outcomes

There is a growing body of research that seeks to examine the impact, if any, of HRM policies and practices on organizational outcomes (for example, the *HRMJ* Special Issue 2005). The most notable studies are those that use large datasets and that interrogate the data using sophisticated statistical techniques. In general, the available studies appear to reveal impressive evidence of robust impacts and outcomes. The now classic studies in the United States include those by Becker and Gerhart (1996), Huselid (1995), Huselid et al. (1997), Ichniowski et al. (1997), and MacDuffie (1995). In Britain studies include those by Guest (1997) and Patterson et al. (1997). A review is made by Purcell and Kinnie (2006).

Debate to some extent has tended to polarize between the competing merits of best practice (universalistic prescription) models and the 'best fit' (contingency) models. But a third hypothesized relationship has been added by Delery and Doty (1996), who argue that in addition to these two there is also the 'configurational' perspectives. This last suggests that what matters is to find the 'themed' collection of HR practices that interact meaningfully together in order to meet the needs of particular situations. The proposition that there are different 'bundles', which, for example, give varying emphases to, say, human capital formation through training and development. Thus, in total, it is possible to say that there are in fact three theories of the linkage between HRM and performance. The extent to which these three are compatible or incompatible is, as we shall see, somewhat open to question. An in-depth analysis is provided in Chapter 4.

The studies testing the *universalistic thesis* (i.e. the hypothesis of a set of best practices in HRM) have been the most popular and the most well supported. Empirical studies confirming this association include those reported by Delaney and Huselid (1996), Huselid (1995) and Huselid et al. (1997). In the UK, researchers at the University of Sheffield Institute of Work Psychology reported results from a 10-year study examining the influences on company performance (Patterson et al. 1997). They found that when compared with a range of other factors (such as investment in R&D, a focus on quality or on business strategy) that one might expect to impact on company performance, a concentration on people management practices has by far the most powerful impact. In addition, it should be noted that the WERS team found that 'workplaces with a high number of "new" management practices and employee involvement schemes were substantially more likely to report high productivity growth' (Cully et al. 1998: 25).

The *contingency/best fit thesis* has also found some support – for example Delery and Doty (1996) reveal a link between Miles and Snow's three types of business strategy and different approaches to HRM. The *configurational thesis* has also been supported (Delery and Doty 1996). The early work by Schuler and Jackson (1987) while primarily conceptual in nature found some support in their later empirical work (Schuler et al. 1989).

Overall, however, there have been relatively more studies of the 'universal best practice' model of HRM and the results of such studies have tended to be more consistently positive. We would seem to have come a long way since Lengnick-Hall and Lengnick-Hall (1988: 671) could observe that 'there is little empirical evidence to suggest that strategic HR directly influences organizational performance or competitive advantage'. In consequence of the new studies and their relative consistency in positive associations, Guest (1997: 263) argues that these more recent studies provide 'encouragement to those who have always advocated the case for a distinctive approach to the management of human resources'. He has also stated: 'We can now say with increasing confidence that HRM works. But this is a skeletal finding and we need to put a lot of flesh on the bones' (Guest 1997: 274). Similar points have been made by others for example Huselid et al. (1997: 186) and it is one we pick up again later because the important point is that simply because a survey-based approach does not reveal the whole picture (for example they are likely to provide little understanding of the actual processes involved) this is hardly a reason to dismiss such approaches entirely.

Another kind of outcome apart from profit and productivity is the impact of HRM policies and practices on workers' responses. Using data from an annual survey conducted by the CIPD, Guest (1999) pointed to the 'surprisingly positive' nature of the workers' verdict on HRM: 'A large proportion of the UK workforce have been on the receiving end of the kind of practices commonly associated with HRM. Furthermore, they like them … the more HR practices they are currently experiencing in their employment, the more satisfied they seem to be' (1999: 22–3).

Hesitations and reservations about the reliability and validity of such large-scale studies have of course been expressed. For example, it has been argued that 'the claim that the bundle of best practice HRM is universally applicable leads us into a utopian cul-de-sac' (Purcell 1999: 36). Questions can be asked about the precise content and comparability of the menues or 'bundles' being evaluated. It transpires that different studies, to a certain extent, use different ingredients in their lists. There are also concerns about the reliability of single-respondent tickboxers who report on behalf of whole organizations. Moreover, the meaningfulness of 'mere' correlations and other statistically derived data in the absence of adequate theory is open to question.

However, even this list of problems is perhaps an insufficient basis to justify the dismissal of such forms of research. Similar statistical approaches are common practice in a whole range of sciences including, for example, epidemiology. The associations found in large-scale surveys while certainly not providing the whole answer or the whole picture are useful additions to the research effort. Subsequently, a number of scholars, many funded by the CIPD, have spent a great deal of time exploring the links between HRM and performance. The CIPD now believes it does have the evidence that there is a positive correlation.

But in what sense is it being suggested that HRM 'works'? Bottom-line financial performance is but one measure; progress in evaluating HRM outcomes might also look more widely across the 'scorecard'. Associated with this last point is the argument about sustainability. It may well be that a quick profit or rise in a company's share price can be achieved by short-term cost-cutting measures – including 'headcount reductions' – which have often been found to gain a favourable response from institutional investors. But this form of accountancy-led management may not deliver long-term growth or innovation. Investigations into longevity have also indicated the importance of human resource policies (Collins and Porras 1998).

Summary

The mesmerizing spell of the one-best-way formula or basket of high-commitment HR practices has influenced not only the statistical testers but has also influenced wider commentary about the validity and viability of the idea of HRM. In consequence, the 'failure' of HRM to 'diffuse' across economies has been not only noted but has been sometimes interpreted as tantamount to proof of failure of the concept in toto. The arrival of the early 1990s' recession also came at a time when academics were trying to figure out the meaningfulness (as well as the meaning) of the new concept. Unsurprisingly, the counterindicators such as the large layoffs at that time, the publicity given to a number of zero-hour contract cases and the rise of the 'McJobs' gave huge cause for caution. But there are dangers in missing the significance of the growth sectors of economies in a rightful concern to remain alert to the low-paid, low-skilled and exploitative segments. The UK government introduced the Gangmasters Licensing Act in 2004 to offer some protection to vulnerable workers in certain parts of the now very diverse economy.

That diversity is throwing up some surprising patterns of growth and exclusion. In India, huge growth has occurred in the electronic and computer software industries. The pool of highly educated workers has attracted numerous international companies such as Microsoft, Oracle and NTT. Nor is it the case that the local computer companies are all foreign owned and reliant on 'outsourced' routine tasks. The European software company, Baan, have headquartered their R&D operations in Bangalore and Novell has opened an R&D centre in Hyderabad. This multibillion dollar industry pays its programmers ten times the average Indian income, has constructed campus-style working environments and is installing employment practices that look very similar to the HR model. Likewise, in Ireland much economic progress has resulted from the planned investment in education and training and the partnership arrangement between government, trade unions and employers. Such instances should give pause for thought.

Clearly, HRM is no panacea; no set of employment policies ever will be. But, as a persuasive account (or narrative) of the logic underpinning choice in certain organizations and as an aspirational pathway for others, it is an idea worthy of examination.

Other new developments and the contributions in this volume

As is perhaps evident from even this brief overview of research and commentary on human resource management, the domain remains lively, vibrant and contested. There are many new initiatives, and analysis at times struggles to keep pace. It is a difficult but intriguing task to make sense of the changes and weigh their significance. For example, significant developments in the way business and work is organized are underway. Notable among these are cross-boundary alliances, outsourcing and networks. Offshoring continues its momentum: there has been an annual average of 300,000 jobs from the UK moving to India, China, the Czech Republic and other low-wage economies for the past six years. Lloyds TSB has signed a 5-year deal to move its finance and accounting operations to India; Deutsche Bank is moving half of its sales and trading operations backroom services to India. Key aspects of the cross-boundary nature of contemporary work organization are explored by Karen Legge in Chapter 3.

The HR function itself is in the midst of further change – the experimentation with the 'business partner' concept is just one example; the whole function is currently subject to reorganization as is explained in Chapter 2 by Raymond Caldwell and John Storey. Developments in e-HR also continue to drive significant change. New technological capabilities are enabling shared services. Boots the chemist has signed a 7-year outsourcing contract for its payroll. NHS Shared Business Services, a joint venture between the Department of Health and the outsourcing provider Xansa, provides finance and accounting services to 100 NHS organizations and the organization is looking at shared HR services. This has already happened in various civil service departments including the Ministry of Defence. The important aspects of e-HR are examined by Emma Parry and Shaun Tyson in Chapter 13. As a final illustration of novel change, the 'agility' of some major growth organizations such as Google is analysed in the new chapter by Dyer and Ericksen. Each of the chapters that follow in this book offer a wealth of insights from leading analysts in their respective fields.

The chapters are organized into five parts. The first part of the book sets the scene with some overall reviews of the state and nature of HRM. The second part focuses on the key theme of strategy and the extent to which, and the ways in which, HR's contribution might be interpreted as strategic – or not. The third part gets to grips with the key practice areas – the heartland activities of HRM. In Part 4, the lens is widened to take in key themes in international and comparative practice. The reader is exposed to the conduct of, and developments in, HR in a range of different countries while, additionally, issues concerning the international management in the sense of cross-border management are tackled. The final part of the book looks to current and future developments in e-HR and ethics.

References

Barney, J. (1991). 'Firm resources and sustained competitive advantage', *Journal of Management* 17(1): 99–120.

Becker, B. and B. Gerhart (1996). 'The impact of human resource management on organizational performance: progress and prospects', *Academy of Management Journal* 39(4): 779–801.

Beer, M., B. Spector, P. Lawrence, D. Mills and R. Walton (1985). *Human Resources Management: A General Manager's Perspective*. New York, Free Press.

Bunting, M. (2000). *Willing Slaves: How the Overwork Culture is Ruling Our Lives*. London, HarperCollins.

Coff, R. W. (1997). 'Human assets and management dilemmas: coping with hazards on the road to resource-based theory', *Academy of Management Review* 22(2): 374–402.

Collins, J. C. and J. I. Porras (1998). *Built to Last: Successful Habits of Visionary Companies*. London, Random House.

Cully, M., A. O'Reilly, N. Millward, J. Forth, S. Woodland, G. Dix and A. Bryson (1998). *The 1998 Workplace Employee Relations Survey, First Findings*. London, Department of Trade and Industry, HMSO.

Cully, M., A. O'Reilly, N. Millward, J. Forth, S. Woodland, G. Dix and A. Bryson (1999). *Britain at Work: As Depicted by the 1998 Workplace Employee Relations Survey*. London, Routledge.

Davenport, T. H., M. Liebold and S. Voelpel (2006). *Strategic Management in the Innovation Economy*. Chichester, Wiley.

Delaney, J. T. and M. A. Huselid (1996). 'The impact of human resorce management practices on perceptions of organizational performance', *Academy of Management Journal* 39(4): 949–69.

Delery, J. and D. H. Doty (1996). 'Modes of theorizing in strategic human resource management: tests of universalistic, contingency and configurational performance predictions', *Academy of Management Journal* 39(4): 802–35.

Donovan, L. (1968). *Report of the Royal Commission on Trade Unions and Employers Associations*. London, HMSO.

Flanders, A. (1970). *Managers and Unions: The Theory and Reform of Industrial Relations*. London, Faber & Faber.

Gennard, J. and J. Kelly (1995). 'Human resource management: the views of personnel directors', *Human Resource Management Journal* 5(1): 15–32.

Guest, D. (1987). 'Human resource management and industrial relations', *Journal of Management Studies* 24(5): 503–21.

Guest, D. (1997). 'Human resource management and performance: a review and a research agenda', *International Journal of Human Resource Management* 8(3): 263–76.

Guest, D. (1999). 'Human resource management – the workers' verdict', *Human Resource Management Journal* 9(4): 5–25.

Hay Group (2006). www.haygroup.com.

Huselid, M. (1995). 'The impact of human resource management practices on turnover, productivity and corporate financial performance', *Academy of Management Journal* 38(3): 635–72.

Huselid, M., S. Jackson and R. Schuler (1997). 'Technical and strategic human resource management effectiveness as determinants of firm performance', *Academy of Management Journal* 40(1): 171–88.

Ichniowski, C., K. Shaw and G. Prenushi (1997). 'The effects of HRM practices on productivity – a study of steel finishing lines', *American Economic Review* 87(3): 291–313.

Kersley, B., C. Alpin, J. Forth, A. Bryson, H. Bewley, G. Dix and S. Oxenbridge (2006). *Inside the Workplace: Findings From the 2004 Workplace Employment Relations Survey*. London, Routledge.

Lengnick-Hall, C. and M. Lengnick-Hall (1988). 'Strategic human resource management: a review of the literature and a proposed typology', *Academy of Management Review* 13(3): 454–70.

Lippman, S. A. and R. P. Rumelt (1982). 'Uncertain imitability: an analysis of interirm differences in efficiency under competition', *The Bell Journal of Economics* 13: 418–38.

MacDuffie, J. P. (1995). 'Human resource bundles and manufacturing performance: organisational logic and flexible production systems in the world auto industry', *Industrial and Labor Relations Review* 48(2): 197–221.

McCarthy, W. E. J. and N. D. Ellis (1973). *Management by Agreement*. London, Hutchinson.

Noon, M. (1992). 'HRM: A map, model or theory?', in P. Blyton and P. Turnbull, *Reassessing Human Resource Management*. London, Sage.

Patterson, M. G., M. A. West, R. Lawthom and S. Nickell (1997). *Impact of People Management Practices on Business Performance*. London, Institute of Personnel and Development.

Pfeffer, J. (1998). *The Human Equation: Building profits by Putting People First*. Boston, MA, Harvard Business School Press.

Polanyi, M. (1966). *The Tacit Dimension*. New York, Doubleday.

Purcell, J. (1999). 'Best practice and best fit: chimera or cul-de-sac?', *Human Resource Management Journal* 9(3): 26–41.

Purcell, J. and N. Kinnie (2006). 'HRM and business performance', in J. P. Boxall and P. W. P. Boxall, *Handbook of Human Resource Management*. Oxford, Oxford University Press.

Scarbrough, H., J. Swan and J. Preston (1999). *Knowledge Management: A Literature Review*. London, IPD.

Schuler, R. and S. Jackson (1987). 'Linking competitve strategies with human resource management practices', *Academy of Management Executive* 1(3): 207–219.

Schuler, R. S., S. E. Jackson and J. C. Rivero (1989). 'Organizational characteristics as predictors of personnel policies', *Personnel Psychology* 42: 727–85.

Sisson, K. and J. Storey (2000). *The Realities of Human Resource Management*. Buckingham, Open University Press.

Storey, J. (1987). 'Developments in the management of human resources: an interim report', *Warwick Papers in Industrial Relations No. 17*. Coventry, University of Warwick.

Storey, J. (1992). *Developments in the Management of Human Resources*. Oxford, Blackwell.

Storey, J. (1995). 'Human resource management: still marching on, or marching out?', in J. Storey, *Human Resource Management: A Critical Text*. London, Routledge.

Storey, J. and K. Sisson (1993). *Managing Human Resources and Industrial Relations*. Buckingham, Open University Press.

Teece, D. J., G. Pisano and A. Shuen. (1997). 'Dynamic capabilities and strategic management', *Strategic Management Journal* 18(7): 509–33.

Ulrich, D. (1997). *Human Resource Champions: The Next Agenda for Adding Value and Delivering Results*. Boston, MA, Harvard Business School Press.

Wernerfelt, B. (1984). 'A resource-based view of the firm', *Strategic Management Journal* 5(2): 171–80.

Wood, S. and L. deMenezes (1998). 'High commitment management in the UK: evidence from the workplace industrial relations survey, and employers' manpower and skills practices survey', *Human Relations* 51(4): 485–515.

threats to the integrationist agendas of HRM? Similarly, has the drive to reinvent personnel roles in terms of more proactive and strategic 'business partner' models disaggregated the precarious specialist expertise of the HR function and fragmented HR roles?

When HRM first emerged as a paradigm its integrationist ambitions were evident both in the pervasive discourses of 'HRMism' and in the search for an all-encompassing approach to workplace management. This partly explains why HRM began to include more and more components of 'people management' within its ever-expanding remit: from 'organizational culture' and 'change management' to 'organizational capabilities' and 'social capital'. But this process was always precarious and it has now begun to fracture. HRM has not delivered on the integration of HR with business strategy and performance, and its ability to exercise 'governance' within the workplace is undermined by policy fragmentation and by the growing challenge of managing employees within and across permeable organizational boundaries (Kaufmann 2004; Marchington et al. 2004). The real danger now is that these already prevalent processes will reinforce the relative powerlessness of the HR function in integrating people management policies and practices while further fragmenting HR organization.

Similar dynamics are at work in the growth of new 'HR business partnering' roles. Ulrich's (1997) multilevel typology of four 'HR business partner' roles (e.g. strategic partner, administrative expert, change agent and employee champion), has gained rhetorical ascendancy among many HR practitioners both in the USA and the UK and the CIPD (2004) has consistently endorsed it as an agenda for the professionalization of the HR function. It is increasingly clear, however, that the broader structural changes that effect the organization and 'disordering' of the HR function have had major implications for the 'core' activities of the function and for the organization of HR roles and responsibilities – often with unintended or negative consequences (Caldwell 2003; Guest and King 2004; Hope-Hailey et al. 2005; Truss et al. 2002). It is no surprise then that Ulrich's (2005) recent 'revisionist turn', in an apparent move away from the rhetoric of business partnering and towards a more rounded reading of the specialist virtues of the HR function, is partly a response to the growing disaggregation of HR organization and the fragmentation of HR roles and responsibilities; an unexpected outcome that came in the wake of the very success of business partnering (Buyens and De Vos 2001; Gratton 2003; Kochan 2004). It is increasingly unclear, however, whether the centrifugal logic of business partnering can be contained or the HR function recentred and strategically reintegrated.

A growing sense of the mounting challenges facing the HR function is gradually leading to a shift in current policy debates. In 2006 the CIPD embarked on a new programme of research examining the HR function of the future. The CIPD has funded some areas of 'HR function' research in the past, but these have rarely been treated as part of a broader holistic exploration and they have been analytically and empirically rather weak (CIPD 2006). It is hoped that some of the new research will seek to consolidate what we know about the major changes to the HR function, and explore their implications for a wide range of organizations, large and small. This policy shift has been necessary partly because the degree of reorganization of the HR function and the redefinition of HR roles continues to provoke heated controversy among practitioners. The CIPD is therefore under increasing pressure to clarify its position on how best to organize and skill the HR function of the future.

Against this background of evidence deficits and policy/practice gaps, what is increasingly needed is a broader, more comprehensive, conceptual framework for the exploration of the HR function that refocuses research on *HR organization* and *HR roles*. HR organization encompasses the relatively stable and fixed elements of HR departmental structures, HR systems, policies and reporting mechanisms, as well as the emergent processes of instability and disorganization that affect all organizations as they undergo transformation and change. The exploration of HR organization is by definition an exploration of the discontinuity, instability and disorder caused by the restructuring, devolution and outsourcing of HR processes and activities. Similarly, HR roles include not only the formal 'roles' that are prescribed by models of instrumental behaviour and strategic action, they also include the disordering and chaotic processes of 'identity' construction and meaning creation that are enacted through 'sensemaking' (Weick 2001). The failure of much of the prescriptive literature on HR roles and business partnering is that they forget 'identity' and treat action one dimensionally as the instrumental realization of clearly defined strategic choices and goals (Ulrich 1997).

From these analytical starting points two very broad and overlapping questions need to be addressed:

1 What changes are occurring to the organizing models, processes of delivery and the boundaries of the HR function? The central focus here is on the impact of new models of HR delivery (e.g. shared services, centres of expertise, self-service e-HR systems and outsourcing) on the function.

2 How are HR specialist and generalist roles changing and what impact have new 'HR business partnering' roles had on the HR function? The central focus here is on the limitations of Ulrich's (1997, 2005) model.

This chapter is devoted to an analysis of these two questions. For completeness, an appendix provides a very brief update on the latest findings from the WERS 2004 (Kersley et al. 2006).

HR organizing models

When 'HRM' first emerged it was assumed that it offered a new and more strategically integrated approach to the management of people (Guest 1987). Invariably most strategic versions of 'HRM' insisted that HR policies and practices must become more internally consistent and more closely integrated with business strategy (Storey 1995). HR policy integration as an ideal presented enormous political and operational challenges, as did the integration of HR strategy and business strategy (Kaufman 2004; Storey 1995, 2001). But these two components represented only part of the picture; there were other important outward mechanisms of business integration: the devolution of HR activities to line managers and HR business partnering with the line. The role of the line was key to early HRM integration debates while HR business partnering was somewhat neglected. These two mechanisms did, however, share an underlying logic; they were both very unpredictable because they were *potentially reversible*. Line managers might resist or reject their new role, but equally they might become positively and negatively empowered by it; they could 'own' HR initiatives, selectively implement them within the workplace or use the offloading of HR to further marginalize the HR function (Cunningham and Hyman 1999; McGovern et al. 1997). Line involvement in HR was partly designed to create 'soft' versions of HR integration by stealth (i.e. 'internalization'), but it was just as likely to engender its opposite: an employer-centred and hard version of HR (Rynes 2004). Similarly, HR business partnering was the generalist frontline in integrating HR into the business, but it could cause confusion among line managers, as well as tensions with HR specialists; and there was always the danger that business partners might 'go native' (Caldwell 2004a).

Another major limitation to the integrationist ambitions of HRM was its structural understanding of HR boundaries. It was once possible to define 'personnel' as a specialist support function organized around a range of core activities and sub-specialties (Legge 1978). In many organizations the personnel function was essentially a centralized administrative or transactional activity focused on expert knowledge, procedural efficiency and compliance; the formal remit of personnel was to somehow limit the scope of line control of personnel matters and its policy reach was invariably remote from business performance issues. With the rise of HRM this functionally ordered yet disengaged model now appears increasingly precarious: the barriers of entry to HR specialist expertise are increasingly porous despite the growth in professionalization. Administrative efficiency and cost is subsumed by effectiveness and value; control of many areas of HR is increasingly devolved to the line managers and employees; once 'core' activities can be outsourced or eliminated; and, perhaps most importantly, 'strategic HR' is counterposed to HR as a centralized support service locked inside a functional box of fragmented administrative routines (Schuler 1990; Ulrich and Brockbank 2005). All these changes have broken the perceived boundaries of internal HR specialist activities and subspecialties.

Despite the growing shift towards more strategic and integrationist models of the HR function, there has been very little systematic empirical research on how the repositioning of HR has affected HR organization; its structures, processes and boundaries (Pettigrew and Whittington 2003). One of the main reasons for this neglect is that HR strategy and performance measurement debates, whether influenced by universal 'best practice' or more contingent 'best-fit' models, have dramatically outweighed research on HR structure and organization (Guest 2003). In most of these models the integration or alignment of HR practices with performance is the primary focus, rather than the possible role HR organization may play in the emergent formulation/implementation of these practices: strategy takes precedence over structure because it 'determines' its deliberate reshaping by managerial action and strategic choice. Accordingly, the implicit assumption of strategic HR is that HR policies and practices can be decoupled from HR organization; it is the strategic analysis of competitiveness, strategy execution or strategic choice that determines the operational and administrative rationale of the HR function (Ulrich and Brockbank 2005: 177).

The rise of 'resource-based' views of organizations began to partly break the hold of the strategy over structure paradigm, while not completely dislodging deliberate notions of strategy formulation (Barney 2001). In resource-based perspectives the conventional 'outside-in' analysis of competitiveness, market positioning and performance is reversed: competitive advantage arises from 'bundles of resources', competences or capabilities (human and technical) that are valuable, inimitable, rare and non-substitutable; they are specific to the organization. From this 'inside-out' perspective, HR organization matters because it is critical to how HR is managed, delivered and measured, both internally and across external organizational boundaries (Barney and Wright 1998).

Despite this potential shift towards the integrity of HR organization, the overall emphasis of the resource-based perspectives is still integrationist: the challenge is to integrate 'bundles of resources' across internal and external organizational boundaries. There are two variations on this perspective. First, within emergent 'networked organizations' and 'N-form companies' it is argued that a strategic HR function is central to 'process integration', 'horizontal networking' and 'organizational integration' (Whittington et al. 1999). Second, the focus alternatively is on creating a 'new architecture' for 'virtual HR' that will facilitate knowledge-based strategic choices as to the appropriate mix of internal and external resources, while allowing for the reintegration of HR 'knowledge stocks and flows' across internal and external boundaries (Lepak and Snell 2002). While the former approach tends to be more concerned with the 'internalization', horizontal resource integration and the dangers of outsourcing going too far, the latter approach is more concerned with the 'externalization' of resources, virtual reintegration from 'outside' and the positive advantages of outsourcing (Barney 2001; Lepak and Snell 2002).

Both sets of ideas must, however, be treated with caution. Resource-based perspectives generally overstate the role on internal resources, knowledge and organizational capabilities in determining competitiveness and they radically underestimate the broader influence of institutional forces on the dynamics of innovation, change and strategic choice (Paauwe and Boselie 2003; Porter 1996). This can lead to an overstatement of the strategic role of the HR function. In practice, the shifting boundaries of HR organization include activities that can be delivered by others as well as activities and processes that can be redefined as 'noncore' and therefore eliminated or outsourced. As the boundaries of HR organization are redefined, the grand HRM challenge of integrating HR within and across organizational boundaries has become much more problematic not less.

As HR organizing comes under scrutiny, it becomes increasingly important to explore the scope and limits of the various models that are emerging. Most of these models consist of four major components: HR shared services; centres of expertise; self-service e-HR; and HR business partnering.

HR shared services

HR shared services are designed to reduce cost and improve service efficiency and delivery by centralizing single or multiple transactional HR services (e.g. payroll, benefit administration), so that they are available to most, if not all parts of an organization (Lee Cook 2006; Redman et al. 2007). The centralizing drive of shared services models is therefore strongly integrationist in terms of HR information systems and processes. But this is 'HR recentralization' with a twist: the internal customer and end user is involved in specifying the level of service and ultimately what is delivered. This process appears unstoppable in many large organizations where homogeneity of HR processes and economies of scale and scope create the conditions for constant improvements in HR delivery outputs (e.g. cost per transaction, cost per unit of HR support). Size also affects the structural options for delivery and system integration in that shared services can be organized divisionally, regionally, nationally or on a global scale. Moreover, because the information processes that are reengineered in shared service models are location neutral and often organization neutral they are open to offshoring and outsourcing, rather than indigenous or local insourcing solutions. This leads to hybrid shared services models whereby some HR activities are provided by specialist in-house service centres while others are being outsourced. Hybridism also allows some relatively small organizations to gain some of the perceived benefits of scalability by mixing insourced and outsourced HR services.

Centres of expertise

Centres of expertise concentrate HR functional areas of expertise (e.g. rewards, performance management, employee communications) so they can be delivered as a specialist design service at the corporate centre or as distributed activity brokered through HR consultancy services to the line. If shared services are designed to achieve economies of scale, centres of expertise are designed to achieve economies of skill. This potential synergy often explains why centres of expertise are embedded in shared services models, as yet another manifestation of the reorientation of HR towards a recentralized, integrated and more customer-facing function. In some cases, however, multiple centres of expertise may be distributed across divisions or business units, especially in highly diversified organizations. Alternatively, if a strong group HR function or specialist HR culture predominates in an organization, a variety of centres of expertise with case management capabilities can be concentrated at the corporate centre.

Self-service e-HR

The rise of 'e-HR' in the form of manager or employee forms of self-service HR, mainly using the internet, is beginning to have an impact on the HR function, especially in larger organizations (Gueutal and Stone 2005; Ruel et al. 2004). Early adopters of e-HR tended to bolt it on to their shared service models in a piecemeal manner, often as an adjunct to their call centre inquiry systems. But the emergence of e-HR is part of a larger shift of business operating models towards web-based systems of delivery (Hawking et al. 2004). This process is still at an early stage and the main driving forces appear to be cost reduction, in the form of reduced HR staff numbers or HR costs per employee. At a more strategic level, however, e-HR is part of the overall push to devolve HR responsibilities to line managers and employees (Hawking et al. 2004). While there is some survey evidence that e-HR is allowing HR to become more 'strategic' by offloading routine HR administration, the process is still very uneven and it often has negative consequences in terms of depersonalizing the HR function in the experience of its users (Lawler et al. 2004: 223).

HR business partnering

HR business partnering continues to be one of the most dominant ideas in current HR redesign. (See HRM in Action Royal Bank of Scotland on page 27). A number of organizations have dispersed 'HR partners' to the business while seeking to strategically realign the HR function and broker HR solutions between the business, transactional HR shared services and centres of expertise (CIPD 2004; Hunter et al. 2006). There is, however, a growing realization that business partnering is not suitable for some organizations, is ineffective in many, and may have negative and unexpected consequences (Gratton 2003; Hope-Hailey et al. 2005; Rynes 2004).

Deciding how to coordinate these four components in an integrated and strategic manner has created considerable challenges for many organizations. HR shared

HRM in Action 2.1   Royal Bank of Scotland

The Royal Bank of Scotland Group: the HR business partnering model

The Royal Bank of Scotland is one of the leading global financial service providers, employing over 136,000 employees. By market capitalization it is currently the third largest bank in Europe and the eighth largest globally. RBS serves more than 30 million customers worldwide, although the bulk of both the group's income and assets continues to be generated in Europe. In the UK the group has more than 20 million personal customers across a range of businesses, including NatWest, Coutts, Direct Line and Tesco Personal Finance and it has over 102,000 UK employees.

With such a large number of employees across a range of businesses and associated staff costs well in excess of £4 billion, RBS was one of the leaders in creating an 'integrationist' shared services model of HR business partnering. The model sought to strategically recentralize HR activities and streamline transactional information processes in order to achieve significant cost savings, improve quality and create new roles for the HR function as a business partner.

Before the transformation an analysis of HR activities revealed that 60% of HR activities were administrative, 25% were advisory and up to 15% were adding value in the sense of HR partnering with the business. In was also estimated that less than 10% of HR staff had the necessary internal consultancy skills, managerial competencies and business knowledge to take on the business partner role.

RBS now has one of the most admired HR functions and the integrationist model of business partnering has been enormously successful. As the bank grew by acquisition, HR shared services allowed HR to move from serving 22,000 employees within RBS to a total employee base of over 120,000 employees. Shared services also provided gains in accountability, measurement and efficiency. HR now spends significantly less time on administrative and advisory work and much more on strategic business activities. On the back of shared services RBS also became an innovator in developing 'human capital' models that correlate a range of HR metrics with business performance indicators. Most notably, 'employee engagement' was identified as a key variable in the HR-business performance linkage.

But the very success of the 'integrationist' model of business partnering has also created new challenges. The shared services model is powerful in delivering economies of scale and measures of efficiency, but it is less successful in terms of measures of business effectiveness and delivery; and outsourcing can achieve similar or even greater cost savings. Shared services as a strategy of HR centralization also has limits in terms of creating the 'commercial mindset' necessary for integrating HR into the business and it can generate new and more demanding challenges for the internal management of the HR function.

services units rarely directly deliver any important sustainable competitive advantages; their success depends more on building lateral relationships with other internal units as well as strong relations with internal customers. This approach can be compromised by strong function-based territorial control over shared service units and a failure to achieve cost reductions or desired service levels, with the result that shared services can quickly become a candidate for outsourcing or restructuring.

to adopt the role of 'HR business partners' in their ongoing search to integrate business strategy and people management (Barney and Wright 1998; Ulrich 1997). The largest ever survey of HR practitioners in the UK by the CIPD (2003) confirmed that this ambition is widely espoused – if not actually practised. Of 1188 practitioners surveyed, 56% indicated that they aspired to become 'strategic business partners', although only 33% were currently performing this role (Caldwell 2004a). Practitioner aspirations are also reinforced by the growing recruitment demand for 'business partners' at all levels and there is some evidence of an emerging 'talent gap' in this area, especially for more senior positions (Lawson et al. 2005).

As an agenda for HR role reinvention and professionalization Ulrich's (1997) ideas on business partnering have been enormously influential in both the USA and the UK, partly because they counter the negative images of a passive, reactive and fragmented personnel function. With a curious mix of universal prescription and practical advice, moral certainty and harsh realism, Ulrich presented a potentially unifying aspiration for the HR professional. But the prescriptive limitations of Ulrich's model and the growing diversity of practice have created considerable confusion for those practitioners who have embraced HR business partnering. In particular, Ulrich leaves many perplexing questions unanswered. What is the scope and nature of the 'strategic partner' role? How does it fit with other more conventional roles performed by HR professionals? How do business partner roles map on to specialist and generalist HR roles? Should all HR practitioners aspire to become business partners – is this realistic? Is the business partner role a strategic boardroom role or an operational role or both? Are HR people best suited to perform a 'change agent' role? Might the business partner roles erode the specialist culture and ethical ethos at the heart of the HR profession (Kochan 2004; Rynes 2004)?

One area of notable confusion has been the 'strategic' remit of business partner roles as vehicles for the delivery of strategy HR. When Ulrich's model first became influential there was an implicit assumption that the business partnering roles must be focused on the real or perceived influence of HR within the boardroom and the accompanying shift of the HR function away from operational-administrative concerns towards 'strategic' or business-driven HR. The 'strategic business partner' role therefore became closely identified with the growing aspiration of HR directors to gain a seat in the boardroom. It soon became evident, however, that the delivery of business-driven HR required a much more intensive focus on operational 'how to' issues of HR practices and effective implementation, rather than the grand intentions of HR strategy and policy formulation. Boardroom influence is certainly important, as it is strongly associated with the inclusion of HR in business planning processes (see Kersley et al. 2006: 64), but it is not the be all and end all of HR business partnering or HR strategy (Kelly and Gennard 2001, 2007).

Another area of uncertainty has been the translation of prescriptive roles into detailed job descriptions for the new holders of the 'HR business partner' job title. These appointments at the business unit, departmental or regional level, often with an operational remit, task defined agenda or local business focus, required the creation of detailed job specifications. But what were the appropriate competencies of HR business partners and how should they be defined (Hunter et al. 2006)? Was it essentially an internal consultancy role designed to broker HR service with the line? Must they really have detailed business knowledge? Was it best to select HR partners from a generalist HR background or could they also be specialists? The response of the HR function to these questions was to produce increasingly more detailed and formalized 'competency profiles' of what business partners should be (for example, Cabinet Office 2005). In contrast, there was little exploration of what the role meant for those who were performing it, with the result that gaps opened up between prescriptive profiles and actual practice, strategic aspirations and performance.

Further complications arose in realizing the central integrationist ambition of business partnering: the alignment of HR with the business. HR partnering involves an erosion of the traditional functional boundaries of HR and a reworking of line–business–HR interfaces and reporting relationships, so much so that partnering with the line versus partnering with HR can become an issue and a source of conflict. The potential for confusion and tension is only too apparent. Should HR business partners report to local business unit heads or HR or should there be dual reporting? Are HR business roles best organized around consultancy-style projects rather than specialist subfunctions? In addition, the possible secondment or assimilation of HR partners into managerial and consultancy roles with a direct business impact raises the question of whether managers can also cross the boundary and become effective HR partners – a further complication in an already complex picture.

One way of potentially avoiding at least some of the mounting confusion surrounding business partnering is to treat it as an all-inclusive 'mindset' for the HR function. The idea is that 'business partnering' is an overall generic descriptor for how HR addresses business issues and problems, often working closely with line managers. The CIPD has often advocated this approach, especially when it seeks to negotiate around the practice gaps that surround the implementation of Ulrich's 'pure' model (Smethrust 2005). The main advantage of this approach is that it makes it clear that the shift needed to make business partnering workable, at least in principle, is a change in mindsets, not just job titles. But this inclusive formulation of business partnering lacks analytical rigour and so the idea can cover a multiplicity of disparate practices that appear to have no internal consistency or coherence. More importantly, from a practice viewpoint, it provides no guidance on how to address the role ambiguities and confusion surrounding business partnering. Mindset models are intrinsically amorphous and ambiguous.

Paradoxically, at the very point where Ulrich's model appears to have gained rhetorical ascendancy in the UK, he has confounded his critics and partly confused his admirers by superimposing a new set of roles on his original model. There were inklings of this revision some years ago when Ulrich insisted that HR practitioners should not just be partners but they must also become active business 'players': partnering always carried connotations of passivity or it assumed somewhat negatively that HR professionals were not already part of the business – a view that has always infuriated some senior practitioners. However, Ulrich's recent revisions (with Brockbank) in *The HR Value Proposition* (2005) appear more substantial. The starting point is the 'delivery of value' and the creation of an 'integrated blueprint for the future of HR', especially in the wake of HR recentralization, the outsourcing of transactional HR and the ascendancy of HR business partnering (Ulrich and Brockbank 2005: viii). This necessitates a major reworking of HR business partnering roles. The HR 'administrative expert' has now become a 'functional expert'; an implicit reinstatement of the enduring importance of a specialist HR function for those who had perhaps 'overlooked' it, or worse, those who contemplated its total demise in the face of outsourcing or downsizing (Ulrich 2004: 32). The change agent role has been absorbed into the 'strategic business partner'. Perhaps most interesting, in a post-Enron world, the 'employee champion' that often appeared as a marginal, business subordinated role, has been enlarged by splitting it into two roles: 'employee advocate' and 'human capital developer'.

Ulrich overlays his reformulated roles with a new synthetic 'HR leadership' role. This is in many ways the replacement for 'business partnering' as an activity that somehow promises to unify his four prescriptive roles; for ultimately the HR function is a centreless cacophony of roles (Ulrich and Brockbank 2005: 218). Yet the new synthetic leadership category is the weakest link in the new model in that it imports some of the worst features of conventional (i.e. American) leadership theory into HR. Ulrich assumes that leadership is essentially influence driven, that leaders simply lead followers and that leadership is defined by a fixed set of competencies. What we are not told is that this leader-centric vision of HR is at a premium in a context where the HR function is becoming more complex and more difficult to manage, especially in large organizations. The spectre of HR losing leadership of the HR function is still a real one and it is likely to intensify as functional authority if dispersed, HR integration/fragmentation becomes more complex and organizational boundaries, both internal and external, become increasingly blurred. HR business partnering contributed to this unravelling; it is unlikely that HR leadership as formulated by Ulrich will resolve it.

Conclusion

The idea of 'integration' has begun to fade as the central ambition of 'HRM', although it still remains powerful in the search for a 'strategic HR function' and a new set of proactive roles for HR practitioners (Buyens and De Vos 2001). But was this ambition ever realistic?

Integrating HR policies and practices has always been a challenge given the economic, political and institutional context of UK employment relations and the HR profession as a stakeholder and interest group has invariably been a very peripheral player in this process. With every push towards long-term strategic interventionism, employee-centred policies and investment in a high-skill, knowledge-based economy, there are even stronger forces arguing for government non-intervention, employer-centred policies and strategies of cost minimization. Equally, bringing HR policies together within an organizational setting and delivering them effectively presents enormous challenges and these have become greater still as the potential scope and boundaries of HR policy expand and shift (see Chapter 5).

Integrating HR policies and practices with business strategy is also enormously daunting. 'Strategy' and the idea of 'integration' are often synonymous in the early 'strategy as positioning' literature, partly because it was assumed that strategy formulation was a relatively coherent process and implementation was simply strategy execution (Beer et al. 1984). These ideas still seem to exercise a powerful hold over some influential proponents of strategic HR (Pfeffer 1998; Ulrich 1997). But strategies are rarely purely instrumental, before and after sequences of action, they also involve emergent processes of practice that are invariably unpredictable with respect to outcomes. It is also increasingly clear that as the competitive dynamics of success change and as organizational boundaries and processes shift, strategies cannot be limited to external or internal analytical schema, they must include both. These ideas are beginning to inspire a rethink of HR-business strategy integration (Purcell 2005). The HR strategy–business strategy linkage must include both an exploration of external competitive imperatives and the idea of organizations as 'unique bundles of resources' – competencies, practices, processes, knowledge – that can be managed both within and across boundaries. But this presents an enormous challenge for more conventional resource-based or organization-specific debates on 'core competencies' and the integrative bundling of key HRM practices, for the analytical focus must shift to the exploration of performance across permeable organizational boundaries. Unfortunately, this new challenge may have a disillusioning outcome for those who defend 'progressive' or 'high-commitment' people management, for it is clear that 'low roads' and 'high roads' to HR are not just alternatives; they can coexist within and across organizational boundaries.

Integrating HR into the line, by devolvement and empowerment, was another essential ambition of HRM, for without it HR practices could not be effectively implemented (Guest 1987). Neither would the HR function become strategic if the line did not take HR policies seriously enough to own them (Ulrich 1997). HR devolution processes have now taken on an enormous variety of forms, but it is increasingly evident that these processes can accommodate both proactive and passive roles for HR, as well as positive and negative outcomes. In practice, devolution processes may integrate HR to some degree, but equally they can fragment it.

Finally, HR business partnering raised hopes that HR would become 'strategic' by integrating HR into the business, mainly as a broker of specialist expertise, strategic knowledge and internal consultancy support to the line. In the most sophisticated cases, business partnering came on the back of shared service, centres of expertise and e-HR which opened up a new strategic space for HR to become 'transformational'. But the process was fraught with dangers: business partnering roles were complex, ambiguous and confusing. HR business partner generalists in partnering with the business came into conflict with HR specialists at the centre, and business partners were often suspected of 'going native'. In practice, the centrifugal logic of business partnering was creating both an agenda for integration and HR fragmentation.

So where does all this leave the HR function? HRM began with an integrationist promise that now looks far more problematical than it once seemed. The belief that integration would deliver the HR–performance linkage has reached its limits as a paradigm for progressive HR practices. The search for strategic HR did not banish the fragmentation of employment policy and practice at the heart of personnel management – ad hocism and pragmatism are still the most powerful guiding principles of practice. Neither was HRM in its various guises a panacea for the deep-seated weaknesses of the personnel/HR function: marginality in business decision making, role ambiguity, limited performance accountability and relatively weak professional power. Instead the rhetoric of HRM and HR business partnering were fundamentally deceptive; they affirmed integration while masking the new centrifugal forces emerging within the HR function.

The question now is what new choices arise after the failures of integration and post-HR business partnering? Is it possible to rebundle HR practices, reorganize HR specialist activities and recentre the HR function or has the disordering of structures, processes and boundaries simply gone too far? Attempting to counter organizational fragmentation with a renewed push toward integration using information systems, the extension of shared services or renewed HR outsourcing may seem natural responses, but they may be unwise. These are the very processes that facilitated fragmentation. The choice has to be posed differently. It has to be asked if the risks of further fragmentation offset the possible benefits of a renewed search for HR–business strategy integration. The answer, given the current state of the HR function, is probably that they do not.

Appendix: evidence from the Workplace Employment Relations Survey 2004

When Keith Sisson made an assessment of the HR function in the first edition (1995) of this book, his judgement was sober. Drawing on the Workforce Industrial Relations Survey (WIRS90) he noted the then limited impact of HRM. Personnel/HR practitioners appeared to constitute a fragmented and poorly qualified grouping of 'clerks' and 'contracts managers' involved in a disparate array of low-level administrative and operational activities (Sisson 1995: 100). They had not appeared to increase their representation or strategic influence in the boardroom, even in large organizations. Moreover, two significant developments – outsourcing, on the one hand, and the devolution of personnel activities to line managers, on the other – may have been further marginalizing their role. But perhaps most decisively and surprisingly, there was little real evidence of a move to include 'human resources' in job titles. Sisson (1995: 107) therefore concluded, that personnel professionals were in danger of espousing 'HRM' as an old-style 'coping' strategy: 'using professionalism in an instrumental fashion to hide the mismatch between a pretentious and abstract model of what they should be doing, and the reality of a relatively fragmented and routine set of activities'.

In the second edition of this book, less than a decade later, Sisson found that the picture had changed in some substantial respects. Drawing this time on the 1998 WERS data he presented an account that catalogued a whole series of significant changes to the personnel function and HR roles. The number of personnel specialists had increased and they were better qualified. The spectre of dramatic outsourcing of HR had appeared to recede, at least temporarily, along with fears about the downsizing of the personnel function. Some HR was being decentralized, although this did not appear to equate with a loss of decision-making authority for the function. Perhaps significantly, there appeared to have been a growth in the use of the 'human resource' job title. In 1990 just over 6% of the people management specialists employed in UK workplaces with 25 or more employees used the HR title, while in 1998 the figure had risen to approximately 30% (Millward et al. 2000; Sisson 2001).

Of course, the change in title in itself may not be of significance unless it is also accompanied by changes in behaviour, influence or, most importantly, a performance effect. Hoque and Noon (2001) demonstrated, using the WERS98 data, that there were important differences between 'personnel' and 'HR' specialists. Their analysis suggested HR specialists were distinct from personnel specialists in four respects: first, level of formal qualifications; second, involvement in strategic planning processes; third, extent to which authority had been devolved to line managers or supervisors; and, fourth, adoption of sophisticated 'high-commitment' practices associated with HRM. In other words, the HR job title was more than simply a change of name, although the reasons for the change and its impact were unclear (Caldwell 2002). Sisson (2001) concluded his review of the WIRS98 data on a more positive if cautionary note. The function was developing 'all-round operational and strategic competence' and it appeared to have 'the quality of people and the structures to deliver what senior managers ask of it' (2001: 93). But there were areas of continuing concern: few workplaces had fully embraced 'high-commitment' managements, there was little evidence of a new strategic approach to HR, cost minimization still predominated in UK workplaces; and the HR function was still espousing HR from the 'touch line'. For Sisson, HRM therefore appeared to have had a 'partial impact' on the personnel function in the UK; it was a case of transition rather than transformation.

What does the latest WERS 2004 data tell us about the changing nature of the HR function since 1998? The WERS research team headed by Barbara Kersley (2006) offers a detailed examination of the changing nature of HR/personnel/employment management function. They assess the idea of the professionalization of the function, the extent of specialists versus generalists, the gender composition, changing roles, the size of the function and overall the question of whether the profile of HR managers differs in any marked respect from that of personnel managers. This appendix concentrates on the findings regarding the HR role.

Large numbers of academic analysts – possibly a majority – have been sceptical about the significance of job title as a proxy measure of HRM. The debate is complicated because the professionalization of the personnel/HR function and the narratives of HRM overlap. New or 'progressive' HR ideas have influence among specialists retaining the apparently old-style 'personnel' job title, while some rebadged functions remain unchanged in anything other than name. And from case study work we know that both instances do occur. To focus on the differences between HR and personnel specialists on the basis of job title can therefore be fraught with hidden dangers.

Evidence of the decline in the personnel job title has been emerging for some years. An analysis of CIPD membership data in 2002 indicated that there were approximately 43,700 members with either the HR or personnel job title. Of these 42% used the personnel title while 58% used the HR title (Caldwell 2002). It is no surprise then that the WERS04 data confirm the ascendancy of the HR title. Whereas in 1998 management 7% of respondents used the human resource manager job title, by 2004 12% were using the title, effectively overtaking the personnel tile, now used by 9% of specialists (Kersley et al. 2006: 38). Bearing in mind that the WERS04 sample is of workplaces and not organizations, this probably understates the significance of HR in employment management.

Kersley et al. use the new data to reopen the question about a possible shift from personnel management to human resource management (2006: 58–61). They note that the increasing numbers of HR managers could be simply a matter of relabelling, but they follow Hoque and Noon (2001) in suggesting that it is something more than this. A series of indicators point to the fact that 'HR managers professional profile differed significantly from that of personnel managers and general managers' (2001: 59). Some differences were found too in relation to job responsibilities with HR managers carrying more responsibility for substantial employment matters such as rates of pay and pensions. They had 'substantially more' autonomy than those using the personnel manager title.

They were also subject to less central monitoring than personnel managers. HR managers were more likely to be qualified in people management (73%) than were those retaining the personnel manager title (52%). Moreover, the latter group tended to have been longer in the same post, whereas the HR managers had been in the specialist post for a much shorter period of time and yet had more qualifications and

(ed.) *Human Resource Management: A Critical Text*, 2nd edn. London, Thomson.

Smethrust, S. (2005). 'The long and winding road', *People Management* 28 July: 24-7.

Storey, J. (1995). 'Human resource management: still marching on, or marching out?', in J. Storey (ed.) *Human Resource Management: A Critical Text*. London, Routledge.

Storey, J. (2001). 'Human resource management today: an assessment', in J. Storey (ed.) *Human Resource Management: A Critical Text*. London, Thomson Learning.

Truss, C., L. Gratton, V. Hope Hailey P. Stiles and J. Zaleska (2002). 'Paying the piper: choice and constraint in changing HR functional roles', *Human Resource Management Journal* 12(2): 39-63.

Ulrich, D. (1997). *Human Resource Champions*. Boston, MA, Harvard University Press.

Ulrich, D. (2004). 'Forces for change', in E. Lawler, D. Ulrich, J. Fitz-enz and J. Madden, *Human Resource Business Processing Outsourcing*. San Francisco, Jossey Bass.

Ulrich, D. and W. Brockbank (2005). *The HR Value Proposition*. Boston, MA, Harvard University Press.

Weick, K. (2001). *Making Sense of the Organization*. Oxford, Blackwell.

Whittington, R., A. Pettigrew, S. Peck, E. Fenton and M. Conyon (1999). 'Change and complementarities in the new competitive landscape: a European panel study', *Organization Science* 10(5): 583-600.

Networked organizations and the negation of HRM?

Karen Legge

Introduction

Through the eye of nostalgia (e.g., Sennett 1998) and with the benefit of hindsight, the age of mass production in western economies may be perceived as a golden one for personnel specialists. This was as a result of Fordism, bureaucratization in both private and public sectors and expanding trade unionism coming together in symbiotic embrace within the political ideology of corporatism. Such a system, based broadly on notions of a collectivist, negotiated settlement between capital and labour, with the state holding the ring for some notion of a fair distribution of the good things in life (health, education, jobs and wealth), stimulated a concern with procedural and distributive justice and consistency in the workplace. Leaving aside the more high-falutin aspirations of personnel management about 'the optimum utilization of human resources in pursuit of organizational goals', personnel managers were guaranteed a role as organizational policemen and women. A major activity and raison d'être of the function – along with welfare provision – was the monitoring of consistency and fairness, enabling the smooth working of a framework of bureaucratic rules and regulations that pertained to stability and order in employment relations and those with trade unions.

And for many HRM specialists and employees, this scenario remains largely true. Despite academics' fondness of speaking in terms of a 'post-Fordist' world, most people in the developed west still work in large, bureaucratic organizations with institutionalized internal labour markets that are policed by personnel departments carrying out much the same activities as their predecessors a generation ago. Certainly, there have been changes, for example, in the move from manufacturing to service sector and the feminization of employment, the eclipse of the trade union movement, the importance of EU labour legislation, but for most employees and personnel departments continuity prevails and change, although ongoing, is gradual.

One consequence of the continuity of this inheritance was that, for years after this world was gradually changing, commentators still tended to write as if the organizational location of personnel management/HRM was solely the large bounded organization, a discrete entity of internalized relationships and activities. Even the recent debate about 'best fit', 'best practice' and HR 'bundles' of practices implicitly took this view (see, e.g. Huselid 1995). Notions of 'fit' suggest that 'the' organization and 'its' environment can be clearly differentiated. Best practice 'bundles' seek their justification in the belief that, embedded in 'an' organization, they can be related to 'its' performance. These ingrained assumptions failed to recognize that such an approach to organizing and its study reflected a particular historical period, of the vertical integration of mature industrialization and Fordism and structural–functionalist approaches to organizational analysis that flourished from the 1920s through to the 1970s. There was little explicit recognition (but cf. Pollert 1991) that Atkinson's (1984) supposedly 'new' model of the flexible firm had more in common with industrial organization pre-1914 than with that of the 1960s and 1970s. Nevertheless, under the impact of globalization and a rightwards shift to neoliberal economic policies in the UK/USA, it is now recognized that changes are afoot, even if they are less extensive than some commentators (Castells 1996; Davidow and Malone 1992; Nohria and Eccles 1992; Piore and Sabel 1984; Powell 1990) might imply.

This may be attributed, first, to empirical observation. Many commentators have recognized the growing importance, in the UK for example, of interorganizational relationships in national and global supply chains and in both manufacturing and in the delivery of public sector services (Colling 2000, 2005; Kinnie et al. 2005; Marchington et al. 2005; Rubery et al. 2002; Scarbrough 2000; Thompson 2005). Few large organizations today can compete successfully without being embedded in a network of insourcing and outsourcing arrangements, strategic alliances, partnerships and joint ventures. The large organization of the twenty-first century is now conventionally described as 'boundaryless' (Ashkenas et al. 1995) or likened to a 'moebius strip' (Sabel 1991).

Second, the present fashion in both organization theory and HRM of neo-institutionalist and resource-based value approaches to the analysis of business systems and strategic choice in organizational design and associated HRM policy and practice promotes this interest (e.g., Boxall 1996; Hall and Soskice 2001; Paauwe 2004; Powell 1998; Whitley 1999). Globalization and its mantra of enhanced competition and the need to secure competitive advantage links empirical observation and theoretical concerns. Thus, globalization stimulates interest in the effectiveness (however defined) of different business systems. The need to achieve competitive advantage in a globalized economy encourages a focus on the rare, valuable and inimitable competencies *and* the processes of cooperation and competition by which firms may add value (e.g., Barney 1991; Castells 1996). Hence the interest in 'extended' and networked organizational forms.

In this chapter, I will use the idea of networked organization rather loosely to cover several different forms and styles of extended organizational interrelations, rather than focus on the classic networked organization as portrayed by commentators such as Castells (1996) and Powell (1990). The classic version assumes that a network of firms is essentially a web of interrelated business processes or value chains where collaboration and competition are in creative tension, enabled by sophisticated and ever-renewing ICTs and driven by mutual interests including knowledge creation and sharing. The vertical, formal hierarchies of bureaucracy are replaced by horizontal linkages of varying degrees of formality and the high levels of mutual dependency are safeguarded from opportunism by high trust relations or 'obligational' as opposed to 'arms length' contracting' (Sako 1992). This is the networked organization as seen through somewhat rose-tinted spectacles. As Marchington et al. (2005) clearly demonstrate on the basis of UK case studies, many interorganizational networks are no strangers to the use of coercive power tactics on the part of their stronger members. For example, arms' length contracting may be the preferred option if the purchaser holds the whip hand and considers it advantageous to off load risk onto the supplier and to engage in regular market testing.

In this chapter, I wish to focus on five issues. First, why has the focus moved from the bounded to the 'extended' or 'networked' organization? Second, what forms do these networks take? Third, what are the costs and benefits associated with these different organizational forms? Fourth, what are some of the contradictions and ambiguities in managing employment relations that arise? What implications do networked forms have for human resource management?

Enter the networked organization

The vertically integrated bureaucracies of Fordism were premised on the assumption that for large organizations seeking economies of scale the transaction costs of hierarchies were lower than those incurred by spot contracting in the marketplace – the classic 'make or buy' decision (Williamson 1975, 1985). The focus was on vertical rather than horizontal relationships. But, by the late 1970s, it was increasingly recognized that Fordism (in its broadest sense) (Jessop 1994) was in crisis, signalled by high inflation and falling levels of profitability and innovation in US mass production. Most important, though, were the perceived causes of this fall: overly diversified, overly centralized and overly functionally differentiated corporations that were too large, too bureaucratic and too unresponsive to a marketplace of rising consumer expectations. This was coupled with perceptions of non-engaged workforces alienated by deskilling and job fragmentation. The rise of political leaders in the USA/UK committed to neoliberal economics and the virtues of deregulation and the marketplace intensified this critique. The upshot was that flexibility, whether intra- or inter-organization, became the new orthodoxy (e.g., Atkinson 1984; Piore and Sabel 1984).

The models of three contrasting business systems were particularly influential in this development: the Japanese, the Italian 'flexible specialization' and the US/UK neoliberal models. The Japanese model (and those of the Asian Tigers) came into prominence in the 1980s and early 1990s due to Japan (erstwhile known for cheap, 'poor quality' commodity products) penetrating US and UK markets with consumer electronics and automobiles. Japan's achievement, in contrast to Fordism where cost reduction had gone hand in hand with standardization and suspect quality, was to achieve cost reduction, rapid product innovation and modification *and* quality (defined as 'conformity to specification') simultaneously. While Fordism had aimed at minimizing production time, the Japanese system sought to minimize time in process and response time to the customer (Best 1990, cited in Rubery and Grimshaw 2003: 59). The Japanese model of 'lean' organization married together both intra- and inter-organizational flexibility. The intra-organizational flexibility is achieved (in theory) by bringing together the 'hardware' of continuous improvement inspired manufacturing techniques (*kaizen*) with the software of 'high-commitment' HRM and work practices (Legge 2000; Rees et al. 1996). The logic is to cut out anything within the organization and its supply chain that does not add value. The corollary is a very fragile work system that is highly dependent on committed, hard working employees, thus rendering the manufacturing 'hardware' and employee 'software' symbiotic (Oliver and Wilkinson 1992). This intra-organizational flexibility (in the 1980s often somewhat mistakenly described as Japanese 'culture') called for flexible teamworking enabled by modularization and individual/team-based and cross-functional learning and, until recently, supported by lifetime job guarantees, promotion by seniority and enterprise unionism. Interorganizational flexibility is inherent in this 'lean' organization model. This is because of its emphasis on process-centred organization, in the context of Japan's dualistic, *keiretsu*-based system of hierarchical networks of relational subcontracting, where the ideal exists of 'co-existence and co-prosperity' (Clark 1979; Dore 1973; Sako 1992 cited in Rubery and Grimshaw 2003: 59).

The Italian 'flexible specialization' model starts from the notion of moving away from standardized mass production to market-responsive, 'designer' small-batch production, enabled by flexible machine tools and a flexible, skilled workforce (Piore and Sabel 1984; for a summary, see Rubery and Grimshaw 2003: 64–7). Such a manufacturing system is seen as embedded in networks of small, decentralized, specialist firms, located in regional proximity (e.g., the oft cited Veneto and Emilia Rogmana in North Italy) and engaged in complex webs of relational, mutually supportive, subcontracting. Such networks are also supported by central services and consortia promoted by regional and local government, allowing some economies of scale. Within these networks of firms, cooperation and competition are finely balanced, encouraging continuous innovation and adaptability.

Although in many ways contrasting, the US/UK neoliberal model also prioritized flexibility, if with a somewhat different emphasis. The emphasis was on a flexible response to the marketplace, whether that of finance, labour or consumers. This approach was encapsulated in rhetoric about 'deregulation', 'freeing up' markets, 'maximizing shareholder value' and 'customer sovereignty'. Two strategies that stimulated networked organization flowed from this model. First, in the private sector, many large conglomerates in the 'old' economy of commodity manufacture and processing abandoned their traditional 'retain and reinvest' in favour of a 'downsize and redistribute' allocative regime (Lazonick 2005; Lazonick and O'Sullivan 2000). This was partly to limit risk and partly to develop tighter performance and accounting controls (Colling 2005: 91). This involved focusing (and sometimes redefining) the core business, massive divestiture and downsizing, with accompanying spin-offs and outsourcing and the distribution to shareholders (and top management via stock options) of the realized value. The idea, echoing the Japanese model, was to produce 'leaner', 'fitter', more 'agile' organizations that, by shedding layers of bureaucracy and noncore business, could get closer and be more responsive to the customer and develop a renewed capacity for innovation. Second (notably in the UK), strategies of privatization of public sector industries and the introduction of market principles in public sector services resulted in large-scale outsourcing and contractual relationships between public and private sector organizations. This is reflected in such initiatives as contracting out, market testing, 'best value', public private partnerships (PPP) and private finance initiatives (PFI). Effectively, this has given rise to complex networks of providers in the delivery of public services.

Finally, a rationale for the networked organizational form may be found in resource-based value theory (see Boxall 1996 and Wright et al. 2001 for good discussions of the relationship between RBV theory and HRM; also, Espino-Rodriguez and Padron-Robaina, 2006 on outsourcing and RBV). In theory, if resources are characterized as rare, inimitable, non-substitutable and appropriable, anything that lacks these characteristics – or activities that do not require organization-specific resources – is not 'core' to the organization and may be acquired 'outside' its legal boundaries through contracting with other organizations. What is not 'core' to one organization may then become the site of another's core competency. At the same time, if resources are defined as any feature of the organization that is value creating, this may include the knowledge to manage complex patterns of coordination and governance inside and outside the organization. Human and social capital are necessary for *and* developed by managing the interfaces between quasi-independent cost centres, supply chains, cooperative alliances, spin-offs, franchises and so on (Nahapiet and Ghoshal 1998). Thus RBV theory underpins the notion that the lean, agile organization should concentrate on developing its competency muscle while shedding the fat of peripheral activities and associated personnel.

Networked organizational forms: some benefits and costs

Colling (2000, 2005: 93–5), using UK government and successive Workplace Employment Relations Surveys (WERS) charts the rise in the incidence of outsourcing in the UK. A particularly revealing statistic, tracking the years 1979–2003, is the reversal in fortunes in terms of numbers employed, between manufacturing industry and financial and business services sectors. The latter, including consultancy services, is heavily implicated in organizational restructuring of all kinds, from business process reengineering to providing the financiers and lawyers essential to drawing up complex partnership agreements.

Storey (2005: 193) provides a useful analytical framework contrasting Fordist bureaucracy with the extended organizational forms. As one moves from bureaucracy through supply chain management and process engineering, through strategic outsourcing, to joint alliances and networked organizations, there is 'a progression towards increasing externalization of relations; to diversified activities [within a network], to performance-based control and to open-market mode of regulation'.

The benefits and costs of these different organizational forms are reflected in their characteristics and the motivations for their adoption. Storey (2005) and Colling (2000, 2005) give a good summary of these.

Supply chain management and *business process reengineering* (BPR), very much in vogue in the 1990s, focus on the notion that organizations (usually, but not exclusively, private sector firms) should organize around their core value adding processes along their entire supply chain. This is with the view to eliminating costs and improving 'quality, flexibility and service delivery' (Storey 2005: 194). Producing value for the customer is the espoused value. In theory and, not surprisingly, this approach to organization involves many of the activities already mentioned with reference to the Japanese model of 'lean' organization. Enabled by ICTs, there should be a move from function-centred to process-centred organization, from linear/sequential work

the same time the latter's work regime demanding that customer service representatives deal with a very high target number of calls per shift.

Joint ventures, *strategic alliances* and various forms of *partnership*, including *franchising* provide a range of benefits. Storey (2005) identifies four benefits of joint ventures. First, a large firm may ally with another firm to quickly acquire expertise in a new product/service area. Large agrochemical companies allying with smaller biotechnology companies is cited as an example. Second, large firms may use their marketing and capital resources to assist a smaller company in bringing a promising new product to the marketplace quicker and more certainly than if it acted independently. Third, partners may reduce their overheads and therefore their cost base by allying. The development of 'shared service centres' is an example of this strategy. The logic of franchising is similar as it 'permit(s) low risk growth by requiring investment from franchisees bound by organizational "franchisor" norms' (Colling 2005: 91). Fourth, investment in some developing countries, notably China and India, requires inward investment to be allied to a domestic partner. A special case, being government led, is the development in the UK of public/private partnerships (PPP), including private finance initiatives (PFI). Advocates for PPP and PFI argue that it enables the public sector to benefit from private sector market-oriented expertise, to accelerate capital investment while diffusing its risks, and to provide new, more flexible and empowering career paths for public sector workers. Critics of these initiatives maintain that it is privatization by the back door, that PFIs will be ultimately very costly to the taxpayer and that the quality of service provision and employment conditions for public sector workers will be eroded (Marchington et al. 2005: 111).

A major challenge for all such initiatives is the bringing together of different organizational cultures and systems and forging a new integrative culture for the new organizational entity. The HR difficulties involved in this will be discussed later.

I have already outlined the characteristics of the ideal type, 'classic' *networked organization*. Storey (2005) provides some useful elaboration. With networks, he maintains, the unit of analysis is the web of relationships between a cluster of highly permeable organizations, not the interrelationship between two organizations. The focus is the value chain of linkages from the conception of the product/service to the end user. To optimize value, network members engage in a free flow and sharing of information, facilitated by ICTs, to create synergies and develop knowledge. It is recognized that no one organization has the monopoly of the knowledge to innovate in product and process effectively and at the speed the market is perceived to require. Strategic and operational planning, logistics, delivery, measurement and auditing systems need to be coordinated with other members of the network and joint problem solving developed. The emphasis is on collaborative, sharing relationships where all parties can 'win', but where roles and relationships are continually evolving in response to the market and consumer preference. Customers and suppliers may come to be treated as partners, while those 'working' for an organization may not be its employees. The complexity of relationships spawn roles unfamiliar to bureaucracies, not only experts in drawing up and managing contracts, but 'brokers, architects, lead operators and caretakers' (Storey 2005: 201) – roles that span boundaries and are concerned with relationship development and maintenance. In networks, as compared with traditional organizations, it is no longer clear who is an 'insider' and who an 'outsider'. The key distinction is the identification of the core organization that informally manages the network, acting as the lead coordinator. Achieving a lead role is likely to depend on the extent to which the core organization is able to control

---

HRM in Action 3.1 Morecambe Bay cockle pickers

On the evening of 5 February 2006, 23 Chinese cockle pickers were drowned on the notoriously dangerous quicksands of Morecambe Bay in northwest England by rapid incoming tides. The workers, mainly impoverished farmers from the Fujian province of China, were all illegal immigrants, working for a gangmaster named Lin Liang Ren. On 24 March 2006, at Preston Crown Court, Lin Liang Ren was convicted of 21 counts of manslaughter (two bodies were never found but presumed drowned) and sentenced to 14 years in prison. He attributed the disaster to 'the top bosses, the English suppliers and their international clients, who put enormous pressure on us to produce'.

The workers resorted to cockling for three reasons: when they couldn't send money home due to the low pay of their regular job, such as working in a takeaway; when seasonal casual work in food-processing factories dried up; when their vulnerable immigration status led to fear of dealing with employers who might check up on this. Gangmasters found Chinese workers to be cheaper and harder working than the locals. But it was prosperous local cockling middlemen who, supplying seafood processing conglomerates such as Penclawdd Seafoods Ltd (owned by Dani Foods), controlled the workload required and set production targets for the 30–40 Chinese cocklers in each team and who were referred to as 'bosses'. Frequent price cutting by labour users also pushed labour providers, such as Lin Liang Ren, to impose a harsher work regime to enhance productivity.

Health and safety was never part of the agenda for cockling labour providers or users. Workers were never told of the dangers of Morecambe Bay, never given tide tables and were not provided with safety equipment. Penclawdd Seafoods Ltd is said to work with 1500 fishermen who use gang labour all over Britain and makes an annual profit of £4m, but does not concern itself with the working conditions of the cocklers.

Today, led by Polish gangmasters working with local businessmen who initiated the recruitment, Polish workers, with no experience of the sea, have taken the place of the Chinese.

(Based on: Hsiao-Hung Pai – Migrant labour – the unheard story in Open Democracy and other internet sources.)

---

resources critical to the performance of other members of the network, thereby creating resource dependency (Kinnie et al. 2005).

All these new forms of extended organization, focusing on the supply/value chain and on process rather than structure, add ambiguity and complexity undreamed of in bureaucracies to the central activity of HRM, managing work and employment relationships. It is to this issue that I now turn.

Contradictions and ambiguities in networked organizational forms[1]

HRM in all organizations confronts the tension that it simultaneously seeks both the control *and* commitment of employees (Legge 1995: 14-19). In networked organizational forms this is rendered additionally problematic as employers seek to exercise control and generate commitment, not only among their own direct employees, but among those working indirectly for them, or within a partnership, who are not legally their employees. Although UK employment law has been broadened to embrace employer–worker relations (as in the UK Working Time Regulations 1998 or the National Minimum Wage Act 1998) there is still much confusion in law about who constitutes the employer in interorganizational relationships.

Marchington et al. (2005) and Rubery et al. (2002) identify three major areas where confusions about employment status combined with multiple employer workplaces generate ambiguities and tensions in managing work and the employment relationship. These involve issues of performance and control, the effort–reward bargain and commitment and the psychological contract.

Performance and control

Rubery et al. (2002: Table 1) list the types of issue over control and performance characteristic of different types of networked organizational form. For example, while an agency may be a worker's employer, the client organization is likely to have control of the work process. The agency, not being present at the workplace, may not be in a position physically or contractually to control work processes, nor to verify the information presented in disciplinary cases of its own employees. Similarly, while workers at a franchised outlet are employed by the franchisee, the franchisor, in protection of the brand and via the franchise contract, may exercise control over working practices and training and provide a disciplinary framework for adherence by the franchisee. In partnerships and supply chain relationships, the partner/client may identify which staff from other partner/client organizations that they are prepared (or not prepared) to work with and may require information on their partners' staff's qualifications and experience in making this selection (see also Swart and Kinnie 2003). There may be ambiguities relating to supervision, performance appraisal and career development (reminiscent of the problems with matrix organization) when staff are seconded to a partner, who is not their employer but who has more detailed knowledge of their work and performance than their employer. Where work is outsourced, employees of the subcontractor may find that their work is being checked and verified by managers in the client organization, if the latter retain responsibility for the outcomes and perceives itself as possessing superior knowledge of the standards required (Marchington et al. 2005).

Such ambiguities are exacerbated when there are multiple employers at a workplace. Legally, the 'main' employer on a site is responsible for the health and safety of all workers on site. However, can managers of the main employer demand that those employed by other employers change behaviour that might endanger health and safety standards and take disciplinary action if it persists (Rubery et al. 2002: Table 2)? What if an agency worker commits an act regarded as a disciplinary offence by the client firm, but not by the agency employer? Can an employee have a grievance against his or her employer if harassed by a manager or employee of another organization at the same workplace? Then there is the situation where employers on a multi-employer work site feel compelled to monitor the employees with whom they have no contractual relationship, but whose performance is crucial to their own effectiveness. Marchington et al. (2005: 23–4) cite the example of an airport, where many organizations (e.g., the airport authority, baggage handling, passenger handling, aircraft and terminal cleaning and airlines)[2] have to collaborate and achieve tight coordination to ensure that planes and

HRM in Action 3.2   Gate Gourmet

Gate Gourmet is one of the world's largest providers of in-flight meals, whose customers include British Airways, American Airlines, Continental, Delta and Qantas. Formerly part of the bankrupted Swissair, since 2002 Gate Gourmet has been owned by the American venture capital firm, Texas Pacific. In the USA, Gate Gourmet has a reputation as a union-bashing employer of cheap, often migrant, labour.

Times are hard for in-flight catering firms because, post-9/11, in an effort to save costs, many airlines have scrapped free meals on shorter flights or offer them on a pay-as-you-go basis. The USA – one of Gate Gourmet's biggest markets – has volumes down by about 40%. Soaring fuel costs and fierce competition among suppliers have exacerbated the situation. In early 2005 Gate Gourmet at London Heathrow lost a valuable contract with Virgin Atlantic after the airline reorganized its in-flight services – including catering – and handed them to a single contractor. It was imperative, then, for the firm to cut its own costs. The alternative was to go into administration.

In June 2005 a rescue package proposed redundancies for 147 workers and was rejected by the workforce, by a vote of nine to one. With the threat of redundancies hanging over the workers' heads, Gate Gourmet then announced that they wished to employ 130 additional temporary staff. On 10 August 2005 the company brought in these new workers without discussion with the union, the Transport and General Workers' Union (T&G). While the union sought to clarify the situation, staff assembled in the canteen in preparation for a meeting. Management then told staff that they had three minutes to get back to work or they would be sacked. They refused. Members due to start the late shift refused to come to work having heard the news. Those in the car park were sacked by megaphone. In all, 667 workers were sacked. The T&G considered that the company had deliberately provoked an illegal, wildcat strike by its provocative actions and because, the day before, it had informed the companies it traded with that there would be a dispute. The T&G considered that the firm's intention was immediately to save on redundancy costs and, ultimately, to substitute cheaper eastern European labour.

The result was that fellow T&G members, employed by British Airways, such as baggage handlers, loaders and bus drivers, walked out in sympathy with the workers sacked by Gate Gourmet. GMB union baggage handlers refused to cover T&G members' work. Further the GMB requested BA to remove GMB members who worked as check-in staff, because of the health and safety implications of potential levels of abuse from passengers. By 11 August all BA flights had been grounded at Heathrow, affecting 17,000 passengers at the height of the holiday season. Over the two-day action more than 100,000 passengers were stranded, costing the airline (in direct costs) an estimated £40m.

(Based on: T&G website, BBC news and other internet sources.)

passengers depart to schedule. In these circumstances the airport may monitor contracts (e.g., of the baggage handling company) to which it is not a party and intervene if performance threatens the airport's punctuality record.

Effort–reward bargain

Major issues concern agency employees and those, largely from the public sector, transferred to private sector companies under Transfer of Undertakings Protection of

Employment (TUPE) Regulations. It is frequently recognized that agency staff are often paid less, irrespective of responsibilities and skill, than the permanent employees of an organization. Rubery et al. (2002: 661–62) argue that wide differentials based on status rather than skill/job description are likely to prove unsustainable in the long term. Although different pay levels may be part of a cost reduction strategy on the part of management, its effectiveness may be eroded by consequent labour turnover and low levels of commitment on the part of the agency staff. Indeed, the problematic nature of this strategy is implicitly recognized when long-serving agency staff are eventually offered permanent contracts with the on-site employer or when the employer uses agency staff as a screening process for entry into permanent employment. Conversely, management may use the lower pay rates of agency staff to argue low increases for their permanent staff on the grounds that they are paid over the market rate.

Similar problems may confront TUPE transferred employees. Although TUPE regulations provide protection of existing pay and conditions when the individual is transferred to a new employer, he or she may remain in the workplace of the original employer working with staff who have not been transferred. This is common practice in public/private partnerships, such as PFI. If the transfer was in the interests of cost reduction, it is likely that transferred staff may receive lower increases than the non-transferred, although working alongside them. If the transferred are now working in a different workplace, their pay and conditions may differ from both new direct recruits and pre-existing employees of the transferee. It is possible too that they may experience tighter performance standards and intensified work.

A further issue is that of equal pay (Marchington et al. 2005: 69–70). The Equal Pay Act 1970 specifies that comparators must be in the same employment or employed by an 'associated' employer (a company controlled by the other company or where both companies are controlled by a third party).[3] Hence, the contradiction is likely to arise that people working alongside each other but with different employers and different pay rates, may simultaneously have good reason to pursue equal pay for work of equal value cases, but be unable to do so for lack of a legally recognized comparator. This means that in TUPE cases, because the transferred now have a new employer, they are unable to bring equal pay cases even in situations where their non-transferred erstwhile colleagues, with whom they still work, receive pay increases while theirs' remain frozen.

At the heart of many of these ambiguities about the effort–reward bargain is that employment status is prioritized over 'felt-fair' pay based on job evaluation.

Commitment and the psychological contract

It is a common place in HRM literature, particularly when discussing 'high-commitment' models, that commitment and integration may result from adherence to a common set of values and a common culture. However, the fragmentation that is inherent in networked organizational forms militates against this. Rather, they are a breeding ground for subcultures, differentiated by employer, employment contracts and business contracts. Furthermore, the development of some measure of a common culture in multi-employer networks is impeded by a major paradox: that networked organizational forms simultaneously may give rise to employment relationships that appear to exhibit low trust (indeed, as suggested earlier, be contrary to felt fair norms) yet expect employees to develop collaborative relationships that require high trust (Rubery et al. 2002: 666).

It is true that some employees, deemed ancillary to their organization's core competencies and transferred to a specialist company, find such a move career enhancing and empowering. This was the case for some IT employees transferred from 'Govco' to 'FutureTech' (Marchington et al. 2005: 272) and the catering workers discussed by Colling (Colling 2003). However, many do not. First, there is the feeling of powerlessness and marginalization at being 'handed over' to another employer with little, if any, role in shaping the contract or choice in the matter, except to accept voluntary redundancy (if on offer) or to leave.[4] Second, employees, having chosen and remained working in their original organization until transfer, may have a great deal of affective commitment to it and a commensurate sense of loss. Many public sector workers, for example, farmed out to private sector subcontractors, lament the loss of a public service ethos that no amount of rhetoric about delivery and responsiveness to the sovereign customer can replace in a contract-driven, profit-oriented company. Third, the fragmentation in networked organizational forms, while providing opportunities for some (see Marchington et al. 2005: Chapter 10) may increase perceptions of job insecurity for the many, particularly those transferred from the public to the private sector. Taken together, these three factors point to the likely disruption of many individuals' psychological contracts with their former employers and a consequent wariness about trusting future employers. As Marchington et al. (2005: 198) point out, in networked organizational forms, good performance is more often due to pride in doing a good job, commitment to a common goal or service and loyalty to colleagues than to commitment to the organization as such. Further, Swart and Kinnie (2003) argue that attempts to develop simultaneously strong employee identities with organization, profession and client may not be possible as each may militate against one of the others.

Whither HRM in networked organizational forms?

Two different scenarios may be painted of the future of HRM in networked organizational forms. The first, optimistic scenario places HRM in a context where interorganizational relationships are based on obligational, relational contracting, where there is a balance of power between or among participants and where opportunities are perceived of mutual, reciprocal gains. This scenario sees the establishment of networked organization in terms of partnership where, rather than cost-savings considerations being dominant, the objective is the synergistic pooling of specialist expertise in the interest of value-adding innovation. An example might be large IT or construction engineering projects, where companies with complementary expertise join together in consortia to bid for and manage a major project.

In these circumstances, where valued, 'core' employees may be seconded to multi-employer project teams, there may be a major strategic role for HRM in areas of management development, performance management and career development. In particular, this may involve initiatives to identify and develop people suited to boundary spanning and negotiating roles and the development of strategies to ensure continuity and succession in the event of turnover. This may be particularly necessary due to the opportunities for poaching talent that is afforded by the close relationship the employee has with the partner organization. Where employees embody the core competencies of the organization, but are 'out of sight', issues of performance management and retention are likely to be perceived as strategic, precisely because of the high investment that has been made in employees. The design and negotiation of individualized reward packages contingent on performance is likely to figure prominently. This may be linked to a business advisor or 'strategic partner' and 'change agent' roles (Ulrich 1997), through which senior HRM specialists may make a major input in advising on the process of developing and maintaining high trust relationships between partners. As generating and maintaining high trust relations is the bedrock of successful partnership, the opportunities and challenges here for HRM are potentially enormous. However, such a role for HR is only likely to be attainable *if* senior HR management have pre-existing power and credibility at board level.

The pessimistic scenario relates to 'run of the mill' outsourcing, based on 'arms' length', low-trust contracting and where cost savings, farming out employee relations 'problems' and offloading risk are the prime motivators on the part of the client organization. Such a context is inimical to either client or provider subcontractor committing to the long-term skill development that lies at the heart of RBV justifications for the strategic nature of HRM. The provider firm is unlikely to invest in long-term training given contracts are primarily won on price and that contract period and tenure may be short due to clients' desire for frequent marketing testing. A client firm that prioritizes cost control may well extend this logic to any activity that is perceived as overhead, which might include an in-house training function. This would be in keeping with the well-known propensity for UK organizations to first cut back training if cost reductions are sought. Certainly there is evidence that a rising number of organizations are outsourcing HR administration, in particular, training and development, recruitment and selection and pay and benefits (Vernon et al. 2000 cited in Cooke et al. 2005). Storey (2005: 198) gives the example of BT's contract with Accenture for HR services. It is an empirical question whether senior HR management in client companies is involved in such decisions as a strategic option, enabling their resources to be focused on the HR dimensions of business strategy or whether the decision to outsource HRM activity is taken as a cost-cutting measure by accountants. In the latter case, the HR function is likely to decrease in size, visibility and authority.

In the pessimistic scenario, HR appears caught in an unenviable position. HR in a client organization faces a number of potential difficulties. If HR takes on a business advisor role in a cost-cutting environment, this may undermine the ability to enact a credible and effective welfare or 'employee champion' role (Ulrich 1997) for existing employees about to be transferred to the subcontractor. Admittedly, the 'employee champion' role does not appear to be a popular choice in this environment (Bach 2005: 15). A role in employee consultation may be undermined by lack of information forthcoming from the transferee.[4] As Colling (2000: 83) points out, in market-driven organizations, whether clients or provider subcontractors, HR services are likely to be driven by service levels agreements with line management, which inhibit a proactive role for HR and places line management firmly in the driving seat. If it is the accountants and lawyers that are primarily involved in providing specialist advice in drawing up contracts, it is largely line managers, in the boundary spanning roles, who take on their management (Marchington et al. 2005: Chapter 6). For provider subcontractors, given the fragmented nature of employment associated with outsourced jobs, the key role of HR in developing coherent and consistent personnel principles and procedures may be seen as unachievable, if not an undesirable inhibitor of flexibility. If the client is in the driving seat, and the subcontractor is reliant on the contract, the client may play a major part in dictating HR policy in the subcontractor organization, whether or not it introduces inconsistencies into the workplace. This is particularly likely if the employees involved are in customer-facing roles, where their perceived identification with the client is deemed important for brand image and the delivery of a 'seamless' service (Swart and Kinnie 2003). Further, unless there is a HR presence on site, the management of the fragmented employment relationship is likely to be located in line management. Because many employees in the subcontractor organizations (except in public/private partnerships) will not be union members, any role for HR involving negotiation with unions will be undermined. In a nutshell, the pessimistic scenario suggests a marginalized role for institutionalized HR in both client and subcontractor provider organizations. In such circumstances, HR specialists may prefer the 'if you can't beat them, join them' stance and seek career development in HR business services consultancies.

Nevertheless, the contradictions about employment status, the presence of multiple employers within a workplace and the influence of the client in shaping the employment relationship (Bach 2005) may present the challenge to HR specialists to develop a role that merges skilled negotiator with administrative expert (Ulrich 1997). This is not a million miles away from the skills required to manage relationships with the unions. Indeed, as the partnership model between weakened unions and organizations becomes predominant, the important skill of generating trust between organizations can be transferred to this arena too. In both cases, the skill is in generating trust with a full recognition of pluralistic assumptions rather than working with unitaristic illusions.

Further, it has been recognized that organizational fragmentation does inhibit the development of commitment to a common organization culture and often involves the disruption of the psychological contract. Trust in the employer may be undermined by the recognition of increasing polarization between the skilled 'haves' and the unskilled 'have nots', symbolized by senior management's lucrative share options, on the one hand, and the pension fraud at Enron, on the other. Bach (2005: 35–7) has suggested that in these circumstances, the HR role should focus less on gaining employees' commitment to the organization and more on their 'engagement' with the customer or brand, framed within an image of 'corporate social responsibility'. In practical terms, Bach suggests, this involves an emphasis on selecting employees whose values and emotions fit the requirements of the job, reinforced by processes of socialization, training and appraisal. This means that for many service sector jobs the emphasis will be on the development of customer-oriented skills, involving emotional and aesthetic labour. Nevertheless, he points out, there is likely to be competition for this role from other functions, such as marketing and corporate communications departments.

Of course, the two scenarios are at either end of a continuum of HR contexts and responses. The rich case study data of Marchington et al. (2005) suggest a far more variegated and nuanced picture. As Scarborough (2000: 16) puts it, in discussing supply chain relationships:

> Attempts to classify such relationships as involving either partnership or exploitation may be neglecting the pervasive effects of tighter logistical integration and the dissemination of key production methods centred on quality and time.

Few networks offer the undiluted 'win–win' outcome of the optimistic scenario as power relations are rarely evenly balanced and the stronger party may be tempted to offload risk and cost onto the weaker party. In the notoriously short-termist UK economy the regulatory environment does little to support a long-term perspective on training and skills development or to assist the development of consistent HR policies in multi-employer contexts. By the very nature of networked organizational forms, each organization is constrained in its choice of HR strategy by other members' requirements, expectations and power (Kinnie et al. 2005). When flexibility is the justification and watchword of such interorganizational relationships, pragmatism, experimentation and learning from operational experience are likely to moderate, if not supplant, a truly strategic approach to HR.

Notes

1. This section rests heavily on the findings of the UK ESRC 'Future of Work' programme's project 'Changing Organizational Forms and the Reshaping of Work' (1999–2002). This research was conducted by Mick Marchington, Jill Rubery, Hugh Willmott, Jill Earnshaw, Damian Grimshaw, Irena Grugulis, John Hassard, Marilyn Carroll, Fang Lee Cooke, Gail Hebson and Steven Vincent. This research explored in depth eight case studies involving agencies, outsourcing, franchising, multiclient and multiemployer sites, public private partnerships and supply chain partnerships. The arguments and examples discussed in this section are derived from Rubery et al. (2002) and from Marchington et al. (2005), to whom I am indebted.

2. Part of the proliferation of separate companies at the airport was due to government requirements for competitive tendering. Services (e.g., baggage handling), previously performed in-house were now provided by wholly owned susidiaries or independent contractors.

3. This constraint does not exist in EU law which allows comparators 'in the same establishment or service' (Marchington et al. 2005: 70).

4. In theory TUPE regulations place an obligation on the tranferor employer to consult employee representatives on the reasons for outsourcing, its implications for employees and on the process of transfer, with the view to seeking agreement to the proposed changes. However, in practice, the consultation process may be constrained by the transferee's unwillingness to share information pertinent to the transfer and future developments in the employment relationship on the grounds of commercial sensitivity. Further, in the past there was confusion as to the scope of its application. Also, employers may attempt to side step its provisions. For example, because only changes imposed as a consequence of the transfer are illegal, employers may seek the consent of employees to changes in their pay and conditions prior to the transfer. This is because these then become the protected ones, being in operation 'immediately before transfer' (Colling 2005: 98–9; Cooke et al. 2004).

References

Ashkenas, R., D. Ulrich, J. Tick and S. Kerr (1995). *The Boundaryless Organization: Breaking the Chains of Organizational Structure.* San Francisco, Jossey-Bass.

Atkinson, J. (1984). 'Manpower strategies for flexible organizations', *Personnel Management* 16(8): 28–31.

Atkinson, J. (1986). *New Forms of Work Organization.* Institute of Manpower Studies Report No. 121. Brighton: Institute of Manpower Studies.

Bach S. (2005). 'Personnel management in transition', in *Managing Human Resources,* 4th edn. Oxford, Blackwell.

Barney, J. (1991). 'Firm resources and sustained competitive advantage', *Journal of Management* 17(1): 99–120.

Best, M. (1990). *The New Competition.* Cambridge, Polity Press.

Boxall, P. (1996). 'The strategic human resource debate and the resource-based view of the firm', *Human Resource Management Journal* 6(3): 59–75.

Castells, M. (1996). *The Information Age: Economy, Society and Culture, Volume One. The Rise of the Network Society.* Oxford, Blackwell.

Clark, R. (1979). *The Japanese Company.* New Haven, CT, Yale University Press.

Colling, T. (2000). 'Personnel management in the extended organization', in S. Bach and K. Sisson (eds) *Personnel Management,* 3rd edn. Oxford, Blackwell.

Colling, T. (2003). 'Managing without unions: the sources and limitations of individualism', in P. K. Edwards (ed.) *Industrial Relations: Theory and Practice.* Oxford, Blackwell.

Colling, T. (2005). 'Managing human resources in the networked organization', in S. Bach (ed.) *Managing Human Resources*, 4th edn. Oxford, Blackwell.

Cooke, F. L., J. Earnshaw, M. Marchington and J. Rubery (2004). 'For better and for worse? Transfers of undertakings and the reshaping of employment relations', *International Journal of Human Resource Management* 15 (2): 276-94.

Cooke, F. L., J. Shen and A. McBride (2005). 'Outsourcing HR as competitive strategy? A literature review and an assessment of implications', *Human Resource Management* 44(4): 413-32.

Davidow, W. H. and M. S. Malone (1992). *The Virtual Corporation: Structuring and Revitalizing the Corporation for the 21st Century*. New York, Harper Business.

DiMaggio, P. and W. Powell (1983). 'The iron cage revisited: institutional isomorphism and collective rationality in organizational fields', *American Sociological Review* 48 (2): 147-60.

Dore, R. (1973). *British Factory-Japanese Factory: The Origins of Diversity in Industrial Relations*. London, Allen & Unwin.

Espino-Rodriguez, T. F. and V. Padron-Robaina (2006). 'A review of outsourcing from the resource-based view of the firm', *International Journal of Management Reviews* 8(1): 49-70.

Grey, C. and N. Mitev (1995). 'Re-engineering organizations: a critical appraisal', *Personnel Review* 24(1): 6-18.

Grint, K. (1994). 'Re-engineering history: social resonances and business process reengineering', *Organization* 1(1): 179-201.

Grint, K. and L. Willcocks (1995). 'Business process re-engineering in theory and practice: business paradise regained?', *New Technology, Work and Employment* 19 (2): 99-109.

Hall, P. A. and D. Soskice (2001). *Varieties of Capitalism*. Oxford, Oxford University Press.

Hammer, M. (1996). *Beyond Reengineering*. London, HarperCollins.

Hammer, M. and J. Champy (1993). *Re-engineering the Corporation: A Manifesto for Business Revolution*. London, Nicholas Brearley.

Harrison, B. and M. Kelley (1993). 'Outsourcing and the search for flexibility', *Work, Employment and Society* 7 (2): 213-55.

Huselid, M. A. (1995). 'The impact of human resource management practices on turnover, productivity, and corporate financial performance', *Academy of Management Journal* 38(3): 635-72.

Jessop, R. (1994). 'Post-Fordism and the state', in A. Amin (ed.) *Post Fordism, A Reader*. Oxford, Blackwell.

Kinnie, N., J. Swart and J. Purcell (2005). 'Influences on the choice of HR system: the network organization perspective', *International Journal of Human Resource Management* 16(6): 1004-1028.

Lazonick, W. (2005). 'Corporate restructuring', in S. Ackroyd, R. Batt, P. Thompson and P. S. Tolbert (eds) *The Oxford Handbook of Work and Organization*. Oxford, Oxford University Press.

Lazonick, W. and M. O'Sullivan (2000). 'Maximizing shareholder value: a new ideology for corporate governance', *Economy and Society* 29: 13-35.

Legge, K. (1995). *Human Resource Management: Rhetorics and Realities*. Basingstoke, Macmillan.

Legge, K. (2000). 'Personnel management in the lean organization', in S. Bach and K. Sisson (eds) *Personnel Management*, 3rd edn. Oxford, Blackwell.

Marchington, M., D. Grimshaw, J. Rubery and H. Willmott (eds) (2005). *Fragmenting Work, Blurring Organizational Boundaries and Disordering Hierarchies*. Oxford, Oxford University Press.

Nahapiet, J. and S. Ghoshal (1998). 'Social capital, intellectual capital and organizational advantage', *Academy of Management Review* 23(2): 242-66.

Nohria, N. and R. Eccles (eds) (1992). *Networks and Organizations*. Boston, MA, Harvard Business School Press.

Oliver, N. and B. Wilkinson (1992). *The Japanization of British Industry: New Developments in the 1990s*, 2nd edn. Oxford, Blackwell.

Paauwe, J. (2004). *HRM and Performance, Achieving Long Term Viability*. Oxford, Oxford University Press.

Piore, M. and C. Sabel (1984). *The Second Industrial Divide*. New York, Basic Books.

Pollert, A. (ed.) (1991). *Farewell to Flexibility?* Oxford, Blackwell.

Powell, W. W. (1990). 'Neither market nor hierarchy: network forms of organization', *Research in Organizational Behavior* 12: 295-336.

Powell, W. W. (1998). 'Institutional theory', in C. L. Cooper and C. Argyris (eds) *Encyclopedia of Management*. Oxford, Oxford University Press.

Rees, C., H. Scarbrough and M. Terry (1996). The People Management Implications of Leaner Ways of Working. Report by IRRU, Warwick Business School, University of Warwick, *Issues in People Management, No. 15*. London, Institute of Personnel and Development.

Rubery, J. and D. Grimshaw (2003). *The Organization of Employment, An International Perspective*. Basingstoke, Palgrave Macmillan.

Rubery, J., J. Earnshaw, M. Marchington, F. L. Cooke and S. Vincent (2002). 'Changing organizational forms and the employment relationship', *Journal of Management Studies* 39(5): 645-72.

Sabel, C. (1991). 'Moebius strip organizations and open labour markets', in P. Bourdieu and J. S. Coleman (eds) *Social Theory for a Changing Society*. Boulder, CO, Westview Press.

Sako, M. (1992). *Prices, Quality and Trust: Inter-Firm Relations in Britain and Japan*. Cambridge, Cambridge University Press.

Scarbrough, H. (2000). 'The HR implications of supply chain relationships', *Human Resource Management Journal* 10(1): 5-17.

Sennett, R. (1998). *The Corrosion of Character*. New York, Norton.

Storey, J. (2005). 'New organizational forms and their links with HR', in G. Salaman, J. Storey and J. Billsberry (eds) *Strategic Human Resource Management, A*

Reader. Milton Keynes and London, Open University and Sage.

Swart, J. and N. Kinnie (2003). 'Knowledge-intensive firms: the influence of the client on HR systems', *Human Resource Management Journal* 13(3): 37-50.

Thompson, G. (2005). 'Interfirm relations as networks', in S. Ackroyd, R. Batt, P. Thompson and P. S. Tolbert (eds) *The Oxford Handbook of Work and Organization.* Oxford, Oxford University Press.

Ulrich, D. (1997). *Human Resource Champions: The Next Agenda for Adding Value and Delivering Results.* Boston, MA, Harvard Business School Press.

Vernon, P., J. Philips, C. Brewster and J. Ommeren (2000). 'European trends in HR resourcing'. Report for William M. Mercer and the Cranfield School of Management.

Whitley, R. (1999). *Divergent Capitalisms, The Social Structuring and Change of Business Systems.* Oxford, Oxford University Press.

Williamson, O. E. (1975). *Markets and Hierarchies: Analysis and Antitrust Implications.* New York, Free Press.

Williamson, O. E. (1985). *The Economic Institutions of Capitalism.* New York, Free Press.

Willmott, H. (1994). 'Business process re-engineering and human resource management', *Personnel Review* 23(3): 34-46.

Willmott, H. (1995). 'The odd couple?: re-engineering business processes; managing human relations', *New Technology, Work and Employment* 10(2): 89-98.

Wright, P. M., B. B. Dunford and S. A. Snell (2001). 'Human resources and the resource based view of the firm', *Journal of Management* 27(6): 701-21.

Strategic issues

This second part of the book is devoted to a closer examination of strategic level issues. Chapter 4 'What is strategic HRM?' by John Storey, presents a review of the strategic HRM literature and locates it within debates about strategic management more generally. The chapter examines the nature of strategy and, using a number of significant examples, reveals the nature and characteristics of strategic HRM in practice. This chapter also shows how cause-and-effect linkages alongside measurement are critical components of a strategic approach.

Chapter 5 'Facing up to the challenges of success: putting governance at the heart of HRM', by Keith Sisson, approaches strategic issues in a new and distinctive way. The chapter has an ambitious aim – to transcend the often ephemeral fads and fashions and to attend to the wider more enduring themes of employment management. In an agenda-setting piece, Sisson argues that other disciplines such as communications, strategy or marketing could lay claim to, and indeed begin to take responsibility for, the core aspects of employment management. Each of these disciplines would put its own stamp on the activity and Sisson contends that HR (as a field of practice and a field of study) can best contribute if it approaches the task from the perspective of 'governance'. This means engaging with the handling of labour services through the dual governance structures of markets and organizations. The latter in particular introduces aspects of contract setting and enforcement, target setting, monitoring, encouragement, negotiation and many other aspects of managerial relationship handling in addition to market relations. Keith Sisson's chapter is strategic in multiple senses – not least of these is the setting out of the fundamentals of the discipline and of the practice.

What is strategic HRM?

John Storey

From the outset, a core characteristic of the idea of human resource management was the notion that 'people management' is capable of being handled in a way which makes it a crucial contributor to competitive advantage. If astute people management, rather than (or more than) technology, finance, marketing or operational efficiency, was the essential source of advantage and not simply a cost to be minimized, then by definition, HRM could be regarded as potentially a strategic process. It could thus be argued that the prefix 'strategic' is not really required because the function is supposed to be inherently strategic. However, as we saw in Chapter 1, HRM is used in both generic as well as specific ways. When used in the generic sense, there will naturally be many different kinds of approach to managing human resources: some of these will be ad hoc while others may be more strategic. The purpose of this chapter is to examine what the strategic types entail.

Debate within the strategic HRM literature is concerned with four main questions and issues: first, what it comprises (for example, how much is it about rational planning and how much about inherent behaviour); second, is the pursuit of 'best fit' or 'best practice' the way to proceed; third, how SHRM fits with the resource-based view (RBV) of the firm; fourth, the 'architecture' of multiple HR strategies within complex organizations. Other key issues concern the methods that are and might be adopted to 'do' strategizing in HR; the kinds of obstacles to its achievement and how these might be overcome.

Many of these debates, and their relevance and urgency in the current environment, stem from the changing nature of competition. The realization of the value of intangible assets has meant that skill in the strategic management of these assets has become crucial and yet uncertain. There are four features to contend with (Kaplan and Norton 2001: 66–7). First, the pathways of value creation are indirect and complex (improved training may lead to higher levels of service and this may lead to improved customer satisfaction and so on – but the chain of cause and effect may be complicated). Second, value is contextual (a star merchant banker may deliver huge gains to one firm but be of little value in a different context such as an internet retail bank). Third, the value of intangible assets is potential not actual until linked with organizational processes such as design and service to realize value. Finally, assets are bundled – intangible assets rarely have value on their own until they are combined with other assets. Taken together, these features suggest not only the changing nature of strategic management but also hint at the potential critical importance of strategic human resource management under the new conditions.

A suitable point of departure to address these issues and questions is the nature of business strategy and the literature on strategic management.

Definitions and interpretations

Strategy

In order to understand what 'strategic HR' might be, it is first necessary to dwell a little on the meaning of strategic management per se and on what it might entail. Problems of definition about strategy are by no means confined to the domain of HR. Different executive teams and different management consulting firms vary massively in the way they approach strategy. As has been noted, some will focus on processes, others will stress shareholder value, or core competences or change management and so on (Kaplan and Norton 2001: 65). Indeed, many board-level managers as well as observers are even unclear about which decisions are strategic and which non-strategic. This is hardly surprising as there is disagreement also among academic specialists in strategic management.

Various definitions have been offered:

> What business strategy is all about, is . . . competitive advantage . . . The sole purpose of strategic planning is to enable a company to gain, as efficiently as possible, a sustainable edge over its competitors.
>
> (Ohmae 1982)

> The direction and scope of an organization over the longer term, which ideally matches its resources to its changing environment and in particular its markets, customers and clients to meet stakeholder expectations.
>
> (Johnson 1987)

> The determination of the long-run goals and objectives of an enterprise and the adoption of courses of action and the allocation of resources necessary for carrying out these goals.
>
> (Chandler 1962)

> A strategy is the pattern or plan that integrates an organization's major goals, policies and action sequences into a cohesive whole. A well-formulated strategy helps marshall and allocate an organization's resources into a unique and viable posture based on its relative internal competencies and shortcomings, anticipated changes in the environment, and contingent moves by intelligent opponents.
>
> (Quinn 1980)

Many more definitions could be cited but these few are sufficient to reveal most of the critical elements. These relate to the objectives of strategy, the nature of strategy and the interplay of external and internal considerations. The objective is, we are told, 'competitive advantage'; the characteristic or desired features are guidelines as to the direction, nature and scope of an organization; the desirable conditions are a match between external opportunities and stakeholder demands, on the one hand, and a firm's resources and capabilities to exploit the opportunities and meet these expectations, on the other.

These then are some of the main features of strategy as viewed from a strategic management perspective. One of our purposes will be to examine what implications these may carry for a strategic approach to HRM. But before we can do that it has to be noted that the analysis of strategy becomes complicated by some further issues.

Since it would be pointless to describe every decision as 'strategic', a distinction has to be made between strategic and tactical decisions. Grant (1998: 14) suggests that a tactic be viewed as a 'scheme for a specific action . . . [a] . . . . manoeuvre necessary to win a battle' whereas strategy 'is concerned with winning the war'. Thus, behind this distinction is the notion that strategic decisions have three common characteristics:

- They are important.
- They involve a significant amount of resources.
- They are not easily reversible.

These three attributes are interconnected. Because the decisions are important (that is they carry significant consequences in terms of risk to the organization as a whole) they usually imply significant decisions about the allocation of resources. For example, an airline, a supermarket chain or hotel chain which takes a decision to occupy a position at the high end of the market would require an allocation of resources that involves commitments in the areas of site location, supply chain, infrastructure, fittings and furnishings, staff quality and staff training and many other related issues. These investments will all become non-viable if the commensurate premium revenues are not attracted. Conversely, an airline, supermarket chain or hotel chain taking a strategic position at the low-cost, no-frills end of the market will require resource allocation decisions which take them to low-cost physical locations (less fashionable town sites for the hotels for example), the airline will need a superfast turnaround regime to keep the fleet in the air, the supermarket will have to operate with poor-quality fixtures, lighting and supply chain relationships and so on. Each of these complementary sets of decisions represents some very considerable degree of 'lock-in' and there will be a whole series of sunk costs. Hence, to prevaricate between the two positions or to seek to revert from one to the other would normally carry very high costs. So, these kinds of interlocking decisions can be regarded as strategic.

Much depends however on the nature of the question one poses. If one asks 'what is the strategy?' to a senior manager, this could mean 'please describe the essence of the strategic intent, the sense of direction, the few core defining elements of market positioning and organizational features assumed necessary to exploit that position'. This version of strategy could well accept that the answer is always incomplete and is awaiting enactment and realization through myriad other decisions and actions. Or, more naively, the question might mean 'what is the full-blown strategic document that foreshadows virtually all implementation decisions and is reflected in or even comprises the current business plan?'

The 'strategic intent' version of the question chimes with Quinn's (1980) approach, which sees strategy as 'a pattern or plan which integrates an organization's policies . . . in the context of a changing environment and moves by intelligent competitors'. One managing director in one of our research projects (Storey and Salaman 2005) referred to strategy as 'a compass not a map'. In other words, it is a sense of direction that allows relatively consistent decisions.

Compass or map, one of the most dominant ideas in strategic management has been the notion of 'positioning' in the market. Porter (1985) famously argued that strategy means finding a competitive advantage. That must mean being, in some way, different from the crowd. He suggests that essentially this means excelling in terms of cost, quality or innovation. It is normally difficult to be a leader on all three fronts. This fundamental idea has been picked up and carried through by a number of writers in strategic management and as we shall see in the next section, also in strategic HRM. Essentially, if a firm has made a strategic choice to lead on one front or another then, it is suggested, its human resource strategy needs to support this choice.

Textbook accounts often contrast two main approaches to strategy. On the one hand, they depict a 'design school', which supposedly views strategy as a linear process. Here strategy is formulated at the apex of the organization following environmental scanning and rational assessment and then communicated vertically for implementation. This is usually categorized as 'strategic planning'. On the other hand, there is the 'process school', which emphasizes the emergent nature of strategy in practice.

But the dichotomy between top-down design and bottom-up emergent strategy is too stark and is essentially a false dichotomy. Naturally, if one shifts from *prescriptions* about how strategy ought to be done, to *descriptions* of how it seems to occur, then the embedded nature of strategy within organizations comes to the fore. Mintzberg (1994) more than anyone has emphasized the importance of 'emergent strategy'. His research revealed how the 'realized strategy' is often only partially in line with the 'intended' strategy. He uses the example of Honda's capture of the US motorbike market. After the event, this appeared to instance astute strategic planning, but in reality it required considerable learning, discovery and surprise along the way. Others have built on this point. And there are practical lessons to be drawn: for example, too strong a dichotomy between strategy and implementation limits the scope for learning.

Nonetheless, some leading thinkers in the strategic management field such as Grant (1998) continue to opt for the rationalistic, analytical approach. Grant says he recognizes the importance of intuition, creativity, learning and experience, but systematic *analysis* is vital as an input to the strategy process: 'Analytical frameworks are not alternatives or substitutes for experience, commitment and creativity but they do provide useful frames for organizing and assessing vast amounts information available on the firm and its environment and for guiding decisions' (1998: 22).

There are merits in paying regard to the insights of both the planning and the process perspectives. Each can usefully inform the other. If too much emphasis is placed on uncertainty and serendipity then the scope for guidance to senior managers becomes much reduced and, incidentally, it becomes difficult to justify the existence of and the rewards allocated to the senior echelons. One of the functions and duties of directors is to set a direction: for example, is this to be a low-cost, short-haul airline such as RyanAir or is it to be a cross-continental, full-service operator, such as Emirates, catering for premier customers willing to pay high fares?

These kinds of choice – the placing of 'bets' (huge investments that carry a significant degree of lock-in for some time) – on one kind of business model or another do not usually just happen by chance. If one traces the steps back far enough no doubt

---

HRM in Action 4.1   Waitrose strategy

In Waitrose, the (planned) strategy is to 'dominate on product and differentiate on service'. The domination on product dimension of the strategy means to have the best fresh food offer (in terms of both quality and range) and to deliver the best product quality consistently across the rest of the range. The 'differentiate on customer service' component means to provide consistently superior service in the areas that are meaningful to customers. Notably, the strategy also means a decision about price – i.e. not to be competitive here but to be able to charge a premium price where quality differentiation justifies it. The emphasis on the product supported by service components is demonstrated in various ways such as the investment in the training of 'product champions' – i.e. in-store staff with high levels of product knowledge in areas such as wines and cheeses. A further support is the investment in the supply chain to ensure that Waitrose buyers have close knowledge of and good long-term relations with known farmers and thus the business can claim to know the 'provenance' of products such as its meats. This assurance of quality in turn becomes a crucial marketing message for its customers.

Historically, this distinctive business model may have in large measure 'evolved' and may have been in that sense 'discovered'. But now it is a firm conscious part of the strategy and it requires clear decisions that meet the three criteria of importance, significant commitment of resources and not easily reversible. The shops are expensive to build, the careful cultivation of suppliers to guarantee the 'provenance' of the meat is a hugely different strategy than that pursued, for example, by Tesco, which has used its huge buying power to drive down supplier cost. Likewise, the staff are carefully selected and are well trained and managed and are offered a wide range of welfare benefits. None of the core elements is now 'accidental' – the business demonstrates its commitment to the strategy by heavy investment in its chosen areas of competitive advantage. At the same time, the strategic management of this business, as is the case with other successful businesses, is alert to changing competitor behaviour, is allowing of learning, is monitoring changing marketplace, government regulation, food scares, spending patterns and many other factors. There is certainly debate between the merits of 'intuitive retailers' and the value or otherwise of analytical frameworks but the attempt to utilize these strategic decision tools is amply in evidence.

---

one could find many instances of incremental learning and a number of false leads. But these do not in themselves undermine the case for attempting a rational assessment of the preferred way forward. Even when launched and in mid-stream, the respective business models require constant review and renewed commitment to keep them viable. Drift will erode the viability of a business model. The case example of the upmarket supermarket chain, Waitrose, indicates some of these features of big choices and commitment; and it also begins to introduce the integral nature of the human resource strategy as well.

Apart from the different approaches to strategic management already mentioned, there have been other developments in that field. There are trends and fashions within the strategic management field of practice and field of study as there are in all others. It is interesting and relevant to note that many if not most of the developments have, in fact, brought the field much closer to the central concerns of human resource management. A significant shift occurred in the 1970s from corporate planning and an emphasis on managing a portfolio of diversified businesses, to a sharper focus on competition and 'strategic management' in the 1980s onwards. In the 1990s, key developments included the role of knowledge in the firm, innovation, organizational learning and dynamic capabilities and the use of cooperative strategies – especially in the form of alliances and interfirm networks and virtual organizations.

One of the more influential (and at times dominating) perspectives has been the resource-based view (RBV). This shifted attention from outside to inside the firm and, as such, underscored the importance of human resources alongside a number of other 'intangible assets' such as corporate culture and reputation. Grant (1998) has explored the nature and value of this perspective. He suggests that 'When the external environment is in a state of flux, the firm itself, in terms of its bundle of resources and capabilities, may be a much more stable basis on which to define its identity' (1998: 107). As Grant maintains, the resource-based view has had a 'profound effect' on the understanding of strategy formation. It redirects attention from selecting market segments to strategies based on differentiation and the exploitation of what Hamel and Prahalad (1992) have termed 'core competencies'. Using this perspective a firm should seek 'self-knowledge' to achieve an understanding of its resources and capabilities. It entails exploitation of these resources over the long term in order to achieve a close linkage between its strategies and its capabilities as exemplified, Grant suggests, by Coca-Cola and Proctor & Gamble. It further requires building the company's resource base by filling significant gaps in its resources and capabilities. Resources comprise tangible assets such as financial and physical resources; intangible resources such as reputation and culture; and human resources including specialized skills and knowledge, motivation and communication and interactive abilities. Together, these resources build organizational capabilities which in turn allow the formulation of a strategy that can deliver competitive advantage.

From a resource-based view, 'human resources are the productive services human beings offer the firm in terms of skills, knowledge, and reasoning and decision-making abilities' (Grant 1998: 116). Economists regard these as constituting 'human capital'. With growing recognition of the strategic potential of this resource, organizations have spent more time identifying competences and seeking to measure them. So, human resources comprise both individual attributes (such as problem-solving ability, commitment and so on) but also organizational resources such as organizational culture and the 'social capital' gained through cooperative and practised patterns of interaction. This concept is reflected in the notion of 'organizational routines' that denote regular and predictable patterns of coordinated activity (Nelson and Winter 1982). Integrated sequences of relevant routines constitute the basis for organizational capabilities. To be useful to a firm, the complementary resources and capabilities must have profit-earning potential and must be sustainable. To be sustainable, these attributes must not be too amenable to being copied (i.e. not too easily replicable by competing firms) and not easily transferable through direct purchase. Another condition is that the resources and capabilities must be 'appropriable' by the firm. When tangible assets are to the fore such as physical materials, plant and equipment, this accruing of returns by the owner is more easily established. But when intangible assets are to the fore, ownership and control are more problematic. As Grant notes, if highly talented individuals and – even more seriously whole teams of talent – leave an organization the threat to appropriability is plain. Professional service firms such as lawyers, architects, advertising agencies and indeed merchant banks are all vulnerable in this regard.

In summary, Grant suggests that there is a sequence of steps that can be advised from a resources and capabilities perspective:

1 Identify the firm's resources and appraise its strengths and weaknesses.

2 Identify capabilities.

3 Appraise the rent-earning potential of these resources and capabilities.

4 On the basis of the previous three steps, select a strategy.

5 Identify the resource gaps that may become evident when a preferred strategy has been selected.

Finally, building on this kind of perspective other writers have increasingly emphasized the importance of 'dynamic capabilities' (Teece and Pisano 1994) in order to keep pace with ever changing environments and the countermoves of intelligent competitors.

On the basis of these ideas from the field of strategic management, we can now turn to an analysis of the concept of 'strategic human resource management'.

Strategic HRM

Interpretations of the meaning of, and potential for, 'strategic HRM' have reflected the debates and uncertainties found in the field of strategic management more generally. Thus, questions of meaning, of description versus prescription, of the scope for choice and so on have all reappeared. But our review of strategic management will offer some guide to the tensions, dilemmas and uncertainties often encountered in the SHRM literature. We start with the meaning of strategy in HRM.

Defining strategy in HRM

HRM or people management more broadly, would normally *not* be described as strategic if decisions about recruitment, selection, pay, job design and so on were taken on an ad hoc basis and without concern for consistency or without reference to the organization's strategy. Conversely, HRM might be regarded as strategic if there is sufficient consistency, that is, if the various elements are mutually supportive. But what needs to fit with what? Two forms of alignment are desirable – *horizontal* integration and *vertical*. The former refers to the consistency, fit and mutual support to be found between the various aspects of HR such as the amount and nature of investment in training and, say, the design of jobs and the rate of remuneration. The notion of vertical integration refers to the alignment of these HR systems with the business strategy. To return to a previous example, if the business strategy is built on a premium end of the market business model, then investment in the various HR elements might need to be substantial – such as upper quartile pay, training and development, pensions and benefits, sophisticated forms of performance management and so on. In general, both horizontal and vertical fit are desirable and will require some thought and action – i.e. some strategizing.

In the light of this, it may be thought that the persistent and recurring debate in HRM between 'best practice' versus 'best fit' is not especially helpful. Strategic choice in the terms discussed earlier naturally assumes difference – or at least some difference. The key to this controversy goes back to the point discussed in Chapter 1, namely, that HRM has both a narrow and a wide (generic) meaning. As explained, the narrow meaning is historically situated: it came to notice and indeed gained prominence because at the time of its emergence it did mark a departure from prevailing beliefs, assumptions and practices in labour management. The model was thus strategic *in that context*. Once the mould had been broken, the universal or common adoption (diffusion) of the model would of course eventually render the model non-differentiating and therefore non-strategic. As there has never been universal adoption this has not arisen. Furthermore, because there are now many diverse labour management practices, there is certainly scope to be strategic in HR by electing for a wide range of approaches. The determining and discriminating factor would not be whether an organization subscribed to a list of policies or even bundles of polices and practices. (Although surveys of the take-up of certain practices may nevertheless be worthwhile for other reasons.)

So, what aspects *do* constitute a strategic approach in HRM? These, in essence, reflect the characteristics described in the first part of this chapter relating to strategic management. But, there are some special aspects. To tease these out we begin with a case example (see HRM in Action 4.2 The Ministry of Defence on page 68).

From this case we can observe the large-scale nature of the shift in HR. The function itself is changing in size (much reduced in numbers) and in function – an abandonment of direct handling of staff management issues and grievances on behalf of line managers and a shift to a remote shared services offering plus a business partner provision. In addition to the restructuring of the function itself, there is also a shift in the approach to people management. The traditional rather paternalistic and civil service-style approach is being reduced and there is an intent to impose private sector-style techniques including incentive pay, a requirement for more individual initiative, clearer accountabilities, measurement and performance management. The wholesale, interrelated nature of the shift indicate some of the attributes of a strategic approach to managing the human resource.

The one element that may possibly be missing or at least be open to some question is the extent to which the MOD's new strategic HR plan is truly consonant with a new business strategy or whether it mainly reflects rather too much a copying of the attributes of what it perceives as leading-edge practice elsewhere. This continues to be a matter of some contention within the organization. In a sense, this is a manifest example of the best practice versus best fit debate. But, in the eyes of the most senior players in HR at this department of state, they are in no doubt that they *intend* a strategic approach, neither are they in any doubt that they have *crafted* a strategic approach. If other observers wish to claim that it is not strategic on the grounds that it does 'not really' fit the organization's wider strategy or on the grounds that its HR approach is too similar to a standard 'best practice' model, then this raises an interesting new level to the debate based on perception and multiple interpretations.

Many – perhaps most – definitions of strategic human resource management tend to be normative and prescriptive. But some are also descriptive statements – they seek to capture and interpret observations of practice. For example, Beer et al. (1985) noted:

We have come to believe that the transformations we are observing amounts to more than a subtle shift in the traditional practices of personnel or the substitution of new terms for unchanging practices. Instead the transformation amounts to a new model regarding the management of human resources in organizations.

The new elements they said were proactive, system-wide interventions; an emphasis on fit linking HRM with strategic planning and culture change; the view that people are social capital; and open communication to build commitment and trust.

It is evident from the wider literature that different criteria have been used to denote 'strategic HRM'. For example, four usages were noted by Hendry and Pettigrew (1986) as a result of their review of the literature at that time:

- the use of planning
- a coherent approach to the design and management of personnel systems based on an employment policy and manpower strategy and often underpinned by a 'philosophy'
- matching HRM activities and policies to some explicit business strategy
- seeing the people of the organization as a 'strategic resource' for achieving competitive advantage.

While it is conceptually possible to identify these separate strands, it may also be appropriate to regard them as aspects of one main idea – namely, the intent to try to manage people in such a way that myriad decisions about people management (how many, where and when available, what skills, how much investment in training, whether to design jobs in narrow or expansive terms, whether to offer career paths, whether to consult and if so with or without representatives and so on) are made with regard to overall organizational goals and methods and not by reference to other considerations.

The notion of matching HR strategy to the kind of Porter (1985) business strategies we touched on earlier has been an influential one in SHRM. A classic example is Schuler and Jackson (1987), who identify the role behaviours and the supporting HRM policies needed to underpin each of the Porter strategies: cost, quality and innovation. For example, to support a business strategy based on product innovation, employees would normally be expected to exercise a high level of creative behaviour, have a longer term focus, be able to cope with risk, have a high tolerance of ambiguity and high levels of cooperative behaviour. In turn, to encourage these behaviours the HR policies would normally include job design that enabled interaction, performance appraisal systems that rewarded longer term and group-based behaviours, compensation systems that allow employees to be stockholders and so on. In contrast, a cost-reduction business strategy might require repetitive and predictable routines that optimized operational cycle times, a focus on short-term gains, a high concern for quantity and pace of output and so on. The HR policies supporting these might include fixed and explicit job descriptions, close monitoring, minimal levels of training and development and perhaps also low pay and minimal benefits.

The 'matching' of packages of HR policies to different contingencies has also been explored by other writers using different business conditions. For example, HR policy choices have been linked to the business lifecycle, that is, from business start-up, through early growth and maturity and eventually to business decline. At each stage, a business might be expected to have different priorities. These will, in turn, require compatible HR strategies. There have been a number of examples of these 'stage' models (Baird and Meshoulam 1988; Kochan and Barocci 1985; Lengnick-Hall and

HRM in Action 4.2   Strategic HR in the Ministry of Defence

The UK Ministry of Defence (MOD) has 80,000 UK non-military staff, mainly civil servants, whose job is to support the military services including air, sea and land forces. The management approach towards this civilian staff has been based on traditional staff management principles. Gradings, progression, pay, training, welfare and so on have all followed formal civil service practices. There has been a large personnel function that has offered line managers and civilian staff personalized service when requested on a one-to-one basis. People management policies were devised at the centre and there were adaptations at service level and at various intervening layers.

Since 2005 the MOD civilian management system has been subject to a major overhaul which is expected to last four years or more to complete. The essence of the transformation is a split between 'transactional service provision' and strategic HR using a business partnering model. The transactional work (keeping personnel records up to date, handling requests for advice about pay, holiday entitlement, processing recruitment and transfers, handling discipline and grievances, health and welfare etc.) has been centralized in a shared services centre. This is an in-house body known as the People, Pay and Pensions Agency (PPPA). This initiative has allowed extensive job cuts among the former personnel staff who used to handle personnel/HR management by being on hand to directly help and advise line managers in their numerous locations.

The PPPA system has 60,000 online and 20,000 offline users. It has 1100 staff offering services to line managers and staff across a range of occupations such as scientists, military police, drivers, logistics, accountants and so on. Much of the work done by the erstwhile personnel/HR specialist was known as 'case work' and this involved direct handling of individual cases on behalf of the line managers (who can be either military officers or civilian line managers). One of the big shifts was to ensure that line managers would assume clear responsibility for managing their civilian staff and that HR should cease doing that for them.

The restructuring of the HR function has been designed to reduce costs (there were 3000 HR staff in 2003 and the aim is to reduce that to 1700 by 2008), to streamline services, to pass more direct management responsibility to line managers, to exploit the potential of IT and to allow an offer of more strategic business-related HR services by the remaining HR staff. In future, the core strategic function at the central MOD will be reduced to about 90 HR specialists and these will set department policy across all three services (army, air force and navy). They will lead national pay negotiations and be responsible for formulation of HR strategy. In addition, the central core team is complemented by 400 'business partners' most of whom are located in the command centres of the various services – plus the joint commands. Their job is to collect and assess all relevant information and to focus efforts so that the senior managers of the services can meet 'business needs including ensuring the right skill mixes'. HR strategic input now is intended to involve, for example, more skills planning. The MOD did consider outsourcing the HR function in a way similar to BT's contract with Accenture which covers 87,000 UK staff. But the MOD decided in the end it wanted to keep the service in-house.

Lengnick-Hall 1988). For example, at the start-up stage, a firm may need HR policies that attract the best technical talent, offers stock options, allows creative work solutions. In the mature to decline stage, the emphasis may shift to cost control, managing headcount reductions and avoiding survivor syndrome. Other theorists have linked HR strategies to different organizational forms. For example, multidivisional corporations will usually require a different HR strategic approach from that of a single product and highly focused business (Fombrun et al. 1984).

Survey evidence

Although the *normative attributes* of SHRM can be described, it may be that many organizations – for a range of different reasons – fail to develop, or choose not to develop, a strategic approach to HR. Evidence from a number of surveys can help shed light on this. In larger companies at least, most HR professionals and indeed most chief executives and top managers from other functions believe that HRM is of strategic importance and ought to be managed more strategically. A CIPD survey of more than 1000 respondents found that 72% of HR managers judged that the influence of HR in the boardroom had increased compared with three years previously (CIPD 2005). Three-quarters of them also reported that they had a written HR strategy. Moreover, other survey evidence also substantiates the idea that chief executives and other senior managers judge that managing human resources is or ought to be a key strategic concern of the business as a whole. Research by Deloitte & Touche found that chief executives ranked investment in people as of equal importance to having an overall business strategy. Indeed, they ranked it as of greater strategic importance than developing new products and services (Touche 2004).

But crucially, while the chief executives recognized the strategic potential, nearly 80% of them did not judge their HR departments to be rising to the challenge. This finding accords very much with our own experience working with organizations in the public and private sectors. Only 17% of the chief executives believed that HR was successful in developing leaders in the organization, only 15% thought that they were effective in motivating and developing the senior team and only 22% thought their HR departments were effective in improving internal communications (Touche 2004).

Some 20 years ago Marginson et al. found in their company-level survey, that most senior management respondents found it very hard to describe their HR strategies and even if they could it was usually vague (Marginson et al. 1988). Arguably, HR executives have learned the talk if not the walk during the intervening decades. Though the examples of 'overarching HR strategies' quoted by Armstrong (2006: 125) may suggest that the nature of these statements indicate a tendency towards generalized statements in place of differentiating clarity. GlaxoSmithKline's is stated as: 'We want GSK to be a place where the best people do their best work.' B&Q 'enhance employee commitment and minimize the loss of B&Q's best people . . . position B&Q as one of the best employers in the UK'. Aegon, 'to ensure that, from whatever angle staff now look at the elements of pay management, performance, career development and reward, they are consistent and linked'. What is revealing about these three examples is that they would seem to be interchangeable; the common themes are 'best people', treated with consistency and seeking commitment. With such shared statements across a pharmaceutical company, a retailer and insurance company, it is hard to see what is strategic about these statements. Armstrong cites seven other organizations and each reflects broadly similar sentiments.

Of course, it could be said these are very high-level statements and hence the differentiating elements may be disguised. But, when moving on to 'specific HR strategies' the same problem seems to persist. Armstrong cites Diegeo (the drinks company) and reports that there are three broad strands to its people strategy:

1 Reward and recognition: use recognition and reward programmes to stimulate outstanding team and individual performance contributions.

2 Talent management: drive the attraction, retention and professional growth of a deep and diverse pool of talented employees.

3 Organizational effectiveness: ensure that the business adapts its organization to maximize employee contribution and deliver performance.

Again, these three elements sound rather bland and very much as though they could equally fit comfortably within the B&Q, Aegon and GSK 'strategies'. Indeed, they sound more like statements of best practice HR than specific business-related strategic choices. The extent to which these various companies truly *deliver* on these aspirations is, of course, another issue entirely.

This is not to say that examples of distinctive HR strategies cannot be found. In the John Lewis Partnership case that follows (see HRM in Action 4.3 on pages 71–72) can be found strategic intent, evidence of planning, a conscious attempt to achieve horizontal integration and a similar intent to achieve vertical integration – i.e. to align the HR strategy with the business strategy.

This case is interesting for two reasons. First, because a great deal of conscious thought has been invested in the HR strategy both at corporate level and as it is played out in the two divisions. Second, because the case illustrates a high-road HR strategy in operation as well as design. The two business divisions each occupy a market position that is targeted in the main at premium customers. The explicit underlying philosophy is to embed an HR strategic approach which is integral to what is seen as the customer–partner–profit chain. The Waitrose business strategy of 'dominate on product and differentiate on service' is commensurate with this HR strategy and vice versa. Likewise the JL department store high-level strategic intent is expressed in its overarching strap line 'We Care'. This is intended to convey a values-based commitment to customers, staff and suppliers.

Strategic human resource management in practice

So far, we have examined the meaning of SHRM and considered a number of examples. But how might the would-be HR strategist (or team) actually set about the *process of formulating and implementing* an HR strategy that aligns with its business or organizational strategy? What practical guidelines are available? In this section we draw on Kaplan and Norton's work (Kaplan 2000; Kaplan and Norton 2001; Kaplan and Norton 2005) to illustrate how organizations can set about, in a practical way, to convert resources and capabilities into outcomes and objectives; and how to build strategy maps to reveal cause-and-effect relationships.

The starting point for Kaplan and Norton is that while most companies have strategic plans with growth targets, the majority fail to achieve profitable growth – i.e. to exceed their cost of capital. The source of the gap between ambition and

HRM in Action 4.3   John Lewis Partnership: an employer of distinction

Over the past few years, the John Lewis Partnership (which comprises the two trading divisions of the John Lewis Department Stores and the Waitrose supermarket chain) has been developing a distinctive HR strategy. JLP has a total workforce of 66,000 – these are termed 'partners' (not 'employees') as the organization is co-owned by the partners. The HR strategy is built around an 'employer of distinction' jigsaw. At the heart of the strategy is a values set known as 'powered by our principles' (PbOP). These principles (honesty, respect, recognition, common purpose) are embedded within the policies and procedures at JLP. They have a presence at each stage of the partners' lifecycle in the organization: recruitment, selection, induction, training, appraisal and so on. Significantly, managers are *assessed* in terms of this enactment of the principles and the regular partnership survey carried out across all 66,000 partners is used additionally to measure their realization in behaviour. A complete review of the competency frameworks at each level of the organization was undertaken to ensure that PbOP behaviours were embodied within them.

Other elements in the HR strategy include progress on work–life balance with an aim to ensure that partners balance home, leisure and work lives. There is a career break scheme for all partners with five years' service. There is a package of leisure benefits from which partners can select known as 'PartnerChoice'. These include residential clubs (private hotels in desirable country locations with their own grounds offering fishing, boating, leisure activities etc.). Another element of the strategy is to maintain competitive pay and benefits along with a bonus scheme based on annual profit. The 15% bonus in 2005 amounted to £1870 for each non-management partner compared with Marks & Spencer's bonus scheme, which paid £500 for each employee.

With regard to pensions, John Lewis is now unique in the retail sector in maintaining a non-contributory, final salary scheme open to new members. (Final salary schemes have been closed at Harrods, Arcadia and even the Co-op). Tesco and Sainsbury require contributions and both have increased their employee contribution rates. The aim and statement of intent is to ensure the Partnership total pay is in the upper quartile of the market. There is an elaborate structure of democracy with elected representatives, at branches, regions and division and corporate. Each of the democratic bodies has the right to hold its appropriate level of managers to account. Thus, managers in John Lewis have to report regularly to a forum of partners and respond to their questions. The main board itself has a number of elected partners. In addition, an elaborate system of journalism communicates regularly to all partners and the organization-wide magazine (*The Gazette*) publishes anonymous letters which openly criticize managers at all levels including the MDs, the board and the chairman. *The Gazette* is enshrined within the constitution of the Partnership. Its aim is to give information to all 60,000 plus partners which is their right as the beneficial owners of the business. Each issue of *The Gazette* carries the following statement: 'The founder, John Speden Lewis identified knowledge and an understanding of our business as one of the keys to a happier working life. Each week the Gazette strives to give Partners a full account of important developments within the Partnership.'

The HR director states that JL aims to be a 'high performing organization' and as part of this a wide range of training and development opportunities are offered. In 2006 a new JLP Senior Academy was launched which offers leading-the-business programmes and career planning.

In addition, it handles psychometrics, 360° feedback, succession planning and career reviews. There is an emphasis on a fair treatment policy with declaration of rights and responsibilities. Finally, in this brief review, JLP strategic HR has also invested in a new IT system which offers direct access to personnel services by partners through 'PartnerLink'. This has involved centralizing HR administration and transactional services in a similar way to that noted in the MOD case in HRM in Action 4.2.

The HR team seeks to benchmark employee management services against other employers. In 2005 it was ranked joint first for pay and benefits and fourth in the *Guardian* Best Employer Awards. Also in 2005 the Partnership came top of a poll of 1500 retail professionals for its reputation as a fair employer.

performance they suggest can be traced to a disconnect between strategy formulation and strategy execution. They report that their research reveals that, on average, 95% of a company's employees are unaware of or do not understand their company's strategy (Kaplan and Norton 2005). As they note, if the people closest to customers and closest to the core operating processes do not understand the strategy then the failure to implement is unsurprising.

Kaplan and Norton suggest the use of 'strategy maps' based on their balanced scorecard methodology. These maps serve three functions: to communicate strategy to the whole organization, to reveal cause-and-effect relationships and to show possible gaps in the strategy. Together, these elements can help bridge the gap between strategy formulation and implementation. They offer a clear line of sight between overall company objectives and the individual's own job. They might show, for instance, how faster process times and enhanced employee capabilities contribute to customer satisfaction and retention and through these to increased revenue growth. Strategy maps offer visual representation of an organization's web of objectives and of the relationships between them to drive organizational performance.

Using the balanced scorecard approach, a company would normally have a series of objectives for four main areas or perspectives: its financial domain, its customer perspective, its internal processes and its learning and growth perspective. Within each of these there will be constituent objectives and associated measurements which allow a monitoring of performance. Kaplan and Norton suggest that senior managers begin with agreement about the 'customer value proposition', in other words, why would a customer choose to trade with this organization rather than another? Normally, there will be a mix of order-winning and order-qualifying factors. The former offer the potential for competitive advantage; the latter are threshold standards. Over time, factors which were once order winners (for example, additional features in cars or extra luxuries in a hotel) may become standard features and migrate into order qualifiers. Having identified the customer value position (such as the low-cost no-frills service on RyanAir or the premium products at Waitrose) the organization is then in a position to design and connect its internal processes to align with these defined customer wants and values.

While Kaplan and Norton give comparatively little direct attention to HR issues, their strategy map approach could be used by senior teams to address their strategic HR needs.

Figure 4.1 shows a simplified version of a strategy map. It reveals how strategy can be translated into implementation.

Tesco steering wheel

An example of the application of at least part of the concept is to be found at Tesco, the UK-based supermarket. Sir Terry Leahy, the chief executive of Tesco, has publicly acknowledged and attributed much of the growth in the company to Kaplan and Norton's balanced scorecard approach. Leahy stated: 'I have paid Robert Kaplan the only compliment he is interested in: putting his teaching into practice.' In its version of the scorecard, Tesco has developed a graphic called a 'steering wheel'. This covers four key areas of the business: finance, operations, people and customers (broadly equivalent to Kaplan and Norton's model but using slightly different terms). (See Figure 4.2.)

Each quadrant of the wheel has a set of objectives attached to it. In the full version of the wheel, these are shown as multiple segments. In turn, targets are set against these objectives. Staff are trained in the steering wheel and its principles, on the basis that they need to understand the interrelationship between different elements of the store and their own activities. Every store also has its own individual steering wheel, which is linked to every person's objectives; through this mechanism it is intended that strategy should be related to day-to-day work.

As mentioned, each segment is driven and monitored by KPIs, which, according to the company, 'set demanding but achievable targets' for the business. Each activity area with such measures is supposed to be backed by a business case quantifying the benefits. Managers are asked to monitor customers, operations, staff and finances using a 'traffic light' system where green indicates that targets are being met and red flags a problem. Where KPIs are not on planned track, a 'steering wheel group'

Strategy map: cause and effect relationships | Figure 4.1

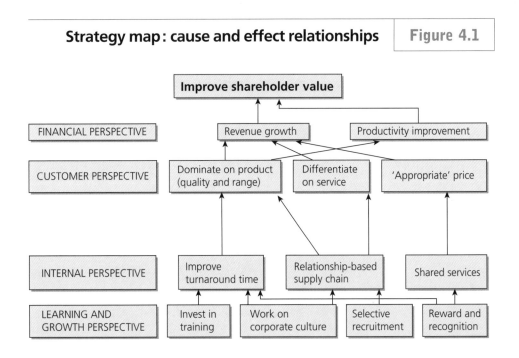

puts in place action plans. Performance is reported quarterly to the board and a summary report is sent to the top 2000 managers in the company to cascade to all staff. The remuneration of senior management is shaped by the KPIs, with bonuses based on a sliding scale according to the level of achievement on the corporate steering wheel.

Assessing the balanced scorecard and strategy maps

This approach clearly has merits: it connects strategy to activity and to measurement; it communicates strategic objectives clearly and simply; and it can reveal how results were achieved. It is however, simply a tool, an aid to planning and implementation. It does not necessarily solve the problems of finding the appropriate strategy or managing the business expertly, still less does it deliver a human resource management strategy.

It is notable that in most expositions of the strategy maps in action, there is very little attention paid to human resource management. Indeed in one of the most celebrated of Kaplan and Norton's cases where they consulted to implement the strategy maps approach, the description of the human resource elements (wrapped up in the 'learning and growth perspective') are the least well-specified elements. The Mobil strategy in the human resource area amounted to 'encouraging' skill development, giving employees access to strategic information and 'involvement' – which they describe in terms of motivation and empowerment. Notably, even with these few (and hardly entirely novel policies) Kaplan and Norton (2001: 39) state that they 'proved to be among the most difficult to specify'. For the involvement objective the tool was an employee survey. We know from extensive use of these that they can be blunt instruments. Further, we also know that executive teams tend not to accord HR policy the same degree of priority and attention as other aspects of business decision making. Scorecards may reveal some indicative measures but these results will be of limited utility unless there is a broader vision about what can be achieved and how it might be achieved in the HR domain.

Figure 4.2	**The Tesco Steering Wheel**

Source: Tesco PLC

Towards a new synthesis in crafting a HR strategy

We noted earlier in the chapter that the controversy about best practice or best fit seems to continue unabated. In addition, the resource-based approach offers yet a further alternative point of departure. Perhaps it should not be a matter of surprise therefore that many HR directors remain uncertain about how to respond to the expectation that they should be able to produce and deliver a HR strategy for their organization. Often, in consequence, they produce a document based on an agglomeration of the current set of policies, practices and initiatives. Alternatively or additionally, they may undertake some environmental scanning and commence their strategic review with some statistical profiles of demographic trends and similar economic, social and legal reviews. The existing suite of policies may then be appended to that analysis, as, with some suitable statement of caveats, it is not normally too difficult to justify the continuance of current policy if it is stated in a sufficiently vague and aspirational manner – as these documents often tend to be.

Work with organizations in both the public and private sectors leads me to suggest that, from a practical point of view, it is possible and indeed usually beneficial for HR directors to craft their strategy through *four simultaneous pathways*. These are shown in Figure 4.3.

An organization's HR strategy can usually be constituted by an amalgam of these four approaches. The first pathway, 'good practices', means the inclusion of policies and practices that, at the very least, accord with current law and codes of practice and, preferably, exceed these. This approach can normally be justified on the grounds that social legitimacy is ensured in this way and further that the organization may avoid the unnecessary expense of high labour turnover or resentment deriving from standards that are out of line with the prevailing norms. Through this pathway the

Four complementary pathways to strategy | Figure 4.3

Good practices

Best fit

Response to analysis of trends, demographics etc.

Build on and exploit resource base

HR STRATEGY

practice strategic human resource management does not mean that they might not benefit from moving in that direction.

The strategy-mapping approach can be used as a tool to help clarify and communicate business strategy, it can also be used to identify gaps in strategy – and these gaps might often be found in the human resource domain. However, cause-and-effect relationships can be hard to prove; the context is often dynamic and so the order-qualifying and order-winning criteria can shift; and the mix of intangible assets work in combination to deliver value and not in a singular manner.

Case examples of strategic human resource management in action were presented. These reveal the possibilities, the risks and the difficulties; organizational politics are never far from the centre of the action. Whether the frame of attention is narrow or wide – as with the cross-boundary idea of a 'HR architecture' – one of the inherent challenges facing those who seek to manage HR strategically is how to stay alongside a shifting business strategy while remaining faithful to an employment deal (psychological contract) carefully constructed with an already existing workforce.

References

Armstrong, M. (2006). *A Handbook of Human Resource Management Practice*. London, Kogan Page.

Baird, L. and I. Meshoulam (1988). 'Managing two fits of strategic human resource management', *Academy of Management Review* 13(1): 116–28.

Beer, M., B. Spector, P. Lawrence, D. Mills and R. Walton (1985). *Human Resources Management: A General Manager's Perspective*. New York, Free Press.

Chandler, A. (1962). *Strategy and Structure*. Cambridge, MA, MIT Press.

CIPD (2005). 'Where we are, where we are heading', London: CIPD Surveys.

Fombrun, C. J., N. M. Tichy and M. A. Devanna (1984). *Strategic Human Resource Management*. New York, Wiley.

Grant, R. (1998). *Contemporary Strategy Analysis*. Cambridge, MA, Blackwell.

Hamel, G. and C. K. Prahalad (1992). *Competing for the Future*. Boston, MA, Harvard Business School Press.

Hendry, C. and A. Pettigrew (1986). 'The practice of strategic human resource management', *Personnel Review* 15(3): 3–8.

Johnson, G. (1987). *Strategic Change and the Strategy Process*. Oxford, Blackwell.

Kaplan, R. S. (2000). 'Having trouble with your strategy? Then map it', *Harvard Business Review* September-October: 167–76.

Kaplan, R. S. and D. P. Norton (2001). *The Strategy-Focused Organization*. Boston, MA, Harvard Business School Press.

Kaplan, R. S. and D. P. Norton (2005). 'The Office of Strategy Management', *Harvard Business Review* October: 73–80.

Kochan, T. and T. Barocci (1985). *Human Resource Management and Industrial Relations*. Boston, MA, Little Brown.

Lengnick-Hall, C. and M. Lengnick-Hall (1988). 'Strategic human resource management: a review of the literature and a proposed typology', *Academy of Management Review* 13(3): 454–70.

Lepak, D. A. and S. A. Snell (2005). 'The human resource architecture: towards a theory of human capital allocation', in S. Little and T. Ray, *Managing Knowledge: An Essential Reader*. London, Sage.

Marginson, P., K. Sisson, R. Martin and P. Edwards (1988). *Beyond the Workplace*. Oxford, Blackwell.

Mintzberg, H. (1994). *The Rise and Fall of Strategic Planning*. London, Prentice-Hall.

Nelson, R. R. and S. Winter (1982). *An Evolutionary Theory of Economic Change*. Cambridge, MA, Harvard University Press.

Ohmae, K. (1982). *The Mind of the Strategist*. London, McGraw-Hill.

Porter, M. E. (1985). *Competitive Advantage*. New York, Free Press.

Quinn, J. B. (1980). *Strategies for Change: Logical Incrementalism*. Homewood, IL, Richard Irwin.

Schuler, R. and S. Jackson (1987). 'Linking competitive strategies with human resource management practices', *Academy of Management Executive* 1(3): 207–19.

Storey, J. and G. Salaman (2005). 'The knowledge work of general managers', *Journal of General Management* 31(2): 57–74.

Teece, D. and G. Pisano (1994). 'The dynamic capabilities of firms: an introduction', *Industrial and Corporate Change* 3: 537–56.

Touche, D. (2004). *Aligned at the Top? A Survey of CEO and HR Directors' Perceptions of HR*. New York, Deloitte & Touche.

Facing up to the challenges of success: putting 'governance' at the heart of HRM

Keith Sisson

HRM is, apparently, triumphant. It appears to have firmly established its supremacy over personnel management – witness the UK's 2004 Workplace Employee Relations Survey (WERS) findings, which show that the preferred title for specialist managers is now 'human resource manager' rather than 'personnel manager', with significant advances in qualifications and responsibilities. It has also become a major department in many business schools, its courses featuring on most MBA programmes. HRM even appears in the title of industrial relations masters' courses as well as being the designation of most recent professorial chair appointments in the area. To cap it all, an increasing number of commentators in both the USA (Ferris et al. 1995) and the UK (e.g. Bach 2005; Boxall and Purcell 2003) are to all intents and purposes suggesting that HRM is supplanting industrial relation as the dominant paradigm in the world of work.

Such success, however, brings with it new challenges. Arguably, in HRM's case there are two that are pressing. One lies in the realm of theory – this one relates to the need to develop an integrated analytical framework. The other, perhaps even greater, challenge is essentially political – this one concerns the need to demonstrate the relevance of the analytical framework to real-world practice and policy issues such as employee engagement and productivity, along with wider concerns such as the contribution of work organizations to social capital development.

These challenges are inextricably linked. Unless HRM is able to develop and articulate a more robust analytical framework, it won't be able to develop a progressive research agenda that embraces clearer conceptual understanding and explanatory accounts of HRM phenomena (Edwards 2003). If it is unable to do this, it will have little to say about the real-world issues that practitioners and policymakers ought to be grappling with. Instead, it will be at the mercy of the latest whims and fancies of these groups.

The stakes are high. The prospects for developing the 'knowledge organizations' that are the key to the future are likely to be seriously affected. It is not too fanciful to suggest that failure to rise to the challenges could mean that HRM is superseded as a significant management function, with implications also for its academic status. Corporate communications or marketing could take over much of the strategic thrust of HRM, with day-to-day administrative routine reverting back to personnel management. In these circumstances, business schools might 'decide' – or rather it may evolve – that a range of other disciplines and subjects (communications, strategy, marketing, organizational psychology and organizational behaviour) rather than HRM, should be home for the subject area.

The theoretical challenge: developing an analytical framework

The theoretical challenge is to make good the lack of an integrated theoretical framework. In Kaufmann's (2004a: 321) words: 'Human resource management remains caught somewhere in the twilight between a science, an applied area of management practice, a heterogeneous collection of administrative tools, and a consulting or ideological statement about how companies should manage their employees.' As in the case of the social sciences (for politics, for example, see Hay 2002), there is need to debate and, hopefully, work towards a measure of consensus around three sets of issues: the focus – the nature and purpose of HRM; the approach – what we can hope to know about HRM; and the methods – how the knowledge can be acquired. In more formal language, these might be labelled HRM's ontological, epistemological and methodological challenges. There is also the need to recognize HRM's industrial relations heritage and to incorporate industrial relations' latest thinking revealed in the references quoted here.

Focus

I believe HRM's core focus needs to satisfy certain basic conditions:

1 It needs to allow us to deal with both *practice and performance*. By this I mean that it doesn't restrict us to description and explanation. It allows us to consider effects as well. In formal terms, more of which below, it has to be capable of being an intervening variable as well as a dependent one.

2 It needs to allow *disciplinary openness*. I will also say more about this in a later section. Such openness, however, is a critical assumption underpinning several of the other conditions and so needs to be made explicit here.

3 It needs to be *inclusive in terms of interests*. I don't believe that HRM can be just about the management interest and concerns for efficiency. Patently the role of management, which HRM can claim much credit for projecting centre stage, is a major strand as are the links with business strategy. Critically important here is the issue of vertical fit – it remains to be established whether business strategy seriously shapes HRM in particular ways or whether HRM largely reflects wider assumptions that managers have about how to manage people. But attention to management cannot be to the exclusion of everything else. Employees' interests must also be taken into account – for example, the significant differences between people's orientations to work, on the one hand, and employment, on the other, should be giving serious food for thought. Key areas are health and personal development

opportunities. Each of these has had its specialist treatment, but each has yet to make much of an impact on or even establish much of a presence on most HRM programmes. There is also a need to recognize that HRM's implications go beyond the immediate workplace – work organizations are a major source as well as beneficiary of 'social capital', with important implications not just for business performance, but also the family, anti-social behaviour, crime and participation in civil society. Indeed, there needs to be greater recognition that many of today's social issues are inextricably tied up with people's employment experience.

4 It needs to be *comprehensive in its subject matter*. Crucially important is that HRM isn't just about 'adapting' employees to existing patterns of work organization. Instead of being taken for granted, these patterns must themselves be a major focus of attention. Some kind of hierarchy may be intrinsic to work organizations. Yet its nature and extent can and do differ, even allowing for very similar technology and market conditions. For example, the proportion of the workforce involved in management/supervision in the UK is four times that in Sweden. It is difficult to escape the conclusion that, rather than technological requirements, differences like these reflect wider assumptions about the role of management.

5 It needs to be rooted in a *realistic understanding of the nature of the employment relationship*. This means recognizing two things. The first is that HRM is essentially about 'governance', i.e. the handling of contractual relations or 'exchange interfaces' (Williamson 1985: 129). In the case of labour services, there are two main types of governance structure – markets and organizations – the choice between the two boiling down to the transaction costs involved in negotiating, drafting and, most critically, administering/enforcing contracts. The former, of which subcontracting is an example, relies on the price mechanism with enforcement in the courts. The latter depends on employment relationships and hierarchy to manage them. The second is that the employment relationship is pretty unique as I try to portray in Table 5.1. The aphorism that 'labour isn't a commodity to be bought or sold like any other' is spot on. 'Human resources' are embodied in people. Also, contrary to the use of contract language, nothing is automatic about the employment relationship. Perhaps the key feature to emphasize for present purposes is the residual control rights afforded to employers to define employees' duties *after* rather than before they have entered into the employment relationship. This leaves a certain open-endedness to the employment contract. This carries implications in the other direction also. What workers 'sell' is their ability to work or, in Marx's phrase, their 'labour power'. Brown and Walsh (1994: 440) put it nicely in suggesting that: 'The act of hiring … is not sufficient to ensure that the job gets done in an acceptable way … The employee has to be motivated – by encouragement, threats, loyalty, discipline, money, competition, pride, promotion, or whatever else is deemed effective to work with the required pace and care.' Essentially, HRM involves managerial rather than market relations.

I suggest, therefore, that the most appropriate focus for HRM is the 'governance of the employment relationship'. By this I mean the 'rules of the game' involved in managing employment relationships. Some practical examples are given later (see HRM in Action 5.1). Crucially, too, in the light of the earlier discussion, I suggest that these rules do not just involve performance management, i.e. the arrangements for recruitment and selection, training and development, the type of payment system and the level of wages, the working time arrangements, the disciplinary arrangements and so on.

Table 5.1	The employment relationship and its implications

The employment relationship's special features	Basic propositions
• Unlike other resources, 'human resources' are embodied in people who, in democratic societies, are citizens with expectations about fair and proper treatment	• The employment relationship has social, psychological and political dimensions as well as an economic one
• For employers, the overriding concern is the efficiency with which resources are used. For employees, there are multiple concerns – fair pay, status, interesting and relevant work, opportunities for personal development	• The employment relationship involves an inbuilt 'structured antagonism', meaning that it is characterized by the potential for conflict as well as cooperation
• The employment relationship is intrinsically open-ended and incomplete – it gives the employer residual control rights to define employees' duties ex post rather than ex ante	• The employment relationship involves considerable uncertainty, fuelling the scope for divergent goals and interpretation
• To enforce the employer's residual control rights, the employment relationship involves a 'governance' structure that is hierarchy rather than contract based	• The employment relationship primarily involves 'managerial' as opposed to 'market' relations – it gives rise to specific 'governance' structures of substantive and procedural institutions or 'rules' that effect both the quality of working life and economic performance
• The employment relationship involves an asymmetrical (unequal) power relationship. The employer is a corporate entity most often with substantial resources at its disposal. The employee is a single individual usually with very limited resources	• The employment relationship not only encourages employees to form collective organizations to influence the 'governance' structure's rules and rule-making processes, but also obliges the state to intervene – to deal with conflict, to ensure a basic floor of individual employment rights and to promote employee involvement in rule making
• A counterbalancing consideration is that, for the employment relationship to be effective, employers require more than the compliance of employees – they require their commitment as well	• The employment relationship depends on the legitimacy employees accord the 'governance' structure, which means a more or less continuous process of 'implicit' and, depending on the presence of trade unions, 'explicit' negotiation'

They also embrace the organization of work and the hierarchy involved, i.e. job design, the grouping of jobs into activities and the structures used to coordinate these activities.

These rules can also be formal or informal. As the examples in HRM in Action 5.1 show, informal norms, expected patterns of behaviour and the 'way things are done here' ('custom and practice') typically sit alongside the formal rules that flow from management decisions, trade union rulebooks, collective bargaining and legislation. Similarly, there can be a mix of formality and informality in the making and administration of the rules. Formal rules, for example, may be interpreted very differently from one department to another – there may even be an informal rule that managers and employees will ignore some formal rules.

As well as individual employees and managers, the organizations involved in making and administering the rules include management and workgroups, works and company councils, trade unions and employers' organizations, employment tribunals courts and the state. The European Council of Ministers, the European Commission and the European Court of Justice also have to be included in the list in the light of the EU social dimension.

A focus on 'governance' means embracing the issue of power. As Table 5.1 suggests, an unequal power relationship is an integral feature of the employment relationship. In theory, there are two equal parties. In practice, employers and employees are very unequal. The employer is a corporate entity most often with substantial resources at its disposal. The employee is a single individual usually with limited resources. Key issues are the extent to which power is ideological as well as economic, legal and political; the extent to which it is a resource capable of advancing common goals; the extent to which it is possessed by individuals or embedded in institutions; and the effect on, and response of, individual employees (Edwards and Wajcman 2005).

A focus on 'governance' similarly means attention to negotiation. Here there are two points to emphasize. The first is that 'negotiation' is as much a feature of individual employment relations as it is of collective ones. Nothing, it must be remembered, is automatic about the employment relationship – to put management decisions, employment rights and collective agreements into effect requires dialogue, consensus building and 'give-and-take'. In a phrase, the work organization is 'a system of negotiated order' (see, for example, Martin 2003). The second is that negotiation is not just about 'exchange'. It is also about influencing relationships, changing attitudes and shaping preferences. Indeed, there are grounds for suggesting that what Walton and McKersie (1965) term 'attitudinal structuring' has become the dominant process, underlining power's ideological dimension.

I appreciate that, along with 'regulation' and rules, institutions have had a very bad press lately: critics say they interfere with the working of markets and get in the way of management's need for flexibility. Arguably, however, the objection to institutions is a very partial one – it largely boils down to employer opposition to individual employment rights rather than rules in general. The exercise of the residual control rights involved in the employment relationship entails a hierarchy-based 'governance' structure, i.e. institutions or rules. Indeed, as Marsden (1999: 1) emphasizes, it is the ability to exercise these control rights that help to explain why the hierarchy-based employment relationship is typically preferred over market-based subcontracting for providing labour services.

Rules, in other words, are the 'stuff' of work organizations. Rules influence norms, beliefs and actions. They do so by establishing both rights and obligations. From one point of view they constrain behaviour, but from another they enable it. Imagine, for example, the implications for most organizations of there being no rules governing attendance.

It is sometimes suggested that the coming of the 'knowledge organization' changes things. True, the setting changes – workplaces tend to be smaller and the boundaries of work organizations more blurred; collectivism and collective bargaining are usually less important; and there is more emphasis on culture, i.e. informal institutions, than formal rules. Even though they may be different, 'rules of the game' there undoubtedly are. 'Knowledge organizations' have hierarchies; recruitment and selection processes; job descriptions; training and development routines; posting and transfer arrangements; performance management systems; disciplinary processes; and so on – all of which have a significant influence.

It is also important to distinguish between the rhetoric and reality of the 'knowledge organization'. High-profile employment tribunal cases involving the finance and IT sectors suggest discrimination, bullying and harassment are far from unknown. The nature and extent of the targets built into many performance management systems also mean that claims for individual initiative and local autonomy have to be taken with a substantial pinch of salt – many employees complain that they have little discretion. Not to be forgotten either is that, through outsourcing and subcontracting many of their support activities, the 'knowledge organization' helps to perpetuate employment in 'traditional' work organizations throughout the service sector, fuelling the growth of an 'hourglass' economy.

To sum up, I believe that a 'governance' focus has significant advantages, bearing in mind the conditions outlined earlier. It makes it possible to embrace issues of both practice and performance. It recognizes that it is managerial rather than market relations that are critically important in HRM. It captures the fact that there is more than one interest as well a number of different types of rule (substantive and procedural, formal and informal, legal and non-legal); different sources of rule making (unilateral, collective bargaining, government and the court system); and different levels at which rules are made (workplace, company, sector, regional, national and international). Indeed, the balance between the different types, sources and levels is one of the main distinguishing features of national systems of HRM. Crucially, it reminds us that institutions involve both rights and obligations and affect both employers and employees. It therefore links, on the one hand, with notions of 'corporate governance' and corporate social responsibility and, on the other, with concepts such as justice, citizenship and industrial democracy – it is difficult, for example, to see how it is possible to operationalize the 'justice' that is being promoted as a key issue (see, for example, Budd 2004; Edwards 2005) in the absence of an overarching 'governance' paradigm. It also brings into play the issue of employee 'voice', trust and legitimacy (Coats 2004). Last, but by no means least, it encourages disciplinary openness. It is consistent with industrial relations' longstanding emphasis on employment or job regulation. At the same time, it connects with the study of 'governance' in other environments and so makes it possible to draw on a wide body of institutional research and analysis (see, for example, the discussion in Campbell 2004; Hall and Soskice 2001; Müller-Jentsch 2004; North 1990; Williamson 1985).

The case for critical realism

As to what might be expected of an analytical framework, there are two main possibilities. Essentially, to paraphrase my former IRRU colleague Richard Hyman (2004: 267), it is a question of a theory 'of' HRM or theory 'in' HRM. It is the ambition of some colleagues, particularly in the USA, to develop a theory 'of' HRM. Kaufman (2004a, 2004b) is a well-known example – indeed, he believes it possible and desirable to have theories of *both* HRM *and* industrial relations. I share Richard's view that it is a matter of theory 'in' rather than theory 'of'. Rather than seeking predictive 'laws', in other words, the ambition should be to 'understand and explain' – to shed light on the mechanisms and processes of HRM, to highlight, explain and draw implications from what 'works' and 'doesn't work'. Arguably, the sacrifices that have to be made in the interest of parsimony to achieve a theory 'of' HRM are far too great given the immense complexity of the phenomena being studied. There is also the danger that a single discipline becomes dominant to the detriment of the insights that others are able to bring.

As Paul Edwards (2006), another IRRU colleague, has suggested, the most appropriate model for the area is that of 'critical' or 'scientific' realism (see Box 5.1). This pays particular regard to agency, action, choice and contingency, emphasizing the sensitivity of behaviour to context. Critically important is that, rather than seeing actors being driven by universally applicable preferences, as the rational choice approach does, it holds that such preferences reflect different experiences.

It is here that the link with institutions comes into play. Individuals help to produce, reproduce and modify institutions. At the same time, however, these institutions have a crucial mediating role in shaping their behaviour.

Box 5.1 Critical realism

Critical realism is an approach to the philosophy of science that seeks an alternative to the two dominant positions. These are *positivism* and an approach variously labelled as *social constructionism* or *interpretism*. *Positivism* seeks explanation in terms of law-like empirical regularities – the *rational choice* approach of economics is an example. It can be faulted for addressing only empirical regularities rather than the underlying mechanisms producing these regularities. Its more or less exclusive reliance on deduction also tends to prevent it from asking *why* things occur as they do. *Social constructionism*, by contrast, focuses on the social processes through which people create meaning. It tends to ignore the influences of structures that lie outside these processes. Revealing generic processes are also stressed over causal explanation. Constructionists rarely ask why construction takes a *particular* form under given conditions.

Critical realism argues that there are real, if unobservable, forces with 'causal powers' and that it is the task of science to understand the relevant mechanisms. The social world is seen as being different from the natural because it requires human intervention, but it does not follow that society is wholly the product of human design or discourse: rules, norms and institutions develop with logics independent of the choices of individual actors. It stresses that causal powers are not necessarily activated and is thus very sensitive to the importance of institutional context. It aims to move beyond the discovery of empirical regularities to understand the mechanisms that not only produce these regularities but also determine when they will occur and when they do.

(Based on: Edwards 2006. See also Hindmoor 2006: Chapter 9.)

Methodology

The territory that HRM seeks to inherit has long been multidisciplinary, with a strong focus on issues rather than methods. In my view, the case for disciplinary openness remains as strong as ever. As Flanders (1970: 85) insisted many years ago in the case of industrial relations, the problem with individual disciplines is that they 'tear the subject apart by concentrating attention on some of its aspects to the exclusion or comparative neglect of others ... a partial view of anything, accurate as it may be within its limits, must of necessity be a distorted one'. Clearly there is danger of being ad hoc. This is not necessarily a feature of multidisciplinarity, however. A framework can be both multidisciplinary and coherent – Walton and McKersie's *Behavioral Theory of Labor Negotiation* (1965) referenced earlier is an excellent example.

I also think that both inductive and deductive approaches should have our support, believing them to go hand in hand. An inductive approach is necessary to ensure that teaching and research is empirically grounded and based on realistic assumptions. At the same time, decisions have to be made about what to look for, which implies a measure of deduction.

As for research methods, I would hope that there is now more or less a consensus. Both qualitative and quantitative methods have their place. An exclusive concern with the quantitative is as one eyed as that which draws only on the qualitative. Understanding evolving developments involving complex, unpredictable processes needs in-depth qualitative methods, the results of which can be checked with appropriate quantitative data. The way that WERS has progressed suggests that the subject has much to be proud of in this respect.

If there is a weakness, it is the lack of a multilevel perspective. HRM tends to focus on the workplace to the exclusion of the sector and national levels. No organization is an island unto itself, however. A more or less exclusive concern with the organization level will inevitably underestimate the significance of the sector and national levels. There is need for an analytical perspective sensitive to the articulation between 'top-down' and 'bottom-up' developments. It becomes absolutely essential the more internationally comparative work in the area becomes.

The political challenge: linking theory to practice and policy

I believe that the second challenge is, if anything, bigger than the first. It is not that persuasive cases cannot be made for the practice and policy relevance of the kind of analytical framework I've sketched out. They can as I will try to do in the case of the UK. Rather it is the nature of the policymaking process that's the problem, along with the prevailing positions of the key players.

Persuasive cases?

Institutions matter. In the UK, academic interest has come together with practitioner and policymaker concerns in the form of work on the links between the high performance workplace and performance outcome. This is an important development that is to be encouraged. The search for the 'holy grail', has, however, tended to blind people to the underlying point – institutions matter. Quoted in HRM in Action 5.1, for example, are three recent cases of interventions involving the senior advisers of ACAS, which is the UK's independent advisory, conciliation and arbitration service. The details differ, but the central points are the same. Long-established ways of doing things (institutions) have led to particular patterns of behaviour. Equally important, relatively basic changes in these institutions can and do make a significant difference to both business performance and people's working lives. The involvement of employees and their representatives in making and administering these changes has also added considerably to their legitimacy.

More controversially, a strong case can be made for the importance of institutions in the engagement problem that British management is increasingly recognized to have (see, for example, Emmott 2005; Syedain 2006). The UK government prides itself on the decline of 'organized' conflict, i.e. strikes and other forms of industrial action (Department of Trade and Industry 2006). Yet 'unorganized' conflict is widespread. Employment tribunal applications have topped the 100,000 mark in recent years, the recent drop having more to do with the administration than underlying state of play. Absence and staff turnover are also telling indicators. It is difficult to believe, but 50 times as many days have been lost through absence in some recent years as through strikes.

Absenteeism, the Confederation of British Industry (2005) reckons, costs around £12.2 billion each year. The UK also continues to lag behind other major countries in the productivity stakes. Moreover, this is true of services as well as manufacturing. Strip out the long hours that many UK employees work and the position worsens. All of this is consistent with survey evidence suggesting that dissatisfaction at work has been growing (Taylor 2002), with many employees reporting that they have little discretion and scope to exercise their initiative (Kersley et al. 2006).

Arguably, the UK is suffering from 'institutional failure'. Overall, it is the decline in collective bargaining that needs to be stressed. Put simply, it has left a legitimacy gap that UK management has failed to fill. The decline of collective bargaining doesn't only mean that large sections of the workforce – especially those increasingly vulnerable workers in the bottom half of the 'hourglass' economy – no longer enjoy the benefits of the additional standards that come from collective agreements. It also means a more general decline in the scope for employee 'voice' – at workplace, company sector and national levels. Furthermore, the role, status and membership of key intermediary organizations such as trade unions and employers' organizations have been seriously affected. Crucially, the UK no longer possesses the networks necessary for coordinating continuous improvement in key areas of human resource development.

One particular result is that, unlike most other EU member countries, the UK has been unable to take advantage of the increasing flexibility built into EU employment directives, reflecting their increasing 'reflexive' and 'procedural' orientation. In the absence of national and sector arrangements for social dialogue, it is effectively restricted to the legislative route in transposing EU initiatives. An unfortunate consequence is a growth of legal dependency. The parties to the employment relationship are encouraged to resort to legislation rather than trying to sort things out for themselves. Given that there is none of the ownership and therefore commitment that comes from being involved in making the rules, the issue of enforcement inevitably rises up the agenda. Hardly surprisingly, none of this helps to promote engagement.

HRM in Action 5.1   Examples of institutions mattering

A case of team working. The first case involves a small manufacturing company with a traditional functional work organization. Demarcation lines were fairly rigid with little or no functional flexibility. Job roles were mainly gender based and productivity levels relatively low. A joint management–trade union programme introduced cell-based teams, with team members responsible for production, cost, quality, engineering and materials movement. Maintenance was also involved with the introduction of a 'total preventative maintenance' programme. A large-scale training programme was conducted to ensure that all team members were able to handle a spread of tasks and share skills. According to key managers and union representatives, both demarcation and direct manning numbers have been reduced, with a number of voluntary redundancies being possible as part of the package. The teams have resulted in improved morale and quality, the latter through the introduction of the maintenance programme. Managers believed that there was a direct and positive link between the programme and improvements in company performance. The new manning scheme had led to an increase in productivity of over 20% and a halving in absence levels from 8 to 4%. There has also been a reduction in rejects, waste and customer complaints.

A case of working time change. The second example involves changes in working time arrangements. This company was characterized by relatively low basic rates and high levels of overtime working. The joint steering group took a two-pronged approach, developing both new shift patterns and a system of 'reserve hours' working. A major management objective was to eliminate the site's 'historic tradition' of the 'end of the month rush', the majority of output being produced in the final week of each month. They aimed instead to work around weekly production targets, in order to provide customers with 'a better flow of product'. Prior to the introduction of the system, employees worked a 37-hour week plus overtime. Under the reserve hours scheme, all employees would receive a salary calculated at 40 hours' work, comprised of 37 basic work hours and three reserve hours per week. The basic salary was increased to compensate for the additional working hours, along with shift premiums, holiday pay, pensionable earnings and redundancy pay. Managers stated that they hoped that employees would 'work smarter and more productive' within the 37 hours. If they met their production targets within the 37 hours, they would not have to work the extra three hours per week, despite being paid for them. Stewards believed that the reserve hours system held certain advantages over the previous system. These included the increase in basic pay for employees going on to the system, which also flowed through to increases in associated benefits; and the fact that it provided employees with a more stable income than having to rely on the vagaries of overtime working.

A case of attendance management. The third case involves the joint working party introduction of a new attendance management system in a Scottish bus company. Both management and union representatives said that relations and communications between them greatly improved as a result of the new arrangements, as did the relationship between the union and the workforce. As one union representative put it: 'Before the new arrangements, there was a lot of mistrust between the troops and us, between the troops and the management, between us and management and between management and everybody. Nobody trusted anybody.' The climate has changed a great deal. As a senior manager stated: 'If you look at day to day relations now, it is hard to believe they were actually as bad as that . . . at the moment there's no real tangible feeling of that terrible hostility that was here two years ago.' The new attendance management policy has resulted in less absence and a reduction in sick pay by about 10%, compared to the previous year. In addition, the new procedure has meant far fewer complaints from the workforce about how absence has being handled. There have also been fewer disciplinary appeals since the new arrangements were put in place. Beforehand, there had been two to four appeals most weeks. Following the new arrangements, the number dropped to one appeal every three weeks. Moreover, the management and the trade union went on to produce a new grievance procedure. As a result of reduced conflict in the workplace, managers felt more able to devote time to handling other issues central to the running of the company. As one senior manager said: 'I wasn't getting the time to look at the areas I needed to address; to improve communication with the workforce and to move the company forward. It has freed up a lot of time.' Union representatives have echoed these sentiments.

In the public services, where collective bargaining remains, there is a very specific issue. The management of change has proved to be especially fraught, with significant investment not producing anything like the return that policymakers hoped for. As authoritative bodies such as the Audit Commission (2003, 2006) and the House of Commons Public Administration Select Committee (2003) have recognized, a key consideration here has been the system of targets. Highly centralized and extremely detailed targets, very often reflecting short-term political pressures, have considerably distorted management priorities as well as riding roughshod over local consultative processes. Similarly, the widespread imposition of individual performance pay in situations where it is difficult to measure individuals' contribution has been more a hindrance than a help.

A key role for corporate social responsibility. In principle, a 'governance' perspective ought to appeal to national policymakers. Not only does it accurately portray the issues they have to consider – much more so than the labour market paradigm they currently work with – but it also enables them to finesse their involvement. Crucially, it enables them to achieve a better balance between the flexibility and fairness that has become the *leitmotiv* of policymaking in the area. As indicated earlier, the decline of collective bargaining means UK governments have had to fall back on a programme of individual rights to deliver fairness at work. This is fine as far as it goes. Such approach has its weaknesses, however, which go beyond the opposition of management discussed later. Not only does legal enactment deal with basic standards rather than the continuous improvement that is needed if the UK is to achieve 'knowledge economy' status, but it also does little to promote the 'give-and-take' necessary to make the employment relationship work smoothly.

A 'governance' perspective suggests more emphasis on 'soft' regulation such as compulsory reporting of policies and practices in key areas of corporate social responsibility. Such emphasis would enable policymakers to set a strong sense of direction without laying themselves open to the charge of imposing a 'one-size-fits-all' approach. At the same time, regular social audits would enable the many benefits of benchmarking to be realized. The spotlight could be on learning and continuous improvement rather than simply a level of minimum rights, which is what legal enact-ment and collective bargaining are effectively limited to achieving. Again, HRM in Action 5.1 offers basic examples of some of the areas that might be involved. Cru-cially, benchmarking offers the prospect of greater downwards as well as upwards accountability – requirements for programmes to be developed in consultation with employee representatives could give a considerable stimulus to much needed dia-logue. There could also be local community involvement on relevant issues with 'naming and shaming' added to the weaponry of those seeking to raise standards. Other things being equal, the overall approach should strongly appeal to businesses that are already pursuing effective HRM polices and practices.

Most immediately, such an approach could help policymakers to promote much more effectively key policy goals such as equality, skills and development and, per-haps above all, high performance working leading to improved productivity. As Porter and Ketels' report (2003) for the DTI pointed out, if UK businesses are to move successfully into the knowledge economy, many have to be encouraged to shift their business strategy from the 'low road' to the 'high road'. There are few signs that the current approach grounded in individual employment rights can/will do much to help – the institutional pressures in favour of short-termism are too strong. In the absence of effective countervailing pressures, little is likely to change.

A mountain to climb?

I do not underestimate the challenge of promoting the concept of 'governance' to practitioners and policymakers. Indeed, I accept that there is little chance of its acceptance in the short term. From time to time, it is possible to get a glimmer of rec-ognition that institutional issues need addressing. Overall, however, the position seems to be that most significant people problems have been resolved. At the risk of repetition, the emphasis of policymakers would seem to be on *the labour market* (DTI 2003a and 2003b). If there are problems inside organizations, these are largely defined in attitudinal terms.

Two underlying considerations are important here. One is the nature of policymak-ing. In practice, this is far removed from the deliberative process with which it is pop-ularly associated. It isn't just that this is very reactive and short term in focus. To paraphrase Schumpeter (1942), national policy tends to emerge largely as the byprod-uct of a competitive struggle for votes. Policies are developed primarily with a view to their attractiveness to voters and/or the media, in other words, rather than a deep analysis of the problems in hand. Arguably, too, this tendency is exaggerated where there is a 'first-past-the-post' electoral system as in the UK – in proportional represen-tation systems, where compromises have to be reached between parties, there is greater pressure to discuss and debate issues on the basis of the evidence. Not unlike some researchers pursuing the deductive approach, policymakers are prone to gauge reaction to their ideas by floating them at a relatively early stage of formulation. Those that find a measure of support are promoted; those that look as though they will arouse opposition are quickly dropped. Either way, there is rarely a serious opportu-nity for a discussion of options. The treatment of evidence is affected as well. Evi-dence that supports policies and policy ideas is enthusiastically promoted; evidence that contradicts them is dismissed or ignored. All of this further entrenches the veto position of powerful interest groups in areas such as HRM.

Although there isn't the same need to appeal to voters, much of this also describes policymaking at the organization level. I am thinking in particular of the way in which senior managers push their ideas, the treatment of evidence and the lack of a serious opportunity for a discussion of options. Additionally important are senior managers' frames of reference. Despite protestations that people are our greatest asset, the evidence suggests that HRM is relatively low down in their priorities and largely seen as an administrative function. The overall patterns of work organization and structures of control are rarely questioned.

The second consideration reinforces the earlier stress on power and ideology. It is the immediate context. Opposition to regulation has become a defining feature of British management, the relative success of organizations such as the CBI in blocking initiatives in recent years having fuelled the stance. 'Soft' regulation may be preferable to 'hard' regulation, but no regulation is considered best of all. Moreover, if the approach outlined here does not directly involve it, many are likely to object that it smacks of a 'stakeholder' approach. The idea that business should embrace human resource development and social capital formation sits very uneasily with the extreme forms of shareholder value that currently prevail. Its practical implications are also very threatening. Many UK businesses are locked into a 'low-road' approach – up-skilling and high-performance working would require little short of a revolution. Even in organizations with a 'high-road' approach, few managers have had the opportunity to develop the social skills that are involved in high-performance working. In the words of the deputy Director General of the Chartered Institute of Personnel and Development (Syedain 2006): 'The British get dictation and they get negotiation, but they don't get consultation.' Also self-management and semi-autonomous team working have significant implications for the numbers, perks and pretensions of managers – far from being agents of change, managers can be a significant barrier.

For many government policymakers, employer opposition is likely to be cause enough for rejecting the paradigm being promoted here – the Treasury, for example, recently dropped plans for compulsory operating and financial reviews for listed companies on the grounds of the regulatory burden, even though some high-profile businesses were in favour. More generally, there is the dominant neoliberal approach to running the economy to contend with. This sees a relatively limited role for government along with the need for low taxation. The emphasis is on markets and ensuring that they work effectively. Significantly, the government department with prime responsibility for the area, the Employment Relations Directorate, sits within the DTI's 'Fair Markets' group, a major task being to encourage confident participants in the labour market. It isn't just that organizations like trade unions and institutions such as collective bargaining tend to be viewed negatively. The significance of the workplace as a key decision-making unit is largely ignored as are the complexities of managing the employment relationship – the workplace is regarded as a 'black box' where participants are expected to respond economically rationally to the broader regional and national economic framework. In the words of Parkinson (2003: 499), 'the company is a private association with which the state ought to have very little to do with'. The idea of 'institutional failure' is rarely entertained – public intervention can only be justified in terms of 'market failure'; if managers are behaving in a particular way, it must be economically rational for them to do so; if not, the 'market' will correct. The status quo is therefore rarely questioned. Crucially, too, there is a premium on macro-level target setting, along with the prioritization of econometric data over other forms of evidence. This means emphasizing what can be measured at the expense of what cannot. Underpinning everything else is the view that sensible governments don't have much choice: globalization is dictating the policy agenda. In Kay's (2003: 310) words, the principles of what is otherwise known as the 'American business model' or 'Washington consensus' (because of the association with the Washington-based International Monetary Fund and World Bank) are 'unavoidable', 'because global business will migrate to the jurisdictions closest to them'.

Self-evidently, these are powerful considerations. Arguably, policymaking at the regional level offers some scope for discussion of evidence-based options. Also not all companies are deaf to arguments about the importance of employee voice and the need for greater legitimacy. At national level, however, short of a 'hung' parliament and a change in electoral arrangements, there seems little prospect of a shift to greater deliberation in policymaking.

At first sight, the dominance of neoliberalism looks equally enduring if not permanent. Here, however, there are perhaps greater grounds for optimism. Perhaps most significantly of these, the Scandinavian countries justly point to evidence that improving working life *and* organizational performance are not necessarily mutually exclusive as neoliberalism often suggests. Rather they can be mutually reinforcing. Improved performance makes it possible for managers to bring about a sustained improvement in working lives. Taking improving working life into account makes it possible for managers to get the motivation, commitment and loyalty that they increasingly need for success. Even the OECD (2006), whose original 1994 *Jobs Study* was especially critical of institutions, has changed its position, recognizing that there is more than one route to performance. In the circumstances, an HRM framework that is rooted in 'governance' may not necessarily sink without trace – it may even help to achieve a better balance in policy thinking.

Conclusion

I anticipate three main strands of criticism to the ideas I have set out here. Surely, some might argue, a 'governance' focus means an unnecessarily broad canvas for HRM. HRM cannot be expected to take on board work organization and personnel practice along with their impact on everything from business performance, to the quality of working life to the state of a nation's social capital – many of these issues are more appropriate to the study of industrial relations than HRM. I have a great deal of sympathy with this view and am more than happy to go along with it. It does carry with it an important implication, however, that returns us to the introduction. If HRM is unable to operate with a broad definition of the management of the employment relationship, it has to give up claims to be supplanting industrial relations as the umbrella paradigm for the field.

I also have some sympathy for the second strand of criticism I anticipate. Many colleagues may agree with the central thrust of my argument that 'governance' should be HRM's core focus. They may object, though, that the mountain to climb to get this accepted in the foreseeable future is just too high – it may even be dangerous to attempt it. HRM would be much better advised to focus on specific issues such as the link between working practices and economic performance before charging off in other directions.

My worry here is twofold. One is that issues such as the link between working practices and economic performance could turn out to be something of a 'holy grail' – the pursuit of econometric evidence at the expense of everything else is already looking as if it could prove to be a false trail (see, for example, the discussion in Godard 2004). The other is that the subject will come under increasing pressure to 'solve' problems on practitioner and policymakers' terms. Here I'm thinking of issues such as employment engagement, which is increasingly being defined in 'attitudinal' rather than 'institutional' terms. Motivation programmes have their place, but are likely to prove to be an expensive failure without institutional change, bringing little credit to those who become involved.

A third group might object that all this talk of 'institutions', 'power' and 'negotiation' is old hat. In Emmott's (2005) words, such language has 'echoes of a historical era that offers few insights into contemporary issues or practice'. The world has moved on and HRM needs to be *more* rather than less exclusive in terms of its subject, interests and disciplinary frameworks. I disagree fundamentally, which is why I have written this chapter as I have. My view is that, unless HRM is able to draw on or develop the kind of analytical framework outlined here, it will continually be vulnerable to the kind of withering attack that Braverman launched against personnel management more than 30 years ago. It may be more appropriate today to talk about the 'world of services', 'human resources' and 'practitioners of HRM and the psychological contract', but Braverman's central thrust will remain:

> Work itself is organized according to Taylorian principles, while personnel departments and academics have busied themselves with the selection, training, manipulation, pacification and adjustment of 'manpower' to suit the work processes so organized. Taylorism dominates the world of production; the practitioners of 'human relations' and 'industrial psychology' are the maintenance crew for the human machinery.
>
> (Braveman 1974: 87)

I hope this will not come to pass. If it does, it will be a massive opportunity wasted. In the era of the 'knowledge economy', the issues HRM deals with assume particular importance. Not only does the rhetoric of 'people are our most important asset' need to become reality. Critically important is that the emphasis of public policy shifts from seeing the workplace as a 'black box' where employers are allowed to treat employees as a commodity to be bought and sold in 'markets' to a place where human beings are given opportunities to grow, develop and contribute. It is here that the 'governance' paradigm comes into its own. It is not so much a question of championing the employee cause. To paraphrase Edwards (2005), it may not be in the interests of a particular employer to promote human resource development and social capital formation, but it is in the interests of society as a whole.

References

Audit Commission (2003). *Targets in the Public Sector. Public Sector Briefing*. Available at www.audit-commission. gov.uk.

Audit Commission/National Audit Office (2006). *Delivering Efficiently: Strengthening the Links in Public Service Delivery Chains*. Available at www.nao.org.uk.

Bach, S. (2005). *Managing Human Resources: Personnel Management in Transition*. Oxford, Blackwell.

Boxall, P. and J. Purcell (2003). *Strategy and Human Resource Management*. Basingstoke, Palgrave.

Braverman, H. A. (1974). *Labor and Monopoly Capital: The Degradation of Work in the Twentieth Century*. New York Monthly Review Press.

Brown, W. and J. Walsh (1994). 'Managing pay in Britain', in K. Sisson (ed.) *Personnel Management*, 2nd edn. Oxford, Blackwell.

Budd, J. (2004). *Employment with a Human Face. Balancing Efficiency, Equity and Voice*. Ithaca, Cornell University Press.

Campbell, J. (2004). *Institutional Change and Globalization*. Princeton, Princeton University Press.

Coats, D. (2004). *Speaking Up! Voice, Industrial Democracy and Organizational Performance*. London, The Work Foundation.

Confederation of British Industry (2005). *CBI-AXA Absence Survey*. London, CBI.

Department of Trade and Industry (2003a). *The Strategy*. London, DTI.

Department of Trade and Industry (2003b). *The Strategy: Analysis*. London, DTI.

Department of Trade and Industry (2006). *Success at Work. Protecting Vulnerable Workers, Support Good Employers*. Available at www.dti.gov.uk.

Edwards, P. (2003). 'The promising future of industrial relations: developing the connections between theory and relevance', invited plenary paper, British Universities Industrial Relations Association, Annual Conference, Leeds, July.

Edwards, P. (2005). *Workplace Justice: Why a New Public Policy Initiative is Needed*. Available from paul.edwards@wbs.ac.uk.

Edwards, P. (2006). 'Industrial relations and critical realism: IR's tacit contribution', Warwick Papers in Industrial Relations, Number 80. Coventry, Industrial Relations Research Unit, University of Warwick.

Edwards, P. and J. Wajcman (2005). *The Politics of Working Life*. Oxford, Oxford University Press.

Emmott, M. (2005). 'What is employee relations?', in *Change Agenda*, London, CIPD.

Ferris, G., D. Barnum, S. Rosen, L. Holleran and J. Dulebohn (1995). 'Towards business-university partnership in human resource management: integration of science and practice', in G. Ferris, D. Barnum and S. Rosen (eds) *Handbook of Human Resource Management*. Cambridge, Blackwell.

Flanders, A. (1970). *Management and Unions: The Theory and Reform of Industrial Relations*. London, Faber & Faber.

Godard, J. (2004). 'A critical assessment of the high-performance paradigm', *British Journal of Industrial Relations* 42(2): 349–78.

Hall, P. and D. Soskice (eds)(2001). *Varieties of Capitalism: The Institutional Foundations of Comparative Advantage*. Oxford, Oxford University Press.

Hay, C. (2002). *Political Analysis. A Critical Introduction*. Basingstoke, Palgrave.

Hindmoor, A. (2006). *Rational Choice*. Basingstoke, Palgrave.

House of Commons Public Administration Select Committee (2003). *On Target? Government by Measurement*. Available at www.publications.parliament.uk.

Hyman, R. (2004). 'Is industrial relations theory always ethnocentric?', in B. Kaufman (ed.) *Theoretical Perspectives on Work and the Employment Relationship*. Ithaca, ILR/Cornell University Press.

Kaufman, B. (2004a). 'Employment relations and the employment relations system: a guide to theorising', in B. Kaufman (ed.) *Theoretical Perspectives on Work and the Employment Relationship*. Ithaca, ILR/Cornell University Press.

Kaufman, B. (2004b). 'Towards an integrative theory of human resource management', in B. Kaufman (ed.) *Theoretical Perspectives on Work and the Employment Relationship*. Ithaca, ILR/Cornell University Press.

Kay, J. (2003). *The Truth about Markets. Their Genius, their Limits, their Follies*. London, Penguin, Allen Lane.

Kersley, B., C. Alpin, J. Forth, A. Bryson, H. Bewley, G. Dix and S. Oxenbridge (2006). *First Findings from the Workplace Employee Relations Survey*. Available at www.dti.gov.uk.

Marsden, D. (1999). *A Theory of Employment Systems. Micro-foundations of Societal Diversity*. Oxford, Oxford University Press.

Martin, R. (2003). 'Politics and industrial relations', in P. Ackers and A. Wilkinson (eds) *Understanding Work and Employment. Industrial Relations in Transition*. Oxford, Oxford University Press.

Müller-Jentsch, W. (2004). 'Theoretical approaches to industrial relations', in B. Kaufman (ed.) *Theoretical Perspectives on Work and the Employment Relationship*. Ithaca, ILR/Cornell University Press.

North, D. (1990). *Institutions, Institutional Change and Economic Performance*. Cambridge, Cambridge University Press.

OECD (2006). *Employment Outlook 2006 – Boosting Jobs and Incomes* (Chapter 7. Reassessing the Role of Policies and Institutions for Labour Market Performance: A Quantitative Analysis). Paris, OECD.

Parkinson, J. (2003). 'Models of the company and the employment relationship', *British Journal of Industrial Relations* 41(3): 481–510.

Porter, M. and C. Ketels (2003). *UK Competitiveness: Moving to the Next Stage*. DTI Economics Papers. London, DTI.

Schumpeter, J. (1942). *Capitalism, Socialism and Democracy*. London, George Allen & Unwin.

Syedain, H. (2006). 'Put out of joint', *People Management*, 7 May.

Taylor, R. (2002). *Britain's World of Work – Myths and Realities*. Available at www.leeds.ac.uk/esrcfutureofwork.

Walton, R. E. and R. B. McKersie (1965). *A Behavioral Theory of Labor Negotiations*. New York, McGraw-Hill.

Williamson, O. (1985). *The Economic Institutions of Capitalism: Firms, Markets, Relational Contracting*. New York, Free Press.

Core practice areas

There are five chapters in this part of the book. Each addresses the heartland components of HR practice. In many large HR departments, practitioners tend to specialize in one or more of these sub-areas such as recruitment, reward management or training. The chapters presented here allow access to the latest developments in each of these areas while also offering expert critical interpretation and commentary.

In Chapter 6, Paul Iles examines employee resourcing and the emerging topic of 'talent management'. Iles points out that many people who work for an organization may not necessarily be direct employees of it because they may be subcontractors or consultants for example – nonetheless, all these workers need somehow to be found and secured. This process occurs, as Iles points out, in a context where various parties such as line managers, recruitment agencies and contractors with possibly different expectations and interests may be competing to secure their own priorities. Consequently, the sub-processes of staffing, appraising, tracking and grading involves HR managers in handling complex issues of power politics and equal opportunities. On top of all this, the attempt to engage in 'talent management' so that special attention can be accorded to those individuals and groups regarded as especially valuable to an organization, confronts HR with a special set of challenges.

In Chapter 7, Alan Felstead, one of the leading authorities in the training and skills domain guides us through the intricacies of training, learning and skills. This is an especially turbulent arena of HR and it involves national policy debates and initiatives as well as organizational-level actions. As Felstead explains, the underlying assumption of the national-level institutional reforms is that human capital is key to economic success. Failures and shortcomings in this regard are seen as contributing to the UK's productivity gap. In this context, this chapter offers a succinct and authoritative guide to the interplay between three crucial aspects to the debate: 'training', 'learning' and 'skills'. The chapter 'navigates a path through the feverish claims and counterclaims' that litter the popular trade magazines and related media.

Chapter 8, by Graeme Salaman, tackles the process of 'change management' – a core theme in the eyes of many strategic human resource management practitioners and analysts. Salaman has for many years been a leading analyst in the areas of the management of change and organizational capability. He has been somewhat unusual internationally in not only providing trenchant critical analyses of popular nostrums of change management but, at the same time, he has acted as consultant at strategic level to many global organizations including Rolls-Royce, Allianz, Morgan Stanley, Willis and Ernst & Young. In this new analysis of the subject, he takes a novel approach by examining change management through the lens of managers' knowledge. He notes that most treatments of the subject focus on change processes rather than the content – or the designers of the content – of change. Drawing on recent research,

Salaman reveals how the underlying theories and knowledge of managers influences the kinds of organizational change that they seek to drive. Utilizing this perspective, many of the paradoxes and contradictions which have characterized the change field are unravelled.

In Chapter 9, Ian Kessler critically assesses the range of reward choices. The idea of tension between the principles of business strategy, external equity and internal equity is examined. These are used to help map recent changes in pay strategies and pay practices. The analysis suggests that the three principles may not be in as much competition as is often imagined.

Chapter 10, by Mick Marchington and Annette Cox, examines the theme of employee involvement and participation. The chapter describes the range of ways in which workers can be involved and engaged. The ways in which different practices operate and vary in degree, scope, level and form are examined, and the outcomes associated with these practices are also scrutinized.

Employee resourcing and talent management

Paul Iles

Introduction: definitions of ER and scope of chapter

In this chapter, we will primarily focus on the 'core' area of 'assessment' in employee resourcing (ER), but will also discuss an emerging issue, talent management (TM). The CIPD standards refer to 'people resourcing' (e.g., Taylor 2002), but we shall continue to call the area ER while recognizing that many 'people' who do work for an organization are not necessarily employees of it (e.g. outsourcing, offshoring, subcontracting, employing consultants).

From the late 1980s, as part of the move from personnel management towards human resource management, many organizations in North America and Europe began thinking of their ER processes as major levers to support strategic and cultural change. As one key way of delivering behaviours necessary to support organizational strategies, ER initiatives therefore became increasingly important: ER processes can be installed to ensure that employees with the requisite skills and qualities are successfully assessed, placed in appropriate jobs or roles, and appraised, developed and rewarded against appropriate competency criteria (Iles 1999, 2000).

Although recent, universalistic 'best practice' models of HRM have also been developed, a 'matching' model of ER is often assumed; different strategies have different implications for the nature, role and importance of ER, with ER practices often seen as secondary processes, 'integrating' with business strategy in a rather reactive manner. At a time when programmes of HRM inspired change often encourage a focus on the 'organizational change lever' of ER, emphasizing the strategic significance of identifying and assessing 'talent' and key managerial and other competencies to support structural and cultural change, it is imperative to analyse what is happening in this area. Understanding the significance of the interrelated ideas, techniques and assumptions that comprise current models of ER and the qualities these schemes typically seek to identify and how they work to define the employee and his/her necessary qualities is necessary.

Most treatments of ER take an avowedly managerialist/practitioner approach to ER and tend not to focus on wider perspectives or the interests of multiple, perhaps competing, stakeholders. For example, Taylor (1998: 12) does not 'attempt to question the legitimacy of the employment relationship as it has developed in modern Western society, excluding literature that takes a critical perspective on this and other issues'. However, the approach taken here does not just focus on advice, prescription and what currently passes for 'best practice', but seeks to acknowledge that there are multiple stakeholders with an interest in ER, including line managers, the HRM function, contractors to whom work may be outsourced, recruiting agencies and search consultants. All these parties may have conflicting or competing demands, values, expectations and agendas.

The ER process involves the assessing, appraising, grading, tracking, sorting, shifting and placing of individuals, not always employees, in order to make staffing decisions and thus raises questions of power, politics, equal opportunity, knowledge and ethics. In part, the current CIPD standards for ER go some way to acknowledge this, as does Taylor (2002). The CIPD for example set out three approaches to ER, namely the 'traditional paradigm', various 'new paradigms' and 'contingency-based' ER.

ER has a far wider significance than the merely technical activity set out in many textbooks of HRM; it involves the embodiment and operationalization of a form of expertise that critically defines the talent, skills, values and qualities (often called competencies or, increasingly, 'talents') required by modern forms of organization. It thus both reveals and represents the form and direction of current forms of organizational change and the working out of the play of power within organizations. In principle, and also in effect, contemporary processes of ER represent the moment when organizational restructuring meets and impacts on individuals. In so doing, ER seeks to define, understand, assess and place people in terms of organizationally defined critical qualities. The issue therefore is not simply, or even perhaps primarily, one of efficiency or rationality, as is often asserted, but of power: the capacity of, and the forms of knowledge and associated technologies through which organizations identify, define and assess individuals against structures of necessary competences or similar behavioural frameworks, including current 'talent management' frameworks.

ER, performance and strategy

A common assertion often made in attempts to link ER with organizational 'performance' (e.g., Guest et al. 2003; Pass 2005) is that ER practices affect employee attitudes such as commitment and motivation, as well as enhance employee competence. A recent case study of ER in Selfridges and Co. at the Trafford Centre, Manchester for example (Pass 2005) shows how the team leader role was redefined by the company and staff had to reapply through a new selection process that focused on behaviours as well as skill sets. In addition, improvements were made to appraisal, linking it to development and career opportunities, ensuring ownership and better implementation. A subsequent survey showed impressive results in terms of enhanced employee commitment, satisfaction and perceptions of team leader behaviour, especially in appraisal performance. Organizational performance also improved, as did turnover. The team leader role was redefined to give more emphasis to people management aspects, especially in such ER activities as recruitment and selection and appraisal.

Whereas recruitment and selection were formerly undertaken by HR, team leaders were now required to interview applicants, advise on job evaluation and make final selection decisions. Team leaders went through eight days of training in 2002, with recruitment revised to look at communication and relationship skills, in line with company policy to recruit for attitude rather than skill so that staff fit with and deliver the culture and values of the organization.

This is an increasingly common stance, also adopted by many low-cost airlines such as the US-based Southwest Airlines. Here, people are selected for their attitudes and 'fit' with the culture, rather than their skills; employee networks are used and teams of employees, managers and customers participate in a 'casting-call'-type selection process, in addition to candidate profiling (Barney and Wright 1998; Baron 2004; Jackson and Schuler 2003). Southwest Airlines has also sought to use 'internal branding' to create not just product/service branding, or corporate branding, but 'employer/employee branding' on the basis of a unique employee value proposition (Edwards 2005; Miles and Mangold 2005).

Assessment and selection

The overall process of resourcing an organization is often termed 'staffing', especially in the USA; a formal process of ensuring that the organization has qualified workers at all levels to meet its short- and long-term business objectives. Through this process the organization tries to decide what kind of employees are needed, obtain the most qualified people, place them in the job and develop them. Assessment is therefore one of the critical functions of effective HRM.

In all areas of life, people make assessment and selection decisions and this is particularly true in organizations; decisions over who to employ, promote, select for further training or select for dismissal. Unless suitable people are assessed and selected, the organization will fail to achieve its strategic objectives and will run into a variety of personnel problems: high turnover, low productivity, high rates of absenteeism and employee stress. The kinds of job offered by organizations differ in terms of their skill and ability demands; the differences between people in terms of their knowledge, skills, personality, motivation and other attributes are therefore clearly relevant to ER decisions (Newell 2005).

In the 'best practice' model, often called 'psychometric–objective' (Iles 1999, 2000), a 'matching' model is often explicit; the aim is to match the 'right' people with the 'right' jobs and to attract candidates who possess the required skills (while putting off those who do not, so as not to overload the process). Selecting those who best fit the job, whose performance in a selection process best predicts future job performance and suitability for the job, is therefore critical. Traditionally, this has required 'job analysis', leading to a 'job description' stipulating tasks, duties and responsibilities. From this, a 'person specification' can be drawn up, defining the kind of person to perform the job effectively (usually described in terms of the knowledge, skills and other abilities/attributes, such as cognitive ability or personality factors believed to be necessary for successful job performance, now often expressed in terms of competencies or competences; an ambiguous term often seen as representing a departure from rigorous psychometric practice). This process will enable applicants to be assessed or measured in some way, through tests, interviews or other 'predictors', in terms of how well they display the essential requirements laid down in the person specification, and enable a best match between job and person. Increasingly, however, organizations such as Selfridges and Southwest Airlines are less interested in fit with 'the job' alone and more interested in 'fit' with the team or organization, and this has led to moves away from 'psychometric' towards 'social process' or 'exchange' models (Anderson and Ostroff 1997; Iles 1999, 2000; Iles and Roberston 1997; Newell 2005). In addition, in reality, recruitment and selection, like strategic planning in organizations in general, is a much more subjective, contested and political process than implied by the 'psychometric–objective', matching model of assessment.

Social process model of assessment

The recruitment and selection process is an exchange, a two-way decision-making process; it is not just the organization that is deciding whether to make an offer of employment to the candidate. The candidate is also making a decision as to whether to enter into an ongoing relationship with the organization, which may be terminated at any stage. Inevitably, then, both 'sides' will be engaging in 'impression management', a process often seen as 'distortion' by psychometric models that seek to minimize 'subjectivity' as much as possible by turning selection methods like interviews into 'tests', using highly structured, scored behavioural, patterned or situational interviews.

This two-way process is not treated as a 'problem', but explicitly recognized by the social process or social exchange model of assessment and selection (Herriot 1989; Iles 1999, 2000; Newell 2005). Here the applicant is seen as an active decision maker; both parties have changing expectations, and the assessment process ideally enables them to exchange information to determine levels of fit or compatibility (one reason for the enduring popularity of the interview, despite decades of negative psychometric research). If the exchange process is successful, expectations will be congruent and a viable formal and social contract will emerge. If not, the process may still be seen as effective, as the organization may feel that the candidate is not suitable (lacking skills, motivation or experience for example) or the candidate may feel that the organization is not suitable, with opportunities and salary level not meeting expectations or the organizational culture seen to clash with personal values. As in the psychometric model, there is an emphasis on 'fit' and 'matching', but this is construed in a different way: the match is not with job demands, but of expectations and needs with culture and values within a process of two-way decision-making and the provision of information. Assessment is therefore a learning process, as both parties learn more about each other and become better able to make informed decisions. In this sense, selection is seen as 'applicant socialization' (Anderson and Ostroff 1997), but if the applicant is made to feel 'too special' in the selection process, expectations of employment may be unrealistically high, leading to inevitable disappointment. This is one reason why 'realistic job previews' are often recommended for effective recruitment.

Knowledge, power and ER

An alternative perspective on ER to the psychometric-objective and social process perspectives views it less as a process of objective 'matching' or as a social exchange process and more as an exercise in power and knowledge (Iles 1999, 2000; Townley 1994). As we have seen, ER essentially involves assessing, appraising, grading, tracking, sorting, sifting and placing employees (and increasingly other kinds of workers) so as to make staffing decisions, including development decisions. Yet despite the need for a fuller understanding of these processes, the bulk of existing HR literature is concerned primarily and solely with assessing the efficiency of these processes, often in rather descriptive, prescriptive and atheoretical ways.

ER has a far wider significance as the embodiment and operationalization of a form of expertise that critically defines the skills, values and qualities and competencies (now increasingly termed 'talents') required by modern forms of organization. ER thus reveals and represents the form and direction of current forms of organizational change and the working out of the play of power within organizations. In principle, and also in effect, contemporary processes of ER represent the moment when organizational restructuring meets and impacts on individuals. In so doing, it seeks to define, understand, assess and place them in terms of organizationally defined critical qualities, such as 'competencies' or 'talents'. The issue therefore is not simply, or even perhaps primarily, one of efficiency or rationality, but of power: the capacity of, and the forms of knowledge and associated technologies through which organizations identify, define and assess individuals against structures of necessary competences or similar behavioural frameworks, such as talent management frameworks.

ER is often concerned with developing prescriptive guidelines, not always based on theory or empirical research, for assessing appraising, grading, sorting, sifting, placing and developing employees, including recent developments such as 360° feedback (Simmons et al. 2005). Townley (1989, 1994) has noted that interest in more rigorous processes of ER can be seen not simply as related to a concern for more efficient staffing, but as integral to what has been identified as HRM. An increasing emphasis is placed on the attitudinal and behavioural characteristics of employees, monitored through selection and performance review (Townley 1989: 92). This emphasis on the strategic significance of identifying and assessing key managerial and other competencies and, increasingly, 'talent' to support structural/cultural change makes it imperative not only to describe what is happening in this area, but to understand the significance of the interrelated ideas, techniques and assumptions which comprise current models of ER and how these work to define the employee and his/her necessary qualities. The limitations of many approaches to ER are that they are almost entirely, if understandably, concerned with improving the efficiency of the processes, and not with understanding their wider provenance and significance. They tend to focus on degrees of, and deviations from, scientific or technical or professional rationality; but they do not address the nature or implications of that rationality. Indeed, they are themselves part of the very discourse they describe, accepting the assumptions of the ER process and interested mainly in supplying technological improvements and evaluations.

From critical theory, we can therefore see ER as part of the government of organizations and the regulation of individuals, including their subjectivity (Miller and Rose 1993; Rose 1990, 1999). The focus is on the role of the appraiser/assessor as both regulator and judge/confessor and the appraised/assessed as an object of power/knowledge, as well as a self-regulating agent. The assessment/appraisal instrument is seen as part of a technology of power and regulation. ER can thus be seen not only in terms of its efficiency or reasonableness, or even in terms of the ways in which reasonableness is constructed and displayed, but in terms of the relationships between these processes, the expertise on which they are based, and the practice of power within organizations (Iles 1999, 2000; Iles and Salaman 1995).

Current developments in procedures and criteria can be explained in terms of changes in the nature of work organization – in particular, as Townley (1989) argues, in terms of 'the importance attached to increased individual discretion, and the implications this has for the administration of work' (1989: 102). Thus assessment and appraisal may be regarded as an element in the 'government' of organizations and the way in which power, knowledge and practice mutually support and reproduce each other. Miller and Rose (1993) following Foucault (1974) use the term 'government' to focus on 'the shifting ambitions and concerns of all those social authorities that have sought to administer the lives of individuals and associations, focusing our attention on the diverse mechanisms through which the actions and judgement of persons and organisations have been linked to political objectives' (Townley 1989: 75-6). This project is greatly enhanced by a further concept – 'governmentality' – used to draw attention to the diverse and various processes and techniques: 'an ensemble formed by the institutions, procedures, analyses, and reflections, the calculations and tactics, that allow the exercise of this very specific albeit complex form of power' (Foucault 1977: 20, quoted in Miller and Rose 1993: 76).

ER therefore offers a striking example of ways in which actions and judgements critical for organizational restructuring and for individual experience are structured and made rational in terms of expert-derived systems and criteria, revealing the interrelationships between knowledge and power. They demonstrate the ubiquity of power/knowledge practices and show the role of a form of organizational governmentality that allows the exercise of power through calculation, assessment and knowledge. Processes of assessment, wherein individuals and employees are 'known' in terms of a set of qualities (competencies/talents), measured against these, and processed in terms of this assessment, are therefore as revealing of organizations as they are of individuals.

This is not simply to argue that assessment practices and knowledge support power in an ideological or legitimating manner; power is that which traverses *all* practices from the 'macro' to the 'micro' through which people are ruled, mastered, held in check, administered, steered, guided, by means of which they are led by others or have come to direct or regulate their own actions (Rose 1990). Foucault's (1977) interest in the construction of knowledge and its relationship to power and 'technologies of power' (disciplinary practices aimed at making behaviour visible, predictable, calculable and manageable, such as assessment (Townley 1994)) enables us to see ER as dividing, partitioning, ordering and ranking employees and imposing and maintaining organizational boundaries through 'hierarchical observation' and 'normalizing judgement'. Partition involves ranking via serial or hierarchical ordering among employees, for example through 'forced distribution' of appraisal ratings. At GE, for example, Welch (Welch and Byrne 2003) adopted the 'vitality curve approach' by which managers were required to identify the top 20% (who enjoyed most investment and identification as high – potential), middle 70% (solid performers) and the bottom 10% of employees (to be managed out of the organization).

This 'partitioning' of employees is taken further in contemporary approaches to 'talent management' (TM), which will be discussed later. Earlier developments in ER often employed variants of the well-known 'Boston Consulting Group Matrix', originally developed for strategic management and business unit portfolio planning. This differentiated, on the basis of relative market share/extent of growth in that market, between 'stars' (high shares of growing markets), cash cows (high shares in low-growth markets), 'wildcats' or problem children/question marks, with low shares in fast-growing markets, and 'dogs', low-growth units with low-market share (Linstead et al. 2004). Application to ER led to substituting market growth for career growth potential and relative market share for current level of performance, leading to such prescriptions for managing people as 'polish the stars, shoot the dogs, milk the cash cows and performance manage the wildcats'.

Power in assessment and appraisal is thus not located merely in the actions of the state or, within the enterprise, in the actions of senior managers; it is present in all knowledge and practice that regulates individuals, including of course their own. This allows us to look for the exercise or practice of power in activities that initially may seem far removed from established centres of power or removed through the nature and exercise of scientific or technical expertise from their interests and values. ER can thus be seen as an example of the exercise of power within the detached and scientific process of competence/talent-based assessment (Hollway 1991); expertise in assessment and appraisal is produced, rather than discovered.

Power is inherent in knowledge itself and in the techniques which that knowledge informs and justifies. Knowledge plays a major role in constructing the individual manager/employee as calculable, discussable and comprehensible in the process of, and as the subject of, senior managerial interventions and decisions in the process of ER. Structures of competence/talent and the process of assessment and appraisal may be based on scrupulous testing instruments. Such expertises are not simply the servants of power, they *are* power itself, having crucial significance for key decisions about promotion, rejection and for the characteristics that are defined – and accepted by all parties – as necessary, and as properly constituting the 'new employee'. This is especially true in most definitions of talent management, which seek to define who is in the 'talent pool' or on the 'fast track' or shows 'high potential'. What is also central to the importance of competence-based talent assessment and appraisal is that it defines key qualities and maintains the necessity and neutrality of these dimensions.

Our concern here is therefore somewhat different from many approaches to ER. The identification of competencies (or more recently 'talents') and the technology of the assessment/appraisal process represent the 'knowing' and constituting of individuals as employees/workers. This discourse consists of a complex of intellectual conceptual frameworks (units of competence/talent identified and distinguished through an elaborate process, involving the opinions of managers themselves, then formulated into discrete 'real' and relevant elements of human action) allied to a technology for the identification and assessment and, crucially, measurement of individuals against these selected competencies/talent frameworks.

Townley (1989) argues that changes in assessment and appraisal processes and criteria are associated with the emphasis, within HRM-style change, on 'the increased emphasis on "flexibility" or the requirement for greater exercise of discretion.... The changes which have been associated with the introduction of selection and HRM generally, have been primarily associated with moves towards "Japanisation" or "flexibility" and the commitment to move away from "bureaucratised" procedures' (Townley 1989: 106); developments in methods for example reflect and channel organizational priorities for HRM/ER change. In a sense, her analysis focuses on the rationality of these developments, albeit one defined in terms of new organizational forms and dimensions of control. Iles (1999, 2000) and Iles and Salaman (1995), however, draw attention not to ways in which developments in assessment/appraisal processes support structural changes in practice, but to the ways in which processes of organizational change and developments in criteria and systems cohere and support each other as a set of related and mutually supportive ideas. This discourse of HRM/ER impacts on employees and demonstrates the practice of power; the effectiveness of this, however, is defined by the discourse itself.

A further and closely related feature of such discourses is that they attend to, and define and constitute, the self – the subject. It is precisely by constituting, rather than opposing, the subjectivity of individuals that the power of organization, and indeed of HR and ER strategies, is exercised. HRM/ER discourse, defining competencies/talent and represented in the technology of assessment/appraisal, creates and shapes individuals as subjects – for example, the constituent competences of the 'new' managers/ employees as 'required' by prevalent forms and directions of organizational change (e.g., entrepreneurial, flexible, etc.). While ER is infused with enterprise (Rose 1990, 1999), it also carries other elements focusing on the importance of 'integration', quality and flexibility, all of which relate to conceptions of key competencies/talents. More recent concerns have been with 'corporateness', as manifested in interest in such areas as corporate identity, governance, branding/reputation, social responsibility and identity (Balmer and Greyser 2003; Edwards 2005; Martin 2006; Martin and Hetrick 2006) as well as with employee commitment and 'engagement' (Harter et al. 2002; Johnson 2004). This agenda stresses such issues as brand, reputation, organizational citizenship and ethics. According special status to enterprise, corporateness and engagement (and associated values such as 'ownership' of individuals' work responsibilities, empowerment, devolution of authority to the lowest level, etc.), ER therefore serves as an overarching set of assumptions, techniques, data, frameworks, models and assessments that make sense of, and guide, the restructuring of organizations and management, to which ER contributes and makes sense.

Furthermore the discourse also constructs a necessary and closed loop of causation: a conception of the environment that requires that organizations develop certain forms of business strategy, which, in turn, needs the support of certain organizational structures, cultures and HR systems, requiring new, competence-based, 'talented' employees. As Rose (1990) remarks, power works, not against, or in opposition to, the subject (the individual versus the state, private versus public, the organization against the employee, etc.) but through the construction, measurement, analysis and treatment of subjectivity – through the ways in which 'subjectivity has become an essential object and target for certain strategies, tactics and procedures of regulation' (Rose 1990: 15). The interest in 'branding', discussed earlier, shows how organizations and ER are becoming more concerned with assessing and managing the private and personal aspects of employees (Alvesson and Wilmot 2002) and enhancing 'employee engagement', concerns reflected also in growing interest in 'emotional intelligence' (Goleman 1996) and the importance of 'emotional labour' (Bolton and Boyd 2003).

Competence/talent itself is therefore presented as a real and deep underlying feature of humans as employees. Further organizational progress (the 'career', most manifest in the close links between talent management and succession planning (CIPD 2006a, 2006b, 2006c)) is based on evidence that an individual is able to offer that s/he has such competence/talent. Frequently, disappointed and rejected candidates from assessment and appraisal may be offered counselling or training in order to support them through the trauma of discovery not simply that they had failed a test, but that they had revealed a lack of key deep qualities or talents. The focus of the discourse, therefore, is the subjectivity of the individual, defined in terms of qualities, talents and competencies, assessed against these and offered support to help develop or compensation and counselling for lacking these qualities. Carter (1996) showed how a regional electricity company's use of assessment centre feedback had important implications for how managers constituted themselves as employees: successful candidates described themselves in such terms, and saw not only their job as vital, but the old management style as anachronistic. Many candidates, though seeing the centre as a 'game', accepted and internalized judgements made about them. The centre represented not only a symbolic cultural break with the past, but the production of knowledge about candidates provided the basis for how they constituted themselves as managers. Efforts to define and measure competencies/talents represent a paradigmatic example of a discourse within an organizational context. To regard these processes in this way helps to illuminate aspects and implications overlooked by more traditional discussions of the topic.

Even ER procedures such as self-appraisal and 360° feedback, often seen as progressive, are mediated through such 'confessors' as mentors, consultants or coaches who interpret, judge, punish, forgive and console, acting to actively construct identity and how individuals see themselves (Simmons et al. 2005). Those who feel assessment or appraisal to be 'a game' may internalize its judgements, welcome its apparent openness and fairness and accept it as symbolizing a break with the past. Du Gay et al. (1996) show how assessment and appraisal activities help reconstitute the nature and conduct of management and managers as proactive, self-regulating and entrepreneurial in a competitive marketplace. Managers are then charged with shaping and normalizing the behaviour of employees in similar directions, in part though competency/talent frameworks and associated ER technologies. As Du Gay et al. (1996: 278) put it, 'contemporary forms of organisational government are premised upon the mobilisation of the subjectivity of managers'.

Talent management and ER

Our analysis thus far, especially the role of 'partitioning', is particularly pertinent to the recent rise of the concept of 'talent management' (TM) in ER, a concept with various meanings; originally linked to recruitment, performance management or performance development, it is now seen in terms of a common approach underpinning all these ER activities (Iles et al. 2006). TM is not new (Adamsky 2003); as we saw, in the 1980s HR managers were urged to employ the BCG matrix to differentiate between star, dead, solid and high-potential employees and manage them differently. A more sophisticated recent approach (Martin 2006) distinguishes between internally focused and externally focused business modes and different kinds of psychological contract, such as transactional, relational and ideological, segmenting human capital into four modes, with different implications for branding. One group, core knowledge workers adding high value and showing uniqueness/firm-specific talents, is typically managed through relational/ideological contracts, high levels of organizational identification and a 'career' focus. Traditional human capital, such as administrators and operatives, can add value, but is not unique; such employees are typically managed through more transactional contracts within full-time employment. Idiosyncratic human capital, people with highly unique skills, is often managed through externalized relationships involving outsourcing, strategic partnerships and portfolio careers. A fourth group, ancillary human capital/contract workers, is often employed on a contract for services basis through outsourcing or payment for work, involving standardized work, ICT and little investment in HRD.

It is unclear whether such models are descriptions, predictions or prescriptions, as TM varies greatly in practice in contemporary organizations. At ConocoPhillips, the key activities of TM include strategic workforce and competency assessments, implementation of recruiting, staffing, career development and performance management strategies and the identification and development of the highest potential technical and leadership talent.

TM is now viewed as a tool to strengthen organizational capability through individual development, performance enhancement, career development and succession planning. Sistonen (2005) argues that TM is the integrated set of processes, programmes and technologies designed to develop, deploy and connect key talent and critical skill sets to drive business priorities; it is the means of identifying nurturing and using high-potential/high-performing people for strategic benefit.

TM grew in the late 1990s in the USA with the explosion of online job boards, equal employment opprtunity applicant tracking, e-recruiting companies and corporate employment websites (Schweyer 2004). A landmark McKinsey & Company study (Michaels et al. 2001) focused on the 'war for talent', a strategic business challenge and critical driver of corporate performance. TM is critical to every company's success and the importance of hiring and nurturing top talent while proactively managing-out low performers is stressed. TM then gained the attention of the US media and HR practitioners, as demonstrated by the front cover treatment by *Fortune* magazine in May 2000 (Stumpf and Tymon 2001) and recent attention in the UK by the CIPD (CIPD 2006a, 2006b, 2006c).

TM can therefore be understood as referring to the identification, development, engagement/retention and deployment of those employees who are particularly valuable to an organization – either in view of their 'high potential' for the future or because they are fulfilling business/operation-critical roles. In some organizations, TM has often become synonymous with leadership development (Iles and Preece 2006) or succession planning for top management; in other organizations, it involves the identification of 'high-potential' new graduate recruits; in yet others, a more inclusive identification of technical and professional 'talent' may be used.

Why the interest in talent management?

New technologies, rapidly changing business models and globalization of markets are all held to have increased the demand for 'talented' people, while an ageing workforce in many western countries is leaving many organizations with their critical talent approaching retirement, often with an inadequate supply of younger talent. Even slowdowns in the economy have not eliminated the talent problem, as workforce reductions may have temporarily slowed the major battles for talent, but put a premium on ensuring that the talent remaining is high performing and well suited to the strategic needs of the business. The dynamic nature of global business is seen as putting pressure on companies to search for exceptional talent in markets where demand exceeds supply (Duttagupta 2005).

According to Michaels et al. (2001), there are three fundamental forces fuelling the war for talent.

Irreversible shift from the industrial to the information age. The increasing impact of technology in the workplace is seen as changing the face of HRM/ER, making the boundaries between organizations more permeable, enabling collaboration and intensifying competition (Reed 2001) and leading to growth in knowledge workers. Workers in traditional blue-collar industries now also need specialized training to operate advanced robotics and computerized production lines (Frank and Taylor 2004).

Intensifying demand for high-calibre managerial/professional talent. The demand for talented people, it is claimed, will far exceed the availability of skilled workers, at all levels, and in all industries, threatening the competitive position of many corporations, with companies competing intensely for the limited supply of very capable managers and professionals.

Growing propensity to switch companies. Demographic trends, an increasing need for and a shortage of skilled labour, the broadened geographic mobility of labour and the obsolescence of the concept of a job for life are also seen as placing power into the hands of workers with transferable skills (Reed 2001); an organization's key assets are also its most mobile assets, with job moves undertaken to increase and enhance knowledge bases, employability and earnings potential (Weddle 2006).

In the UK, a tight labour market, skills shortages in certain areas and the changing demographics of the UK will cause additional challenges in the future (Moynagh and Worsley 2005). The expectations of the workforce are also changing, with more workers placing value on the concept of work–life balance when considering career decisions. There is also lack of confidence in the leadership potential of the existing workforce; a dearth of formal internal succession plans for even senior positions; and continued diversity issues, for example recruiting women into board positions. In this context, TM appears to be a priority for many British HR practitioners (CIPD 2006a, 2006b, 2006c).

Defining, identifying and assessing 'talent'

As we have seen, it is widely assumed that talent has become more important, but also that it remains in limited supply. Yet those who advance such views often find it difficult to define what is meant by 'highly talented' employees, and different organizations have different talent targets – for example, Microsoft UK focuses attention on its A list, the top 10% performers, regardless of role and level, Six Continents targets executives below board level and high-potential individuals as the two cadres likely to provide their leaders of tomorrow, while Philips is upgrading culture and talent to shape its vision of being a high-growth technology company (Duttagupta 2005).

'Talent' is often seen as the sum of a person's abilities, while often remaining elusive to measurement (Michaels et al. 2001). However Stainton (2005) also cites opportunity, because talent requires opportunity to be displayed; talent is an attribute that needs direction for it to be used constructively and effectively.

Components of talent management

Different components of TM models put forward by different authors are quite similar to each other and often not very different from what many organizations were doing before TM became fashionable. For example, Morton (2006) identifies eight categories, based on the experiences of 30 organizations: recruitment, retention, professional leadership, HIPO development, performance management, feedback/ measurement, attending to workforce planning and culture; while Fitz-enz (2005) argues that TM encompasses six HR services: staffing, leadership development, succession planning, performance management, training and education and retention. Iles et al. (2006) argue that comprehensive TM involves attracting talent (recruitment and selection), retaining talent, developing talent and transitioning talent. A strong and easily identifiable brand image that reflects the core values of the organization is often asserted to help attract potential talent (Edwards 2005; Martin 2005). The talent requirements of the organization must be clear and accurate in order to promote a suitable match between a potential applicant, the organization and the role. However, the recruitment process will need to be flexible enough to ensure that talent is not overlooked during a particular recruitment process. Talented people are likely to stay with a company only if they feel it has the right culture and provides them with self-fulfilment, a sense of accomplishment and emotional attachment. In essence, this is a variation of the *psychological contract*; long-term commitment to an organization is seen chiefly driven by some kind of emotional attachment or engagement. Bones (2005: 6) argues that this can be achieved by recruiting and developing employees who share the same values, attitudes and beliefs that the organization's success is built on; developing those employees so that they have true commitment and a sense of belonging; ensuring that talented individuals achieve a sense of fulfilment and accomplishment in their employment; and fostering relationships via mentoring/ coaching while encouraging networking between business departments (Johnson 2004).

A transparent PM system that supports the provision and continuous development of talent is also necessary; the process of succession planning historically lacked transparency and was often undertaken behind closed doors, focusing on past performance rather than future potential. TM is longer confined to a small pool of employees who, early in their careers, demonstrated that they had talent.

Talent management in practice

The capital markets and investment banking sector distinguishes between direct revenue generators, the 'front office', and those that support them, the 'middle and back offices'. Two ER challenges faced in managing front-office personnel are managing 'stars' and the development of 'player–managers' (Aldrich 2005). Front-office personnel are often very visible, well paid and sought after by competitors. Stars are in critical jobs whose performance is crucial to organizational success, including younger professionals as well as seasoned executives. These carry various titles and have a record of past accomplishments, but also the potential to continue contributing to their firm's success, with the highest future value to their organization. How much this value is realized depends on the alignment between the stars and their organization and whether organizational practices and structures simultaneously fit the strategic requirements of a business and the needs of its key employees. Stars are mobile and it is expensive and inefficient to hire front-office staff from competitors. When a company hires a 'star', the star's performance often plunges, with a sharp decline in the functioning of the group or team the person works with, and the company's market value may fall, as is often found with sports teams. In addition, stars do not often stay with organizations long, and therefore companies do not gain competitive advantage by hiring stars from outside. Performance is not just attributable to individuals, but groups and context, and uprooting them from this context may prove counter-productive (Groysberg et al. 2004). External social networks and company-specific factors such as resources and capabilities, systems and processes, leadership, internal networks, training and membership of teams can impact on success, and competitive advantage is mediated by the complex organizational systems within which people work. Many skills and competencies reside instead in the collective skill sets of employees or within special routines embedded more broadly in the firm's operations and knowledge base.

'Player–managers' are significant decision makers in the sector, often the 'star' heads of business areas with responsibility for managing their team. Experienced and successful front-office performers are, however, often promoted to run teams without any management training and often without any consideration for their ability to perform successfully in their new role.

The banking sector illustrates the increasing importance placed on TM. The Royal Bank of Scotland (RBS), for example, has launched the second phase of its human capital strategy with a human capital 'toolkit', an online suite of resources available to human resource staff in the UK launched in 2005 to deliver access to key information to help the HR function quickly identify business issues. The new toolkit is split into five main work streams; surveys, measurement, research, benchmarking and reporting (CIPD 2006b). HRM in Action 6.1 discusses this case in more detail, based on CIPD 2006a, 2006b, 2006c.

RBS is interesting in that it seems to have embraced TM, but has recognized that it brings forward various challenges. These include bringing in a global dimension, reducing administrative burdens, embedding it throughout the organization and recognizing and rewarding 'talent managers'. It employs an integrated approach to assessment, development and deployment, and while focused on 'high potentials', identified as senior management successors, appears to recognize possible drawbacks in terms of the reactions of those not seen in that way; it seems to be trying to adopt a more inclusive approach that recognizes that talent can be found at all levels.

This focus on senior management succession is also found in the TM programme in the Swiss-based UBS, based on the UBS Leadership Institute set up in 2002 to serve the top 600 in the organization. It includes a strategic leadership conference for the top 500 and a mentoring programme. The Global Leadership Experience involves three development programmes targeted at senior management, and with the Accel-erated Leadership Experience, a group-wide high-potential programme first run in 2004, makes up the TM initiative. Each business unit also has its TM team, and TM has a growing priority as a critical strategic process. Line managers are seen as key 'owners of talent', and a line management engagement strategy involving strategic direction, appraisal and HR support is used to implement TM. Unlike some TM pro-grammes, the focus is not just on the top 10%; UBS takes the view that everyone has the opportunity for development (Roebuck 2006).

This more diverse TM focus on all levels is endorsed by Pfeffer (2001), who argues that the view put forward by Michaels et al. (2001) holds that organizational perfor-mance is essentially the aggregation of individual performances; if you attract/retain people who do well individually you can win the competitive battle (Gladwell 2002). As with the psychometric–objective view, people are held to be essentially unchanged, at least by the time they are adults in the workforce, in terms of their

HRM in Action 6.1   Talent management in Royal Bank of Scotland

RBS is currently (CIPD 2006a, 2006b, 2006c) trying to move away from succession planning to 'action-oriented talent management', which is seen as a more fluid, holistic concept of ER than the more passive, limited concept of 'succession planning'. The TM process is seen as about identifying, developing and utilizing talent; rather than search for external talent, the current focus is on ensuring that leadership roles are being filled internally.

RBS has also tried to develop a corporate, group-wide set of principles and language to discuss TM and leadership capability. The belief is that talent exists at all levels in its organizations, and RBS wishes to provide 'talent' with opportunities to develop. However, it also wishes to show everyone that they are still valued group members. It recognizes that individual potential, ability and aspirations change over time, just as RBS's leadership needs and requirements will change over time; consequently TM is recognized as a dynamic, negotiated process. One requirement is to fill senior vacancies with internal talent; another is to share talent across the group. Calculated risks are taken with high-potential employees by appointing them to stretching roles, but with the necessary support.

Around three years ago, 'talent forums' were introduced to each division in order to make collective decisions about who the senior manager talent for the future is and define clearly what will make them ready for such positions. A full review takes place annually, with a six-month interim review. The process is guided by succession plans, input from independent assessors who assess people against leadership excellence and profiling competencies in 'talent assessment' workshops inviting general discussion, given the prevalence of matrix management in RBS.

The RBS executive and line managers are seen as accountable for building a stream of future leaders, focusing on the implementation of TM. HR acts as facilitators of the talent forums. TM success criteria include the percentage of successors identified and progress made in ensuring their readiness. An overall aim is to have 'adult–adult' dialogue with all employees, not just with 'high potentials', requiring honesty and transparency.

Current TM challenges include how to become more international, given the spread of operations across Asia, the USA and Europe, embedding TM throughout the organization including call centres, reducing administration, and recognizing and rewarding managers who most effectively manage talent.

abilities and capabilities; selecting, and keeping the right people is therefore crucial. Pfeffer (2001) argues that the system in which the person works, as shown by Groysberg et al. (2004), is critical; teams can outperform groups of more talented individuals and people can perform above or below their natural abilities depending on the situation, including the leadership they receive and the help they get from others in their immediate environment.

This emphasis on networks, teams and social processes in TM, in contrast to the 'individualistic' focus of Michaels et al. (2001) is echoed by Iles and Preece (2006), who argue that leadership development, as both theorized and practised, has too often been equated with leader development, resulting in a focus on the individual rather than the social, political and collective contexts of action and meaning. Leadership development, and TM by extension, is about the development of leadership/

TM processes in context, as well as the development of leaders/talents as individuals. Leader/talent development can be seen as involving the enhancement of human capital, while leadership development/TM is about the creation of social capital (Day 2000). Thus, TM involves extending the collective ability of people to effectively undertake talent roles and processes, and is centrally about helping them to understand how to join and build social networks, develop commitments and access resources. TM should not be conflated with 'managing individual talent'; TM involves the development of TM processes, in addition to the development of individual talents. Whereas most current TM focuses on human capital development, skills development and attitude change, TM as social capital is oriented to building organizational capacity in anticipation of unforeseen challenges. Rather than seeing TM in terms of individual-level/intrapersonal skills and abilities, this approach involves the analysis of the complex interactions between 'talent' and the social and organizational environment. TM therefore involves using social/relational processes to help build commitments among members of a community of practice (Wenger 1998), which may be internal and/or external to the organization.

Recent empirical research in the UK has pointed to practitioner confusion in this area. Most respondents to the CIPD 2006 Learning and Development Survey believed 'talent' to be inclusive and applicable to all (Bones 2006; CIPD 2006c): 71% did not agree that TM should be focused on only a small, privileged group and 67% thought that 'talent' to describe a specific group was demotivating to those not selected, inhibiting their engagement. However, paradoxically, most organizations would seem to be resourcing elites only: only 28% included all employees in their TM strategy and nearly 50% said that it covered only a minority. Succession planning and MBA programmes were commonly used tools, despite their perceived ineffectiveness; in practice, such schemes are often used solely for top management or high potentials. 'Inclusive' activities such as action learning, secondments or external roles were much less commonly employed. In addition, showing that rhetoric and consultant prescription seem to be ahead of practice, 60% of organizations had no formal TM strategy and 80% no formal definition of talent, while 49%, mostly SMEs, undertook no TM of any sort.

Conclusion

ER is crucial to many constructions of effective HRM and has been increasingly linked to organizational performance. This is particularly true of recent developments in 'talent management'. Most such approaches, whether to 'competencies' in the 1980s and 1990s or to 'talent' in this century, have taken an individualistic model, most fully embodied in the 'psychometric–objective' model of assessment. However, these models neglect the social context of ER, whether the process of mutual exchange of communication, information and decision making stressed in 'social process' models or the intersection of power and knowledge emphasized by critical theories of ER. This neglect of the context seems to be repeated in leading current conceptions of 'talent'; as Martin (2006) puts it, talent matters, but managing talent matters more. Different groups, whose value to the organization differs, may need to be treated differently, as they differ in their potential to add value or risk the corporate brand; different HR/ER practices may be required for each talent segment. However, comparisons and IR problems may then ensue as the 'losers' in the 'war for talent' resent the 'winners'. In addition, a focus on talented individuals may inhibit team working; and performance may not be attributable to individual talent, but to groups of staff and the organizational context in which they work. Many issues and questions in TM therefore remain, including: how is a 'TM' approach different from other approaches to ER, how is talent defined/identified/assessed, who in an organization needs to own/get involved in TM and succession planning for it to be successful and how does TM link with areas such as business strategy, the employer/employee brand and capacity building? In addition, how can organizations measure the success of TM initiatives, how do they decide a best-fit approach for their organization and culture, such as whether to use the external or internal labour market or adopt a 'closed' or 'open' approach to TM? In particular, future research needs to address possible 'downsides' to TM, especially the more elitist/exclusive approaches, such as the possible negative effect on the psychological contract/engagement of those not on an organization's TM programme, the threat to effective team working and the possible conflicts between 'winners' and 'losers' in the war for talent and between those in the talent pool and those not selected for it or excluded from it.

References

Adamsky, H. (2003). *Talent Management: Something Productive this Way comes.* Available at www.erexchange.com.

Aldrich, P. (2005). 'Analysing the management of human resources in the capital markets and investment banking sector: complexity and credibility in talent portfolio management', presentation to the British Academy of Management Annual Conference, Oxford University, September.

Alvesson, M. and D. Wilmot (2002). 'Identity regulation as organizational control: producing the appropriate individual', *Journal of Management Studies* 39: 619–44.

Anderson, N. and C. Ostroff (1997). 'Selection as socialisation', in N. Anderson and P. Herriot (eds) *International Handbook of Selection and Assessment.* Chichester, Wiley.

Balmer, J. T. and S. A. Geyser (2003). *Revealing the Corporation: Perspectives on Identity, Image, Reputation, Corporate Branding and Corporate-level Marketing.* London, Routledge.

Barney, J. and P. Wright (1998). 'On becoming a strategic partner: the role of human resources in gaining competitive advantage', *Human Resource Management* 37(1): 31–46.

Baron, J. (2004). *Aligning HR Strategy with Business Strategy.* Available at www.stanford.edu/-baron/epso2004.ppt.

Bolton, S. C. and C. Boyd (2003). 'Trolley dolly or skilled emotion manager: moving on from Hochschild's managed heart', *Work, Employment and Society* 17: 289–308.

Bones, C. (2005). *Managing Talent – Exploring the New Psychological Contract.* Henley, Henley Management College (www.henleymc.ac.uk).

Bones, C. (2006). 'The talent management paradox', in CIPD, *Reflections on the 2006 Learning and Development Survey.* London, CIPD.

Carter, C. (1996). 'Rethinking the assessment centre: a technology of power', presentation to the *British Academy of Management Conference,* Birmingham September.

CIPD (2006a). *Learning and Development Annual Survey Report 2006.* London, CIPD.

CIPD (2006b). *Reflections on Talent Management: Change Agenda.* London, CIPD.

CIPD (2006c). *Reflections on the 2006 Learning and Development Survey.* London, CIPD.

Day, D. (2000). 'Leadership development: a review in context', *Leadership Quarterly* 11(4): 581–611.

Duttagupta, R. (2005). *Identifying and Managing Your Assets: Talent Management.* London, Pricewaterhouse-Coopers.

Edwards, M. (2005). 'Employer and employee branding: HR or PR?', in S. Bach (ed.) *Managing Human Resources: Personnel Management in Transition,* 4th edn. Oxford, Blackwell.

Fitz-enz, J. (2005). *Talent Management Intelligence: Solving the People Paradox.* Available at www.humancapitalmag.com.

Foucault, M. (1974). *The Archaeology of Knowledge*. London, Routledge.

Foucault, M. (1997). *Discipline & Punish*. London, Tavistock.

Frank, F. and C. Taylor (2004). *Talent Management: Trends that will Shape the Future*. Available at www.talentkeepers-services.com.

du Gay, P., G. Salaman and B. Rees (1996). 'The conduct of management and the management of conduct: contemporary managerial discourse and the constitution of the "competent" manager', *Journal of Management Studies* 33(3): 263–82.

Gladwell, M. (2002). 'The talent myth: are smart people over-rated?', *The New Yorker*, 22 July.

Goleman, D. (1996). *Emotional Intelligence*. New York, Bantam Books.

Groysberg, B., A. Nanda and N. Nohria (2004). 'The risky business of hiring stars', *Harvard Business Review* May 82(5): 92–100.

Guest, D. E., J. Michie, N. Conway and M. Sheehan (2003). 'Human resource management and corporate performance in the UK', *British Journal of Industrial Relations* 41(2): 291–314.

Harter, J. M., F. Schmidt and T. L. Hayes (2002). 'Business unit level relationships between employee satisfaction/engagement and business outcomes: a meta-analysis', *Journal of Applied Psychology* 87: 268–79.

Herriot, P. (1989). 'Selection as a social process', in M. Smith and I. Robertson (eds) *Advances in Selection and Assessment*. Chichester, Wiley.

Hollway, W. (1991). *Work Psychology and Organizational Behaviour*. London, Sage.

Iles, P. A. (1999). *Managing Staff Selection and Assessment*. Buckingham, Open University Press.

Iles, P. A. (2000). 'Employee resourcing', in J. Storey (ed.) *HRM: A Critical Text,* 2nd edn. Oxford, Blackwell.

Iles, P. A. and D. Preece (2006). 'Developing leaders or developing leadership? The Academy of Chief Executives' Programmes in the North-East of England', *Leadership* 2(2): 317–40.

Iles, P. A. and I. T. Robertson (1997). 'The impact of personnel selection procedures on candidates', in N. Anderson and P. Herriot (eds) *International Handbook of Selection and Assessment*. Chichester, Wiley.

Iles, P. A. and G. Salaman (1995). 'Recruitment, selection and assessment', in J. Storey (ed.) *HRM: A Critical Perspective*. London, Routledge.

Iles, P. A., D. Preece and C. Xin (2006). 'Talent management and succession planning – a comparison study between the UK and China', paper presented to KSSS Conference, Beijing, September.

Jackson, S. E. and R. S. Schuler (2003). *Managing Human Resources for Strategic Partnership,* 8th edn. Cincinnati: Southwestern.

Johnson, M. (2004). *New Rules of Engagement*. London, CIPD.

Linstead, S., L. Fulop and S. Lilley (2004). *Management and Organization: A Critical Text*. New York, Palgrave Macmillan.

Martin, G. (2005). *Technology and People Management: Transforming the HR Function or the Function of HR*. London, CIPD.

Martin, G. (2006). 'Driving corporate reputations and brands from the inside: a strategic role for HRM', paper presented to the *British Academy of Management Annual Conference*, Belfast, September.

Martin, G. and S. Hetrick (2006). *Corporate Reputations, Branding and People Management: A Strategic Approach to HR*. Oxford, Butterworth Heinemann.

Michaels, E., H. Handfield-Jones and B. Axelrod (2001). *The War for Talent*. Boston, MA, Harvard Business School Press.

Miles, S. J. and W. G. Mangold (2005). 'Positioning Southwest Airlines through employee branding', *Business Horizons*, 48: 535–45.

Miller, P. and N. Rose (1993). 'Governing economic life', in M. Gane and T. Johnson (eds) *Foucault's New Domains*. London, Routledge.

Morton, L. (2006). *Talent Management: A Critical Way To Integrate and Embed Diversity*. Available at www.workinfo.com.

Moynagh, M. and R. Worsley (2005). *Working in the Twenty-first Century*. Swindon, Economic and Social Research Council.

Newell, S. (2005). 'Recruitment and selection', in S. Bach (ed.) *Managing Human Resources*, 4th edn. Oxford, Blackwell.

Pass, S. (2005). 'Missing links in the causal chain between HR practices and organizational performance', paper presented to *CIPD Professional Standards Conference*, Keele University.

Pfeffer, J. (2001). 'Fighting the war for talent is hazardous to your organization's health', *Organizational Dynamics* 29(4): 248–59.

Reed, A. (2001). *Innovation in Human Resource Management: Tooling up for the Talent Wars*. London, CIPD.

Roebuck, C. (2006). 'Talent management should be a business issue', *Personnel Today* 16 May.

Rose, N. (1990). 'Governing the soul', paper presented to conference on *The Values of the Enterprise Culture*, University of Lancaster.

Rose, N. (1999). *Governing the Soul,* 2nd edn. London, Free Associations Books.

Schweyer, A. (2004). *Talent Management Systems*. Chichester, Wiley.

Simmons, J., P. A. Iles and M. Yolles (2005). 'Identifying those aboard the moving train: towards a stakeholder-focused methodology for organizational decision-making', *Systems Research and Behavioral Science* 22: 41–53.

Sistonen, S. (2005). *Talent Management*. New York, Deloitte & Touche Oy.

Stainton, A. (2005). 'Talent management: latest buzzword or refocusing existing processes?', *Competency & Emotional Intelligence* 12(4): 39–43.

Stumpf, S. and W. Tymon (2001). 'Consultant or entrepreneur? Demystifying the "war for talent"', *Career Development International* 6(1): 48–56.

Taylor, S. (1998). *Employee Resourcing.* London, IPD.

Taylor, S. (2002). *People Resourcing,* 2nd edn. London, CIPD.

Townley, B. (1989). 'Selection and appraisal: reconstituting "social relations"', in J. Storey (ed.) *New Perspectives on Human Resource Management.* London, Routledge.

Townley, B. (1994). *Reframing Human Resource Management.* London, Sage.

Weddle, P. (2006). *Manage Talent Needs with a Sound Strategy.* Available at www.careerjournal.com.

Welch, J. and J. Byrne (2003) *Jack: Straight from the Gut.* New York, Warner Books.

Wenger, E. (1998). *Communities of Practice: Learning, Meaning and Identity.* Cambridge, Cambridge University Press.

Measure for measure: Mapping the terrain of the training, learning and skills debates

Alan Felstead

Introduction

The only constant in the field of training, learning and skills is change. This is a fact of life that HRM practitioners and researchers have to deal with. The institutions of vocational education and training (VET), for example, have been subject to frequent alterations, mergers and even abolition. In 1999, the Further Education Funding Council (FEFC) and training and enterprise councils (TECs) in England were both abolished and replaced by the Learning and Skills Council (LSC), which has 47 local arms (see Felstead and Unwin 2001). National training organizations suffered a similar fate in 2001 when they were replaced by the Skills for Business Network covering the whole of the UK. The network comprises 25 employer-led sectors skills councils (SSCs) each with its own sector 'footprint' for which it is responsible. SSCs are, in turn, overseen and supported by the Sector Skills Development Agency (SSDA).

Despite these institutional changes, the principle of a largely voluntary system of VET delivery in which employers decide when, who and how they train their staff remains intact. Although the introduction of a compulsory training levy was considered by the Labour Party before its election in 1997, this idea was quickly dropped when Labour came to power. Such a policy was considered too risky in that it would have prompted resistance from industry and would have dented the incoming government's 'business-friendly' image (Senker 1995; Smith 1998). Nevertheless, the list of changes to the VET system over recent years is lengthy (see Table 7.1). Yet the UK's policy overdrive in this area is not unique; other countries, too, have placed similar emphasis on the VET system and consequently they have also made changes to the institutional architecture over which they preside (see Sung et al. 2006).

The presumption that underlies all of these initiatives and bouts of institutional change – in the UK and beyond – is that the development of human capital is the key to the economic success of the nation, organizations and individuals. Substantial research support can, it is argued, be called on to justify such a position. A stream of articles from the National Institute for Economic and Social Research (NIESR), in particular, has highlighted Britain's relatively lowly ranking in the world skills league as measured by qualifications of a comparable standard. This, it is argued, hinders labour

Table 7.1	Policy development and reform since 1990

1990	Investors in People established to encourage employers to invest in human capital (Alberga et al. 1996; Hoque 2003; Spilsbury et al. 1995)
1992	Further and Higher Education Act creates the Further Education Funding Council (FEFC), the Office for Standards in Education (OfSTED) and legislation to free further education colleges from local education authority control (LEA) (Ainley and Bailey 1997)
1994	Modern apprenticeships introduced (Fuller and Unwin 2003)
1997	Processes for establishing devolved administrations in Scotland, Wales and Northern Ireland begin, including responsibility for education and skills (devolved administrations begin from 1999) (Felstead 2002, 2005)
1998	Individual learning accounts (ILAs) and the University for Industry (UfI) launched (DfEE 1998)
1998	Department for Education and Employment launches the Skills Task Force (DfES 2000)
1999	Creation of the Learning and Skills Council (Felstead and Unwin 2001)
1999	Training Standards Inspectorate becomes the Adult Learning Inspectorate (Hughes 2002)
2001	Replacement of national training organizations (NTOs) with Skills for Business Network comprising sector skills councils (SSCs) and the Sector Skills Development Agency (SSDA)
2002	Centres of vocational excellence (CoVEs) established (Statz and Wright 2004)
2003	Skills strategy launched jointly by DfES, Department of Trade and Industry, Department of Work and Pensions and HM Treasury
2004	Modern apprenticehips relaunched as apprenticeships (Apprenticeship Task Force 2005)
2004	Tomlinson Report into qualification reform published (Tomlinson Report 2004)
2004	Foster Review of Further Education and Leitch Review of Skills established (HM Treasury 2005)
2005	14–19 White Paper published which launches new vocational diplomas
2005	Skills Strategy White Paper which launches skills academies, Union Learning Academy and the Next Step consultation process

This table presents a summary of changes to the VET system. Devolution of the responsibility for education and training means that not all these changes apply throughout the UK.

Source: Amended and adapted from HM Treasury 2005: Box E.1

productivity and weakens Britain's economic performance (Daly et al. 1985; Mason and Finegold 1995; Mason et al. 1992; Prais et al. 1989; Steedman 1988; Steedman and Wagner 1987). On this basis, policymakers have latched onto the idea of increasing the qualifications of the workforce. The argument is that a more qualified workforce will increase the competitiveness of companies and thereby raise the competitiveness of the nation as a whole. Similarly, international comparisons of participation rates in education and training are frequently used as justification for policy interventions that boost participation rates and close the gap with the UK's major competitors.

Policymakers' explanations for a country's relative economic standing – and in particular, its productivity performance – are couched in terms of a nation's take-up of 'training', its exposure to 'learning' and its 'skills' level. Both episodic international employer-level studies – such as the European Commission's Continuing Vocational Training Survey (CVTS) – and more regularly conducted individual-level polls – such as the European Union Labour Force Survey (EULFS) – encourage these kinds of explanation. They also prompt the compilation of league tables and international scoreboards (Eurostat 2002; Felstead et al. 1998). Perhaps as expected, policymakers have been quick to seize on these international benchmark studies, but have been far less interested in the intellectual basis of the data they report. The aim of this chapter is to reveal the different conceptual, analytical and measurement dimensions to these data. The chapter pays particular attention to uncovering some of the complexities inherent in the terms 'training', 'learning' and 'skills'. Furthermore, it shows how, in some respects, the debates surrounding these terms have shifted, while the nomenclature and language of the discussion has remained much the same. The chapter is therefore structured around these three terms with each meriting a section of its own. The chapter ends by identifying some of the gaps in our existing knowledge about training, learning and skills and therefore sketches out a future research agenda.

Training

Statistics on 'training' are frequently reported in a number of government publications that review the state of the British labour market and promote regular commentary in the national press (see HRM in Action 7.1). For example, the 2006 edition of *Social Trends*, an annual compendium of over a dozen areas of social policy, presents data on the receipt of job-related training by age, sex and qualification (ONS 2006: 44). Similar statistics are available on a quarterly basis on the ONS website (www. statistics.gov.uk). They have also formed the basis of government commentaries in the past (e.g., DfES 2000; HM Treasury 2005) and are set to do so in the future. For example, an analysis of the labour market towards the end of the twentieth century was bullish in concluding that:

> Training activity has increased substantially since 1985, most rapidly in the late 1980s. There was a decrease during the recession and then an increase reaching a peak in 1994 . . . it is possible to conclude that training activity in the UK in Spring 1996 may be higher than at any previous time.
>
> (DfEE 1997: 64)

The available evidence suggests that the picture has improved even further since then with the proportion of employees receiving some job-related training in the four weeks prior to interview rising from 14.8% in 1996 to 16.2% in 2005 (see Figure 7.1).

These data can be compared with similar data collected across the European Union since member states are required as part of their membership to carry out a labour force survey (LFS) at least once a year (see Box 7.1). This must include a list of common questions, the adoption of a common coding framework for the replies received and the use of agreed definitions. However, the data collection agencies appointed by each member state are responsible for selecting the sample, preparing the questionnaires, conducting the interviews among households and forwarding the results in accordance with the common coding scheme. The compilation of comparable statistics on the labour force at the community level has been a priority task since the formation of the European Community in 1958. Although labour market statistics – including training data – existed in most countries before they became fully fledged members of the EU, comparison across Europe was problematic. The sources used, the definitions adopted and the methods of data collected deployed differed to such an extent that 'like with like' comparisons were virtually impossible. For this reason, the Statistical Office of the European Communities (Eurostat) has regularly organized the EULFS.

| Figure 7.1 | **Training incidence in Britain, 1984–2005** |

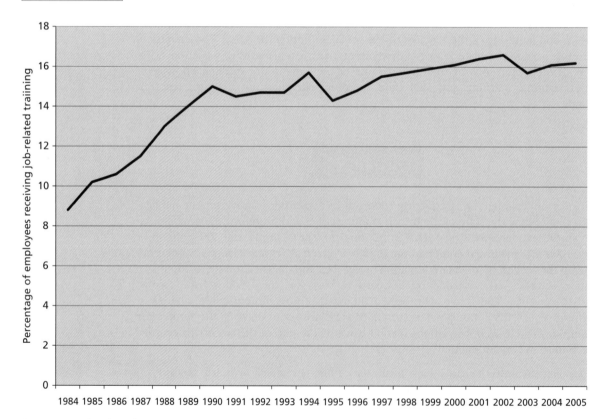

Source: Data taken from the *Labour Force Survey (LFS) Historical Quarterly Supplement*, Table 28; www.statistics.gov.uk, accessed 25 May 2006

> ## Box 7.1   What is the Labour Force Survey?
>
> The Labour Force Survey (LFS) is a survey of individuals living in households. In the UK, the LFS is carried out every quarter with almost 60,000 households contacted and survey information collected on around 150,000 people. Of this total, around 65,000 are 16 and above and are in work. The design of the LFS involves an element of overlap between survey quarters. Each quarter's sample is made up of five waves, each consisting of about 12,000 households. Every sampled address in a wave is interviewed in five successive quarters, such that in any one quarter, one wave will be receiving their first interview, one wave their second and so on, with one wave receiving their fifth and final interview. Thus, there is an 80% overlap between successive quarterly surveys.

International training comparisons of the type reported in Table 7.2 are now possible. The results produce apparently comforting and reassuring evidence for policymakers whose mantra is that 'education is the best economic policy we have' (Prime Minister reported in DfEE 1998: 9). The UK is well above the EU average and is ranked fourth in terms of the extent to which its adult population receives education and training. However, closer examination of the data begins to call into question the robustness of the evidence. Training incidence, for example, varies wildly between countries with some reporting participation rates well into double figures (e.g., Denmark, Finland, Sweden and the UK), while others are well below the European average (e.g., Greece, Hungary and Slovakia). Furthermore, countries renowned for the emphasis they place on continuing professional development such as France, through its training levy, and Germany, through its apprenticeship system, are in the bottom half of the league table. These variations may reflect some of the differences in training activity across Europe, but also suggest that the meaning of 'training' may differ between member states in ways not easily picked up in household surveys of this type (see Campanelli et al. 1994; Méhaut 1992). As a result, one must be cautious about placing too much weight on comparisons of training activity across the EU despite the fact that the stated intention of the EULFS is to provide a 'harmonized and synchronized' labour force survey of households of persons living in each Member State' (Eurostat 1992: 53). Furthermore, analysis of the UK LFS (see later) – from which the UK data contained in the Eurostat series are derived – suggests that reliance on a *single* indicator can paint a misleading picture of training activity within a single country, let alone across 15 or 25 member states.

Previous research (Felstead et al. 1999) has examined in detail the nature of the sharp rise in the training participation before the turn of the century. Within the space of just over a decade, training incidence almost doubled, rising from 8.8% in 1984 to 15.5% in 1997. Nevertheless, this picture of upward movement is called into question when other trends based on the same survey series are examined.

Policymaking interest in the trajectory of training activity is founded on the economic benefits training is expected to generate for individuals, organizations and the nation. This presumption is based on human capital theory, which conceives of training as an investment made by individuals, organizations and/or the state. Hence, the *quantity* of training inputs – in terms of numbers of employees, their time and expenditure – evidently constitutes a basic measure of training effort. Yet, time series evidence based on training *incidence* can only tell part of the story since individuals are asked to respond to the question: 'Have you taken part in any education or training connected with your job, or a job that you might be able to do in the future?' This is first asked of the three months before being interviewed and then of the four weeks

Table 7.2	Training incidence across the European Union, 2004

Country	Percentage of the adult population (25–64) participating in education and training
Sweden	35.8
Denmark	27.6
Finland	24.6
United Kingdom	21.3
Slovenia	17.9
Netherlands	16.5
Austria	12.0
Belgium	9.5
Cyprus	9.3
Latvia	9.1
France	7.8
Ireland	7.2
Estonia	6.7
Lithuania	6.5
Czech Republic	6.3
Luxembourg	6.3
Germany	6.0
Poland	5.5
Spain	5.2
Malta	5.0
Portugal	4.8
Italy	4.7
Hungary	4.6
Slovakia	4.6
Greece	3.7
EU-15	10.1
EU-25	9.4

Source: Adapted from European Communities 2005: 105

prior to interview (the latter has been asked since 1984 and so provides a longer data series than the 3-month question, which was first asked in 1994).

Although knowing the 4-week participation rate is important, on its own it is far from adequate as a measure of how much training is going on. Training episodes vary substantially in *length* and therefore the volume of training delivered cannot simply be read across from participation rates. If the average length of time spent in training changes over time, then this will have a bearing on the quantity of training. Unfortunately, there is no information in the LFS on the amount of training undertaken by trainees during the four weeks prior to interview. Therefore, it is hard to draw any meaningful conclusions from the LFS about the trend in the quantity of training taking place over the 4-week period.

However, the LFS does ask respondents the number of hours training they received during the week immediately before the interview, when a respondent's memory is at its most reliable. From this information it is possible to plot the 1-week participation rate and compare it with the trends for the equivalent 4-week question. This reveals that while the 1-week participation rate rose more or less in parallel with the 4-week participation until 1988, it subsequently stabilized and then fell. The result is that, taking the 1985–1994 period, there was only a small increase in the 1-week training participation rate. This casts immediate doubt on the presumption that there was a substantial increase in training volume over the period.

An additional advantage of looking at the 1-week participation rate is that, combined with the measure of the actual number of hours training undertaken, we can arrive at an estimate of the total amount of training undertaken off the job. Although not ideal, because of the exclusion of on-the-job training (OJT), this measure is the only valid indication of trends in training volume in Britain over the period under focus. Remarkably, it shows little or no overall increase between 1985 and 1994 with a mere 4% rise in the volume of off-the-job training compared to a 54% rise in 4-week training participation rate.

Taken together, these two trends suggest that while in any 4-week period more people were receiving training than did before, the amount they received fell. Consistent with such an interpretation is another LFS finding on the length of education and training courses. These were reported as falling: in 1985, 26% of those in training were on courses lasting less than 1-week, while the corresponding figure for 1994 was 45%. It is just such a trend that can, at least in principle, drive a wedge between the movements in the 4-week and 1-week participation data series. To illustrate the point, consider a hypothetical situation in which a proportion β of the population on a 2-week training course is replaced by a proportion 2β on a 1-week course. Assuming that the date of survey interview is random, consider what would happen to the observed 4-week participation rate in these circumstances. With the 2-week course, there would be five weeks during which course participants would be able to answer 'yes' to the 4-week participation question (i.e. it would capture those who started the course five weeks before the interview as well as those who started the course within the 4-week reference period). With the 1-week course, there would be only four weeks during which a 'yes' answer could be elicited from each participant. Although the training volume is the same in both scenarios, shorter and more numerous courses (in this example, twice as numerous) are more likely to be recorded by the 4-week rather than 1-week participation rate. The results are suggestive of a pattern of training activity in which training opportunities are spread more thinly among a higher proportion of workers. Hence, training incidence is rising while training intensity is falling. This raises uncertainty about the actual volume of training activity received. None of these analytical complications is noted in the published sources. Nevertheless, an uncritical reading of the available data can give a misleading picture of training activity. A similar approach could be applied to the EULFS data series as well as the datasets of other countries outside of Europe.

If published statistics concerning the quantity of training leave something to be desired, information about its quality is thinner on the ground. Nevertheless, debates on the extent to which Britain has undergone a training revolution relates to the sort of training being delivered – for example, a sceptical reading of the rise in the incidence of training is that much of it is defensive (to meet health and safety regulations, for instance) and concerned with teaching 'low-grade' computing and customer care skills. However, some progress has been made on investigating this issue. For example, a postal survey of CBI members asked respondents to select up to three out of a possible seven training outcomes commonly mentioned in the literature as motivating employers' training activities. The results reveal striking variations according to occupation (Felstead et al. 1997). Enhancing problem-solving skills is a strong motivator for the training offered to managers (37%) and associate professional employees (47%), but is also a significant outcome for those who employ and train craft workers (33%). For those dealing with customers, enhancing customer care is an important motivation for training. As expected, a high proportion of clerical employers (74%) report that training results in improved computing skills among their clerical staff. A slightly lower, but still high, proportion of associate professional employers (62%) report likewise. Teamworking outcomes are consistently on the high side across all occupational groups.

Making workers more punctual or reliable and getting them to work to deadlines might not be regarded as a technical skill outcome. Neither would raised enthusiasm for the company be seen as a technical skill. Nevertheless making workers more punctual is a significant training outcome for those who train craft (24%) and routine (22%) staff. Increasing enthusiasm for corporate objectives is a strong outcome for those who train sales (35%) and professional staff (41%). These findings throw an interesting light on the common interpretation of the word 'training'. In much of the economic literature, it is seen as involving an improvement in some particular well-defined competence. In fact, this is explicitly stated in the definition used by government statisticians when compiling training statistics: 'intentional intervention to help the individual (or the organization) to become competent, or more competent, at work' (Clarke 2002; HMSO various). However, as is well known to the HRM practitioner, training also involves massaging attitudes and behaviour and particular training episodes can be exclusively designed to have such effect. As a result, research has begun to suggest that employers may protect their investment in 'general' training by including elements designed to raise employees' commitment to the organization and thereby minimize the extent to which job mobility is enhanced (Green et al. 2000).

Learning

Where once policymakers would have used the word 'training', they now use the word 'learning'. Learning has become the new buzzword and is often prefaced according to its location (workplace), duration (lifelong) or breadth (lifewide) (Stern and Sommerlad 1999). However, its use serves to acknowledge that learning can arise in a variety of settings, including the demands and challenges of everyday work experience and social interactions with colleagues, clients and customers. To reflect this change of emphasis, survey results and sometimes their titles have simply been rebadged to reflect this policy spin. Despite its billing the Learning and Training at Work (LTW) survey, for example, is still mainly focused on measuring training based on a concept first used in 1987 (Spilsbury 2003). This defines training as 'the process of acquiring the knowledge and skills related to work requirements by formal, structured or guided means' and specifically *excludes* 'general supervision, motivational meetings, basic induction and learning by experience' (Training Agency 1987: 14). Equipped with this definition, employers are asked a series of questions about the training activities they provide to workers. In other words, the LTW survey remains rooted in a tradition of measuring the additional productive capacity of individuals in terms of whether or not they have attended certain courses or have followed a structured programme of activities under the guidance of others.

The same goes for many surveys that focus on the narrow interpretation given to 'training' by respondents. If unprompted, individuals regard training as formal courses and employers view it as an activity they fund and/or initiate (Campanelli et al. 1994; Felstead et al. 1997). Cognitive tests of what survey respondents refer to when presented with particular words suggests that 'training' tends to focus the minds of respondents on critical incidents or salient episodes that are divorced from normal everyday practice. In order to elicit information on implicit learning, slow gradual learning or tacit knowledge (see Eraut 2000) a case study approach is often considered more appropriate. In these circumstances, interviews typically focus on how people learn to do what they are doing. Respondents are initially invited to describe their work in great detail and to recall their activities over a number of weeks and in particular how their work varied, if at all, over this period. Only then do these interviews move on to discuss the type of knowledge, skills and competences required to do the job. Finally, interviewers probe in order to reveal how these capabilities are acquired in the workplace (Eraut et al. 1998, 1999). The implication is that training statistics underreport learning activities and therefore provide a poor measure of lifelong learning.

Prompted, in part, by cognitive testing, case study research and the results of other surveys (e.g., Park 1994; Sargant et al. 1997), survey questions have been widened to go beyond the intentionality of training events and hence capture unstructured and incidental learning activities. The most notable change came with the launch in 1997 of the National Adult Learning Survey (NALS). The survey was commissioned by the Department for Education and Skills and used to monitor progress towards the national training target of reducing the proportion of non-learners to 24% of the adult population by 2002 (NACETT 1997). The survey was repeated in 2000 and 2001 and then again in 2002. Many of its questions are now carried in the LFS and elements also appeared in the ad hoc European-level survey on lifelong learning carried out in 2003 (*Official Journal of the European Communities* 2002).

The NALS series broke new ground by collecting information on a wider range of learning activities than previous surveys. It does not restrict its focus to 'education and training as conventionally understood – viz. periods of instruction received from a teacher or trainer' (Beinart and Smith 1998: 33), but instead collects information about respondents' involvement in both taught and self-directed learning through a series of wide-ranging questions. The survey instrument asks respondents about 10 specific types of learning; six are defined as taught learning, four as self-directed learning. They are asked: 'in the past three years have you [been engaged in a series of learning activities]'. Respondents are asked about each activity in turn. Taught learning comprises: taught courses intended to lead to qualifications; taught courses designed to develop job-related skills; courses, instruction or tuition in driving, playing a musical instrument, arts and crafts, sport or any practical skill; evening classes; learning from packages; and any other taught course, instruction or tuition. Self-directed learning comprises: independent study for qualifications without taking part in a taught course; supervised on-the-job training; time spent keeping up to date with job-related developments by reading books, manuals or journals or attending seminars and talks; and deliberately trying to improve knowledge by means other than taking part in a taught course. All these types of learning are characterized as vocational if they are initiated in order to help respondents' current or future employment and as non-vocational if they are not.

Despite the upsurge of interest in workplace learning, there is little evidence to suggest that data collection methods are informed by an *explicit* conceptual framework (OECD 1997). A host of writers have, therefore, set about revealing the *implicit* conceptual frameworks that lie behind existing research studies. As such they have mapped the various approaches to the study of workplace learning (Billett 2002; Fevre et al. 2001; Hager 2004; Sfard 1998). Two camps have been identified by this literature: those who view 'learning as acquisition'; and those who regard 'learning as participation'.

Theorizing learning as 'acquisition' underpins strategies that seek to address employees' skills and knowledge deficits through the provision of courses, usually leading to qualifications, which are then assumed to signal that the individual (or at the aggregate level, the workforce) has become more skilled. An important aspect of the 'learning as acquisition' approach is the tendency to treat knowledge and skills transfer as unproblematic. It is assumed that the knowledge and skills gained are well defined and readily codified. It therefore follows that once individuals have acquired bundles of specified knowledge or skills sets (signalled by qualifications), they will be able to apply what they have learned in new contexts without difficulty.

An alternative standpoint is provided by the 'learning as participation' metaphor. It challenges the 'learning as acquisition' approach in three ways. First, it legitimizes the workplace itself as a site for and source of, teaching and learning and, therefore, acts as an antidote to the view that privileges formal educational provision over 'informal' processes (see Billett 2002). Second, it conceives learning as a process that is primarily social and situated (Lave and Wenger 1991). Hence, the approach is interested in explaining how people learn at work in what appears to be a relatively naturalistic way, through helping each other, by performing tasks and through experience in general. Importantly, such learning often occurs without recognition and this helps account for the historical lack of theoretical and empirical interest in the area. Third, the issue of learning transfer is treated as problematic: if learning is conceived as a process embedded in particular social activities, it follows that learning cannot be transported easily from one situation to another.

It is possible to detect a schism in the empirical literature drawn around these two conceptual camps. On the one hand, much of the policy-led research takes human capital theory as its frame of reference and implicitly adopts a 'learning as acquisition' perspective. This is evident in the analytical measures used. These include qualification attainment, years spent in formal education and the incidence of training. These indicators are often referred to as 'human capital endowments' and are used to explain why the better endowed are higher paid and vice versa. They are also easy to measure – the number and type of qualifications a person has can be counted, the number of years spent in full-time education can be calculated and individuals can recall whether or not they took part in a training event in the preceding weeks/months (however, powers of recall diminish the longer the period). Such measures are commonly found in national surveys throughout the world with tried and tested question formulations now standard (OECD 1997).

However, case study research on workplace learning tends to adopt a 'learning as participation' approach. In-depth studies of a wide variety of jobs – such as engineers, accountants, nurses, miners and teachers (Boud and Middleton 2003; Eraut et al. 1998; Fevre et al. 2001; Hodkinson and Hodkinson 2004) – suggest that a great deal of learning goes on at work that is not picked up by standard survey questions. Nevertheless, this learning is often crucial to the effective execution of tasks. While these studies recognize that learning at work is ongoing (Leman 2003), they limit its reach by only including 'significant changes in capability or understanding, and exclude the acquisition of further information when it does not contribute to such changes' (Eraut 1997: 556).

Despite their conceptual and methodological differences, there have been some attempts to incorporate the lessons of case study research with its emphasis on 'learning as participation' into survey design that has traditionally been dominated by the 'learning as acquisition' mode of thinking. One such survey was carried out in 1999 and comprised some 1500 telephone interviews with employees living in Norway (Skule and Reichborn 2002). More recently, the 'learning as participation' approach to learning has been used to shape the learning at work survey in Britain (Felstead et al. 2005). Its particular novelty lay in the rejection of notions of incidence and length – frequently used to measure training (see previous section) – in favour of questions that focus on respondents' evaluations of the effectiveness that certain activities have on improving their own work performance.

In the British survey, over half (51.8%) reported that simply doing the job had helped them learn most about how to improve. This was corroborated elsewhere in the survey. Almost nine out of 10 respondents said that their job required them to learn new things and pass on tips to colleagues and a similar proportion agreed that they had picked up most of their skills through on-the-job experience. However, not all work activities proved to be as helpful. The use of the internet, for example, to download materials, participate in e-learning and seek out information was regarded as being of no help at all to almost half the sample (49.7%). Despite the emphasis placed on training course attendance and the acquisition of qualifications, both were lowly rated by our respondents in terms of their helpfulness in improving work performance. Activities more closely associated with the workplace – such as doing the job, being shown things, engaging in self-reflection and keeping one's eyes and ears open, i.e. facets associated with learning as participation – were reckoned to provide more helpful insights into how to do the job better. All of these factors were rated as more helpful sources of learning than attending training courses or acquiring qualifications. These results suggest that codified knowledge is at its most useful when gaining *initial* competence at work, but its potency declines as a means of *improving* performance. At this stage, the workplace – and the everyday activities it comprises – provides the most highly rated source of learning.

Skills

Like other terms reviewed in this chapter, there is no agreement on what is meant by 'skills'. On close examination, it becomes clear that 'skills' are conceived, analysed and measured in different ways from author to author. To navigate a path through this minefield, it is first necessary to examine 'skill' according to the unit of analysis adopted. The literature suggests that skill can reside in: people; jobs; and/or settings. These three levels are considered in turn and are depicted in Table 7.3.

Analyses focused on the skills possessed by individuals concentrate on the attributes and capacities individuals have for carrying out particular activities. These activities may be undertaken at work, but do not have to be. Classic examples here are the skills of women that are more underused at work than those possessed by men (Bynner et al. 1997). This definition casts the skills net widely and has the potentiality to report on patterns of skill underutilization in the workplace.

Where the focus is on jobs, analysts examine the demands of the job rather than the capacities individuals possess. It therefore has a much narrower focus. Job demands refer to the complexity of jobs and/or the discretion job holders exercise in

Table 7.3	**Three principal approaches to skill definition**

Focus	Principal area of concern	Typical method of analysis	Typical users
Person	A person's individual attributes acquired through: • education • qualifications • training • experience	Questionnaires Administered tests Behavioural observations	Economists Psychologists
Job	Task requirements: • complexity • discretion	Questionnaires Job analysis Job evaluation Case studies	Occupational psychologists Management/ employment relations theorists Sociologists
Setting	Social relations	Case studies of occupations and industries	Sociologists Social historians

Source: Adapted from Noon and Blyton 2002

carrying out the tasks involved (DfES 2000: Chapter 2; Spenner 1990). Complexity varies according to the nature of the job such as the abilities and techniques required, the intricacies of the steps involved and the knowledge of equipment, products and processes needed for competent performance. In addition, some authors argue that skill levels vary according to the extent to which job holders exercise discretion and judgement at work (e.g., Braverman 1974; Zuboff 1988). While all jobs are carried out within prescribed rules – whether set by law, occupational standards or custom and practice – an element of choice/judgement remains. The greater this is, the higher the skill of the job in the overall skill hierarchy.

Other authors place their focus on the historical and political setting and the ways in which skill is constructed, defended and maintained by different interest groups. The approach of these authors is on the group rather than the individual or the job. Social historians and sociologists are among those most attracted to such an approach. Particular use has been made of the social construction of skill approach in historical accounts of the impact of technological change (e.g., Elbaum et al. 1979; Griffin 1984).

The measurement tools correspondingly vary (as indicated in Table 7.3). The main measures are: occupational profiling; self-assessed abilities; qualification levels; job complexity; and discretion exercised at work.

Occupational profiling

A common approach to skill measurement is to monitor changing occupational profiles. The reason for such an approach is that 'skills levels' are a central derivation of the standard occupational classification (SOC) system or their equivalent in other countries such as the dictionary of occupational titles (DOT) in the USA. These systems are hierarchically derived and are based on the level of formal qualifications required for a person to get a particular job and the duration of training and/or work experience normally required for occupational competence (Elias 1995: 43–5; OPCS 1990: 3). It, therefore, makes sense to examine how the profile of employment is changing over time according to these occupational classifications.

However, analysing skills trends by SOC alone is extremely hazardous since it fails to pick up changes *within* the various SOC categories (Kelleher et al. 1993). For example, the rising proportion of high level SOCs need not necessarily indicate rising skill levels since these SOCs may demand lower level skills than in the past. As a further complication, the basis on which occupations are classified has changed and so we have breaks in the series in 1990 and 2000. SOC2000 was introduced because SOC90 had become outdated. The extensive revisions to the SOC include a tighter definition of managerial occupations and moving many job titles between major groups to reflect the repositioning of certain jobs. Also new occupations have been introduced in the fields of computing, environment and conservation, and customer service occupations (covering call centre operators).

Self-assessed abilities

Direct testing of individuals' abilities is one of the most effective ways of assessing their skill levels. However, it is also one of the most expensive. One example of such an approach is the International Adult Literacy Survey (IALS) (OECD and Statistics Canada 1997). This study was able to test respondents directly about a limited range of particular skills – 'prose', 'document' and 'quantitative' literacy skills – as well as question them about the frequency with which these skills were used at work. However, a less expensive option is to ask respondents to make a self-assessment of their own abilities and then question them about whether these abilities are used at work or not. This approach was adopted by recent cohort studies such as the National Child Development Study (NCDS) and the British Cohort Study (BCS). A total of 15 questions were asked in the 1991 sweeps (when individuals were 33 and 20 years old respectively). These included two questions on verbal abilities, four on construction skills, three on caring abilities, two on keyboard skills and four on organizing capabilities (Bynner et al. 1997). They were asked how good they were at each ability, whether they used these abilities at work and whether they had got better or worse at each of them over the last 10 years.

Qualifications

Qualifications are often taken as an indication of the skills people have. Many academics and policymakers agree on this score:

> Because we have no direct measure of skills, it is accepted practice to take certificated education and training outcomes as a proxy for skills.
>
> (Green and Steedman 1997: i)

> The existence of people with qualifications is not necessarily the same as the availability of skills in the workplace – but can be used as a key indicator.
>
> (DfEE 1998: 27)

One aspect of the skills debate, therefore, has been to compare the qualifications of the British workforce with those of competitor nations. This is a complex and difficult task since adjustments have to be made that take into account different qualification standards, norms and scope between nations. However, it can be done (see DfEE and Cabinet Office 1996; HM Treasury 2005). This type of research identifies the strengths and weaknesses of the British educational system. Its strength lies in the production of graduates – approaching one-quarter of the population now have qualifications above National Vocational Qualification (NVQ) level 3, a proportion that has more than doubled over the last decade. However, the UK has more people with low qualification levels than many of its major comparators and is ranked 18th across the Organization for Economic Cooperation and Development (OECD) on this measure. Five million people have no formal qualifications at all. It also has a smaller than average proportion of people with intermediate-level qualifications which puts it 20th out of the 30 countries in the OECD (HM Treasury 2005: 43).

Job complexity

Another way of measuring skills is to focus on the complexity of the jobs that people occupy. While this method has the merit of anchoring people's minds about the jobs they do and therefore minimizes exaggeration inherent in self-assessment (a phenomenon known as social desirability), it can only be focused on those in paid work since it is focused on skills in the job not the person. There are two ways in which job complexity can be measured. The first is to ask respondents a number of questions about their jobs. These typically revolve around the level of qualifications required to get and do the job, the length of training required for the job and the time taken to learn 'the ropes' of the job. The second measure – and one pioneered by the 1997 Skills Survey and carried on in the 2001 and 2006 Skills Surveys (Felstead et al. 2000; Felstead et al. 2002) – is based on asking individuals in work about the importance of a range of generic activities to their jobs. These cover technical as well as social skills and have even been extended to capturing emotional and aesthetic skills that case study research suggests are becoming more prevalent as we move towards a more service-oriented economy (Bolton 2004; Payne 2006).

Discretion exercised at work

Another aspect of skill is the extent to which job holders can exercise discretion and judgement at work (this aspect is emphasized by writers such as Braverman (1974) and Zuboff (1988)). One way of assessing the extent of discretion individuals have at work is to ask them about the amount of choice they have in carrying out their job and the extent to which they are able to exercise personal influence over how hard they work, what work tasks they do, how tasks are carried out and what standards they are expected to achieve.

Not surprisingly, the stories that these skill measures tell of change over time are not entirely consistent with one another (Felstead et al. 2004). By way of contrast, the data suggest a consistent upward movement in the complexity of jobs carried out in Britain. This is evident in the significant rise in the qualification requirements of jobs. Notably, the proportion of degree-level jobs rose from 10% in 1986 to 17% in 2001. Similarly, fewer jobs in 2001 needed a cumulative training time of less than three months than in earlier years; in 1986 66% fell into this category, but by 2001 this had fallen to 61%. By the same token, fewer jobs required less than one month 'to learn to do well'; these jobs accounted for 27% of the total in 1986 compared with 20% in 2001. A rise in the complexity of jobs is also evident in the rising importance ratings given to a range of generic activities carried out at work. Most notably, the importance of computer skills has risen more rapidly between 1997 and 2001 than any other job skill. Movement towards greater equality is also evident in these trends. While there are substantive differences between the skills used at work by men and those used by women, the differences appear to be narrowing over time. For example, the proportions of jobs held by men requiring no qualifications fell from 31% to 24% over 1986–2001, while the equivalent decline for women's jobs was from 48% to 29%. Moreover, it is women part-timers who are benefiting more from the narrowing of the gender gap.

However, the rise in job complexity has *not* been accompanied by a corresponding rise in the control workers can exercise over their jobs. Rather, there has been a marked decline in task discretion. For example, the proportion of employees reporting 'a great deal' of choice over the way they do their job fell from 52% in 1986 to 39% in 2001. The proportions reporting a 'great deal' of influence over what tasks are done fell from 42% in 1992 to 30% in 2001. This decline occurred for both men and women. Nevertheless, the level of task discretion in jobs declined much faster for women part-timers than for women full-timers, thereby exacerbating rather than alleviating existing inequalities in the quality of women's working lives.

Conclusion

The main purpose of this chapter has been to shed light on the complexities inherent in conceiving, analysing and measuring 'training', 'learning' and 'skills' that are regular features of commentary by politicians and practitioners (see HRM in Action 7.1). The pages of *People Management*, for example, are replete with references to these key elements of HRM. The role of the research community – through chapters such as this – is to navigate a path through the feverish claims and counterclaims that are particularly associated with trend analysis and international comparisons. As readers of the chapter will now be aware, none of the claims and measures used is without its merits. Instead different conceptualizations, analytical foci and measurement proxies lie behind many of these disputes.

Nevertheless, there remain gaps in our knowledge. For example, it is far from clear what training actually involves. Instead, we know quite a lot about who gets it, how long it lasts and whether it leads to a qualification or not. Our knowledge of what is actually taught is much patchier (for exceptions, see Fevre et al. 2001; Felstead et al. 2007). More research is, therefore, required on what training means in particular sectors of the economy in order to understand fully its cognitive impact on those who receive it. Inevitably, this kind of research question lends itself to a case study approach since the role and function training plays in a productive system and how this has changed over time can best be examined from such a perspective.

Case studies, however, have been the preferred research method for studies on workplace learning. Here, the need is for more translation of the ideas and concepts generated from this research to be built into the design of survey instruments that can give broader insights. Useful analytical concepts such as 'learning as participation', for example, need to mainstreamed into survey designs. Similarly, other education-born concepts such as 'communities of practice' – namely, colleagues committed to joint learning – have rarely been examined by survey researchers.

Sociologically inspired concepts of skills have suffered a similar fate. The explosion of interest in emotional and aesthetic labour, for example, has concentrated its attention on particular sectors of the economy such as hotels, restaurants, call centres and the airline industry. While this has produced a wealth of evidence along with a conceptual debate about whether these job aspects constitute 'skills' (e.g., Bolton 2004; Payne 2006), few attempts have been made to quantify the extent to which this type of labour is present in today's jobs, where it is most prevalent and how it has changed over time. We have surprisingly little robust evidence about these matters.

The fact that academics take different positions on conceptualization, analytical focus and measurement tools used to study training, learning and skills is not unique. Indeed, it is a key feature of many of the HRM debates reviewed in other chapters in this book. However, what sets this chapter apart is the political weight now attached to getting more workers trained, exposed to more learning opportunities and better skilled. What is more, many of the issues reviewed in this chapter are played out in public debates in quality press, in radio reports and in television commentaries. It is hoped that this chapter has provided readers with a set of intellectual tools that allows critical appraisal of the growing body of evidence now available on this important element of HRM.

HRM in Action 7.1 Conceptual, analytical and measurement issues played out in journalistic commentaries

---

The following excerpts are taken from recent newspaper commentaries. They highlight a number of issues reviewed in this chapter.

Excerpt 1: 'Industry gets the big quiz', *The Guardian*, 11 March 2003

The mammoth survey ... will seek to analyse the economy's training needs. Employers will be asked how much training actually goes on in their workforces and how relevant it is for business ... Employer bodies such as the Confederation of British Industry maintain that industry is spending in excess of £20bn a year on staff training, but labour market analysts urge caution on this figure. They point out that it includes the salary costs of staff carrying out in-house training and the salaries of those being trained. Training is a very broad concept and can include, for instance, being shown where the factory's fire exits are.

This excerpt problematizes the concept of 'training' by highlighting the elasticity of the training expenditure figures that are often bandied around in policy documents. It suggests that we need to thoroughly investigate how 'training' is defined, measured and the data on it are collected (Ryan 1990; Spilsbury 2003).

Excerpt 2: 'Why Nellie has the answers', *Financial Times*, 26 September 2002

While smaller companies provide less formal training than larger ones, they are nevertheless substantial providers of informal training, encapsulated in the phrase 'sitting by Nellie'. Policymakers, however, are nervous about such informality since, in their minds, training and qualifications are synonymous. The problem is that while day release at a college can lead to a

qualification, sitting by Nellie does not – even if it is in fact a much more effective way for employees to gain skills.

The key issue here is the difficulty policymakers have with skills that can only be acquired and improved in the workplace through everyday work experience. While qualifications and periods spent being trained are easily measured – and converted into targets (see NACETT 2000; OECD 1997, 2003) – informal learning presents more of a challenge.

Excerpt 3: 'We all kill a few patients as we learn', *The Guardian*, 18 May 2004

I made a mistake at work today. We all do. But what if I said that I was a doctor? When a plumber gets it wrong, he leaves you with a flooded kitchen; when a doctor gets it badly wrong, he leaves you dead or crippled for life ... Airline pilots learn to fly the plane before they have to carry passengers. Due to limited training opportunities, doctors gain experience by treating patients. We are carrying passengers before we know how to fly the plane.

While it is commonly recognized that the most effective learning is by trial and error, it is shocking to think that this kind of learning goes on in many occupations with sometimes fatal consequences. However, this excerpt alerts us to this possibility and to the importance of 'learning by doing' across a range of occupations (Eraut 2004).

Excerpt 4: 'Fewer employers report gaps in skills', *Financial Times*, 13 March 2006

The proportion of companies reporting that workers lack crucial skills has fallen by over a quarter in the past two years, according to a survey of more than 70,000 employers ... slightly fewer than 1.3 million workers were described as not fully proficient last year compared with 2.4 million in 2003 ... the greatest proportion of workers lacking skills in 'lower level' occupations such as sales and customer services and elementary jobs such as farm workers, labourers, cleaners and catering assistants ... Some of the biggest skills gaps reported by employers were 'soft skills', in particular teamworking and customer handling skills.

This excerpt suggests that skills include a host of abilities, many of which are unlikely to be recognized in formal qualifications. Indeed, today's jobs may be demanding different abilities of jobholders that extend far beyond technical know-how (Payne 2000).

Excerpt 5: 'Youngsters hope to nail success at the Skills Olympics', *Financial Times*, 18 May 2006

Britain's gold medal hopefuls are to receive intensive training to ensure that the country avoids national humiliation when London plays host to the 'Skills Olympics' in 2011 ... For Phil Hope, the skills minister, London 2011 is more than just a competition. It is a key element of the government's fixation with improving the quality of the British workforce ... the 'skills agenda' has been at the centre of feverish government activity, designed – among other things – to make vocational education more palatable to parents and children. But the general public, Mr Hope said, suffered from a 'cultural attitude that thinks academic qualifications matter more than vocational training'.

This highlights, once again, the emphasis placed on qualifications, and academic ones in particular, over vocational training. However, apart from events such as the Skills Olympics, the international skills scorecard rarely strays from measuring the stock of qualifications held by individuals living and working in a country (HM Treasury 2005).

References

Ainley, P. and B. Bailey (1997). *The Business of Learning: Staff and Student Experiences of Further Education in the 1990s*. London, Cassell.

Alberga, T., S. Tyson and D. Parsons (1996). 'An evaluation of the Investors in People Standard', *Human Resource Management Journal* 7(2): 47–60.

Apprenticeship Task Force (2005). *Final Report*. London, Apprenticeships Task Force, DfES.

Beinart, S. and P. Smith (1998). 'National Adult Learning Survey 1997', *Department for Education and Employment Research Report No. 49*. London, Department for Education and Employment.

Billett, S. (2002). 'Critiquing workplace learning discourses: participation and continuity at work', *Studies in the Education of Adults* 34(1): 56–67.

Bolton, S. (2004). 'Conceptual confusions: emotion work as skilled work', in C. Warhurst, I. Grugulis and E. Keep, (eds) *The Skills That Matter*. Basingstoke: Palgrave Macmillan.

Boud, D. and H. Middleton (2003). 'Learning from others at work: communities of practice and informal learning', *Journal of Workplace Learning* 15(5): 194–202.

Braverman, H. (1974). *Labor and Monopoly Capital*. New York, Monthly Review Press.

Bynner, J., L. Morphy and S. Parsons (1997). 'Gendered skill development', in H. Metcalf (ed.) *Women, Skill Development and Training*. London, Policy Studies Institute.

Campanelli, P., R. Thomas, L. Channell, L. McAulay and A. Renouf (1994). 'Training: an exploration of the word and the concept with an analysis of the implications for survey design', *Department for Education and Employment Research Series No. 30*. London, Department for Education and Employment.

Clarke, A. (2002). 'Who trains? Employers' commitment to workforce development', *Labour Market Trends* 110(6): 319-34.

Daly, A., D. M. Hitchins and K. Wagner (1985). 'Productivity, machinery and skills in a sample of British and German manufacturing plants', *National Institute Economic Review* 111: 48-61.

DfEE (1997). *Labour Market and Skill Trends 1997/1998*. Sheffield, Department for Education and Employment.

DfEE (1998). *The Learning Age: A Renaissance for a New Britain*. London, Department for Education and Employment.

DfEE and Cabinet Office (1996). *The Skills Audit Report: A Report from an Interdepartmental Group, Occasional Paper*. London, HMSO.

DfES (2000). *Skills for All: Research Report from the National Skills Task Force*. London, Department for Education and Skills.

Elbaum, B., W. Lazonick, F. Wilkinson and J. Zeitlin (1979). 'The labour process, market structure and Marxist theory', *Cambridge Journal of Economics* 3(3): 227-30.

Elias, P. (1995). 'Social class and the standard occupational classification', in D. Rose (ed.) *A Report on Phase I of the ESRC Review of the OPCS Social Classifications*. Swindon, ESRC.

Eraut, M. (1997). 'Perspectives on defining "the learning society"', *Journal of Education Policy* 12(6): 551-8.

Eraut, M. (2000). 'Development of knowledge and skills at work', in F. Coffield (ed.) *Differing Visions of a Learning Society: Research Findings. Volume 1*. Bristol, The Policy Press.

Eraut, M. (2004). 'Informal learning in the workplace', *Studies in Continuing Education* 26(2): 247-73.

Eraut, M., J. Alderton, G. Cole and P. Senker (1998). 'Learning from other people at work', in F. Coffield (ed.) *Learning at Work*. Bristol, The Policy Press.

Eraut, M., J. Alderton, G. Cole and P. Senker (1999). 'The impact of the manager on learning in the workplace', in F. Coffield (ed.) *Speaking Truth to Power: Research and Policy on Lifelong Learning*. Bristol, The Policy Press.

European Communities (2005). *Europe in Figures: Eurostat Yearbook 2005*. Luxembourg, Office for Official Publications of the European Communities.

Eurostat (1992). *Labour Force Survey: Methods and Definitions, 1992 Series*. Luxembourg, Office for Official Publications of the European Communities.

Eurostat (2002). *European Social Statistics: Continuing Vocational Training Survey (CVTS2)*. Luxembourg, Office for the Official Publications of the European Communities.

Felstead, A. (2002). 'Putting skills in their place: the regional pattern of work skills in late twentieth century Britain', in K. Evans, P. Hodkinson and L. Unwin (eds) *Working to Learn: Transforming Learning in the Workplace*. London, Kogan Page.

Felstead, A. (2005). 'The geography of work skills: a focus on Wales', *Briefing Paper No. 6 for the Rees Review*. Cardiff, Welsh Assembly Government.

Felstead, A. and L. Unwin (2001). 'Funding post-compulsory education and training: a retrospective analysis of the TEC and FEFC systems and their impact on skills', *Journal of Education and Work* 14(1): 91-111.

Felstead, A., D. Ashton and F. Green (2000). 'Are Britain's workplace skills becoming more unequal?', *Cambridge Journal of Economics* 24(6): 709-27.

Felstead, A., A. Fuller, N. Jewson, K. Kakavelakis and L. Unwin (2007). 'Grooving to the same tunes? Learning, training and productive systems in the aerobics studio', *Work, Employment and Society* 21(2): forthcoming.

Felstead, A., A. Fuller, L. Unwin, D. Ashton, P. Butler and T. Lee (2005). 'Surveying the scene: learning metaphors, survey design and the workplace context', *Journal of Education and Work* 18(4): 359-83.

Felstead, A., D. Gallie and F. Green (2002). *Work Skills in Britain, 1986-2001*. London, Department for Education and Skills.

Felstead, A., D. Gallie and F. Green (2004). 'Job complexity and task discretion: tracking the direction of skills at work in Britain', in C. Warhurst, I. Grugulis and E. Keep (eds) *The Skills That Matter*. Basingstoke, Palgrave Macmillan.

Felstead, A., F. Green and K. Mayhew (1997). *Getting the Measure of Training: A Report on Training Statistics in Britain*. Leeds, Centre for Industrial Policy and Performance, University of Leeds.

Felstead, A., F. Green and K. Mayhew (1998). 'Interpreting training statistics in Europe: issuing a health warning', *European Vocational Training Journal* 14: 62-9.

Felstead, A., F. Green and K. Mayhew (1999). 'Britain's training statistics: a cautionary tale', *Work, Employment and Society* 13(1): 107-15.

Fevre, R., S. Gorad and G. Rees (2001). 'Necessary and unnecessary learning: the acquisition of knowledge and "skills" in and outside employment in South Wales in the 20th century', in F. Coffield (ed.) *The Necessity of Informal Learning*. Bristol, The Policy Press.

Fuller, A. and L. Unwin (2003). 'Learning as apprentices in the contemporary UK workplace: creating and managing expansive and restrictive learning environments', *Journal of Education and Work* 16(4): 406-27.

Green, A. and H. Steedman (1997). *Into the Twenty First Century: An Assessment of British Skill Profiles and Prospects*. London, Centre for Economic Performance, London School of Economics.

Green, F., A. Felstead, K. Mayhew and A. Pack (2000). 'The impact of raining on labour mobility: individual and firm-level evidence from Britain', *British Journal of Industrial Relations* 38(2): 261-75.

Griffin, T. (1984). 'Technological change and craft control in the newspaper industry: an international comparison', *Cambridge Journal of Economics* 8(1), March: 41-61.

Hager, P. (2004). 'The conceptualization and measurement of learning', in H. Rainbird, A. Fuller and A. Munro (eds) *Workplace Learning in Context*. London, Routledge.

HMSO (various). *Training Statistics*. London, HMSO.

HM Treasury (2005). *Skills in the UK: The Long Term Challenge - Interim Report*. London, HM Treasury.

Hodkinson, H. and P. Hodkinson (2004). 'Rethinking the concept of community of practice in relation to schoolteachers' workplace learning', *International Journal of Training and Development* 8 (1): 21–31.

Hoque, K. (2003). 'All in all, it's just another plaque on the wall: the incidence and impact of the Investors in People Standard', *Journal of Management Studies* 40(2): 543–71.

Hughes, M. (2002). *Making the Grade: A Report on Standards in Work-Based Learning for Young People*. London, Learning and Skills Development Agency.

Kelleher, M., P. Scott and B. Jones (1993). 'Resistant to change? Some unexplained omissions in the 1990 standard occupational classification', *Work, Employment and Society* 7(3): 437–49.

Lave, J. and E. Wenger (1991). *Situated Learning: Legitimate Peripheral Participation*. Cambridge, Cambridge University Press.

Leman, S. (2003). 'Participating in adult learning: comparing the sources and applying the results', in N. Sargant and F. Aldridge (eds) *Adult Learning and Social Division: A Persistent Pattern, Volume 2*. Leicester, National Institute of Adult Continuing Education.

Mason, G. and D. Finegold (1995). 'Productivity, machinery and skills in the United States and Western Europe: precision engineering', *National Institute of Economic and Social Research Discussion Paper No. 89*.

Mason, G. S. J. Prais and B. van Ark (1992). 'Vocational education and productivity in the Netherlands and Britain', *National Institute Economic Review* 140: 45–63.

Méhaut, P. (1992). 'Further education, vocational training and the labour market: the French and German systems compared', in A. Castro, P. Méhaut and J. Rubery (eds) *International Integration and Labour Market Organisation*. London, Academic Press.

NACETT (1997). *Skills for 2000: Supplement to the Report on Progress Towards the National Targets for Education and Training*. London, National Advisory Council for Education and Training Targets.

NACETT (2000). *Aiming Higher: NACETT's Report on the National Learning Targets for England and Advice on the Targets Beyond 2002*. London, National Advisory Council for Education and Training Targets.

Noon, M. and P. Blyton (2002). *The Realities of Work*, Basingstoke, Palgrave Macmillan.

OECD (1997). *Manual for Better Training Statistics: Conceptual, Measurement and Survey Issues*. Paris, Organization for Economic Cooperation and Development.

OECD (2003). *Beyond Rhetoric: Adult Learning Policies and Practices*. Paris, Organization for Economic Cooperation and Development.

OECD and Statistics Canada (1997). *Literacy, Economy and Society*. Paris, Organization for Economic Cooperation and Development.

Official Journal of the European Communities (2002). 'Commission Regulation (EC) No. 1313/2002', 20 July: L192/16-L192/21.

ONS (2006). *Social Trends 36*. London, Office for National Statistics.

OPCS (1990). *Standard Occupational Classification, Volume 1*. London, HMSO.

Park, A. (1994). 'Individual commitment to learning: individuals' attitudes', *Employment Department Research Series No 31*. Sheffield, Employment Department.

Payne, J. (2000). 'The unbearable lightness of skill: the changing meaning of skill in UK policy discourses and some implications for education and training', *Journal of Educational Policy* 15(3): 353–69.

Payne, J. (2006). 'What's wrong with emotional labour?', *SKOPE Research Paper No. 65*. SKOPE, Universities of Oxford and Warwick.

Prais, S. J., V. Jarvis and K. Wagner (1989). 'Productivity and vocational skills in services in Britain and Germany: hotels', *National Institute Economic Review* 130: 52–74.

Ryan, P. (1990). 'How much do employers spend on training? An assessment of the "Training in Britain" estimates', *Human Resource Management Journal* 1(4): 55–76.

Sargant, N. with J. Field, H. Frances, T. Schuller and A. Tuckett (1997). *The Learning Divide: A Study of Participation in Adult Learning in the United Kingdom*. Leicester, National Institute for Adult Continuing Education.

Senker, P. (1995). 'Training levies in four countries: implications for British industrial training policy', *EnTra Research Report RR105*. London, Engineering Training Authority.

Sfard, A. (1998). 'On two metaphors for learning and the dangers of choosing just one', *Educational Researcher* 27(2): 4–13.

Skule, S. and A. N. Reichborn (2002). *Learning-Conducive Work: A Survey of Learning Conditions in Norwegian Workplaces*. Luxembourg, Office for Official Publications of the European Communities.

Smith, D. (1998). 'Skills shortage: we're learning (at last)', *Management Today* July: 34–5.

Spenner, K. I. (1990). 'Skill, meanings, methods and measures', *Work and Occupations* 17: 399–421.

Spilsbury, D. (2003). 'Learning and Training at Work 2002', *Department for Education and Skills Research Report No. 399*. London, Department for Education and Skills.

Spilsbury, M., J. Moralee, J. Hillage and D. Frost (1995). 'Evaluation of Investors in People in England and Wales', *Institute of Employment Studies Report No. 263*. Brighton, Institute of Manpower Studies.

Statz, C. and S. Wright (2004). 'Emerging policy for vocational learning in England: will it lead to a better system?', *Learning and Skills Research Centre Research Report*. London, Learning and Skills Development Agency.

Steedman, H. (1988). 'Vocational training in France and Britain: mechanical and electrical craftsmen', *National Institute Economic Review* 126: 57–70.

Steedman, H. (1998). 'A decade of skill formation in Britain and Germany', *Journal of Education and Work* 11(1): 77–94.

Steedman, H. and K. Wagner (1987). 'A second look at productivity, machinery and skills in Britain and Germany', *National Institute Economic Review* 122: 84–94.

Stern, E. and E. Sommerlad (1999). *Workplace Learning: Culture and Performance*. London, Chartered Institute of Personnel and Development.

Sung, J., A. Raddon and D. Ashton (2006). 'Skills abroad: a comparative assessment of international policy approaches to skills leading to the development of policy recommendations for the UK', *Research Report 16*. Wath-upon-Derne, Sector Skills Development Agency.

Tomlinson Report (2004). 14–19 Curriculum and Qualifications Reform: Final Report of the Working Group on 14–19 Reform. London, Department for Education and Skills.

Training Agency (1987). *Training in Britain: A Study of Funding, Activity and Attitudes – Employers' Activities*. Sheffield, Training Agency.

Zuboff, S. (1988). *In the Age of the Smart Machine: The Future of Work and Power*. New York, Basic Books.

Managers' knowledge and the management of change

Graeme Salaman

Organizational change is now regarded by management writers as a dominant and constant feature of organizational life (Ghoshal et al. 2000; Kotter 1996). Practitioners and consultants alike contend not only that change is necessary to ensure movement away from the dysfunctions of bureaucracy but also that *post* the demise of bureaucracy (an assessment which is itself somewhat premature – see Salaman 2005) change must be not an episodic event but a continuous process of adaptation and improvement. Furthermore these claims – certainly for the frequency of change if not for the successful achievement of the identified effects – have some empirical basis. Surveys of managers indicate that more than 60% of UK managers report a major restructuring in their organization (Worrall et al. 2000).

But the literature on organizational change reveals a puzzle. On the one hand, it is claimed that the successful management of change – especially when this achieves the degree and quality of change known as the 'learning organization' or the 'adaptive organization' – represents a major source of competitive advantage (Hamel and Prahalad 1993; Pettigrew and Whipp 1991). On the other hand, it is claimed that most change programmes fail to achieve their objectives. How can we explain the fact that change is increasingly frequent and pervasive, that it could offer real competitive advantage when designed and managed well, yet fails to do so? What are the sources of this failure? Why do managers fail to achieve the benefits that change could offer them even when they apparently recognize the possibility of these benefits by making unsuccessful attempts to change?

This puzzle has certainly received attention (Beer et al. 1990; Beer and Nohria 2000; Brunnson and Olsen 1993) but it merits more. It is possible that the sources of the persistence of the puzzle lie in the relative neglect of the processes that underpin and inform decisions on the design and implementation of the change projects and their methodologies. These processes are the responsibility of management, often indeed – depending on the nature of the proposed change – senior management. They depend on the judgement of managers. The processes that determine managers' decisions on the design of change – and on the need for change and its scope and timing – like other strategy processes – consist of what Whittington calls 'practices': 'shared routines of behaviour, including traditions, norms and procedures for thinking, acting and using things' (Whittington 2006: 619). Like all organizational processes involving the identification of problems, options and the choice of solutions, these processes require 'skills and tools' (Whittington 2002: 119). And these tools include assumptions, values and views about how the organization works and what needs to be done to make it work differently. But these 'tools' have some distinctive qualities. One of them is that they may be tacit – taken for granted. Another is that they not only define what needs to be done and how, they also shape the reality that is to be changed. Nonaka and Takeuchi note how managers share: 'schemata, mental models, beliefs and perceptions so ingrained that we take them for granted. The cognitive dimension of tacit knowledge reflects our image of reality (what is) and our vision of the future (what ought to be)' (Nonaka and Takeuchi 1995: 310).

This chapter will propose that some light can be shed on the way managers design and manage change and when and if they seek to initiate change by examining an aspect of change which has hitherto received relatively little attention in the current literature. This literature remains somewhat unbalanced, being predominantly concerned less with analysis and more with prescription, more with operational issues than with issues of strategy and more with issues of implementation than questions of design. One consequence of this is that the role of management choice in change programmes is underplayed. Yet since the content and processes of change programmes are designed or chosen by management, it seems sensible to enquire into the nature and bases of these decisions and choices.

This chapter aims to shift the focus from implementation and the operational to the decisions surrounding the design of change. It aims to understand the bases on which managers make design decisions – especially the assumptions, logics and knowledge that underpin processes of executive judgement and decision making. This chapter and our research (Storey and Salaman 2005a, 2005b) argues that managers play a much more active part in the design of change. The argument has three elements:

1 Managers design change.
2 They design it in the light of their 'theories' or logics of organization.
3 The nature of the design is affected by the nature of the logics available to the top team and to the nature of the dynamics among these logics.

It is argued here that managers play an active and key role in decisions on organizational change and that these decisions on issues of organizational capability are made possible by, and informed and sustained by, the logics and assumptions that make these decisions sensible and acceptable. In other words, this chapter attempts to theorize managers' decisions about organizational change by understanding how these decisions themselves are dependent on and informed by managers' own theories of organization.

Managers and the design of change

Existing accounts of the role of managers in change focus predominantly on their role as managers of change processes rather than as designers of the content and process of change projects. More significantly, accounts of the role of managers as designers of change or as people responsible for choosing change initiatives tend to assume a somewhat reactive, passive role for managers, stressing their subordination to larger societal forces and movements. This tendency is apparent in two separate debates about the nature and implications of change both of which define the role of management in change in a passive manner as 'carriers' or 'relays' in the transmission of ideas about the direction and form of change arising outside the organization and both of which address the forces or ideas that inform the direction of organizational change.

This tendency to define the role of senior managers in the design of change programmes as mere transmitters of larger societal forces and movements – 'relays' for larger macro causal factors and pressures – is illustrated by the analysis of the work of management consultants (whose recommendations often drive and inform processes of organizational change) that defines the relationship between consultant's recommendations and managers' decisions on the design of organizational change in terms of 'fads and fashions' (Abrahamson 1996; Keiser 1997). It is certainly not unreasonable to highlight the way in which, on occasion at some time and place, certain widely publicized change initiatives (for example, business process reengineering, outsourcing, knowledge management, etc.) dominate the change agenda. To see the introduction, acceptance, installation and dominance of changing forms of organizational change as a succession of fads and fashions is understandable and even illuminating since it draws attention to the ways in which a particular type of organizational change becomes attractive because of its pervasiveness and popularity. It becomes part of what is seen as 'normal' or 'modern' as Brunsson and Olsen (1993) have noted. These changes become defined as the available and acceptable solutions to organizational problems. So there is little doubt that the pattern of incidence and distribution of types of organizational change, the way in which different types of change emerge, dominate, decline are replaced by new types of organizational change, the way in which during a period of 'popularity' a particular form of organizational change assumes major dominance and unquestioned authority, all these features of organizational change initiatives support a view of change in terms of fashion and fads.

But this view, although compelling, also implicitly contributes to a conception of the role of management in change that this chapter will question and seek to modify since, in effect, it reasserts the longstanding polarity in social and organizational theory between the social and the individual whereby one or the other of these dichotomized entities is seen as dominant over the other. When organizational change initiatives are described and explained in terms of the dominance of larger, societal fads and fashions, in effect the 'social' – the external, macro, discursive world of authoritative conceptions of organizational structures and processes – is seen to dominate over and indeed to leave no space for choice or decision on the part of the individual. Organizational reform becomes as Brunsson and Olsen (1993) note 'institutionalized'.

The implications for senior management are not simply and solely that they are now defined as 'cultural dopes', accepting and applying dominant ideas and exhortations and thus losing the capacity of intervention and choice, but equally seriously, that defining organizational change as driven by fashion leads to a neglect of, possibly even defines as unnecessary and irrelevant, an understanding of the ways in which senior managers understand, invoke, use, negotiate available ideas when thinking about organizational change in practice – the ways they 'make do', make sense. The result could be that as Whittington notes, managers are seen as automata rather than in their practical work on strategy, as artful and creative interpreters. A result could be that the subtle and highly significant processes whereby managers 'do strategy' – in this case strategies for organizational change – the processes of analysis and negotiation, the logics, tools and assumptions that are used, the routines of behaviour, the nature and role of authorities that are invoked to support or challenge proposals, the dynamics of the groupings, alliances and conflict that underpin the emergence of strategies would be missed.

This tendency to define managers' role in change design issues as dominated by the social, as 'oversocialized' into wider societal discourses, is also evident in the debate about the role of enterprise in organizational change.

For 20 years there has been an important and influential debate about the role and importance of enterprise as a dominating discourse of organizational change within employing organizations in the public and private sectors. Enterprise is identified as a major and underpinning principle of the reforms of economy, government public sector and society initiated in the UK by Margaret Thatcher, whose advocacy of economic liberalism with its glorification and sanctification of market structures and relationships was increasingly associated with a focus on the cultural values seen as necessarily implicated in and supportive of the efficiency of markets, the liberation of individuals and the non-interventionist state. Thatcher's programme of reform extended the domain of the market (albeit not always in straightforward ways) and 'encouraged or required the reconstruction of the institutions concerned along the lines suggested by the model of the commercial enterprise' (Keat 1990: 3). The paradigmatic status of the *enterprise* operating in a market context competitively to identity, develop and meet the needs of the identified, differentiated segmented category of consumer, is further associated with another sense of enterprise – 'the kind of action or project that displays enterprising qualities or characteristics on the part of those concerned ... characteristics such as initiative, energy, independence, boldness, self-reliance, a willingness to take risks and accept responsibility for one's action' (Keat 1990: 3). Thus enterprising forms of organization are seen to generate enterprising employees.

One of the attractions of enterprise is its claim to encompass analysis and critique at the societal/political, the organizational and the individual levels and to identify the ways in which these three levels are interrelated. It argues that there exist linkages between the political, the organizational and the personal and claims to demonstrate how developments at the level of societal and political discourse impact on the identities of individual employees. 'Enterprise' offers a way of identifying and understanding the connections between these levels of dimensions. As du Gay et al. note in a discussion of the implications of discourse for the construction of the new manager – 'a complex series of links has been established through which the economic priorities of politicians and business persons have been articulated in terms of the required personal characteristics of managers' (du Gay et al. 1996: 265).

However, although the notion of enterprise is central to processes of organizational change, like much of the change literature, the analyses of enterprise remains abstract – at the level of analysis of the ideas and prescriptions of advocates of enterprise and focuses less on the ways in which these have been translated into actions or critically on the ways in which managers have used the notion of enterprise in devising change programmes. Empirical studies tend to focus on the analysis of the assumptions and implications of the organizational measures recommended by advocates of enterprise or on the implications of these structures and processes for employees' identities.

A result of this is that although enterprise has been a major focus of consultants' recommendations and academics' analyses for many years we know a great deal more about what the proponents are recommending than we do about how senior managers are making sense of, and applying, these recommendations. Even if and when they are installing the various changes recommended by the advocates, the critical organizational link between external encouragement and internal, management decision making is relatively neglected. Once again we lack knowledge and understanding of how managers use and actively understand and interpret (or indeed reject and ignore) these exhortations in their actual strategy practices.

So crucial questions about the ways in which and the extent to which these discourses of enterprise are translated into practices at the organizational level remains relatively underexplored. The link between societal level discourses of enterprise or consultants' recommendations and organizational change programmes is asserted rather than explored and the crucial role of managers in making these linkages neglected. The result is that a critical juncture or relay in the process of linkage between discourse – organization – and employee subjectivity; the knowledge, assumptions, analyses and decisions of senior organizational decision makers remains largely neglected. As Fournier and Grey note, rather like the work of Braverman some years ago, these 'overdetermined' analyses of enterprise overlook the role of management as active agents in processes of decision making; instead defining senior managers in an abstract and formalistic manner as a passive category whose role is simply to recognize and implement enterprising strategies and organizational forms (Salaman 1982). Interestingly, it could be argued that recent discussions of enterprise rely on an extremely unenterprising – indeed passive – conception of managers.

Management is – or should be – central to the processes whereby enterprise is installed within organizations. Management is a critical link in the series of linkages that connect societal discourses with organizational changes and with employee subjectivity. If the 'management of conduct' depends on the 'conduct of management' (du Gay et al. 1996) then it is crucial to understand the thinking that determines managers' 'conduct' with respect to enterprise – especially senior managers who are authorized to make decisions about strategy and organization and crucially the links as they see them between the two. Yet although some work on managers' understanding of and intentions towards enterprise has taken place – on how managers actually make sense of enterprise – for example, du Gay et al. 1996; Newman 2005; Salaman 2005 – the role and contribution of management itself as a key decision-making role in processes of organizational change has been largely neglected. Not for the first time, management has been treated as something that is 'either self-evident and unproblematic . . . or, more commonly, black-boxed and unexplicated' (Alvesson and Karreman 2001: 100). To the extent that management is conceptualized and positioned within the enterprise literature it is simply assumed to be an unproblematic mechanism or relay in the processes of application of enterprise within the organization.

The focus of this chapter and the research it reports is on how senior managers – strategic level individuals and teams – understand, make sense of, interpret their organizations and the pressures they face and how these can best be handled when thinking about and making decisions about issues of corporate strategy or organizational structures and processes. This requires analysis of assumptions, theories and beliefs that executives hold which make their decisions about organizational strategies and the appropriate organizational forms for the achievement of the strategic objectives they have chosen for their organization, sensible, reasonable, even necessary and inevitable – which influence and underpin their choices of organizational structures and systems – the 'changing conceptions of how organizations work and the associated technologies and practices through which these conceptions are instrumentalised' (du Gay et al. 1996: 265).

This chapter attempts to redress the balance between the manager and wider social pressures which surround the manager – between the individual and the social, between structure and agency – by using the insights generated by a number of recent debates – the process approach to strategy, the focus on strategy as practice, the cognitive approach to strategy and others – to focus on the micro-activities and cognitive assumptions that managers use when making choices and decisions about organizational change – what Chia and Holt (2006) describe as 'the internal life of organizational routines' which not only addresses the 'micro-practices of organizing', but also acknowledge that in practice, senior management work on issues of strategy and change is likely to differ significantly from the at least implicit model of strategizing in the traditional strategy literature. In practice, with issues of change design as of strategy development, Mintzberg and Water's (1985) description of strategy as a pattern in a stream of actions, will apply, with strategies emerging from the dynamics and relationships of management interactions and the logics and assumptions held by the managers.

In summary, current analyses of change which seek to explain executive decision making on the nature and design of change tend to underplay and neglect the role of managers as active, interpretive agents and instead to define them, if implicitly, as simply relays of larger societal forces. Some years ago Child noted that organizational strategies and structures can only be understood in terms of 'the process whereby strategic decisions are made which directs attention onto the degree of choice which can be exercised in respect of organizational design' (Child 1972: 2). But much of the change literature in effect neglects the critical role of managers as active decision makers exercising choice about the direction and nature of the organization (if in some cases by choosing to retain existing strategies and structures), even though such a recognition is critical to the SHRM literature with its emphasis on 'alignment' or 'fit'. Much of the literature that addresses the role of managers in the design of change in effect defines managers as passive.

Managers' decisions underpinned by logics

It may seem excessive or inappropriate to introduce the notion of managers' 'theories' of change, on two grounds. First, that evidence suggests that managers are strongly focused on action rather than on reflection and that therefore 'theory' would be unappealing to them. But to be concerned with action in no way excludes commitment to theory (although it may discourage explicit discussion of theory or result in low value being placed on activities that are deemed 'theoretical'). On the contrary, ultimately all purposeful organizational action is based on some form of theory in terms of which the action taken (or the change that is designed) is judged to be likely to achieve the desired effect. Second, it could be argued that management activity tends to consist less of large-scale strategic analysis and planning (which being based on cause-and-effect assumptions could be judged theoretical) and more of ad hoc adjustments and small-scale decisions. But as many commentators have noted this argues not against the existence of a broader underlying pattern (of the sort that could be described as an underpinning model or theory) and more that this theory or pattern emerges from and is apparent less in explicit determinant form and more through the actions and decisions managers take. It remains important (Chia and Holt 2006).

It is important to understand the logics which underpin senior decisions on organizational change since these determine the nature (size, shape, internal processes and relationships, location of boundaries, etc.) of the organization. While it is understandable that commentators have pointed to the fashionable even faddish nature of change initiatives, this delineation in itself is not enough because, while it stresses the nature and role of dominant logics, it also overestimates the dominance of these ideas (Storey and Salaman 2005a).

The nature and importance of these phenomena have received attention from other researchers in ways with which our study is consistent although this body of work is not usually referenced or used in discussions of enterprise in organizations. Within the strategic management literature Spender's (1989) exploration of 'industry recipes' and Bettis and Prahalad's (1995) concept of a 'dominant logic' are important precursors of this approach. Spender, for example, argues that managers 'turn to a body of judgement which is shared by those socialised into the industry' (1989: 214). Although it must be noted that the focus here is on the internal organizational 'body(ies) of judgement', not the logic shared across an industry. The cognitive approach to strategy also shares a number of features with this approach. This literature, addresses and analyses processes in strategic management 'through which those responsible for all aspects of strategizing, acquire, store, share and act upon information, knowledge and beliefs concerning those issue that have an ultimate bearing on the longer-term direction of the organization as a whole' (Hodgkinson and Sparrow 2002: 6).

Similarly, Ranson et al. (1980) point to the important role in organizational strategic decision making of an underlying 'interpretative scheme' that underpins and is embodied in organizational strategies, structures and systems (Greenwood and Hinings 1993; Ransom et al. 1980). Karpik (1978) notes the key role of what he terms 'logics of action', which consist of criteria of evaluation, and 'tools of rationality', which orient behaviour towards the external world (and influence how it is classified, defined and understood) but which do not arise from the external world but have a prior existence and which are symbolic and potentially differentiated (Karpik 1978: 46–59).

This literature supplies the point of departure for the analysis of this chapter. It aims to identify and understand the possible implications of the knowledge of senior managers by exploring not the knowledge per se, but the implications for their strategic analysis and decision making and commitment of some key features of the knowledge on which this analysis is based. Two key polarities that characterize the knowledge of groups of executives are regarded as important knowledge variables – factors that help shape how and if and when executives think about and make decisions about change – that influence decisions on the business model and the model of business.

Understanding and analysing this sort of senior-level strategic organizational knowledge must involve not only a focus on organizational and managerial systems of knowledge production, acquisition, movement, retention and application and not only a focus on the assumptions and knowledge that create the way organizational realities are defined and options identified and analysed and interpreted. It also means a concern with the characteristics of the knowledge of the top team that influences – or may influence – how options are identified, analysis is conducted and decisions made. This requires a focus on and an attempt to achieve, *reflexivity* – the organization's ability to understand how it understands – with 'practical rationality' (Habermas 1971) – the surfacing and analysis of underlying issues and assumptions and the identification of alternatives – and which focuses on the notion of tacit knowledge and the importance of researching and understanding the inherent limitations of organizational processes of knowing. As Nonaka and Takeuchi have noted, organizations systemically develop and embed ways of defining the world and organization which become institutionalized.

This means reconceptualizing the kinds of knowledge addressed in this chapter as the sets of assumptions, beliefs and working models and, in particular, in terms of the key and differentiating features of this underpinning strategic knowledge. This kind of knowledge 'provides a framework for evaluating and incorporating new experiences and information' (Davenport and Prusak 1998: 5). This involves and enables judgement. It is 'the capacity to exercise judgement on the part of an individual which is either based on an appreciation of context or is derived from theory, or both' (Tsoukas and Vladimirou 2001: 976).

Tacit knowledge and explicit knowledge; consensual knowledge and differentiated knowledge

Analysis of senior executives' knowledge reveals and explores the implications of two important and characteristic features of this organizational knowledge. These features have been noted before but the use of both sets of features together to allow an exploration of their interrelationships (see later) is both new and productive.

The first distinction is between tacit and explicit knowledge. That knowledge can be tacit may now be accepted almost as a truism but it remains highly significant especially for the type of knowledge addressed by our study. The importance of the tacit/explicit distinction will be revealed in our analysis. Tacit knowledge for example, raises the possibility that executives may feel very strongly about a particular proposal – their own or another's – and yet in a sense not recognize or fully recognize the assumptions and beliefs they have about what their organization should do or what it needs to be like to do it or why their views seem so obvious (at least to them).

Nonaka and Takeuchi (1995) in a much quoted argument have insisted that organizations contain both explicit and tacit knowledge and argue that the latter – consisting of technical knowledge and of beliefs and schemata – needs to be converted into explicit knowledge. This notion of tacit knowledge in some ways comes close to what writers such as Berger and Luckmann have called the *social construction of reality* – at least in its emphasis on its being taken for granted and tacit. But Nonaka and Takeuchi's definition of tacit knowledge introduces a new dimension: that this knowledge is necessarily positive, useful and functional in terms of the organization's aims and priorities. This assumption is questionable.

The other key polarity is that between consensual and differentiated knowledge. Whether executives share the same assumptions and beliefs about strategy and capability or hold different sets of underpinning logics is highly significant to the dynamics of the top team, the nature and quality of decision making and very possibly ultimately to the performance of the organization as will be shown.

The knowledge management (KM) literature assumes knowledge as neutral, consensual, unitary, technical operational knowledge which (if tacit) once surfaced and managed and organized impacts positively on performance. Problems associated with knowledge, when they occur, are technical issues requiring organizational or technical solutions. The KM approach defines organizations as rational instruments for the achievement of shared goals and stresses cooperation, consensus, order and hierarchy.

But this overlooks and defines away inherent and fundamental organizational issues of power, conflict and difference. Knowledge in organizations is often differentiated. These differences in ways of seeing the organization, its structure and the outside world reflect organizational differences and reveal differences in interest and power. It is misleading to assume a priori that organizational knowledge is unified. Grant has suggested that a key feature of an organization's ability to create value from knowledge is its capacity to aggregate knowledge – the 'ability to add new knowledge to existing knowledge' (Grant 1996: 111). This ability is unquestionably valuable (see Teece et al. 2002) and indeed can be a major source of innovation when the combination reconfigures an established system or arrangement to link together existing elements in new ways. Henderson and Clark (2002: 321) call this *architectural innovation*.

But it cannot be assumed that knowledge can always be aggregated, not only because this requires a common language or framework such as that supplied by business planning frameworks, management competences, accountancy systems and standards and so on, but more fundamentally because some organizational knowledge – and especially knowledge about core organizational issues of purpose, structure, markets, customers competitors, mission etc. – is differentiated, even oppositional. It cannot be added together because each set of knowledge rejects and seeks to undermine the other, sometimes vigorously and vehemently. Storey and Salaman's work (2005a) on managers' theories of innovation found that in some organizations, managers held very different and opposed notions of how innovation should be organized and managed.

Differences in what differently situated members of organizations know and what they know about arise naturally within organizations that are hierarchical, power systems where power and benefits are distributed unequally. Differences in organizational circumstances, location, power position and benefits underlie differences in interpretive knowledge frameworks and knowledge and are expressed in differences in and struggles over knowledge and over the respective status (or authority) of knowledge. An approach to knowledge in organizations must incorporate this possibility. As Giddens has remarked: 'Any sociological theory which treats such phenomena as "incidental" or "secondary and derived" and not as structurally intrinsic to power differentials is blatantly inadequate' (Giddens 1968: 264).

A major tradition of analysis of organizations focuses on organizations as sites of contention and conflict where power and knowledge are deployed to achieve or maintain dominance or to critique and reduce it. 'Organizations are ... arenas in which coalitions with different interests and capacities for influence vie for dominance' (Palmer et al. 1993: 103). Many studies have shown how differences in interests and organizational location and situation relate to differences in knowledge – ways of seeing the organization and its purposes expressed through different sectional viewpoints and interpretative frameworks. Much of the work on differentiation and conflict in organizations (see Lawrence and Lorsch 1967) 'shows how technical boundaries between departments and sections are reinforced and buttressed by cognitive boundaries' (Greenwood and Hinings 1996: 1033).

In conflicts of and around knowledge, groups will seek to impose their own view of reality. And they will seek to develop and disseminate knowledge which legitimizes their position and their view of the organization's priorities. They will seek to undermine or rule as invalid dangerous or, worse, rival views. They will seek legitimacy by claiming consistency with accepted or proposed sources of moral authority: the founding fathers, the original charter, the organization's accepted prime purpose (usually 'vaguely ambiguous'). But power is inherent in knowledge itself. And that a particular body of knowledge establishes dominance within an organization is not a result of its correspondence with objective truth but more that in one way or another it has managed to achieve political dominance which establishes truth. Truth comes from power.

The research project reported in this chapter[1] is based on the proposition that executive team thinking about, and formulation of, corporate strategies and organizational structures is significantly informed by the models and theories of organization and strategy which are held by members of senior teams. These theories inform both what senior managers propose for the business – strategically and organizationally – and how they react to other's proposals. They inform and potentially limit all stages of the strategic process – definitions of the environment, environmental scanning, data analysis, the identification of acceptable strategic possibilities and the design of appropriate organizational forms. Yet, despite their critical role in underpinning discussion of (and possibly in generating differences of views about) and informing decisions on, fundamental issues of direction and organization, these underpinning theories and convictions are all too frequently left implicit and unexplored.

The research project reported on here surfaces and analyses the models and theories that senior managers hold and use when contributing to the formulation of critical organizational decisions on strategy and organization.

Research methods

The research project concentrated on executive teams. The knowledge work undertaken by the chief executive and the other executive directors was the focus of attention. Ten organizations were studied. These were drawn from a variety of sectors including retail, construction, business services, healthcare, facilities management, banking and pharmaceuticals. Three mutually reinforcing methods formed the heart of the study: in-depth one-to-one interviews with each member of the respective executive teams; direct observation of management meetings of all kinds including, in some cases, executive board meetings; and scrutiny of secondary sources including, most notably, executive board agendas and minutes plus internal company reports. The observations of meetings allowed insight into the naturally occurring conversations of directors and senior managers and facilitated the observation of non-verbal signals passing interactively between them. While researchers naturally strive to observe boards in action these, we found, were not necessarily the settings that revealed most about managers' knowledge. Usually, debates had occurred outside and prior to the boards. These last events when running 'normally' were relatively staged affairs with managers' positions and interpretative frameworks heavily disguised.

The questions explored in one-to-one interviews with senior teams focused on an exploration of executives' views on what their organization needed to do and what it needed to be *like* to do it effectively and their view of the inherent capabilities and historic capabilities of the organization and of any critical authorities that should determine the nature and future of the business (for example, the organization's history or its core market segment or its core competences or values or traditions or its duty to its shareholders or employees).

Research access to executive boards is, not surprisingly, difficult to negotiate. There are obvious issues about commercial confidentiality. In addition, directors are wary about revealing too much about their work, which they regard as sensitive at the interpersonal level. In order to overcome these serious reservations held by directors that have impeded research of board in action, it was necessary for our study to offer some advantage to the participants. Our study assisted senior teams to recognize, evaluate and make sense of the implications of different and possibly competing conceptions held by members of senior teams about what their organization should be doing and what it should be like in order to attain required goals. We made these fundamental issues more discussible (we found they are usually not adequately discussed). Moreover, we allowed such discussion to take place in less personalized and less subjective ways than very often tends to be the case during the normal conventions of business. Our executive subjects usually found the research intervention useful in terms of both content as well as process analysis of their work.

Findings about executive managers' strategic knowledge

This study could help senior teams to recognize, evaluate and make sense of the implications of different and possibly competing conceptions held by members about what their organization should be doing and what they should be like in order to attain required goals. It helps to explain what is otherwise an important but sometimes puzzling phenomenon: that senior managers seem unable to develop new strategies and directions for their business or to find new and improved ways of organizing their business to improve its efficiency. One certainty amidst the uncertainties facing businesses is that sooner or later the business model will fail: what brought success will sooner or later begin to fail. Yet executives frequently find it hard not only to recognize the signs of failure but more seriously to see the sources of failure in the historic business model or to be able to conceive of a direction and form for their business outside of the historic pattern.

This phenomenon is sometimes defined as 'path dependency' or as indicating the role of 'success recipes'. But these terms simply redescribe the phenomenon. Our project aims to explain it by accessing and analysing the underlying and underpinning theories that executives use when defining, analysing and making recommendations about the problems they see as facing their business.

The knowledge of executives that underpins their views on strategies and capability could be located on two axes. It is the core argument of this chapter that the four positions generated by the interplay of these axes have significant implications for the nature and processes of senior decision making on these matters. Each type carries its own implications and many carry dangers (see Table 8.1).

The two cross-cutting dimensions give rise to four types of knowledge state. By this we mean the types of condition that characterize the ways in which executives can deploy their knowledge. Thus, under Type 1 conditions, executives face circumstances where they have few opportunities to scrutinize and challenge their colleagues' knowledge base or to have their own assumptions challenged. Moreover, because there is broad consensus the team can act in unison and goodwill tends to prevail. Under Type 2 conditions, their knowledge of business and their business models also remain relatively unexamined and unchallenged but they are conscious, that differences exist. Where these circumstances obtain suspicion is fuelled that difference can be attributed to malfeasance or stupidity. Under Type 3 conditions, knowledge is displayed more openly and consensus is reached through negotiation. Under Type 4 conditions, knowledge is also made explicit but the evident differences leads to manifest conflict that may for various reasons – as discussed later – be difficult to handle constructively. In the section that follows, we elaborate these types and we give examples of their operation and consequences.

Type 1: common understandings

Executives in organizations where there was a common but unexplored understanding about most if not all key strategic issues drew heavily on their shared tacit knowledge. This generated easy, familiar and deep levels of agreement – often of long standing – about what the business was doing and had been doing and should do and what it needed to be like in order to pursue its proper and historic role and objectives. These assumptions usually centred on distinctive normative models of organization, customer proposition and employment relations.

The tacit consensus of the top team in this first case illustrates some interesting points about the way in which teams in these kinds of organizations think about and discuss change. Since such top teams are not used to identifying, exploring and accepting differences in viewpoint, they find difficulty in managing difference, disagreement and conflict. They have problems in distinguishing healthy difference

Table 8.1	**Four types of executive knowledge state**

	Tacit	*Explicit*
Consensual	*Type 1* Common, submerged/ unexplored understandings	*Type 3* Negotiated action
Differentiated	*Type 2* Divergent, submerged/ unexplored conflicts	*Type 4* Manifest conflict

HRM in Action 8.1   The clothes retailer

In Clothes Retailer Co., the top team operated with a high level of tacit consensus. This was based on a series of shared but largely unsurfaced well-established historic assumptions. These were largely unstated except by general references to a shared and taken-for-granted set of business and organizational 'principles', 'values' and models. These were hallowed and given authority by history and by the intentions of the founders (who were often quoted as a way to legitimate a preferred stance). There was frequent reference to 'our way of doing things'. This was often played as a kind of trump card to de-legitimate alternative proposals which were thus tarnished by their wider market connotations.

Executives had a real pride in the business model and their model of business but neither was fully stated explicitly. There was a conviction that with respect to strategy and organization the business was different and distinctive (which was true but probably not as true as executives thought). But this historic consensus was beginning to come under pressure as performance problems became more and more evident. This proved to be a fascinating moment from a knowledge research point of view because it provoked some unusual reactions among the executives. A number of them preferred to try to ignore the negative market and financial signals. The performance indicators that would have focused attention on the fundamental issues were often marginalized. Instead, alternative less threatening and diverting issues were attended to – reorganizations, restatements of values, new store openings and so on.

Eventually, other executives alarmed by the growing evidence and by the lack of forthright action or sense of urgency began to question the common understanding. The erstwhile consensus that had been reassuring and had served to reduce conflict and disagreement was beginning to be seen as problematic. This was not only because it now seemed possible that it was less distinctive than previously thought but also because it now seemed that it might no longer be effective for employees or customers and also because it tended to exclude other options.

But because executives shared so many assumptions and beliefs they found it hard not only to think about new possibilities but even to envisage ways in which such innovations could be generated. At this stage the executives almost literally did not know what to do.

In the event, the new circumstances (declining performance, significantly increased competitive pressure, indications of disquiet within the business, problems around senior succession) were initially addressed by two types of activity. On the one hand, there was a piecemeal introduction of modern management processes (development and training, cautious and limited executive team-building initiatives, performance management, supply chain redesign) which did not constitute a significant change in the assumptions underlying either business model or model of business and therefore were broadly acceptable to all members of the top team because they were not seen as at odds with the historic business model/model of business. On the other hand, there was an initiative to revive and refresh and re-emphasize the historic values and unique features of the organization through the relaunch of the business's values and the communication of these throughout the business. In short a major strategy was to surface, revive and reassert the historic assumptions and models. This initiative could be seen, in terms of the model used here, as an attempt to make the tacit model more explicit.

from conflict. Disagreement is seen as potentially 'conflict' partly because they are not used to disagreement and, partly, because they are not sure of, and are wary about, where it might lead.

Second, such teams usually have difficulty discussing and making decisions about strategy and organizational change because they have not had practice in having these discussions. Conventionally, key strategy and capability issues are resolved simply by applying the historic models. So, strategy issues are resolved simply by invoking the accepted and taken-for-granted models. Also, because of this historic lack of attention to strategy issues, such organizations have not usually developed the necessary structures to discuss and develop strategy. Top teams collectively in these organizations are unsure about their responsibilities for the development of strategies. Individual members do not feel sufficient responsibility for setting and monitoring strategy. As a result, governance issues become ambiguous and confused and the top team spend time addressing issues that are either in the distant future or in the near past. Also members of these teams have not usually developed the confidence and knowledge and experience to engage in debates about strategy – even if they see these as legitimate and as part of their responsibilities.

When, as a result of external performance pressures, the top team in the retail case was forced to acknowledge the need for a discussion of issues of both strategy and organizational change, a third issue arose that troubled them. On one level, it looked little different from the same issue facing any business: what should we do, how should we change? But it had an added dimension since these questions were not and in their view could not be answered simply in terms of market opportunities and their organizational requirements. For this organization, with its deep-seated tacit taken-for-granted assumptions about strategy and capability any decision on these issues had to be 'legitimate'. This was a favourite term of the chief executive when discussions about future directions were initiated: not only were the discussions themselves questionable, but the outcomes of any such discussion must be assessed not only or even primarily in terms of their likely business and organizational impacts but also in terms of their but being true to the historic models and assumptions of the business. This raised a serious, persuasive and as yet unresolved dilemma: should the business try to compete with the competition by being like them or by being different from them (and true to its tacit models)?

Organizations where the top team share strong tacit assumptions find it easy to generate commitment, but this could be at the expense of the quality of analysis. Under these circumstances, option for change are limited by the dominance of the historic model and the possibility of path dependency is strong. Those who advocate a review of the historic model or who advocate a break with it are likely to experience issues of legitimacy. Change if it is possible at all probably raises two difficulties. First, it occurs only within the tight constraints of the original model – that is, as *incremental revitalization*. Or, because the top team has little experience of analysis and assessment of options for strategy and organization, there may be a tendency to embrace too quickly and too uncritically new alternatives.

Type 2: divergent, submerged/unexplored conflicts

In many of the organizations, executives worked on the basis of divergent knowledge bases and divergent interpretive schemas. These differences were important enough:

but what made them even more important was that the existence, cause and consequences of these radically different cosmologies about how to manage at a strategic level coexisted in a tacit, implicit, unsurfaced and unexplored way. Managers found it difficult to understand why others took such radically different (and in their view misguided) approaches to a whole range of issues that they saw as critical to the success of the organization. Because the underlying assumptions and logics which informed and generated the fundamental differences were tacit, managers explained these differences in often personalized ways. This tendency fuelled suspicion and mistrust. The conflict was displaced from root issues and translated into arguments about the personal shortcomings and the merits of specific initiatives and proposals.

In circumstances such as those in the second case, while a range of assumptions and theories about business models and models of business coexist within the top team, these models are not brought forward for explicit examination. Those who try to surface differences are often described as 'poor team players'. People disagree – often passionately – but don't understand why they disagree and they may not even fully recognize or understood the theory that guides their own and others' convictions.

The existence of tacitly different sets of assumptions underpinning views on strategy and capability produces a number of consequences in these types of organization. First, diversity of views tend not to be positive in these circumstances because when disagreements occur neither side can understand the provenance of or grounds for the proposals for the other. They lack a common language and they lack a way of discussing that they lacked this language. In these sorts of case, differences become moralized and personalized.

Second, disagreement, because it is masked and distorted, creates mistrust and alienation. It tends to result in groups being even less able to communicate with each other.

Third, the issues at stake can be fundamental and in these cases it is crucial that a way be found to surface and assess the differences which exist within the top team. But since the source of the differences is usually unacknowledged, this debate does not usually take place. Each side simply explains the attitudes of the other by reference to stereotypes: 'old fashioned', 'traditional', 'reactionary', 'irresponsible', 'lacking understanding of our distinctive proposition' and so on.

Type 3: negotiated action

Executive knowledge under Type 3 situations is characterized by consensus around an explicitly stated knowledge of strategy and of business. In these cases – often characteristic of small to medium businesses where the original owner entrepreneur's vision of strategic and organization (and the links between the two) has generated success – all members of the top team are committed to this clear philosophy.

One clear example of this type of situation was found in a medium sized and rapidly growing engineering consultancy.

There are some inherent dilemmas for the design of change that characterize this third type based on the consensus/explicit model. First, because there is just one model, senior staff in these situations are often unable to think of alternate ways of achieving their ends. For example, if values are placed so centrally as in the engineering case, then management tends to be defined negatively. Hence, all issues of growth and development have to be resolved by normative methods. Hence, the dominant model limits the ability to think of other models. It also stymies the ability to think of alternative ways of achieving the same ends.

HRM in Action 8.2   The retail bank

The senior team in HighStreet Bank was committed to a strategy of innovation and were committed to ensuring the organization was geared up to achieve this strategy by encouraging innovation, a core strategic value. But members of the top team differed radically but implicitly in what they meant by innovation and in their view of the necessary organizational arrangements to achieve it. Two key features of the assumptions about strategy and capability held by members of the top team – that they were different but tacit – were displayed by the evident frustration felt by each camp about the views and actions of the other and by the inability of each group to understand the position and rationale of the other group and by the way that they assumed their own position was obvious and self-evident.

The result was a situation of considerable conflict, distrust, disappointment and frustration but these emotions were not directly expressed. There were few efforts made to understand the origins of the different approaches in different theories of business and organization.

Conflict between the two groups centred on the outputs of or proposals arising from the different models – actions taken or proposed by each side – not on the theories which informed these different positions. One group was guarded and conditional in their approach to innovation and saw it as potentially risky, irresponsible, childish. They saw the sort of organization necessary to achieve innovation as formal, structured, and controlling, containing many safeguards against the dangers of innovation: for example an elaborate and comprehensive innovation management system to filter out unworkable ideas. Innovation was defined by this group as a specialist function which needed to be tightly controlled by the market – facing product businesses. The necessary organizational culture was and should be deferential, hierarchical, cautious, compliant. The role of leadership was to preserve the business against the risks of unnecessary change and from unsuccessful and expensive innovation; to ensure that any permitted innovation did not threaten and could be subsumed by the organization and its historic features and strengths.

The other group saw innovation as central to everything the organization did. It was valued in the highest possible way. The necessary form of organization was one that did not stress controlling and filtering innovation but encouraged it. Innovation should be 'normal' and not the prerogative only of specialists. The culture should be enterprising, encouraging, positive, creative, tolerant of deviancy. The structure of the organization should be flat, changeable, fluid, with reduced numbers of and scope for senior managers.

Second, where there is a dominant single model accepted by all members of the top team, there is a tendency to inhibit creative and divergent thinking about change options. Decision making becomes easy – possibly too easy. As long as the model brings success, all is well, but when new ways of working are required these types of top team may have difficulty in identifying or objectively assessing proposals that are radically at odds with the historic models. They may also have difficulty dealing with difference and disagreement. The usual response to dissent is either to convert the dissenters or to remove them. When a situation arises that requires strategic management to 'appropriately adapt, integrate and reconfigure internal and external organizational skills, resources and functional competences to match the requirements of a

---

HRM in Action 8.3 The engineering consultancy

Engineering Consultancy undertakes sophisticated design work for all branches of the construction industry. The firm was formerly organized as a partnership but it is now a plc. The founder is still the CEO. Most of the senior staff are significant owners of equity. Most have been with the firm from the beginning. The firm has a clear and highly explicit philosophy – both business model and model of business – and sees the latter as critical to the former and views the former as the reason for the firm's success. These views on what the business should do and what it had to be like to achieve its goals have been developed and polished and refined over many years. Employees who do not accept these ideas are quickly identified as outsiders and deviants. The business model is built on innovation, flexibility, responsiveness, quality and valued-adding engineering. To be able to produce work of this sort required an organization which could attract, recruit retain and develop high-quality highly intelligent and creative people and to get the best out of them by not suppressing them with formal systems and management. Management was reduced to a minimum, the normal working organizational unit or cell is no more than 25 engineers. Control is exercised through a combination of high-profile charismatic leadership modelled on the founder; an accountancy system which enabled management to monitor the progress of all projects; and a strong set of shared values explicitly communicated: innovation, quality, responsiveness.

All executives agreed that the secret of the business's success stems from these closely related models of business and organization. Consensus is not only explicit it is celebrated; and the shared model is seen as a source of organizational strength. Commitment to the model is a prerequisite for membership of the team. The MD remarked of the top team: 'Over the years we've smoothed off the round edges.' Decision making is relatively easy because executives share a way of seeing the business, the organization and the marketplace. The problem with this model stems from an inherent contradiction: in order to ensure the continued ability of the firm to develop and retain its key staff it had to grow, because only growth would ensure that there were sufficient promotion opportunities to reward and retain the key staff who were actively encouraged to be ambitious and seek promotion. And the model required that able staff be encouraged to use their skills. But growth exposed the basic organizational model to strain – it raised the risk that the values would not be enough to hold together a larger organization, that new staff – possibly staff in a partner organization – did not develop commitment to the core values which were critical to organizational control (the risk, as one executive put it, that local staff would 'go native'). Growth in size coupled with greater geographical spread (growth was taking place through expansion in the Middle East) could also require more explicit management controls that were counter to the basic normative model. So, the steps necessary to sustain the model might actually threaten the model because these steps required the model to work in new and adverse circumstances.

---

changing environment' (Teece et al. 2002: 183), executives in explicit/consensual situations are likely to face a huge difficulty.

Finally, as in religious groups, the commitment of top teams to an explicit and dominant organizational/business model is often associated with a charismatic founder/entrepreneur who individually or through/with the top team develop the model. This makes for a series of possible problems for such organizations when the founder finally

leaves – issues of succession, problems associated with the inevitable institutionaliza-
tion of charisma and the possibility that, post the exit of the founder, disputes will
break out about the status and legitimacy and relevance of the original model.

Type 4: manifest conflict

In this type of executive team, knowledge is explicitly stated and multiple formulations come into conflict. This type – explicitly different view and approaches to
organization and business – is in theory the most functional and healthy of the four:
the existence of differences allows the possibility of innovation and the analysis of different models and scenarios theoretically opens up the possibility of calm and objective search for the most useful model. Difference, diversity, disagreement are
legitimate and explicit in this model. Openness to new possibilities, freedom from
historic recipes, the ability to think outside historic restraints should all be most possible under these circumstances.

This type in some respects seems to proffer the most favourable of options; there
can, nonetheless, be problems. A multiplicity of models can create a level of uncertainty and ambiguity that creates difficulty. There are too many choices and too few
ways (and not enough time) to choose between them. Executives need to make decisions about key issues facing their business. But, as Brunsson (2002) has usefully
noted, for decisions to initiate action, they require not only analysis but also motivation
and commitment, especially when the consequences of the decision are very great, as
they are for strategic and organizational decisions. Under these circumstances executives, according to Brunsson, certainly need to assess options but they also need and
seek to create certainty and there is evidence that focusing for too long on the complexities and choices of decision making can evoke uncertainty and hesitation.

Executives face two pressures: to make the right choices and to mobilize the team
and the organization to get things done. Achieving the balance between thorough discussion of differences and underlying models and mobilizing and motivating coherent
and consensual teams is difficult and not always achieved. As Brunsson and Olsen
(1993: 5) note, 'organizations face two problems: to choose the right thing to do and
to get it done'. Although the explicit/difference model supplies fertile ground for the
identification and analysis of different options, it also raises the risk that if there is
excess of choices this makes decision making difficult and also emphasizes analysis
and choice at the expense of commitment and action – outcomes which, of course, are
emphasized by the consensual models, although in turn raise other possible problems.

Conclusion

The emphasis in this chapter is on sense making and relationships at the top team
level and their implications for thinking about and decisions on change (Alvesson and
Karreman 2001). The chapter has argued that a focus on and an understanding of the
knowledge that underpins senior management thinking and decision making on
issues of strategy and organizational change (and of the perceived links between
these) are important for an understanding not only of the direction of organizational
change but of decisions about if and when change is necessary. The chapter has
argued for a view of managers' knowledge as *theoretical* knowledge – knowledge

---

HRM in Action 8.4   The high street retailer

Managers' knowledge: type 4

In this case, only one member of the top team had spent his career in the organization. All the others had joined in the past couple of years from outside and each from very different types of firm. Each of these firms of origin was highly successful and each therefore represented a viable, plausible, model. Moreover, their firms of origin had clear, explicit and dominant business models. These newly recruited senior executives brought with them their experiences of these successful ways of doing business. Indeed, their recruitment was impelled partly because of the experience they brought, from these competitors, of alternative models.

This retailer was, at the time of the research, undergoing a performance crisis as the historic boundaries between types of retailer and product specialization were aggressively eroded: food retailers moved into non-food, or into books, cosmetics and so on and so, for this retailer, this wealth of detailed knowledge of alternative business models was at once both liberating and confusing. Previously, the retailer had operated with an explicit and consensual business model and model of business, which was strongly historically based with clear normative elements. But performance issues had caused the top team to conclude that new models were necessary – hence the recruitment of executives from outside bringing with them clear but very different models and experience.

---

asserts causal connections between forms of structure and identified organizational effects: knowledge that generates understanding and interpretation and underpins judgement, or 'propositional statements' (Tsoukas and Vladimirou 2001: 983).[2] This form (or view) of knowledge, was, as Tsoukas and Mylonopoulos (2004: S2) point out, anticipated many years ago by Bell when he remarked that in the post-industrial society what is decisive for the organization is 'the centrality of theoretical knowledge that ... can be used to illuminate many different and varied areas of experience' (Bell, 1999: 20).

Executives' decisions on issues of strategy and capability are informed and justified by their views of what is best and how to achieve it – their propositional knowledge about their organization, how it 'works' and its efficiency. Although strategy and change are frequently presented as if they are a direct and unmediated organizational response to changing environmental circumstances this chapter has argued for a reinstatement of managers as active and creative agents in decision making about the future of their businesses (Brunsson 2002: 215).

This chapter has not focused on the specific content of managers' theories of organization but instead has offered a classification of some key features of this knowledge which, it is argued, play an important role in influencing how and when, indeed if, change is considered and how it is considered. This framework comprises four categories based on the cross-relationship of two key distinctions. One of these distinctions – tacit/explicit – is a familiar one but it has not previously been applied to strategic-level knowledge, though Polanyi does note that our skills in the use of tools – including intellectual tools – i.e. knowledge – can become so taken for granted that we no longer realize we are using them. What he calls 'indwelling' (Polanyi 1962: 59; Tsoukas and

Vladimirou 2001). The other distinction, consensus/differentiated, although familiar from the organizational literature, is less common within the KM literature but this too can be a source of interpretative insights, we believe.

The research reported here confirms not only that senior managers hold (often very strongly) knowledge that underpins and informs their views on what their organization should (and should not) seek to achieve and on how their organization should be structured to achieve these purposes – which, in turn, inform their views on the need for change and the type of change that is required – but also suggests that the two key distinctions, tacit/explicit and consensual/differentiated, when combined, are useful for understanding how senior managers think about, analyse and make decisions on key issues of business strategy and organization (and for how they see the linkages between these) and thus how and when they think about change. Many analyses of senior management strategic thinking with reference to attitudes to change have noted the obstacles to innovative thinking; the vulnerability to path dependency and other barriers to clear, open and well-based strategic thinking; or have noted the strategic errors that such obstacles generate or extolled the virtues of the ability to think strategically and organizationally beyond the constraints of established routines and recipes. This research helps us understand both the nature of these obstacles or, possibly, the sources of the ability of strategic management to achieve the sorts of radical reconfiguration of strategy, organization and competence defined by Teece et al. and others as the source of competitive advantage (Teece et al. 2002: 183). The research suggests that the nature and quality of top team thinking may well be influenced by the features of the knowledge that underpins it.

Since issues of organizational structure and performance are important for senior members, differences in views on how or if and when the organization should be changed will be held intensely and, since organizations frequently involve and invoke values in their structure, objectives and dynamics, will be defined in moralized terms as well as in terms of efficiency. If, as Tsoukas and Mylonopoulos (2004) argue 'the ongoing development of organizational knowledge is, or can be a dynamic capability that leads to continuous organizational development of knowledge assets', then the analysis of the knowledge underpinning key strategic decisions and of the degree and ways in which this knowledge is tacit, explicit, consensual or differentiated is critical to an understanding of the possibility of executives achieving this critical capability.

Brunsson (2002) has usefully noted that for decisions to initiate action, they require not only analysis but also motivation and commitment, especially when the consequences of the decision are very great, as they are for strategic and organizational decisions. Under these circumstances, executives, according to Brunsson, certainly need to assess options but they also need and seek to create certainty and there is evidence that focusing for too long on the complexities and choices of decision making can evoke uncertainty and hesitation.

The change literature displays some puzzling features: that change is critical to success, that senior managers seem to recognize this (judging by the frequency and quantity of change initiatives) but still many/most change programmes fail. This chapter has argued that one way of illuminating this puzzle may be to focus on the way in which (and the occasions on which) change is designed by senior managers and thus to reinstate managers to their full and proper role as agents of change and not as mere relays in the transmission of pervasive or fashionable ideas about organizational restructuring. The chapter has argued that two features of the knowledge held by members of the senior executive team have a significant influence on some key dynamics of management thinking on issues of strategic and organizational change – encouraging or discouraging open analysis of issues and options and decisions. The key to the ability of the top team to design change that supports future success organizational change – lies in the ability of the top team to understand, reflect on and move beyond the sets of propositional knowledge and established logics that have underpinned historic success and to define their own routes through the many siren voices that surround them – whether these are the voices of history or the external choruses with 'the power of truth, the potency of rationality and the promises of effectivity' (Miller and Rose 1990: 51).

Notes

1. The ideas explored in this chapter were developed within the ESRC project entitled 'Managers' roles in the evolution of business knowledge' led by John Storey, Graeme Salaman and Richard Holti: 2003–2006 part of the Evolution of Business Knowledge Programme, ESRC project code RES-334-25-0008.

2. Tsoukas and Vladimirou (2001) suggest that judgement requires two steps: judgement involves a series of steps. It requires ordering phenomena into categories and it requires an assessment of these by criteria. It could be argued that the structure of the argument of this paper involves precisely these steps.

References

Abrahamson, E. (1996). 'Management fashion', *Academy of Management Review* 21(1): 254–85.

Alvesson, M. and D. Karreman (2001). 'Odd couple: making sense of the curious concept of knowledge management', *Journal of Management Studies* 38(7): 995–1018.

Beer, M. and N. Nohria (2000). 'Cracking the code of change', *Harvard Business Review* May/Jun 78: 3.

Beer, M., R. A. Eisenstadt and B. Spector (1990). 'Why change programs don't produce change', *Harvard Business Review* Nov/Dec: 158–66.

Bell, D. (1999). *The Coming of the Post-Industrial Society*, New York, Basic Books.

Bettis, R. A. and C. K. Prahalad (1995). 'The dominant logic: retrospective and extension', *Strategic Management Journal* 16: 5–14.

Brunsson, N. (2002). 'The irrationality of action and action irrationality: decisions, ideologies and organizational actions', in G. Salaman (ed.) *Decision Making for Business*. London: Sage.

Brunsson, N. and J. P. Olsen (1993). *The Reforming Organization*. London, Routledge.

Chia, R. and R. Holt (2006). 'Strategy as practical coping: a Heideggerian perspective', *Organization Studies* 27(5): 635–56.

Child, J. (1972). 'Organizational structure, environment and performance: the role of strategic choice', *Sociology* 6: 1–21.

Davenport, T. and L. Prusak (1998). *Working Knowledge: How Organizations Manage What they Know*. Boston, MA, Harvard Business School Press.

du Gay, P., G. Salaman and B. Rees (1996). 'The conduct of management and the management of conduct: contemporary managerial discourse and the constitution of the "competent" manager', *Journal of Management Studies* 33: 263–82.

Ghoshal, S., G. Piramal and C. A. Bartlett (2000). *Managing Radical Change*. New Delhi, Viking.

Giddens, A. (1968). '"Power" in the recent writings of Talcott Parsons', *Sociology* 2(3): 257–72.

Grant, R. M. (1996). 'Towards a knowledge-based theory of the firm', *Strategic Management Journal* 17 (Special issue): 109–22.

Greenwood, R. and C. R. Hinings (1993). 'Understanding strategic change: the contribution archetypes', *Academy of Management Journal* 36(5): 1052–81.

Greenwood, R. and C. R. Hinings (1996). 'Understanding radical organizational change: bringing together the old and the new institutionalism', *Academy of Management Review* 21(4): 1022–54.

Hamel, G. and C. K. Prahalad (1993). 'Strategy as stretch and leverage', *Harvard Business Review* Mar–Apr: 75–83.

Habermas, J. (1971). *Towards a Rational Society*. London, Heinemann.

Henderson, R. M. and K. B. Clark (2002). 'Architectural innovation: the reconfiguartion of existing product technologies and the failure of established firms', in M. Mazzucato (ed.) *Strategy for Business*. London, Sage.

Hodgkinson, G. and P. Sparrow (2002). *The Competent Organization*. Buckingham, Open University Press.

Karpik, L. (1978). 'Organizations, institutions and history', in L. Karpik (ed.) *Organization and Environment*. Sage, London.

Keat, R. (1990). 'Introduction', in R. Keat and N. Abercrombie (eds) *Enterprise Culture*. London, Routledge.

Keiser, A. (1997). 'Rhetoric and myth in management fashion', *Organization* 4(1): 49–74.

Kotter, J. P. (1996). *Leading Change*. Boston, MA, Harvard Business School Press.

Lant, T. K., F. J. Milliken and B. Batra (2002). 'The role of managerial and interpretation in strategic persistence and reorientation', in G. Salaman (ed.) *Decision Making for Business*. London: Sage.

Lawrence, P. R. and G. S. Lorsch (1967). *Organization and Environment*. Boston, MA, Harvard Business School Press.

Miller, P. and N. Rose (1990). 'Governing economic life', *Economy and Society* 19(1): 9–31.

Mintzberg, H. and J. A. Waters (1985). 'Of strategies deliberate and emergent', *Strategic Management Journal*, 6: 257–72.

Newman, J. (2002). 'Managerialism and social welfare', in G. Salaman (ed.) *Decision Making For Business*. London, Sage.

Newman, J. (2005). 'Bending bureaucracy: leadership and multi-level governance', in P. du Gay (ed.) *The Values of Bureaucracy*, Oxford, Oxford University Press, pp. 191–210.

Nonaka, I. and H. Takeuchi (1995). *The Knowledge-Creating Company: How Japanese Companies Create The Dynamics of Innovation*. New York, Oxford University Press.

Palmer, D. A., P. D. Jennings and X. Zhou (1993). 'Late adoption of the multidivisional form by large US corporations: institutional, political and economic accounts', *Administrative Science Quarterly* 38: 100–31.

Pettigrew, A. and R. Whipp (1991). *Managing Change for Competitive Success*. Oxford, Blackwell.

Polanyi, M., (1962) *Personal Knowledge*. Chicago, Ill., The University of Chicago Press.

Polanyi, M. (1967). *The Tacit Dimension*. Garden City, NY, Anchor Books.

Ranson, S., C. R. Hinings and R. Greenwood (1980). 'The structuring of organizational structures', *Administrative Science Quarterly* 25: 1–17.

Rose, N. (1989). *Governing The Soul*. London, Routledge.

Salaman, J. G. (1982). 'Managing the frontier of control', in A. Giddens and G. Mackenzie (eds) *Social Class and the Division of Labour*, Cambridge, Cambridge University Press, pp. 46–62.

Salaman, J. G. (2005). 'Bureaucracy and Beyond: Managers and Leaders in the "Post-Bureaucratic" Organisation', in P. du Gay (ed.) *The Values of Bureaucracy*, Oxford, Oxford University Press, pp. 141–64.

Spender, J. C. (1989). *Industry Recipes: The Nature and Source of Managerial Judgements*. Cambridge, MA, Blackwell.

Spender, J. C. and R. M. Grant (1996). 'Knowledge and the firm: overview', *Strategic Management Journal* 17 (Special issue): 5–10.

Storey, J. and G. Salaman (2005a). *Managers of Innovation*. Oxford, Blackwell.

Storey, J. and G. Salaman (2005b). 'The knowledge work of general managers', *Journal of General Management* 31 (2): 57–73.

Teece, D. J., G. Pisano and A. Shuen (2002). 'Dynamic capabilities and strategic management', in M. Mazzucato (ed.) *Strategy for Business*. London, Sage.

Tsoukas, H. (1996). 'The firm as a distributed knowledge system: a constructionist approach', *Strategic Management Journal* 17 (Winter Special issue): 11–25.

Tsoukas, H. and N. Mylonopoulos (2004). 'Introduction: knowledge construction and creation in organizations', *British Journal of Management* 15: S1–S8.

Tsoukas, H. and E. Vladimirou (2001). 'What is organizational knowledge?', *Journal of Management Studies* 38 (7): 973–93.

Valentin, E. K. (2002). 'Anatomy of a fatal business decision', in J. G. Salaman (ed.) *Decision Making for Business*. London, Sage.

Whittington, R. (2002). 'The work of strategising and organising: from a practical perspective', *Strategic Organization* 1(1): 119–27.

Whittington, R. (2006). 'Completing the practice turn in strategy research', *Organization Studies* 27(5): 613–34.

Worrall, L., C. Cooper and F. Campbell (2000). 'The impact of organizational change on UK managers' perceptions of their working lives', in R. J. Burke and C. L. Cooper (eds) *The Organization in Crisis*. Oxford, Blackwell.

Reward choices: strategy and equity

Ian Kessler

Introduction

Around a decade ago, one of the leading US academics on reward, Gomez-Mejia (1993: 4) stated that

> The emerging paradigm of the (pay) field is based on a strategic orientation where issues of internal equity and external equity are viewed as secondary to the firm's need to use pay as an essential integrating and signalling mechanism to achieve overarching business objectives.

Capturing the essence of the 'new pay' approach, it was a statement that highlighted an interest in the link between rewards and corporate performance among practitioners, researchers and other commentators. This accorded with a more general concern among these stakeholders about how HR practices related to competitive 'success', while clearly privileging pay as a particularly powerful means of achieving it. As presented by Gomez-Mejia, this strategic approach to pay was based on a number of premises: first, that there were three fundamental principles on which pay systems and structures might be founded: business strategy, external equity and internal equity; second, that these were competing or alternative principles that organizations might choose to weight in different ways; and third, in terms of emerging practice, that organizations were increasingly attaching importance to business strategy at the expense of the principles associated with equity.

The statement and these premises might be interpreted and used in furthering debates on reward in different ways. If one accepts that the three pay principles are distinct and competing, they provide a useful means of reviewing changes in organizational approaches to reward in recent years. Has organizational practice shifted, as predicted, from equity to business strategy? The statement might also be seen to shed light on the analytical approaches adopted in the mainstream SHRM literature to reward. It is tempting to view the assumption that business strategy competes with internal and external equity as misconceived; thus, one might argue that 'fairness' of treatment in pay (or other) terms is likely to play an important part in generating the kinds of employee attitudes and behaviours needed to further business goals. However, the presentation of the pay principles in this way is indicative of a research approach that placed limited emphasis on issues of equity and process in looking at the relationship between pay and business strategy. To what extent do these analytical assumptions still hold in studying pay within the broader SHRM context?

The chapter uses the pay principles to map recent changes in pay practice in Britain. It is divided into four main parts; the first outlines how pay systems and structures can be related to business strategy, internal equity and external equity; the succeeding three take each in turn and consider how and to what extent they are reflected in current pay practice. It will be argued that, rather than a pay paradigm principally based on business strategy, internal and external equity are assuming increasing importance. As a subtext, the chapter considers research approaches to the study of pay and corporate performance. It will be suggested that the plausibility of a statement that views equity and business strategy as competing pay principles has been overtaken by a perspective that regards them as closely related.

Definitions and practices: strategy and equity as pay principles

The principles of business strategy, internal and external equity have informed but rarely structured conceptual frameworks related to reward. A traditional starting point has been the recognition that reward can be broadly defined. As Bloom and Milkovich (1992: 22) note reward is a 'bundle of returns offered in exchange for a cluster of employee contributions'. This draws attention to the wide range of benefits available to management in compensating employees, although such a broad definition necessitates some refinement to distinguish different types of benefit. The distinction between intrinsic and extrinsic reward acknowledges that benefits may be more or less tangible, in the latter case taking the form of concrete, material goods and in the former less solid outcomes such as a positive feeling or emotion. Extrinsic rewards can be further divided into pay and non-pay benefits, but while a considerable array of non-pay benefits are available, including medical insurance, company cars, leave and welfare facilities, it is pay that has traditionally been the centrepiece of the reward package.

The design of pay systems and structures has typically (Mahoney 1989) been seen to revolve around three key contingencies – job, person and performance – but an attempt can be made to map Gomez-Mejia's principles onto them. This is relatively unproblematic in the case of *internal and external equity*. Pay structures have normally been founded on the job, comprising grades that embrace occupations of equivalent value to the organization; the more valuable the job to the organization, the higher the grade and the pay. The key issue confronting organizations is how to determine job value and it is in this context that consideration is often given to internal and external equity.

In general, internal equity relates to the ranking of jobs found within the organization according to their relative worth. Typically, this is established by the application of job evaluation techniques. In its most systematic form this emerges as analytical job evaluation, a process that identifies key dimensions of a role, for example knowledge required, levels of responsibility, problem-solving activity and then measures each using a standard scoring system to arrive at a points total. However, the importance of the job to the organization might equally be founded on external equity, in others words, be related to the state of the labour market for a given occupation. Clearly, occupational groups in high demand and short supply assume a higher value to an organization than those more readily available and on these grounds may receive a higher rate of pay.

The principles of internal and external equity often complement one another. Having established a pay structure based on internal job worth, an organization might set the pay rates for this structure by positioning itself in the external labour market, paying say at the median or upper quartile rate for comparative jobs in the area or region. However, the principles of internal and external equity can sometimes be in tension. It may, for instance, be easier to recruit and retain those from an occupational group rated highly in a job evaluation exercise than it is to acquire and keep those from a group rated less highly. In such circumstances, an organization might pay a market supplement to the latter group, reflecting their higher external labour market worth, but preserving the broader integrity of a pay structure founded on internal equity.

The relationship between *business strategy* and pay can be seen to equate more directly to person and performance than to job. Business strategies in large part depend on the employment of workers with the necessary skills, attitudes and behaviours to deliver the product or service and, in general, organizations seek to ensure that they acquire these through linking pay to person and/or performance. This linkage is usually the basis for the organization's pay system, a mechanism by which employees progress within and between job-based grades. Progression within grade occurs in two main ways. First, pay systems allow for movement up a grade, either according to fixed incremental points or, more flexibly, between single minimum and a maximum scale points. Such movement is usually consolidated into base pay. Second, they generate one-off, non-consolidated payments, often seen as constituting

Pay principles and contingencies | Figure 9.1

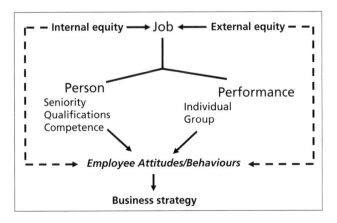

the variable element of pay. Such payments may be in addition to increases in base pay or assume the sole means of pay up-rating.

Progression in both senses can be linked to person and or performance. Employees might be paid according to the personal characteristics they bring to the job or develop over time. Pay is being related to employee inputs whether in the form of qualifications, experience, skills or capabilities. In relating pay to performance, the emphasis shifts from inputs to outputs. These outputs might derive from the activities of the individual or the collective, providing the foundation for different types of pay system; in the case of the former, for instance, piecework, sales commission and merit-based schemes and in relation to the latter profit sharing, share ownership and team-based pay. Depending on the nature of the performance being rewarded, different attitudes and behaviours are being encouraged or reinforced. In crude terms, piecework schemes, for example, encourage volume production; profit sharing and share ownership schemes might be seen to foster loyalty and commitment; while merit-based schemes seek to ensure the completion of clearly defined, individual work-related objectives.

In summary, business strategy, internal and external equity can crudely be seen to relate to the pay contingencies – job, person and performance – often seen as the basis for pay structures and systems. As Figure 9.1 indicates, the relationship between internal and external equity is key to establishing job worth, the foundation of pay structures; while business strategy has been tied to performance and person, the criteria driving the operation of pay systems and ensuring that attitudes and behaviours are tied to the pursuit of business goals. It is a picture that needs to be qualified in two respects. First, issues of equity, and particularly internal equity, can additionally be seen as important in understanding the operation of pay systems as well as structures, not least in relation to how performance is given effect in this context. Second, issues of pay equity as they relate to job worth also have a significant bearing on employee attitudes and behaviour and by implication the pursuit of a business strategy. These qualifications will be returned to in the succeeding sections.

Business strategy

The 'new' or 'strategic' approach to pay, heralded by various commentators in the early 1990s (Lawler 1995), retains a strong hold over prescriptive approaches to reward and continues to influence practitioners as they frame their policies. As Peter Reilly, from the Institute of Employment Studies recently noted: 'All organisations should develop remuneration systems aligned with business needs and are adaptable to changing circumstances' (CIPD 2006). More compelling perhaps is evidence to suggest that corporate discourses on pay are still informed by such language. Over the last five years CIPD reward surveys have consistently indicated that among organizations with a reward strategy, 'supporting business goals' is by far the most common objective. In 2005, for example, almost 80% suggested this was the primary reward objective (CIPD 2005). This is reflected in Table 9.1, which presents the importance attached by organizations to different sorts of reward goal. While some significant differences in emphasis between private and public sector organizations are highlighted, in general, these findings appear to provide support to Gomez-Mejia's suggested ranking of principles; the support of business goals and a concern with high employee performance outscore concerns with external market rates or internal equity as reward objectives.

Given the apparent importance of business strategy as a pay goal, the most immediate question to pose is what is meant by this support? Most typically, such support emerges as a presentational attempt to ensure that the principles underpinning the reward system support broader organizational values and beliefs. In introducing a new pay structure in 2005, BT announced that 'in line with strategic priorities, this approach to reward increases our ability to motivate our people and live the values, while achieving competitive advantage through cost leadership' (EReward 2005: 10). More specifically, the pay-strategy link comes to the fore in a merger situation where a company uses pay to help to manufacture a new corporate culture by aligning pay principles with broader corporate values. GlaxoSmithKline, for instance, put in place an approach to reward that embodied the new GSK 'spirit of entrepreneurship, innovation and performance'. This 'prioritised the importance of individual performance', the previous reward system placing much less emphasis on this criterion (EReward 2003: 5).

The pursuit of this kind of alignment is even more tangibly reflected in attempts by organizations to use rewards to encourage particular employee attitudes and behaviours that advance corporate objectives. Over the last 20 years these attempts have been informed by a prescriptive rhetoric that has shifted emphasis. The mid 1980s saw the emergence of individual performance-related pay, which in its most structured and robust form was seen as a means of locking the employee into the organization by linking pay to the achievement of individual objectives derived from those set at the corporate level. The mid-1990s' 'backlash' against what was increasingly seen as a rigid approach to pay, placing weight on the single-minded pursuit of such objectives regardless of the consequences for interpersonal relations with colleagues or customers, took the form of a heightened interest in competency-based pay. Rewarding employees for the acquisition and application of 'soft' capabilities or 'harder'

Importance of reward strategy goals — Table 9.1

	%	
	Public	Private
Support business goals	71	85
Reward high performance	66	79
Recruit and retain high performers	49	75
Achieve/maintain market competitiveness	34	64
Manage pay costs	63	54
Link pay to market	23	53
Ensure internal equity	60	30
[n = 323]	60	30

Source: CIPD 2003

accredited skills, it was premised on the belief that *how* tasks were achieved was as important as *what* was achieved in narrow, output terms. Rewarding capabilities assumed particular significance in service sector organizations involving regular customer interaction and in production industries and beyond where team working demanded cooperation with colleagues. Indeed, the apparent growth of team working encouraged an interest in linking pay not only to team behaviours but to team outputs as well. Such an approach found strong endorsement in the Makinson Report (2001) on the civil service pay and encouraged the adoption of team pay on a pilot basis in some of the largest civil service executive agencies such as the Benefits Agency and Customs & Excise.

By the new millennium, however, interest had turned to an approach that recognized the need to link pay to person and performance, both being seen as essential to the pursuit of business strategies. Captured by the term 'contribution-based pay', it was an approach that suggested that to leverage pay to 'best effect' in pursuing business goals pay should be linked to various input *and* output measures at individual and group level. As Brown and Armstrong (1999: xiii), noted: 'Pay for Contribution should form part of an integrated and strategic approach to reward. This needs to flow from and support, the business strategy; be related to the needs of all stakeholders; and use an appropriate mix of total rewards.'

On closer inspection, however, serious doubts emerge as to how meaningfully and effectively organizations have been able to link pay to business strategy. These doubts take different forms. First, they relate to the extent to which organizations are actually pursuing a top-down, rational approach to pay. While most of the organizations in the CIPD (2003) survey with a reward strategy seek to relate reward to business goals, well under half (45%) of the organizations in this survey actually had a written reward strategy or were in the process of devising one. Even more striking is the fact that only 6% of the respondents in this survey felt their reward strategy was 'fully aligned' with their business strategy. Moreover, other evidence indicating that few organizations appear to evaluate whether pay objectives have been met is hardly suggestive of a strategic approach (Corby et al. 2002).

More profoundly, care is needed in assuming that organizations adopt an economic rationale for the design of their pay systems; in other words, that they seek to relate pay to business strategy in some kind of means–end way. While research attempts to explore the normative pressures on organizational approaches to the selection of pay systems remain limited, there is evidence to suggest such influences. External isomorphic pressures, particularly of a mimetic kind, are reflected in the fashions that have been associated with payment systems such as IPRP and can be seen at work in the shared pay practices adopted by civil services executive agencies on pay devolution in the mid-1990s (PTC 1996). The strength of internal norms is highlighted in Ahlstrand's (1990) Esso Fawley case study, where productivity pay agreements became so deeply embedded in the 'fabric' of the organization as a symbol of constructive management action, that they continued long after any proven link between pay and productivity in the plant had vanished.

Second, doubts on the pay–strategy link relate to the actual use of these different practices, with evidence suggesting the low take-up of some of the newer systems. As Table 9.2 indicates, few organizations have adopted pure forms of team-based or competency pay. It is equally striking that a limited proportion of organizations, barely a quarter, have adopted an approach to salary progression purely based on individual performance. Certainly the data in this table focus on base pay, therefore excluding consideration of variable pay. Indeed, it is striking that the same CIPD (2005) survey showed that a significant proportion (44%) of organizations relate cash bonuses to individual performance. However, these data confirm the picture presented in other recent surveys (EReward 2004), which suggest that there are certain barriers to the adoption of systems that relate pay to the team performance, competence and even individual performance.

Third, there are doubts that relate to the operational difficulties confronting these pay schemes. These difficulties have been well rehearsed and do not require a detailed restatement. However, in brief, team pay has faced difficulties in establishing standards of team performance that could be linked to pay and problems in identifying viable teams for pay purposes (Armstrong 1996). The implementation of competency pay has been plagued by measurement difficulties, especially where competencies have been defined in 'soft' behavioural terms (Sparrow 1996). The operational difficulties associated with individual performance related pay have been even more intensively discussed. Drawing on various types of research evidence, these have ranged from broad concerns that IPRP is likely to create instrumental forms of compliance from employees, so undermining creativity and discretionary behaviour (Kohn 1983), to more detailed, technical concerns about the 'efficacy' of procedural elements associated with objective setting, performance appraisal and pay determination (Kessler and Purcell 1992).

In a more general sense, the ways in which operational difficulties readily undermine the pay–business strategy link connects to a longer standing research literature on the subversion and decay of pay systems. Classic ethnographic studies focusing, in particular, on piecework schemes in manufacturing industry, have highlighted the way in which pay systems are invariably subject to social and political pressures (Lupton 1963; Whyte 1955). Pay systems, as a series of rules that have to be applied in situated contexts, are inevitably modified and subverted to meet local circumstances. Indeed, in practice, they become subject to pressures from groups, most obviously employees and line managers, seeking to control and manipulate them in pursuit of their own interests.

Criteria governing pay progression	Table 9.2

	% of organizations
Individual performance and skill/competency	63
Linked to market rates	44
Wholly based on individual performance	27
Service-related increments	20
Linked to team performance	12
Wholly based on skills	6
Wholly based on competences	5

Source: CIPD Reward Survey 2005: 5

Finally and perhaps most fundamentally, doubts about the link between pay and business strategy revolve around the theoretical plausibility and empirical strength of the relationship. It is implicit in discussion about the pay–strategy link that the adoption of a pay practice related to person or performance will generate employee attitudes and behaviours likely to advance the pursuit of business objectives. Indeed, this is in line with assumptions underpinning a broader SHRM literature on the association between various HR practices and business performance. Debate has raged about the nature of this association. Attention has increasingly focused on the impact of bundles of such practices, somewhat at odds therefore with the 'champions' of the 'new pay' approach, which privileges remuneration as the key lever. More significant, however, has been the tension between competing models of SHRM with different implications for pay practice.

A 'best practice' model, suggesting that business 'success' is dependent on fostering employee commitment, has sparked debate about which reward systems create committed employees. The absence of consensus on this issue is reflected in the range of different reward practices included within lists of high-commitment bundles (Kessler 2001). Individual performance-related pay, in particular, has attracted considerable attention in this respect. Some have seen it as a harsh, judgmental approach, likely to elicit only temporary compliance (Wood 1996), while others have viewed it as at least likely to generate a calculative commitment.

The 'best fit' model suggests that 'competitive success' is dependent on matching HR practices including those related to pay to different contingent circumstances. It is a model that has a somewhat stronger 'pedigree' in pay terms than the 'best practice' model in representing the most recent manifestation of Lupton and Gowler's (1969) contingency approach. This suggested that the 'appropriateness' of a pay system is likely to reside in matching the pay system to the managerial objectives and the organization's internal and external circumstances. It is a model which, in a general sense, has some plausibility and empirical support. The prevalence of certain types of payment system in industries over a number of years, such as piecework in the clothing and footwear industries, is indicative of a match between such systems and particular technologies. In its more recent manifestations, this model has posited a relationship between pay practices and competitive strategy (Schuler and Jackson 1987) and the organizational lifecycle (Kochan and Barrochi 1985).

The 'best resource' approach, drawing on the resource-based view of the firm to explore the relationship between HR practices and corporate performance, has less explicitly highlighted the role played by pay systems in this respect. Looking more generally at how employees as a rare, inimitable, non-substitutable and value-adding resource contribute to 'sustained competitive advantage', it is an approach that might, nonetheless, be seen to have implications for the relationship between pay and business strategy. For example, in terms of 'human capital advantage' (Boxall 1996) the 'attractiveness' of a reward package might clearly be expected to play a role in attracting and retaining employees with distinctive capabilities. Indeed attention has been drawn to the use of deferred forms of reward – pension schemes, share options and even standard seniority pay – in helping to build the 'resource mobility barriers' (Mueller 1996) needed to ensure that key employees remain in the organization. Less tangibly pay systems might contribute to 'human process advantage', supporting distinctive employee routines through the reward of the relevant attitudes and behaviours.

While based on competing assumptions, these models share a failure to theorize and test the relationship between a given pay practice, employee responses and the pursuit of business objectives. Limited attention is given to how or why any given pay practice might elicit employee commitment or generate behaviours compatible say with a cost- or quality-based competitive strategy. The debate over the status of IPRP as a high-commitment practice is testament to the theoretical complexities surrounding the relationship between pay, individual and organizational performance. However, it is a debate that somewhat misses the point about the nature of these complexities. To argue over whether IPRP is or is not a HCM practice is to overlook the fact that it could be either depending on managerial intention. By proposing a mechanistic link between a given pay practice and employee outcomes, meaning is ignored and, more importantly, why such a relationship might exist. But, at a more basic level, much of the research founded on these models simply fails to test this link. This is apparent in research exploring the best practice model, which has often revealed a positive relationship between such practices and various organizational outcomes (Richardson and Thompson 1999), but has not sought to establish whether such practices have generated the assumed employee attitudes and behaviours. Such an approach to pay practices and outcomes helps explains Gomez-Mejia original statement. If pay practices, variously related to person or performance, are assumed to generate the necessary worker attitudes and behaviours in a mechanistic and unproblematic way, any concern with equity, which might affect such employee responses, remains incidental. It is only when attempts are made to theorize the relationship between pay and the achievement of business goals that issues of equity, process and meaning re-emerge as important.

External equity

External equity is an organizational imperative. Organizations cannot survive if they fail to pay 'competitive' labour market rates to attract employees with the skills needed to provide a service or manufacture a product. This is not a purely mechanistic task of paying the equilibrium market clearing rate where the supply of labour meets demand as classical labour economist would have us believe. Institutional labour economists have consistently highlighted a range of pay rates for a given occupation within defined geographical area, suggesting that there is a zone of pay discretion (Gerhart and Rynes 2003). Indeed various models have been presented, such as efficiency wage theory, to suggest why employers might pay above the market rate.

However, this section argues that beyond the ongoing need for organization to give careful consideration to how pay relates to the market, over recent years there have been labour market pressures pushing external equity to the top of the pay agenda. The centrality of this is reflected in Table 9.1, which indicates that in the private sector almost two-thirds of organization view 'achieving and maintaining market competitiveness' as an 'important' reward goal. There are a number of very real pressures that lend credence to it.

For over a decade labour markets in Britain have been tight, with levels of unemployment at historically low levels. The National Employers' Skill Survey (Learning and Skills Council 2005: 24) found that 18% of organizations had a vacancy in 2004, up from 14% in 2001. The proportion of establishments reporting 'hard to fill vacancies' is lower at one in 10, but this is a figure that has remained stubbornly constant in the last few years. Labour market pressures have been intensified by a skills gap with one in five establishments (20%) in the survey revealing a skill shortage in their work-force. These difficulties do vary somewhat between industry and occupation, with shortages among professionals such as nurses, teachers and social workers in the pub-lic service receiving a particularly high profile among policymakers and commenta-tors. Organizational sensitivity to the external labour market has also been affected by the changing nature of the workforce, which has seen a growth in service sector employment and, partly related, in female participation in the workforce (Robinson 2003).

These external labour market pressures have been apparent in a number of developments in pay practice. First, they have encouraged organizations to place greater weight on comparing their wages with external rates in the process of pay determination. As a recent review of the pay scene noted, 'Benchmarking salary lev-els has been given more priority in the past few years as unemployment has fallen and labour markets have tightened' (IDS 2004). This sensitivity to external rates has weakened the emphasis on relating pay to individual performance in some organiza-tions. As this same review continues: 'Employers dissatisfied with the PRP systems have altered them to reflect more of the market influence.' A more recent report reinforces these observations: 'Prompted by tightening labour markets … many employers have moved away from one dimensional approaches to [pay] progres-sions towards more complex schemes involving two or more measures' (IDS 2006a). Moreover, in times of low inflation modest annual increases in the paybill have been 'eaten away' by the need to maintain competitive salaries, leaving little left for individual performance. This has been highlighted as a particular problem in the finance sector where 'employers are struggling to fulfil employees' expectations with pay systems which remain hybrids of market based and performance related approaches' (IDS 2003a).

Second, attention has increasingly focused on how to cope with uneven external labour market pressures, particularly as they relate to region and or occupation. It was a concern that received high prominence in the public sector when in April 2003 the Chancellor announced that: 'In future remits for pay review bodies and pub-lic sector workers will include a stronger local and regional dimension.' Such an approach clearly threatened to subvert national pay arrangements in different parts on this sector, a prospect that not only enraged the trade unions on the grounds that it undermined 'transparency and fairness', but many public sector employers, espe-cially in local government (Local Government Pay Commission 2003). Local govern-ment employers did not deny uneven pressures but saw them as more nuanced, relating to local 'hot spots' rather than to region or to generic occupational groups. Indeed, the character to these pressures has encouraged 'light touch' and flexible responses. In the private service sector, where 'outside of London and the South East there is not a great deal of variation [in pay] which is intrinsically regional', allowan-ces have often been used to complement national arrangements. At Barclays Bank, for example, a London allowance has been extended across much of the south with a decreasing amount paid as the distance from central London increases (IDS 2003b). The 'modernization of pay' in the public sector has typically made provision for recruitment and retention supplements to be paid at the discretion of local employ-ers. These supplements have been available within the context of national framework arrangements for pay as with Agenda for Change in the NHS and agreements for uni-versity staff and teachers.

Third, responses to external labour market pressures have emerged in the modification of internal grading structures. In moves that echo the development of internal labour markets originally designed to hoard labour as a protection against the competition for it in tight labour market circumstances, organizations have been developing pay structures that can attract and retain staff. A grading structure provides a map for the employee through the organization, highlighting how and in what ways progression is possible. As such, organizations have sought to establish grading structures that clarify and enhance employee opportunities. This link between the redesign of grading structures and external labour market pressures is again particularly apparent in the public sector where it has taken different forms. In education, the advanced skills teaching grade provides a chance for teachers to progress in career and pay term by deepening and extending their professional capabilities. In social care, grades are being developed that facilitate movement from the support roles into social work. Such moves might be seen as part of broader trend in to the public service that seeks to deal with professional shortages by providing career pathway into such roles, a move that has assumed its most sophisticated form in the NHS 'skills escalator'.

In the private sector, similar moves can be seen in the creation of job families, a discrete hierarchy of roles from a particular service or production function embedded in a wider set of organizational pay arrangements (IDS 2006b). The incidence of job families should not but overstated. A recent CIPD (2005) reward survey noted that 14% of organizations had developed job families, with 19% indicating that they are used in combination with other grading arrangements. Nonetheless, they are seen as a particularly effective way of dealing with external labour market pressures, providing greater clarity than might otherwise have been apparent in a broadly based grading structure, while also sharpening the process of benching marking in establishing competitive pay rates. For example, a recent report noted that: 'Mobile phone operator O_2 has adopted a reward strategy of differentiating pay by major job family with a view to more clearly matching market rates for particular groups of employees' (IDS 2005).

Finally, external labour market pressures have encouraged organizations to review and in some cases restructure their total reward packages, in other words, the non-pay as well as the pay elements. Some care is needed in assuming that they have unambiguously improved the proposition to employees. Perhaps the most important element of the reward package beyond the immediate wage, the occupational pensions, has been under considerable attack with companies closing final salary schemes and facing deficits in their pension funds. At the same time, organizational attempts to use the compensation package as a means of attracting and retaining employees has been apparent in the notion of 'total reward'. Seeking to highlight the wide range of returns on offer to employees for their contributions, a total reward approach has assumed different forms, serving slightly different purposes. Addressing managerial concerns that employees perhaps underestimate the true worth of non-pay benefits, it has emerged as a simple restatement of the existing remuneration package, but more clearly attaching a monetary value to it. Public sector employers, for example, have long held the view that their staff undervalue 'generous' pension entitlements encouraging an increased emphasis on this benefit. As part of a more flexible approach to benefits, captured by the term 'cafeteria benefits' it is an approach which has been seen to lend distinctiveness to the organizational employment offering. Indeed, it is a tool that has been viewed as a way of addressing the changing nature of the workforce, providing scope for employees to select benefits which accord with different lifestyles choices. Total reward packages might include the opportunity to select more flexible hours and family friendly benefits such as childcare facilities and help with childcare. As a recent report on Astra Zenaca's flexible benefits schemes noted, 'The scheme is seen as recognising the diversity among staff by allowing individuals to choose benefits according their life style' (*People Management* 2002).

Internal equity

If a heightened sensitivity to external equity as a response to developments in labour markets beyond the organization characterizes the contemporary reward agenda, then it is equally apparent that internal equity has emerged as a key consideration. Its importance has assumed at least three different forms: one related to the regulation of pay at the extremes of the labour market; another associated with the pursuit of pay equality, principally in gender terms; and a final one linked to the issue of pay process. Each dimension of internal equity is considered in turn.

It may seem somewhat perverse to highlight the increased significance of pay equity following a 20-year period when wage inequality has increased (Machin 2003: 91). However, New Labour governments have attempted to regulate pay at the top and bottom ends of the labour market, by implication, seeking to encourage organizations to narrow the gap between their high and low earners. At the top end, concerns about senior management pay among various interested parties have rumbled on over a number of years, assuming a high public profile at various times as what are seen by some as inflated remuneration packages come to light. Researchers have not been immune from this interest, drawing heavily on the level and nature of senior management pay to explore the tenets of principal-agent theory (Jensen and Meckling 1976). Highlighting the need to align the interest of senior managers as the agents and shareholders as principles through pay mechanisms, such research in the UK suggests a relationship between executive salaries and bonuses and corporate performance, although more general evidence suggests that remuneration packages are primarily determine by firm size (McKnight and Tomkins 1999). In public policy terms, attempts to regulate senior management pay can be traced back to the Cadbury Report in 1992, which recommended the establishment of remuneration committees made up of non-executive directors to determine senior managers' pay. The operation of such committees in terms of makeup and disclosure of their activities was then considerably tightened with the publication of codes of practice following the recommendations of the Greenbury and Hampel Reports in the late 1990s.

Concerns have not, however, abated. Indeed they have been fuelled by evidence indicating that the median base pay for the highest paid directors among the FTSE 100 companies increased from £301,000 in 1993 to £579,000 in 2002, an increase of 92% over a period in which inflation had risen by just 25% (Select Committee on Trade and Industry 2003). The most recent government intervention has further increased transparency, for the first time making remuneration committees accountable to shareholders. The Directors' Report Regulations 2002 now requires listed companies to produce a remuneration report to be approved by resolution at the annual general meeting. Although this resolution is only advisory, it has already provided shareholders with scope to articulate concerns, reflected in the fact that only 67% of W.H. Smith's shareholders voted in favour of the 2004 remuneration report, which provided a multimillion pound 'golden hello' for the new chief executive.

Government attempts to regulate pay at the bottom end of the labour market have been more incisive. The National Minimum Wage (NMW), introduced in 1998, for the first time in the UK established a statutory basic pay entitlement, which through recommendations from the standing Low Pay Commission has been regularly up rated. From October 2006 the NMW has been set at £5.35 for those over 22 years of age, £4.45 for those between 18 and 21 and £3.30 for employees between 16 and 17. It is an intervention that has attracted criticism from different quarters. Viewing the NMW as a legitimate means of addressing poverty, trade unions and community groups have been concerned about its calculation and level. Unison, for example, has called on the use of the European Threshold of Decency to set the NMW a measure that yields a much higher rate than the NMW. Others have challenged whether the NMW provides a 'living wage' and sought a much higher rate for this purpose (Greater London Authority 2006). At the same time, the LPC has calculated that by 2006 5% of the workforce would have benefited from the NMW. Moreover, the HM Revenue and Customs & Excise, responsible for enforcing the NMW, has handled around 16,000 complaints about non payment and has identified over £21 million in pay arrears.

From the other side of employment relationship, employers have been concerned at the affect of the NMW on competitiveness, raising the spectre of increased labour cost, as workers seek to reimpose differentials, and consequent job losses as businesses fail. There have been instances, particularly in the hospitality and retail sectors, of organizations being forced to reorganize their grading structures as differential become squeezed. Tesco, for example, has cut its grades from five to two, while the retail co-operatives merged four grades to create a multiskilled position of customer service assistant (Willman 2006). The government, however, has been sensitive to such concerns, seeing the NMW less as a means of dealing with poverty and more as a way of providing a minimum protective floor without detrimentally affecting competitiveness, productivity, levels of employment and wage inflation. This is reflected in the terms of reference of LPC which require it to monitor the consequences of the NMW in these terms and in research findings which suggest that the NMW has not undermined competitiveness as predicted.

Over recent years pay equality, particularly between women and men, has emerged as a significant public policy concern. This has been in response to evidence which suggests that the pay gap between women and men in the UK remains stubbornly wide and one of the 'worst' in the European Union. Thirty five years on from the passing of the Equal Pay Act 1970, full-time women workers are still earning 17% less than men, while the gap between female and male part-time workers is even wider, at 38%. A range of interest groups has sought to put pressure on the government and employers to address this issue. Various unions have launched campaigns, including the TGWU with its 'Pay Up' call and Unison with its 'Getting Equal' drive. Moreover, in 1999 the Equal Opportunities Commission (EOC) set up an equal pay taskforce, which reported two years later with its 'Just Pay' report.

Yet, to a degree, these groups have been 'pushing at an open door'. Equal pay is an issue that has resonated with New Labour's 'Fairness at Work' agenda and prompted a number of initiatives. In 2001 the government set up a review headed by Denise Kingsmill, Deputy Chair of the Competition Commission, to look at the pay gap and in 2005 established a Women and Work Commission, also concerned in large part with this issue.

These different reporting bodies have consistently suggested that the reasons for the pay gap are varied and complex, but much attention has focused on the potentially discriminatory consequences of pay systems and structures. Concerns have been raised about whether the kinds of individual objective established under performance-related pay might work against women; more subtle forms of discrimination have been suggested as residing in extended incremental scales that detrimentally affect women whose careers are more likely to be punctuated by breaks; while the lack of transparency in the operation of broad job bands has encouraged worries that discriminatory practices may 'creep in'. Yet much of the attention in addressing pay discrimination has focused on internal job worth, particularly given the legislation's concern with ensuring equal pay for work of equal value. Indeed, under the legislation one of the surest ways of guaranteeing protection from an equal pay claim is to ensure that jobs have been assessed under a factor-based job evaluation scheme. In response the Kingmill report, in particular, called for pay audits to 'root out' such discrimination and set a target for 50% of large organizations to have completed one before the end of 2003 and 25% of all employers by the end of 2005.

These public policy concerns have unevenly impacted on the organizational pay agenda. According to Table 9.1, there appears to be a marked contrast between the private and public sectors in the importance attached to 'internal equity', with around one-third of private sector employers viewing it as an important reward goal compared to almost two-thirds in the public sector. Certainly, private sector employers cannot ignore the fact that the cost of discrimination in equal pay cases can be high. A ruling from the European Court of Justice, enshrined in an amendment to the Equal Pay Act in 2003, extends the period when arrears from unequal pay can be received from two to six years. However, the relative lack of urgency among private sector employers is apparent in the slow progress made on the conduct of pay audits. In 2005, only 34% of large private sector organizations had completed pay audits (Adams et al. 2006).

The limited private sector activity may reflect the perceived limits on the scope for employers to address the pay gap through tackling pay discrimination. In explaining the pay gap the Women and Work Commission placed particular emphasis on deep-rooted horizontal and vertical job segregation in the labour market which was, in turn, related to gendered patterns of training and skill formation. It was a finding which led the commission to resist the call for mandatory pay audits.

The importance attached to issues of internal equity in the public sector comes as no surprise. In a sector where a majority of the employees are women and where occupationally diverse workforces have always raised issues about the comparative worth of different job roles, pay equality has long been a latent cause for concern. In the last few years, a combination of factors has brought this issue to the fore. There has been frustration, particularly among the public sector unions, at the slow progress made in achieving pay equity. In local government, the difficulties in implementing the 1997 single status agreement covering over 1½ million local authority workers, at the centre of which was a review of pay structures on the basis of equal pay principles, culminated in a national strike in 2002 and the establishment of a commission to take the issue forward. A timetable has now been established to restructure pay systems by 2007. It is a timetable the local authority employers are keen to meet as female employees begin to take equal pay claims to tribunals with some success and costly awards. Similar tribunal decisions have placed pressures on NHS employers, although these have been overtaken somewhat by Agenda for Change. This agreement, covering most of the 1 million employees in the service, has at its

---

HRM in Action 9.1   NHS Agenda for Change

Covering 1.2 million workers in the NHS, Agenda for Change took effect from 1 October 2004. It brings together most occupational groups, formerly covered by an array of Whitley and Review Body arrangements, under a single structure and system. It relates pay to performance, person and job in various ways, highlighting the importance attached to internal and external equity and, by implication, how these have been used to further the NHS's strategic objectives. The key features of the agreement include:

- establishment of eight bands, covering doctors, nurses and other health professionals and non-review body staff, on a single pay spine
- all staff are assigned to one of the bands on the basis of job as measured by an equality-proof job evaluation scheme

- staff move up the band on an annual incremental basis subject to 'satisfactory performance'. However, there are gateway points along the scale where assessment of knowledge and skills is necessary to progress
- all leads and allowances are replaced by a higher basic pay 'This supports simplification of the pay systems and is consistent with the principle of equal pay for work of equal value.'
- where there are external market pressures on jobs, those in these roles are paid a long-term recruitment and retention premium
- a system of London weighting and range allowance is replaced by a 'high-cost area supplement'
- new arrangements are implemented at trust level in partnership with the recognized trade unions.

---

heart a requirement for individual hospital trusts to assess jobs using an equality-proof job evaluation scheme (see HRM in Action 9.1).

The concern with pay equality has also been responsible for encouraging an interest among practitioners and researchers in internal equity as it relates to 'fair' pay processes. As pressures grow to avoid discrimination in pay structures and systems, so organizations are giving greater thought to transparency in the processes underpinning pay determination. It is striking, for example, that a recent survey found that the factors rated most important by organizations in the design of contingent pay schemes were 'simple and easy to understand' and 'equitable and consistent'. These were factors placed well ahead of aligning pay with business goals and being able to differentiate pay according to performance (EReward 2004).

In addition, this focus on process has encouraged researchers from within the mainstream SHRM literature to explore whether and how HR practices, including pay, affect employee attitudes and behaviours in ways that may further business strategy. The search for the 'missing link' between HR practices and business performance has been labelled by Purcell and his colleagues (2003) as 'unlocking the black box'. They suggest that the capacity of HR practices to further business goals is dependent on whether these practices can improve employee performance by providing them with the necessary skills and the opportunity and the motivation to use them. This approach has value in encouraging a focus on the relationship between HR practices and employee attitudes and behaviours, but fails to fully theorize this relationship. How and why might pay generate these 'desired' attitudes and behaviours?

There is a range of theoretical frameworks, particularly from an organizational psychology tradition, which provide some help in addressing this question. Various process theories, for example, have been drawn on to consider the circumstances in which pay might motivate. For example, expectancy theory suggests that pay will motivate when achievable performance targets are set; pay is clearly related to them; and employees value pay. It is a model effectively used by Marsden and Richardson (1994) in examining the dysfunctional workings of individual performance related pay in the Inland Revenue. Similarly equity theory (Adams 1963) has been drawn on to explore how the relative treatment of employees under different reward systems, in terms of distributive, procedural and interactional justice, can affect employee motivation. For instance, in noting much lower theft rates among employees who had received a pay cut but with an accompanying apology and explanation than among those who had arbitrarily been give such a pay cut, Greenberg (1990) revealed how procedural justice might moderate the consequences of distributive injustice.

The notion of procedural justice connects with a literature on workplace voice that suggests that pay systems are more likely to generate 'desired' attitudes and behaviours if an inclusive approach to their design and implementation is adopted. Over 20 years ago, Bowey and her colleagues (1982) found that the more extensive the consultation and negotiation with a range of parties – trade union representative, line managers and employees – over the design and implementation of productivity pay schemes the 'better' their performance. It is a finding which has considerable plausibility given the range of groups with an interest in pay systems. In light of this finding, it is perhaps depressing for those interested in pay system effectiveness to note evidence indicating that meaningful employee involvement in pay decisions remains low. Certainly, there are examples in the public sector, particularly in local government and the NHS, where pay reform has explicitly been based on a partnership arrangement with the unions. However, the Workplace Employee Relations Survey (2004) revealed that in only 18% of the workplaces covered was there negotiation over pay related matters, in 5% there was some consultation, in 6% information was provided and in 70% none occurred (Kersley et al. 2005).

There are other frameworks that might be used to explore the relationship between pay, and indeed other HR practices, and employee attitudes and behaviours. Much recent attention has focused on a psychological contract model (Conway and Briner 2005), which relates the fulfilment or violation of the employment expectations to such outcomes as employee commitment and organizational citizenship behaviour. A recent qualitative study using such a model has highlighted how it is the breach of promises on salary-related issues that are most likely to prompt feelings of contract violation with the resultants negative consequences for employee attitudes and behaviours (Perzfall 2006). The psychological contract model and others from the field of organizational psychology have limitations, often being based on employee cognition rather than actual practice and giving limited consideration to institutional context that might be seen as important not only shaping these practices but responses to them as well. However, they do seek to explore how and why given pay practices affect employee attitudes and behaviours. In so doing, they suggest that internal pay equity is best seen not as a principle which competes with business strategy, but one that may be crucial to its 'effective' pursuit.

Conclusion

This chapter has had two main objectives: to explore changes in pay practice in Britain over recent years and to assess how approaches to the study of pay within a broader SHRM literature have developed. In drawing on the pay principles distinguished by Gomez-Mejia, it has become clear that the suggested primacy of business strategy over internal and external equity in pay practice has failed to emerge; indeed, if anything it is equity, in both senses, which has come to dominate the pay agenda. The privileging of business strategy as a pay principle was found to have some surface support. The contemporary prescriptive pay rhetoric continues to stress the need to align pay with business goals, while many practitioners remain wedded to this language in formulating their pay policies. However, the balance between the pay principles proposed by Gomez-Mejia fails to capture the British pay scene for two reasons. First, beyond the pay rhetoric, organizational attempts to relate pay to business strategy are highly problematic. The use of pay systems that seek to relate person and performance to corporate goals is fraught with difficulties as design flaws and workplace influences create considerable uncertainty as to likely outcomes. Second, there have been very real societal pressures that have propelled external and internal equity to the centre of the pay agenda: the tight and changing nature of labour markets; the regulation of top and low pay; and the public policy impetus behind achieving equal pay, reflected in a range of initiatives.

At the same time, shifting analytical approaches to the relationship between pay and corporate performance suggests that it may be misconceived to view business strategy, internal and external equity as competing pay principles. Gomez-Mejia's statement might be seen to reflect assumptions in the broader SRHM literature on a mechanistic relationship between HR practices and business outcomes; a perspective that assumed that pay practices would change employee attitudes and behaviours in ways that furthered business goals, but without theorizing or testing whether this was indeed the case. The search for explanations of the relationship between pay and other HR practices, employee responses and corporate outcomes has increasingly (re-)focused on the importance of 'fair' and inclusive processes; if employees are treated equitably by pay practices, they may well think and act in ways more likely to progress corporate objectives. Such a view suggests that rather than being alternatives, business strategy and equity may well be crucially related.

References

Adams, J. (1963). 'Inequity in social exchange', in L. Bekowitz (ed.) *Advances in Experimental Social Psychology*, Vol. 2. New York, Academic Press.

Adams, L., K. Carter and S. Schafer (2006). *Equal Pay Review Survey, 2005*. Manchester, EOC.

Ahlstrand, B. (1990). *The Quest for Productivity*. Cambridge, Cambridge University Press.

Armstrong, M. (1996). 'How group efforts can pay dividends', *People Management* 25 January: 22–7.

Bloom, M. and G.T. Milkovich (1992). 'Issues in managerial compensation research', in C. Cooper and D. Rousseau (eds) *Trends in Organizational Behavior*. Chichester, Wiley.

Boxall, P. (1996). 'The strategic HRM debate and the resource-based view of the firm', *Human Resource Management Journal* 6(3): 59–75.

Bowey, A., R. Thorpe and F. Mitchell (1982). *Effect of Incentive Payment Systems*. London, Department of Employment.

Brown, D. and M. Armstrong (1999). *Paying for Contribution*. London, Kogan Page.

CIPD (2003). *Reward Survey Report*. London, CIPD.

CIPD (2005). *Reward Survey Report*. London, CIPD.

CIPD (2006). *Reward Management Symposium Report, 13 July 2005*. London, CIPD.

Conway, N. and R. Briner (2005). *Understanding Psychological Contracts at Work*. Oxford, Oxford University Press.

Corby, S., G. White and C. Stanworth (2002). *Does it Work? Evaluating a New Pay System*. London, University of Greenwich.

EReward (2003). *UK Total Reward and Pay for Performance Drives: GSK Merger, Report No. 15*. Manchester, EReward.

EReward (2004). *What is Happening on Contingent Pay Today, Part 1, Research Report No. 18*. Manchester, EReward.

EReward Research (2005). *Pay at BT*, Report No. 35. Manchester, EReward.

Gerhart, B. and S. Rynes (2003). *Compensation*. London, Sage.

Gomez-Mejia, L. (1993). *Compensation, Organization and Firm Performance*. San Francisco, Southwestern.

Greater London Authority (2006). *A Fairer London: The Living Wage*. London, Greater London Authority.

Greenberg, J. (1990). 'Employee theft as a reaction to underpayment of inequity', *Journal of Applied Psychology* 75: 55-61.

IDS Report (2003a). *Markets Driving Pay in Banking*, 892 November: 6-8.

IDS Report (2003b). *Regional Pay*. January: 15-16.

IDS Report (2004). *Pay Trends*, 907 June: 10-11.

IDS Report (2005). *Case Study Pay Development at O₂*: 16-17.

IDS Report (2006a). *Pay Trends*, 945 January: 15-16.

IDS (2006b). *Job Families*, HR Studies No. 814.

Jensen, M. and W. Meckling (1976). 'Theory of the firm: managerial behaviour, agency costs, ownership structure', *Journal of Financial Economics* 3: 305-60.

Kersley, B., C. Alpin and J. Forth (2005). *Inside the Workplace*. London, DTI.

Kessler, I. (2001). 'Reward system choices', in J. Storey (ed.) *HRM: A Critical Text*. London, Thomson.

Kessler, I. and J. Purcell (1992). 'Performance related pay – objectives and application', *Human Resource Management Journal* 2(3), 34-59.

Kochan, T. and T. Barrochi (eds) (1985). *HRM and Industrial Relations*. Boston, MA, Little Brown.

Kohn, A. (1983). 'Why incentive plans cannot work', *Harvard Business Review*, Sept-Oct: 54-63.

Lawler, E. (1995). 'The new pay: a strategic approach', *Compensation and Benefits Review* July: 14-20.

Learning and Skills Council (2005). *The National Employers' Skill Survey*. London, LSC.

Local Government Pay Commission (2003). *Report*. London, LGPC.

Lupton, T. (1963). *Money for Effort*. London, HMSO.

Lupton, T. and D. Gowler (1969). 'Selecting a wage payment system', research paper III. London, Engineering Employers' Federation.

Machin, S. (2003). 'Wage inequality since 1975', in R. Dickens, P. Gregg and J. Wandsworth (eds) *The Labour Market Under New Labour*. Basingstoke, Palgrave.

Mahoney, T. (1989). 'Multiple pay contingencies: strategic design of compensation', *Human Resource Management* 28(3): 337-47.

Makinson Report (2001). *Incentives for Change*. London, HMSO.

Marsden, D. and R. Richardson (1994). 'Performance pay? The effects of merit pay on motivation in the public services', *British Journal of Industrial Relations* 32(2): 243-61.

McKnight, P. and C. Tomkins (1999). 'Top executive pay in the United Kingdom', *International Journal of Economics of Business* 6: 233-43.

Mueller, F. (1996). 'Human resources as strategic assets', *Journal of Management Studies* 33(6): 757-85.

Perzfell, M. (2006). 'Exploring the role of reciprocity in psychological contracts', unpublished PhD thesis, London School of Economics.

People Management (2002). 'Pick 'n' mix', 7 November: 44-5.

PTC (1996). *Whatever Happened to National Civil Service Pay?* London, PTC.

Purcell, J., N. Kinnie, S. Hutchinson, B. Rayton and J. Swart (2003). *Understanding the People and Performance Link*. London, CIPD.

Richardson, R. and M. Thompson (1999). *The Impact of People Management on Business Performance: A Literature Review*. London, IPD.

Robinson, H. (2003). 'Gender and labour market performance in the recovery', in R. Dickens, P. Gregg and J. Wandsworth (eds) *The Labour Market Under New Labour*. Basingstoke, Palgrave.

Schuler, R. and S. Jackson (1987). 'Linking competitive strategies with human resource management practices', *Academy of Management Review* 1(3): 199-213.

Select Committee on Trade and Industry (2003). *Sixteenth Report*. London, HMSO.

Sparrow, P. (1996). 'Too good to be true?', *People Management* 5 December: 22-9.

Whyte, F. S. (1955). *Money and Motivation*. New York, Harper.

Willman, J. (2006). 'Minimum wage reaches tipping point', *Financial Times* 12 May.

Wood, S. (1996). 'High-commitment management and payment systems', *Journal of Management Studies* 33(1): 53-77.

Employee involvement and participation: structures, processes and outcomes

Mick Marchington and Annette Cox

Introduction

Employee involvement and participation (EIP) is typically a major component of the bundle of practices associated with high commitment or 'best practice' HRM (see, for example, Appelbaum et al. 2000; Guest et al. 2003; Godard. 2004). It is seen in a variety of guises – such as information sharing, quality circles, teamworking and consultation – but irrespective of the precise form of EIP, it is thought to contribute to improved levels of worker satisfaction and commitment and, subsequently, organizational performance. A key problem is that neither EIP nor HRM is defined adequately. Other chapters in this book show that HRM is capable of being interpreted in multiple, conflicting and contrasting ways. Similarly, depending on the managerial philosophy underpinning EIP, it can take a range of forms, even where it has the same title.

Focusing at the organizational level alone, however, only takes us part way in attempting to understand how EIP works. To appreciate that better, we have to take into account the way in which institutional forces – such as legal provisions, social policy and sector-level influences – shape EIP within organizations. Comparative business and employment systems literature (Rubery and Grimshaw 2003) tells us that such forces influence the ways in which employers deal with labour and, indeed – unlike the UK where any social intervention tends to be interpreted in negative terms – can actually help to improve both business efficiency and workers' rights. As Boselie et al. (2003) note, in the Netherlands, many components of high-commitment HRM, including EIP, are taken for granted as part of the employment package whereas in the UK they are practised only by some organizations.

As well as recognizing the influence that macro-level forces have on how EIP is practised at workplace level, we are also interested in exploring how it is shaped by more micro-level factors. The examination of micro-factors by Ferner et al. (2005) is helpful but needs to be extended in our view, beneath the level of the organization, to examine how EIP might vary due to the degree to which it is embedded within organizations, to the extent to which it is seen as central to managing people and to the frequency of its practice. This distinction is simple if we compare the annual attitude survey with the day-to-day influence that workers might have through self-managed teams. But embeddedness can also vary with each form of EIP depending on the number of workers covered, its regularity of occurrence and the subject matter with which it deals. Moreover we still need to appreciate how EIP is influenced or implemented by specific managers or supervisors. The processes of EIP have been largely ignored in recent times given an obsession with formal structures and an increasing reliance on large survey sets – such as WERS – to produce data about how HRM has evolved across the economy as a whole. While it is clearly important to know the proportion of workplaces in different countries or sectors that use a particular form of EIP, it is also critical to understand how these are influenced by the dynamics of worker–manager relations at workplace level. Accordingly, we could find that a specific EIP practice is underpinned by legislation, is a key component of organization-wide policies, is clearly embedded within the HR framework at establishment level yet still fails to impact on workers because their line manager shows little interest in implementing the policy as intended. Of course, the converse could also apply, where a line manager may be very good at consulting her/his staff in the absence of an embedded EIP policy framework, but we would argue this is less likely and comprises a much more fragile ecosystem.

This sets the framework for the remainder of the chapter. In the next section, we attempt to deconstruct the meanings of EIP by examining the extent to which different practices can vary in relation to degree, scope, level and form. Thereafter, we explain how different practices actually operate, providing some data on extensiveness both in the UK and in some other countries, as well as analysing their essential features. We then move on to develop the notion of embedded EIP (Cox et al. 2006b), examining what this means in practice and differentiating between its breadth and depth. Recent evidence from a variety of sources (Bryson 2004; Cox et al. 2006b; Delbridge and Whitfield 2001) shows that more broadly and deeply embedded EIP is associated with positive perceptions of employee influence, managerial responsiveness and higher levels of worker commitment and satisfaction. After this we examine the process of implementing EIP through the lens of leader–member exchange (LMX) theory (Liden et al. 2004; Sparrowe and Liden 1997). It also uses data from WERS 2004 to illustrate the substantial influence that management style has on worker perceptions. Finally, we bring the chapter together by concluding that more research needs to be done both at a comparative and at a micro-level in order to tease out how EIP actually operates in practice.

Charting the terrain of EIP

Despite its popularity as a concept, EIP lacks a clear and unambiguous definition. This is problematic because research and practice refers to a multitude of different practices, with a range of names but which often have little in common. For example, while some would regard industrial democracy as the only true form of EIP because workers have the potential to control their organizations, others regard two-way communications between line managers and their staff as more meaningful as it relates to their everyday working experiences. Similarly, while some might feel EIP is only achievable when trade unions are able to protect workers' rights and channel their contributions through an independent, representative body, others feel that workers can only really be involved through opportunities to exercise discretion at work. In short, because participation is such an elastic term greater precision is required if we are to analyse it properly.

This task is made more problematic because the dominant terminology – workers' control, industrial democracy, workers' participation, employee involvement, empowerment, social partnership – has changed over time, to some extent reflecting different fads and fashions but also conveying contrasting motives (see, for example, Cotton 1993; Harley et al. 2005; Heller et al. 1998; Marchington et al. 1992; Poole 1975; Stuart and Martinez Lucio 2005). At one level, no one could possibly be 'against' workers participating in the organizations within which they are employed; after all, the alternative is autocracy and the unfettered exercise of managerial power or indeed slavery. However, once we move beyond such a simplistic dichotomy and start to analyse the nature and impact of participation, as well as the motives of those who propagate it, the picture becomes more complex and multifaceted. In order to make progress EIP needs to be deconstructed into degree, scope, level and form.

The *degree* of EIP indicates the extent to which workers – or their representatives – are able to influence management decisions. This can range from merely being provided with information, through two-way communication, consultation, codetermination and control (see Figure 10.1). Managers retain ultimate control over decisions in most of these categories and despite being accorded the right to be consulted about an issue workers' views can be ignored if management sees fit. Of course, while managers would be foolhardy to discount strong worker opposition, even if the latter lack the power and resources to prevent action being taken, nobody would seriously argue that rights to consultation have the same force as codetermination or control.

If the degree of participation is a vital aspect in any definition, then so too is the *scope* of the decisions in which workers might be involved. Scope relates to the type of subject matter dealt with, ranging from the trivial to the strategic. Examples of the former might include the venue for the office Christmas party or the colour of the office wallpaper. Conversely, strategic issues typically relate to broader questions about organizational goals, plans for new products and services and investment

The escalator of EIP   Figure 10.1

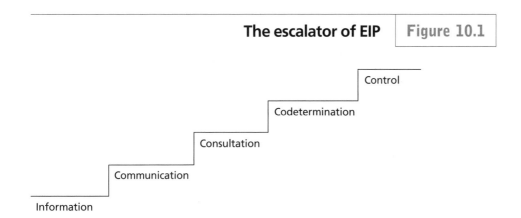

decisions, all of which can have major consequences for work organization and work-ers' future job prospects. These sorts of decisions are routinely taken by senior man-agers alone and at best worker representatives are consulted before plans are finally approved or informed in advance of their implementation. The combination of scope and degree can lead to inconsistencies in EIP, such as where employees are given extensive rights over trivial issues but provided with little (or no) information about major changes.

The *level* at which workers (or their representatives) are involved in management decisions is the third category. This can vary substantially, ranging from workplace or departmental level through to establishment, division and headquarters. This distinc-tion is useful because it acknowledges that management does not operate in a unified way and decisions taken at more senior levels – especially those by a foreign-owned multinational – are beyond the scope not only of shopfloor or office workers but also of local managers, and even governments in the host country. There is often a link between scope and level, in that the more trivial decisions tend to be made at work-place level whereas the more strategic are taken at corporate headquarters without any employee involvement.

Finally, EIP takes quite different *forms*: it may be direct or face to face, as is the case with many of the recent initiatives in most developed countries, or it may be indirect or representative – as occurs when trade unions represent workers on high-level con-sultative committees or works councils. Some would argue direct EIP is explicitly designed to weaken the collective will of workers by individualizing their actions and getting them to identify with employer goals. Yet, an alternative perspective would suggest that direct EIP provides workers with a route straight to managers. Moreover, job redesign and self-management can offer workers opportunities to exert consider-able control over their daily working lives. However, influence and involvement at workplace level is meaningless if decisions taken further up the corporate hierarchy lead to its closure.

It is therefore essential to classify different participation schemes according to this matrix of degree, scope, level and form. At present, as evidence from a number of countries demonstrates (Freeman et al. forthcoming 2007), the most widely used forms of EIP are communication and consultation, either at shopfloor or organiza-tional level. Most – such as briefing or problem-solving groups – are dilute on degree and very few team-working initiatives offer any real opportunity for workers to man-age themselves. Employers are clearly the main drivers of EIP and schemes are there-fore likely to be designed with their objectives in mind; improved quality and productivity, enhanced worker commitment and satisfaction or reduced levels of absence or labour turnover (Dundon et al. 2004). There is more evidence of indirect EIP in mainland Europe (Gill and Krieger 1999), largely due to legal and institutional forces that shape HRM, but in Anglo-Saxon economies such as Britain this tends to be restricted to larger (often, multinational) firms and public sector organizations. Most organizations operate with a mix of formal EIP schemes, so it is more appropriate to conceive of participation in the plural rather than the singular. With this in mind, we can now turn to review briefly different types of EIP. Table 10.1, drawn from Cully et al. (1999) and Kersley et al. (2005, 2006), compares the extensiveness of different forms of EIP in Britain in 1998 and 2004. These results indicate that downward com-munications have continued to grow in popularity while other forms of EIP have declined slightly (representative and task-based participation) or both grown and declined (upward problem solving).

Of course, any cross-sectional survey cannot measure change per se, but data from the panel survey (Cox et al. 2006a) show that, in continuing workplaces, there had been significant increases in the proportion of workplaces using downward communication techniques over the previous six years. Interestingly, in these same sorts of workplace, there had also been increases in upward problem solving and in representative participation via JCCs – contrary to the overall data that are influenced by the changing composition of workplaces.

Downward communications is currently the most extensive form of EIP in Britain, with more than 90% of workplaces claiming to have some form of briefing system and almost two-thirds saying they make use of the management chain to cascade information to workers. However, it is also the most limited in degree and scope, largely because communication is downward but also it is typically bolted on to work processes and takes up a limited amount of worker time. It takes several forms in practice – such as formalized written documents to all workers, regular briefing groups and face-to-face interactions between line managers and their staff. These techniques share the common purpose of seeking to inform and 'educate' employees in order to enhance commitment and satisfaction and ultimately improve their performance. Depending on how EIP is practised, this can be viewed as nothing more than a neutral device to inform workers about specific issues or as an instrument to reinforce management prerogatives by shaping worker expectations.

Face-to-face communications systems rely on small groups of staff being brought together regularly (say, once a week/month) to hear about new developments direct from their line manager. Although briefings themselves are intended as one-way, downward communications, there is often provision for feedback up the line management chain in order to clarify issues and ensure that senior managers are aware of

The extensiveness of EIP in Britain, 1998 and 2004		Table 10.1

EIP technique	% of workplaces (1998)	% of workplaces (2004)
Downward communications		
Team briefings/meetings with entire workforce	85	91
Systematic use of management chain	52	64
Regular newsletters	40	45
Upward problem solving		
Suggestion schemes	31	30
Problem-solving groups	16	21
Representative participation		
Workplace JCC	20	14
JCC above the level of the workplace only	27	25
Task-based participation		
Some core workers in formally designated teams	74	72
Some core workers trained to be functionally flexible	69	66

workers' feelings. Although there is widespread support for team briefings in principle, in practice they can run into many problems – such as line managers not being able to communicate effectively, the information lacking relevance or not being timely and trade unions seeing briefing as a device to undermine or marginalize their role (Marchington and Wilkinson 2005).

Upward problem solving incorporates a range of voice mechanisms that tap in to employee knowledge and ideas, typically through individual suggestions or through ad hoc or semi-permanent groups brought together for the specific purpose of resolving problems or generating ideas. These offline schemes tend to be 'bolted on' rather than integral to the work process (Batt 2004) but they are now much more widespread in most developed economies (Benson and Lawler 2003; Kessler et al. 2004). They complement notions of high-commitment HRM because upward problem solving is predicated on assumptions that employees are a major source of competitive advantage. These practices are designed not only to increase the stock of ideas, but they are also expected to increase cooperation at work; evidence suggests that workers like being involved (Freeman and Rogers 1999). Despite offering a greater degree of active voice than communications cascaded down the management hierarchy, some critics view these practices as problematic precisely because they encourage workers to collaborate with management in helping resolve work-related problems, so reducing their ability to resist changes with which they disagree.

Problem-solving groups typically comprise small groups of workers meeting on a regular basis to identify, analyse and solve quality and work-related problems. Members may be drawn either from the same team or from a range of different work areas, with a leader and, in some cases, facilitators. While management's objective is to enhance productivity, quality or service through the appropriation of workers' ideas, problem-solving groups can also increase satisfaction and commitment if workers feel their views have been taken seriously. However, doubts are expressed about sustaining groups beyond the initial phase of active involvement, as questions are raised about whether or not gains will be maintained (Handel and Levine 2004) or whether there will be job losses if groups are too successful in identifying cost savings (Osterman 2000). Moreover, workers can be criticized for acting as management stooges, helping organizations to improve performance without any commensurate increase in worker rewards. By the same token, employers subject to severe product market pressures might disapprove of any activity allowing workers productive time away from their work station (Cappelli and Neumark 2001).

Representative participation was seen 25 years ago as well nigh synonymous with EIP. At that time, JCCs were more extensive than nowadays (34% of workplaces had them in 1980 compared with 14% in 2004) and they were much more common in unionized than non-union workplaces (Cully et al. 1999: 100). JCCs were seen as operating as an adjunct to collective bargaining or as an alternative (Marchington 1994). In the former case, employers sought to involve workers through their trade union representatives in a variety of different forums, using JCCs as a sounding board for ideas or providing managers and shop stewards with the opportunity to talk to each other in a relatively cooperative environment. In the latter case, JCCs were seen as a device to undermine or deter trade union organization and to persuade workers that issues were better dealt with in the consultative rather than the negotiating arena. Recently, both non-union representative participation and direct forms of EIP have assumed greater prominence and JCCs are often considered to lack relevance at workplace level, especially if they operate solely at higher levels in the organization. The decline in joint consultation can be overstated however. Between 1990 and 1998, there was a rise in the proportion of private sector workplaces with JCCs (Gospel and Willman 2005: 131) and in 2004 three-quarters of larger workplaces had a JCC and over 40% of workers were employed at workplaces where one still operated (Kersley et al. 2006: 127).

There are also other – alternative or supplementary – mechanisms by which employers have consulted employees through their representatives. Partnership schemes have become more prominent since the mid-1990s and these are just as likely in non-union as in unionized workplaces (Ackers et al. 2005). Of course, in non-union firms, concerns are raised about independence of representation and whether or not it is possible in such circumstances for workers' interests to be adequately protected. In hybrid committees, which union and non-union representatives attend together, there are questions about divided loyalties or how people are chosen to sit on the committee in the first place (Guest and Peccei 2001). In many other European countries, and also in large multinationals, representative participation is found in the form of European works councils and the implementation of the Information and Consultation of Employees Regulations (ICER) is likely to stimulate further interest.

Task-based participation has become more significant since the 1980s, although the WERS data suggest it had actually levelled off by 2004. Through practices such as team working and self-managed teams, it is an obvious component of the high-commitment HRM model, largely because these forms of work organization provide workers with opportunities to use their discretion rather than be subject to close supervision by managers (Appelbaum et al. 2000). This form of EIP is integral to the job, forming a part of everyday working life, rather than only being experienced when managers choose to involve workers or through union representatives. It can occur both horizontally and vertically. The former refers to the number and variety of tasks that workers perform at the same skill level in an organization and in some cases it can lead to a wider range of activities that helps to provide workers with a greater knowledge of the work process and, arguably, more meaningful work. However, this form of EIP might serve solely to alleviate the boredom associated with repetitive routines by doing something different, if only for a short period of time. Via vertical task-based participation, workers are trained to undertake tasks at a higher skill level or given some supervisory responsibilities, such as taking over the planning and design of work as well as its execution. Team-working combines both horizontal and vertical task-based participation and the chance for workers to manage their own teams (Benders 2005).

While there is strong evidence that task-based participation provides benefits for employers, there are also arguments that even if workers feel they are working harder under team-working regimes they can also be more satisfied with their jobs (Osterman 2000; Wilkinson et al. 1997). Although much depends on the organizational and managerial context, teamwork does have the potential to deliver satisfaction *and* control. It can also provide more interesting work if managers are serious about making jobs more meaningful. However, while some would regard task-based participation and especially team working, as the ultimate in EIP, others view it as work intensification. For example, Barker (1993: 408) suggests that self-managing teams produce 'a form of control more powerful, less apparent and more difficult to resist than that of the former bureaucracy'. Under a team-working regime, pressure for performance comes from peers as well as managers, prompting the fear that this is control at its most subversive because team members assume responsibility for peer surveillance (Sewell 2005).

In summary, it is clear that EIP takes a range of forms – communications, problem-solving groups, representative and task-based participation – both in the UK and in other developed economies. The popularity of different practices varies over time and at present direct forms of EIP are generally more extensive, while representative forms vary due to factors such as governmental and legal influences, trade union power and workplace size. As Freeman et al. (forthcoming 2007) note, even among the Anglo-American countries that share much in common, differences still remain due to specific path-dependent legal and institutional developments. However, it is also apparent that, even at the smallest workplaces, there is a mix of EIP practices in operation (Forth et al. 2006), with some achieving greater prominence than others. Most commentators believe a mix of direct and representative EIP provides benefits for organizations and workers (see, for example, Bryson 2004; Delbridge and Whitfield 2001; O'Creevy and Wood 2005).

Embedding EIP within the organization

Our discussion so far makes clear the need to consider different types and dimensions of EIP in understanding its impact within workplaces. We now advance this argument by analysing the associations between the embeddedness of EIP practices and employee outcomes. The idea of 'embeddedness' derives from the work of Granovetter (1985), which situates economic activity and decision making within a network of social pressures and structures. This network of influences might include other structures and practices within organizations, the quality of relationships among staff, organizational politics and external relationships with customers and suppliers. It is evident that different configurations of these pressures experienced in workplaces will shape the degree of embeddedness of EIP, which is, in turn, likely to affect the strength of its impact. For EIP external and internal organizational influences are likely to be important and it is worth exploring types of embeddedness to begin to understand how the concept might apply to EIP. Recent work by Cox et al. (2003–2006b) developed ideas from a study by Van Emmerik and Sanders (2004), who used a threefold categorization of institutional, network and temporal embeddedness, in order to analyse the breadth and depth of EIP.

Breadth adopts the principle of network embeddedness and can be measured by the number of EIP practices operating at the workplace. Single EIP practices are likely, other things being equal, to have less effect than a number of practices operating together because they lack reinforcement. They can be more easily dismissed as 'bolted on' or out of line with other HR practices and not taken seriously by workers. Combinations of EIP provide the potential for employees to be involved in different ways. For example, employees can receive information from and ask questions of their line managers through team briefings, give their views on aspects of work via surveys, resolve issues about quality through problem-solving groups and interact with their representatives who can exercise collective influence at establishment level through meetings with senior managers. Information received in one forum can be used in others and influence on decision making at a more senior level can help to shape employment relations at workplace level. If managers show they value employee views and share information on organizational performance, this may help to build trust. These processes are likely to foster organizational loyalty, and opportunities to influence work processes may enhance worker satisfaction with their immediate job roles.

Depth utilizes the principle of temporal embeddedness, indicating how embedded each separate EIP practice is within the workplace. This can be assessed by, among other things, the frequency with which meetings take place, the opportunity for employees (or their representatives) to raise issues and the relevance and importance of subjects considered at meetings. The more frequent the meetings, and the more that employees are directly involved in the process – for example via their contribution to team briefings or to problem-solving groups – then the more embedded the practice is at workplace level and potentially the stronger and more positive its association with employee perceptions. Without regular meetings to discuss views, issues may be forgotten and without opportunities for upward communication, employees may assume their views are not sincerely valued. Conversely, regular and frequent use of EIP mechanisms builds up expertise and familiarity with their operation among managers and employees so both parties may commit more to and gain more from the process. Survival of the mechanisms in an organization over a period of time may indicate commitment to making them worthwhile and useful. Greater depth reduces the likelihood of techniques being superficial and provides greater possibilities for EIP to make a difference to employee attitudes.

Institutional embeddedness includes elements both of breadth and depth and it measures how seriously EIP is taken by managers and employees in contrast to superficial 'bolted on' mechanisms. The proportion of employees participating in EIP, the amount of time managers allocate to employees for their input to EIP and the overall effort put into EIP in terms of the number of practices used contribute to the degree of importance it has in the organization. Management style, sincerity and commitment to the spirit of EIP mechanisms, which we discuss later in relation to informal EIP, are also important indicators of institutional embeddedness.

Studies have examined the impact of embeddedness of EIP both implicitly and explicitly. In analysing WERS 98, Delbridge and Whitfield (2001) confirmed that employee perceptions of job influence were greater when more than 25% of each team briefing was allocated to their comments and questions and when workers experienced higher levels of representative participation over issues beyond their daily tasks. Bryson (2004), also using WERS data, examined links between different forms of EIP and employee perceptions of managerial responsiveness to their suggestions. His results distinguished between the effectiveness of different forms of EIP but also found a positive significant relationship between employee perceptions and EIP breadth in terms of numbers of direct EIP practices used.

Our own work (Cox et al. 2006b) has used WERS 98 to examine associations between EIP embeddedness and employee outcomes. It showed that the *breadth* of EIP had consistently positive and significant associations with organizational commitment and job satisfaction. Indeed, combinations of EIP practices had a substantially stronger association with employee perceptions than single practices alone. The *depth* of EIP also showed significant positive associations with organizational commitment and job satisfaction. In short, the more embedded EIP is within the organization – measured through frequency of meetings, proportion of staff covered by an EIP practice or potential influence – the more positive are levels of organizational commitment and job satisfaction. Testing separately for links between depth of *direct* EIP and *indirect* EIP and employee perceptions showed that additive combinations of

HRM in Action 10.1   Multichem: investing in multiple forms of EIP

Multichem is a large multinational firm with sites throughout the world. Each site is given considerable discretion in how to implement HR practices provided they fit with the overall company values. EIP mechanisms are seen as desirable in principle but they take rather different forms at each establishment depending on local, regional and national factors. At its Scottish site, there is a wide range of formal EIP practices, covering both direct and representative forms. The latter includes monthly meetings between senior shop stewards and the manufacturing director and each of the unions also meets with management on a regular basis to explore ideas. The senior stewards also sit on a communications group with senior managers, including the managing director. In effect the plant operates with a partnership approach and it has received funding from the IPA (Involvement and Participation Association) for training and development.

At the level of direct EIP, downward communications are well established for all employees through monthly team briefings and there is an annual brief reporting on financial results. Teamworking and team-building activities are extensive at the plant, as the nature of the production process requires very close working and the need for production workers to use their discretion if problems arise. Staffing levels are maintained at a high level because it is seen as desirable for workers to attend regular training sessions to update skills and learn how to work effectively in groups.

EIP is supported strongly by senior managers and representative and direct EIP are both seen as critically important. They also interlock and it is unlikely that direct EIP would have developed to the extent it has without the presence of mutually agreed forms of representative participation.

direct EIP that were embedded in the workplace had positive and statistically significant associations with both organizational commitment and job satisfaction. This suggests that worker attitudes are more positive if EIP practices have a close and immediate impact on them.

Establishing EIP through the line

In the previous section, we discussed how the formal structures of EIP seem to be linked with positive employee outcomes. However it is also important to analyse the role that line managers may – or may not – play in reinforcing or developing EIP at workplace level, especially given the increasing prominence of direct EIP. Research into the implementation of 'best practice' HRM (Purcell et al. 2003) has shown the crucial role played by line managers in delivering HR practices. Guest and Conway's survey (2002) demonstrates that, according to HR managers, different forms of EIP – in this case, communication from junior managers in particular – have a significant impact on the psychological contract held by employees. The importance of the relationship in shaping employees' attitudes and behaviours is promoted by Sparrowe and Liden who argue that the employee–line manager relationship is 'a lens through which the entire work experience is viewed' (1997: 523).

However, line managers often appear as a weak link in the implementation of HRM practices and much research has indicated a gap between strategic intentions and workplace reality. For example, Khilji and Wang's (2006) multilevel study in the banking industry in Pakistan showed major discrepancies between intended and implemented HRM in that sector. A large volume of literature exists to explain why managers may not implement both HRM and specifically EIP practices as intended by senior management because they lack the intrinsic and extrinsic motivation to do so or due to lack of skills, shortage of time and competing priorities (see, e.g., McGovern et al. 1997; Whittaker and Marchington 2003). Perhaps more than any other aspect of HRM, EIP raises particular problems in so far as line managers may not believe in its principles, believing that workers only need to be informed or consulted in highly specific circumstances or when organizations are forced to by legal pressures or trade unions. Moreover, even if they agree in principle with EIP, they may lack the skill to make team briefings or problem-solving groups operate effectively and are not able to pick up on suggestions from workers; research suggests that managers are not always trained in how to run these sorts of sessions (Dundon et al. 2004). Furthermore, EIP tends to come a long way down the list of managerial priorities when compared against the more immediate production or service pressures. In other words, line managers are absolutely crucial to the implementation of EIP and its reinforcement at the workplace.

In examining the reasons why line manager commitment to EIP might be important for its success, we can use leader–member exchange (LMX) theory to evaluate what line managers' roles might be in the implementation of EIP. This provides an explanation for why employees in the same organization might have different experiences of HR practices, including EIP, by arguing that the quality of relationships between employees (members) and their line managers (leaders) vary (Liden et al. 2004). The relationship between the two is thought of as an exchange between two parties or 'dyad' whereby employees experiencing high LMX gain access to higher levels of resources, support and advice from their line manager, which in return elicits desirable discretionary behaviours and attitudes from employees. The significance of high LMX is supported by Gerstner and Day's (1997) meta-analysis which showed that the quality of the LMX relationship was positively and significantly related to employee job performance, satisfaction and commitment.

The nature of the 'exchange' process and how it is triggered is not particularly well defined (Coyle-Shapiro and Conway 2004) but to apply LMX to the implementation of EIP it is necessary to analyse how this might work. Maslyn and Uhl-Bien (2001) have proposed that effort made by each half of the line manager–employee dyad is determined by how far the other party has met expectations, so if line managers meet employees' expectations with respect to HR practices that are important to them – such as performance appraisal or advice on promotion, support for training or a personal difficulty – employees may be more likely to engage in EIP. This then raises questions about how line managers implement EIP; in other words, how far can they capitalize on the reciprocal effort yielded by employees in a positive exchange process?

Trends discussed earlier show growth in direct EIP and some evidence of continued decline in indirect, representative forms. It is the former techniques, such as team briefing and cascading information, that create growing line management responsibilities for implementing EIP. We reported earlier that EIP techniques are sometimes treated as optional extras that are less embedded than other elements of HRM, so one could argue that line managers have large amounts of discretion in whether or not to implement EIP techniques compared to decisions over allocating pay, recruiting and disciplining employees. Managers may or may not be thorough in conducting team briefings regularly, providing sincere answers to employees when they ask questions, or ensuring that they understand the financial information, productivity and performance data they are given. Furthermore, Liden et al. (2004) argue that line managers play a very important role in socializing employees, not simply by ensuring that they understand the formal content of their job description but also in initiating them into group cultures, introducing them to contacts within their own social network and shaping their understanding of the cultural norms of the workplace. This means that

---

HRM in Action 10.2   Restaurant Co.: managing EIP across small workplaces

Restaurant Co. is a large non-unionized company with more than 300 branches located throughout the UK. HR support is provided from a centralized head office and a branch manager runs each restaurant, sometimes with assistants. The restaurants operate long opening hours, seven days a week and have unpredictable trade patterns with many of the workforce on non-standard contracts. Line managers have a large amount of discretion in how they implement EIP. Restaurant managers often view key members of staff as the 'glue' holding the branch together and as such they tend to be involved more in what goes on.

The main focus of formal EIP is an information cascade system from head office to branches via communications from operations managers, an area meeting of restaurant managers and a weekly bulletin highlighting sales performance and operational issues. Team meetings for the entire establishment are held every one to two months and they are usually very informal, often centring on an event such as a wine tasting or group tasks and sometimes concluding in a night out. This format helps to entice people on non-standard contracts to attend meetings without

resenting coming in on their day off and they are used as a team-building or training exercise.

Staff are consulted informally by line managers in a busy restaurant. This is viewed as more immediate and less time consuming than regular team briefings and it avoids disrupting business. Informal EIP is seen as more useful where matters arise that relate only to certain individuals or workgroups and it is also seen as a more practical way to involve staff on variable start times. Managers recognize that positive relationships with staff are vital in eliciting discretionary behaviour, ensuring good customer interaction and gaining both commitment to them as managers and to the Restaurant Co. brand.

It is clear that, while top-down communications are reasonably effective, informal EIP is relied on for achieving input from frontline employees. Consultation is far more likely for day-to-day operational issues, such as waiters choosing their own sections or problems affecting kitchen processes, but even here managers retain the final say, especially if they think employees might not come to the 'right' decision.

even where EIP practices (such as JCCs, attitude surveys and suggestion schemes) are beyond the immediate control of line managers, the importance they accord to these practices is significant. The degree to which line managers encourage or discourage employee participation in EIP will help to shape worker perceptions of the importance attached to EIP in the workplace or organization and also the extent to which they feel they wish to engage in EIP techniques available to them.

Beyond ensuring employee commitment to formal EIP structures, line managers are also responsible for the practice of informal EIP. The practices reviewed so far in this chapter are contained within formal structures, initiatives or programmes but Strauss (1998: 16) notes that 'informal participation differs from its formal counterpart in that there are no explicit mechanisms involved'. Instead, informal participation can be characterized as a product of management style or a particular set of leadership behaviours, based on whether or not managers actively seek and respond to the views of employees or delegate when taking decisions about workplace matters. Involving employees in decision making could take place within or outside the remit of formal EIP so there is an overlap between the two dimensions. Line managers may choose to consult employees about the introduction of a new work practice during a team briefing or in a less formal setting, such as during rest breaks or even outside the workplace. Much less research attention has been given to informal EIP (Suter 2003), although it may be just as significant as formal practices in its impact on workers. Informal EIP is not, by its nature, amenable to

Links between employee perceptions of management effectiveness in consultation, satisfaction with involvement in decision making and organizational commitment/job satisfaction				Table 10.2

	Workplaces 10–24 employees		Workplaces 25 employees	
	Commitment	Satisfaction	Commitment	Satisfaction
Managers are good or very good at seeking employee views (0/1)	0.546** (0.135)	0.854** (0.129)	0.509** (0.057)	0.840** (0.059)
Managers are good or very good at responding to suggestions from employees (0/1)	0.370** (0.124)	0.796** (0.138)	0.496** (0.059)	0.824** (0.054)
Employees are either satisfied or very satisfied with the amount of involvement in decision making (0/1)	1.143** (0.119)	1.462** (0.111)	0.876** (0.050)	1.321** (0.052)
Number of observations	2135	2134	14,292	14,195

**significant at 1%

measurement through the presence or absence of particular schemes. However, the general approach is encompassed by the term participative decision making (PDM), for which a number of studies suggest a positive impact on a range of individual and organizational outcomes (e.g. Cotton et al. 1988; Kessler et al. 2004). Recent analysis, using WERS 2004, of the links between management adherence to the spirit of PDM processes and worker outcomes supports these findings (see Table 10.2).

Table 10.2 shows strong relationships between organizational commitment and job satisfaction and employee perceptions of managers' attempts to seek their views and respond to their suggestions, as well as their satisfaction with involvement in decision making. All these links are positive and highly significant. These results suggest that the *quality* of EIP processes, critically those associated with involvement of employees in decision making, have particularly strong connections with job satisfaction and organizational commitment. The way in which EIP is implemented and/or reinforced at workplace level is therefore likely to be just as important as the practices themselves. Consequently, the role of line managers in enacting the spirit of EIP through both formal and informal means is extremely important.

As the line management role in implementing EIP relates both to formal and informal practice, which could overlap, we also need to consider the relationship between each form; in other words, do formal and informal EIP co-exist and benefit each other in the same workplace and which, if any, takes precedence? Strauss (1998) argues that a pre-existing culture of informal EIP is likely to be helpful for the introduction of formal EIP practices. However, formal EIP could be argued to offer the structures and

Table 10.3	**Links between employee perceptions of helpfulness of formal EIP practices and organizational commitment/job satisfaction**

	Workplaces with 10–24 employees		Workplaces with 25 + employees	
	Commitment	Satisfaction	Commitment	Satisfaction
Notice boards	0.239*	0.447**	0.471**	0.524**
	(0.108)	(0.121)	(0.050)	(0.058)
Email	0.239	0.150	0.314**	0.225**
	(0.130)	(0.124)	(0.069)	(0.066)
Intranet	−0.151	−0.008	0.045	−0.068
	(0.157)	(0.159)	(0.062)	(0.059)
Newsletters	0.133	0.138	0.364**	0.388**
	(0.128)	(0.142)	(0.052)	(0.053)
Union/employee reps.	0.179	0.091	0.170**	0.153**
	(0.180)	(0.184)	(0.062)	(0.057)
Meetings	0.971**	1.043**	0.683**	0.935**
	(0.111)	(0.129)	(0.053)	(0.057)
Number of observations	2123	2128	14,411	14,279

*significant at 5%
**significant at 1%

processes that provide guidance and inspiration for informal EIP so it could be questioned whether the latter can exist without the support of formal structures. This is an important issue because variations in the degree of EIP (in)formality are likely to be found within and between different workplaces, between workplaces of different sizes and across different sectors and institutional regimes. Data that illuminate this point are shown in Table 10.3, again based on analysis of WERS 2004.

This shows some significant differences between very small workplaces and the rest of the survey sample. For employees in workplaces with 25 or more employees, there are positive and highly significant links between employee perceptions of the helpfulness of all of the EIP practices – except intranets – and organizational commitment and job satisfaction. For workplaces with 10 to 24 employees, positive significant links were found for fewer EIP practices. One inference is that significant links between employee perceptions of EIP techniques and job satisfaction and organizational commitment will only be found for EIP techniques that are most likely to be practised in the smallest workplaces. Face-to-face meetings, for example, are likely to be extremely important in these establishments but may take many forms. For example, 'meetings' could comprise a talk from the managing director to the whole workforce but it could also be a 10-minute chat with a line manager, a chance discussion with a colleague or a long unscheduled debate among a work group. They might also take place as part of the work process rather than carrying the label of EIP. Contrariwise, email and newsletters may be inappropriate in small organizations, and unionization is much less common in SMEs. This would explain why there are many more significant associations in larger establishments. In small workplaces, informality is likely to be driven by the types of EIP practices used but it may well be that informal processes can oil the wheels of formal EIP machinery in larger establishments. In short, this evidence supports our argument that the influence of micro-level factors is critically important in trying to understand the ways in which EIP is practised.

Conclusion

It is to be hoped that this chapter has illustrated the complexity of EIP and analysed the plurality of techniques available and the massive variations in the ways in which it is applied. This is due in no small measure to the fact that both the adoption and the application of EIP are shaped by influences within and beyond the workplace. At a macro level different legislative regimes, political orientations and cultural norms influence – more or less strongly – forms of EIP adopted, so producing widely differing systems of worker participation. For example, central European and Nordic countries have enshrined employee rights to worker voice in an array of indirect consultation and codetermination machinery founded on a belief in consensual employment relations. In contrast, the United States and UK history, of rather more antagonistic relationships between workers and employers and lower levels of state support for collective forms of EIP, has meant that in recent years lower levels of unionization have allowed much greater use of direct EIP. At workplace level, these macro-level factors combine with product, labour market, technology and skill levels, worker interests and management style to produce specific combinations and applications of EIP (Marchington forthcoming 2007). This shows EIP is promoted or impeded by specific configurations of factors at both national and local level and it raises questions of whether the interplay between the practices adopted leads to tensions or mutual reinforcement. Our chapter has charted a continuing trend to use direct EIP at the expense of indirect methods but the latter still retain a substantial presence and influence. There appears to be growing evidence of complementarity between these multiple methods, at least across the Anglo-American world (Boxall et al. 2007; Teicher et al. forthcoming 2007) but where MNCs are operating, tensions are also likely due to the interaction of home and host country effects.

It is arguable, however, that understanding the application and outcomes of EIP at workplace level is where most research attention is still needed. Our evidence shows a link between EIP and employee outcomes of organizational commitment and job satisfaction and that line managers' roles in applying and reinforcing EIP principles in the workplace are critical. As Purcell and Georgiadis bluntly put it: 'merely adopting the structures of EI is not enough' (forthcoming 2007). The problem of providing sufficient guidance and incentives for line managers to embed EIP thoroughly is well known and seemingly intractable. However, the fragile case often found for the impact and effectiveness of EIP no doubt lies partly in shallow implementation, so senior managers need to recognize that they are likely to reap what they sow. Few benefits are likely to be found where EIP structures are superficial and not embedded via dedicated management practice. For academics, there is a need to develop both the application of LMX theory to the field of EIP and to analyse further the interactions between formal and informal EIP. This would be helpful in explaining the interaction between line managers and employees in fostering employee engagement with EIP and it could contribute to discussions about how line managers might be trained to improve the application of formal and informal methods.

The future for EIP, at least in the immediate European context, is dominated by the progressive implementation of the Information and Consultation of Employees Regulations. By 2008 these will require all organizations with at least 50 workers to provide data and seek worker views on all major changes affecting them. In the UK, proponents of indirect representative EIP see opportunities to bolster the role of unions through the regulations (Veale 2005) while others are keen to stress the flexibility that the legislation affords to employers and workers to accommodate local preferences (Yeandle 2005). The regulations are indeed capable of a fairly elastic interpretation. However, they should stimulate employee awareness of their rights to be consulted at the workplace and make employers at least question whether they are doing enough to satisfy employees' desires to be informed about workplace change and to voice their views on it. This therefore places us at a point in the development of EIP where there is now an implicit renewal of support for indirect methods following a period of sustained growth in direct techniques. Questions about how direct and indirect, and formal and informal, EIP can co-exist in the future will now need to be addressed by academics and practitioners alike.

References

Ackers, P., M. Marchington, A. Wilkinson and T. Dundon (2005). 'Partnership and voice, with or without trade unions: changing UK management approaches to organisational participation', in M. Stuart and M. Martinez Lucio (eds) *Partnership and Modernisation in Employment Relations*. London, Routledge.

Appelbaum, E., T. Bailey, P. Berg and A. Kalleberg (2000). *Manufacturing Advantage: Why High Performance Work Systems Pay Off*. Ithaca, Cornell University Press.

Barker, J. (1993). 'Tightening the iron cage: coercive control in self-managing teams', *Administrative Science Quarterly* 38(3): 408–37.

Batt, R. (2004). 'Who benefits from teams: comparing workers, supervisors, managers', *Industrial Relations* 43(1): 183-212.

Benders, J. (2005). 'Team working: a tale of partial participation', in B. Harley, J. Hyman and P. Thompson (eds) *Participation and Democracy at Work*. Basingstoke, Palgrave.

Benson, G. and E. Lawler (2003). 'Employee involvement: utilization, impacts and future prospects', in D. Holman, T. Wall, C. Clegg, P. Sparrow and A. Howard (eds) *The New Workplace: A Guide to the Human Impact Of Modern Working Practices*. Chichester, Wiley.

Boselie, P., J. Paauwe and R. Richardson (2003). 'Human resource management, institutional and organisational performance: a comparison of hospitals, hotels and local government', *International Journal of Human Resource Management* 14(8): 1407-29.

Boxall, P., P. Haynes and K. Macky (2007). 'Employee voice and voiceless-ness in New Zealand', in R. Freeman, P. Boxall and P. Haynes (eds) *What Workers Say: Employee Voice in the Anglo-American World*. Ithaca, Cornell University Press.

Bryson, A. (2004). 'Managerial responsiveness to union and nonunion worker voice in Britain', *Industrial Relations* 43(1): 213-41.

Cappelli, P. and D. Neumark (2001). 'Do high-performance work practices improve establishment-level outcomes?', *Industrial and Labor Relations Review* 54(4): 737-75.

Cotton, J. (1993). *Employee Involvement: Methods for Improving Performance and Work Attitudes*. Newbury Park, CA, Sage.

Cotton, J., D. Vollrath, K. Froggatt, M. Lengnick-Hall and K. Jennings (1988). 'Employee participation: diverse forms and different outcomes', *Academy of Management Review* 13: 8-22.

Cox, A., M. Marchington and S. Zagelmeyer (2003). 'The embeddedness of employee involvement and participation (EIP) and its impact on employee outcomes - an analysis of WERS 98', paper presented to EGOS Colloquium, Copenhagen, 3-5 July.

Cox, A., M. Marchington and J. Suter (2006a). *Embedding the Provision of Information and Consultation in the Workplace*. Draft paper to the Department of Trade and Industry.

Cox, A., S. Zagelmeyer and M. Marchington (2006b). 'Embedding employee involvement and participation at work', *Human Resource Management Journal* 16(3): 250-67.

Coyle-Shapiro, J. A.-M. and N. Conway (2004). 'The employment relationship through the lens of social exchange', in J. Coyle-Shapiro, L. Shore, M. S. Taylor and L. Tetrick (eds) *The Employment Relationship: Examining Psychological and Contextual Perspectives*. Oxford, Oxford University Press.

Cully, M., A. O'Reilly, N. Millward, J. Forth, S. Woodland, G. Dix and A. Bryson (1998). *The 1998 Workplace Employee Relations Survey: First Findings*. Department of Trade and Industry. London, HMSO.

Cully, M., A. O'Reilly, N. Millward, J. Forth, S. Woodland, G. Dix and A. Bryson (1999). *Britain At Work: As Depicted by the 1998 Workplace Employee Relations Survey*. London, Routledge.

Delbridge, R. and K. Whitfield (2001). 'Employee perceptions of job influence and organizational participation', *Industrial Relations* 40(3): 472-89.

Dundon, T., A. Wilkinson, M. Marchington and P. Ackers (2004). 'The meanings and purpose of employee voice', *International Journal of Human Resource Management* 15(6): 1149-70.

Ferner, A., P. Almond, T. Colling and T. Edwards (2005). 'Policies on union representation in US multinationals in the UK: between micro-politics and macro-institutions', *British Journal of Industrial Relations* 43(4): 703-28.

Forth, J., H. Bewley and A. Bryson (2006). *Small and Medium-sized Enterprises: Findings from the 2004 Workplace Employment Relations Survey*. Department of Trade and Industry. London, HMSO.

Freeman, R. and J. Rogers (1999). *What Workers Want*. Ithaca, Cornell University Press.

Freeman, R., P. Boxall and P. Haynes (eds) (forthcoming 2007). *What Workers Say: Employee Voice in the Anglo-American World*. Ithaca, Cornell University Press.

Gerstner, C. and D. Day (1997). 'Meta-analytic review of leader–member exchange theory: correlates and construct issues', *Journal of Applied Psychology* 82(6): 827-44.

Gill, C. and H. Krieger (1999). 'Direct and representative participation in Europe: recent survey evidence', *International Journal of Human Resource Management* 10(1): 572-91.

Godard, J. (2004). 'A critical assessment of the high performance paradigm', *British Journal of Industrial Relations* 42(2): 349-78.

Gospel, H. and P. Willman (2005). 'Changing patterns of employee voice', in J. Storey (ed.) *Adding Value through Information and Consultation*. Basingstoke, Palgrave Macmillan.

Granovetter, M. (1985). 'Economic action and social structure: the problem of embeddedness', *American Journal of Sociology* 91(3): 481-510.

Guest, D. and N. Conway (2002). 'Communicating the psychological contract', *Human Resource Management Journal* 12(2): 22-33.

Guest, D. and R. Peccei (2001). 'Partnership at work: mutuality and the balance of advantage', *British Journal of Industrial Relations* 39(1): 207-36.

Guest, D., J. Michie, N. Conway and M. Sheehan (2003). 'Human resource management and performance', *British Journal of Industrial Relations* 41(2): 291-314.

Handel, M. and D. Levine (2004). 'The effects of new work practices on workers', *Industrial Relations* 43(1): 1-43.

Harley, B., J. Hyman and P. Thompson (eds) (2005). *Participation and Democracy at Work: Essays in Honour of Harvie Ramsay*. Basingstoke, Palgrave Macmillan.

Heller, F., E. Pusić, G. Strauss and B. Wilpert (eds) (1998). *Organizational Participation - Myth and Reality.* Oxford, Oxford University Press.

Kersley, B., C. Alpin, J. Forth, A. Bryson, H. Bewley, G. Dix and S. Oxenbridge (2005). *Inside the Workplace: First Findings from the 2004 Workplace Employment Relations Survey.* Department of Trade and Industry. London, HMSO.

Kersley, B., C. Alpin, J. Forth, A. Bryson, H. Bewley, G. Dix and S. Oxenbridge (2006). *Inside the Workplace: Findings from the 2004 Workplace Employment Relations Survey.* Department of Trade and Industry. London, HMSO.

Kessler, I., R. Undy and P. Heron (2004). 'Employee perspectives on communication and consultation: findings from a cross-national survey', *International Journal of Human Resource Management* 15(3): 512-32.

Khilji, S. and X. Wang (2006). 'Intended and implemented HRM: the missing linchpin in strategic human resource management research', *International Journal of Human Resource Management* 17(7): 1171-89.

Liden, R., T. Bauer and B. Erdogan (2004). 'The role of leader–member exchange in the dynamic relationship between employer and employee: implications for employee socialization, leaders, and organizations', in L. Shore, S. Taylor, J. Coyle-Shapiro and L. Tetrick (eds) *The Employment Relationship: Examining Psychological and Contextual Perspectives.* Oxford: Oxford University Press.

Marchington, M. (1994), 'The dynamics of joint consultation', in K. Sisson (ed.) *Personnel Management,* 2nd edn. Oxford, Blackwell.

Marchington, M. (forthcoming 2007). 'Employee voice systems', in P. Boxall, J. Purcell and P. Wright, *Oxford Handbook of Human Resource Management.* Oxford, Oxford University Press.

Marchington, M. and A. Wilkinson (2005). 'Direct participation and involvement', in S. Bach, *Managing Human Resources: Personnel Management in Transition,* 4th edn. Oxford, Blackwell.

Marchington, M., J. Goodman, A. Wilkinson and P. Ackers (1992). *New Developments in Employee Involvement.* Employment Department Research Paper No. 2.

Marchington, M., A. Wilkinson, P. Ackers and T. Dundon (2001). *Management Choice and Employee Voice.* London, Chartered Institute of Personnel and Development.

Maslyn, J. and M. Uhl-Bien (2001). 'Leader–member exchange and its dimensions: effects of self and other effort on relationship quality', *Journal of Applied Psychology* 86(4): 697-708.

McGovern, P., L. Gratton, V. Hope-Hailey, P. Stiles and C. Truss (1997). 'Human resource management on the line?', *Human Resource Management Journal* 7(4): 12-29.

O'Creevy, M. and S. Wood (2005). 'Benefiting from a multichannel approach', in J. Storey (ed.) *Adding Value through Information and Consultations.* Basingstoke, Palgrave Macmillan.

Osterman, P. (2000). 'Work restructuring in an era of restructuring: trends in diffusion and effect on employee welfare', *Industrial and Labor Relations Review* 53(2): 179-96.

Poole, M. (1975). *Workers' Participation in Industry.* London, Routledge.

Purcell, J. and K. Georgiadis (forthcoming 2007). 'Why should employers bother with worker voice?', in R. Freeman, P. Boxall and P. Haynes (eds) *What Workers Say: Employee Voice in the Anglo-American World.* Ithaca, Cornell University Press.

Purcell, J., N. Kinnie, S. Hutchinson, B. Rayton and J. Swart (2003). *Understanding the People and Performance Link: Unlocking the Black Box.* London, CIPD.

Rubery, J. and D. Grimshaw (2003). *The Organisation of Employment: An International Perspective.* London, Palgrave.

Sewell, G. (2005). 'Doing what comes naturally? Why we need a practical ethics of teamwork', *International Journal of Human Resource Management* 16(2): 202-18.

Sparrowe, R. T. and R. C. Liden (1997). 'Process and structure in leader–member exchange', *The Academy of Management Review* 22(2): 522-52.

Strauss, G. (1998). 'An overview', in F. Heller, E. Pusić, G. Strauss and B. Wilpert (1998) *Organizational Participation - Myth and Reality.* Oxford, Oxford University Press.

Stuart, M. and M. Martinez Lucio (eds) (2005). *Partnership and Modernisation in Employment Relations.* London, Routledge.

Suter, J. (2003). 'An analysis of formal and informal employee involvement: a case study of a National Health Service Trust', unpublished MSc dissertation, Manchester School of Management, UMIST.

Teicher, J., P. Holland, A. Pyman and B. Cooper (fothcoming 2007). 'Employee voice in Australia', in R. Freeman, P. Boxall and P. Haynes (eds) *What Workers Say: Employee Voice in the Anglo-American World.* Ithaca, Cornell University Press.

Van Emmerik, H. and K. Sanders (2004). 'Social embeddedness and job performance of tenured and non-tenured professionals', *Human Resource Management Journal* 14(1): 40-54.

Veale, S. (2005) 'Information and consultation: a TUC perspective', in J. Storey (ed.) *Adding Value through Information and Consultation.* Basingstoke, Palgrave Macmillan.

Whittaker, S. and M. Marchington (2003). 'Devolving HR responsibility to the line: threat, opportunity or partnership?', *Employee Relations* 25(3): 245-61.

Wilkinson, A., G. Godfrey and M. Marchington (1997). 'Bouquets, brickbats and blinkers: total quality management and employee involvement in practice', *Organization Studies* 18(5): 799-819.

Yeandle, D. (2005). 'An employers' organisation perspective', in J. Storey (ed.) *Adding Value through Information and Consultation.* Basingstoke, Palgrave Macmillan.

International HRM

This part of the book contains two chapters, which, in their distinct ways, cover the twin pillars of international HRM: comparative HR, on the one hand, and the management of international enterprises, on the other. These two chapters are written by two sets of analysts who have for many years been leading researchers in these two domains.

In Chapter 11 Chris Brewster reviews the field of comparative HRM. Chris is the founder of and was, for many years, Director of Cranet the international survey of HRM practice across many countries. The central focus of this chapter is the variation in HR practice across the world. In an increasingly global context for business, knowledge of how management of people varies in different territories becomes correspondingly more important. The chapter provides an excellent coverage of the key debates in comparative HRM and of the main conceptual paradigms that are used in its study.

Chapter 12, by David Collings and Hugh Scullion, examines global staffing in the context of multinational enterprises. Unlike the chapter by Chris Brewster, which focused on comparative HR, the purpose of this chapter is to focus on the critical strategic and operational staffing issues that international organizations must confront. The authors have been at the forefront of empirical research on international talent management and the varied use of parent country expatriates and locally sourced staff. The growth of emerging markets such as China and India makes this set of themes of increasing importance.

HRM: the comparative dimension

Chris Brewster

Introduction

Human resource management (HRM) is universal. Every organization has to utilize and, hence, in some way, to manage, human resources. Two of the classic texts identified four areas (employee influence, human resource flow, reward systems, work systems, in Beer et al. 1985) or a five-step cycle (selection, performance, appraisal, rewards and development, in Fombrun et al. 1984), which they imply can be used to analyse HRM in any organization anywhere in the world. These approaches, or variations of them, are used in, perhaps, most universities and business schools. However, approaches to HRM, and the practice of HRM, vary across the world. This chapter focuses on the extent to which the concepts and practice of HRM vary country by country. Are the models converging and, if so, towards which model? The US case is particularly important, given the power of the US version of HRM. Are countries in the increasingly unified Europe developing a distinctive and converging pattern of European HRM? Or are there identifiable differences in the way they manage human resources?

Some of the old cinemas, with what was then high-tech, wrap-around screens, used to show a sequence that started with a bird's-eye view of a small child. Then, through the use of telephoto lenses merging with satellite pictures, the camera slowly pulled back so that the child lost a little definition and became first one of a group of children and then gradually disappeared, as the group became part of a street scene. The camera continued to pull back to reveal the street to be successively part of a suburb, a city, a conurbation, a country, a continent and eventually an invisible dot on planet Earth. Each picture is in itself accurate: each helps us to understand some things better while blurring others. This chapter uses this extended focus pulling as an analogy for examining the differences in the way human resource management (HRM) is practised in different countries. The focus of much of the research and analysis of HRM, particularly in the UK, has been at workplace level. There is also a strong tradition comparing HRM in organizations of different size, sector or ownership within one country. At the other extreme, there are commentators who state, or imply, that their analysis is universal. This chapter adopts a mid-focus position, concentrating on comparative HRM: the differences between countries. The main area of focus is comparisons between countries, but occasionally the focus will be changed to note differences between regional groups of countries (such as the European Union or groups within that) or differences within countries. As with the cinema metaphor, this picture is no more or less accurate than the others: it just helps us to understand some things more clearly.

This chapter is based on the belief that we have increasingly to take an international and comparative view of these issues. There is a growing internationalization in the field of business. The concept of globalization has taken a firm hold in the management literature as it has in the political and cultural literature. This holds true not only for the large multinationals in the private sector, but also for smaller employers and for organizations in the public sector. Through the emergence of large trading blocs like the European Union, this trend has been accelerated. Hence, an increased knowledge about the specifics of management across borders (Sparrow et al. 2004), including knowledge of how human resource management issues are handled in various countries, has become a prominent issue for social scientists as it has become a key issue for all kinds of managers.

This chapter addresses this issue, first, by exploring some of the key debates in comparative human resource management. These are the conceptual paradigms that underlie how the topic is understood; the issue of convergence and divergence; and the issue of the explanatory factors for the differences that are found. These conceptual distinctions provide a platform on which to explore some of the differences in the way that human resources are managed in different countries.

Universalist and contextual paradigms in HRM

Things are done differently in different countries. This includes differences in the way that human resource management is conceptualized; the research traditions through which it is explored; and the way HRM is conducted. In conceptual and research terms two different (ideal type) paradigms have been classified as the *universalist* and the *contextual* (Brewster 1999). The notion of paradigm is used here in Kuhn's (1970) sense as an accepted model or theory and with the corollary that different researchers may be using competing models or theories. This notion of paradigms has been applied to HRM elsewhere (Delery and Doti 1996; Wright and McMahan 1992). There will, of course, be other paradigms. Many of these will, like the two ideal types explored in more detail in this chapter, have originated in particular geographical areas; though like them they will have adherents now in many countries. Thus, there is a strong Latin paradigm of research into HRM which, building on the French sociological and Marxist traditions and the focus on Roman law, is concerned with the establishment of large-scale concepts, societal level and political interactions and the nature and detail of the law. There are different approaches to the notion of HRM in Japan, and so on. For our purposes here, the universalist and contextual paradigms will serve as good examples, building as they do on the significant US and northern European traditions.

HRM in Action 11.1   Lidl in Finland

Peltonen (2006) explores what happened when the German supermarket chain, Lidl, opened up in Finland. An employers' association official explained:

> When Lidl first came to Finland and contacted us, we got the impression that it wanted to operate as a regular Finnish retailing chain . . . Furthermore, in my opinion Lidl does not even stand out among the international retailing companies operating in Finland: there are numerous foreign chains that have subsidiaries in Finland, and I think we can ignore the conclusion that the foreign companies were somehow different or special in the human resource management sense. All the firms I know follow the strategy of adapting to the local environment and that is why most international retailing companies have joined our association before they have started their operations in Finland.

As part of Lidl's strategy, the company joined the employer's association in order to acquire the knowledge needed for the adjustment of its HR policies to the national context. But, of course, Lidl also wanted to take advantage of the strategies that had led to success in Germany and that were not common in Finland. A trade union official saw it as follows:

> Some store managers and regional executives at Lidl seem to be more competent than others and, as a whole, things work very well in these shops from our point of view. My theory is that many of the problems are created as corporate level HR strategies are implemented at regional and store levels and the knowledge of the proper way of managing people is lost in the process. It is not appropriate for us in our role to start training and helping Lidl middle managers to become better at managing human resource issues, although I must admit that we have been doing that to some extent.

It is to some degree the difference between these paradigms, lack of awareness of them and the tendency for commentators to drift from one to another, which has led to the confusion about the very nature of HRM as a field of study as pointed out by many of its leading figures (see, e.g., Storey 1992, 1995).

The *universalist paradigm,* which is dominant in the USA, but is widely used elsewhere, is essentially a nomothetic social science approach: using evidence to test generalizations of an abstract and law-like character. As in other related areas of the social sciences, the universalist paradigm tends to seek convergence. This paradigm assumes that the purpose of the study of our area of the social sciences, HRM, and in particular strategic human resource management (SHRM) (see, e.g., Ulrich and Smallwood 2005; Wright and McMahan 1992), is to improve the way that human resources are managed strategically within organizations. The ultimate aim of this work is to improve organizational performance, as judged by its impact on the organization's declared corporate strategy (Huselid 1995; Tichy et al. 1982), the customer (Ulrich 1989) or shareholders (Becker and Gerhart 1996; Huselid 1995). Further, it is implicit that this objective will apply in all cases. Thus, the widely cited definition by Wright and McMahan states that SHRM is 'the pattern of planned human resource deployments and activities intended to enable a firm to achieve its goals' (1992: 298).

The value of this paradigm lies in the simplicity of focus, the coalescing of research around this shared objective and the clear relationship with the demands of industry. The disadvantages lie in the ignoring of other potential focuses, the resultant narrowness of the research objectives and the ignoring of other levels of analysis and other stakeholders in the outcomes of SHRM (cf. Brewster 2004; Legge 1995).

Arguably, there is greater coherence in the USA as to what constitutes 'good' HRM: a coalescing of views around the concept of 'high-performance work systems'. These have been characterized by the US Department of Labor (1993) as having certain clear characteristics:

- careful and extensive systems for recruitment, selection and training
- formal systems for 'sharing information with the individuals who work in the organization'
- clear job design
- participation procedures
- monitoring of attitudes
- individual performance appraisals
- properly functioning grievance procedures
- promotion and compensation schemes that provide for the recognition and financial rewarding of high-performing members of the workforce.

It would appear that, while there have been many other attempts to develop such lists (see, for example, Storey 1992, 1995), and they all differ to some degree, the Department of Labor list can be taken as an exemplar of the universalist paradigm: few US researchers in HRM would find very much to argue with in this list, though they are likely to label their studies as SHRM. Both researchers and practitioners in other countries, however, find such a list contrary to experience and even to what they would conceive of as good practice. Thus, they might argue for information being shared with representative bodies such as trade unions or works councils, for flexible work boundaries, for group reward systems. And they might argue that attitude monitoring, appraisal systems and so on are culturally inappropriate.

Common to this debate is the assumption that SHRM is concerned with the aims and actions of management within the organization. Perhaps in a country like the USA which has as an avowed aim of most politicians the objective of 'freeing business from outside interference', it makes sense to develop a vision of human resource management that takes as its scope the policies and practices of management. (Although here too it is worth pointing out, so that the argument is not misunderstood, that there are American commentators who do not accept this limitation on their analysis.)

Methodologically, research based on this vision of HRM is deductive: it involves generating carefully designed questions that can lead to proof or disproof, the elements of which can be measured in such a way that the question itself can be subjected to the mechanism of testing and prediction. Built into this paradigm is the assumption that research is not 'rigorous' unless it is drawn from existing literature and theory, focused around a tightly designed question that can be proved or disproved to be 'correct', and contains a structure of testing that can lead on to prediction. The research base is mostly centred on a small number of private sector 'leading-edge' exemplars of 'good practice', often large multinationals, generally from the manufacturing even specifically the high-tech sector.

The *contextual paradigm* by contrast is idiographic, searching for an overall understanding of what is contextually unique and why. In our topic area, it is focused on understanding what is different between and within HRM in various contexts and what the antecedents of those differences are. Hence, the research mechanisms used are inductive. Here, theory is drawn from an accumulation of data collected or gathered in a less directed (or constrained) manner than would be the case under the universalist paradigm. Research traditions are different: focused less on testing and prediction and more on the collection of evidence. There is an assumption that if things are important they should be studied, even if testable prediction is not possible or the resultant data are complex and unclear. The policies and practices of the 'leading-edge' companies (something of a value-laden term in itself) which are the focus of much HRM research and literature in the USA are of less interest to the contextualists than identifying the way labour markets work and what the more typical organizations are doing. Among most researchers working in this paradigm, it is the explanations that matter – any link to firm performance is secondary. It is assumed that HRM can apply to societies, governments or regions as well as to firms. At the level of the organization (not 'firm' – public sector and not-for-profit organizations are also included) the organization's objectives and strategy are not necessarily assumed to be 'good' either for the organization or for society. There are plenty of examples where this is clearly not the case. Neither, in this paradigm, is there any assumption that the interests of everyone in the organization will be the same; or any expectation that an organization will have a strategy that people within the organization will 'buy in to'. The assumption is that not only will the employees and the unions have a different perspective to the management team (Kochan et al. 1986; Purcell and Ahlstrand 1994), but that even within the management team there may be different interests and views (Kochan et al. 1986; Lepak and Snell 1999).

These, and the resultant impact on HRM, are issues for empirical study. As a contributor to explanation, this paradigm emphasizes external factors as well as the actions of the management within an organization. Thus it explores the importance of such factors as culture, ownership structures, labour markets, the role of the state and trade union organization as aspects of the subject rather than external influences on it. The scope of HRM goes beyond the organization to reflect the reality of the role of many HR departments, particularly in Europe: for example, in lobbying about and adjusting to government actions, in dealing with such issues as equal opportunities legislation or with trade unions and tripartite institutions. This paradigm is widespread in the UK and Ireland, Australia and New Zealand and in many of the northern European countries and has some adherents in North America. Furthermore, if one were to judge by the journals and newsletters put out by the HR societies and consultancies, HR practitioners in the USA are as interested in many of the same legislative and labour market issues as those elsewhere. This seems to apply particularly to the US public sector where, perhaps, the pressures of compliance are greatest. Interestingly, there are increasing calls from North Americans for a contextual paradigm or, to be precise, approaches that have considerable resonance with this paradigm, to be used in the USA (see, for example, Dyer and Kochan 1995).

Outside the USA, much of the research is located squarely in the contextual paradigm, concerned to develop a critique of the relationship between owners and/or managers used and the employees and the society in which the organizations operate. There is less likelihood of the researchers assuming that the purposes of the power holders in the organization are unchallengeable and that the role of research is to identify how HRM contributes to those purposes.

The universalist model has been subjected to significant critique in Europe, particularly. Looking at the UK, Guest sees 'signs that … the American model is losing its appeal as attention focuses to a greater extent on developments in Europe' (Guest 1990: 377); the same author is elsewhere sceptical of the feasibility of transferring the model to Britain. The point was also noted in the Germany: 'An international comparison of HR practices clearly indicates that the basic functions of HR management are given different weights in different countries and that they are carried out differently' (Gaugler 1988: 26); and 'a single universal model of HRM does not exist' (Pieper 1990: 11). Critiques have also come from France; arguing that 'we are in culturally different contexts' and, that 'rather than copy solutions which result from other cultural traditions, we should consider the state of mind that presided in the search for responses adapted to the culture' (Albert 1989: 75, translation in Brewster and Bournois 1991).

Many of the seminal management and even HRM texts are written as if the analysis applies at all levels: what Rose (1991) called 'false universalism'. These texts are produced in one country and tend to base their work on a small number of by now well-known cases. This only becomes a problem when the analysis or prescriptions in those texts are adopted unthinkingly elsewhere. But the world, including the academic world of HRM, is becoming ever more international. This is a major problem in relation to the US literature. The cultural hegemony of US teaching and publishing, particularly in the US journals, mean that these texts are often utilized by readers and students in other countries. US-based literature searches, now all done on computer, of course, tend to show little writing outside the universalist tradition. For analysts and practitioners elsewhere with interests in different sectors, countries and so on, many of these descriptions and prescriptions fail to meet their reality. It is not that either paradigm is necessarily correct or more instructive than others, but that the level and focus needs to be specified to make the analysis meaningful (Brewster 1999).

Convergence and divergence in HRM

Early management theorists were generally clear that practice would converge towards the most efficient and therefore, they argued, the US model (see, e.g. Drucker 1950; Harbison and Myers 1959). More recently, the convergence thesis has received support from transaction cost economics: this too contends that at any one point of time there exists a best solution to organizing labour (Williamson 1985). 'Most transaction cost theorists argue that there is one best organizational form for firms that have similar or identical transaction costs' (Hollingsworth and Boyer 1997: 34). A widespread emphasis on the benchmarking practices of organizations, and attempts at the diffusion of 'best practices' have been noted (Marchington and Grugulis 2000; Wright and Brewster 2003). They have doubtless contributed to shaping similar forms of organization across countries as well as similar curricula in business education.

Most of these views centre around convergence towards a US model – the model of the most powerful country in the world (Smith and Meiksins 1995). One theoretical possibility, therefore, is that as policies of market deregulation and state decontrol are spreading from the USA to Europe, firms everywhere move towards North American HRM.

Another possibility is that different regional models of HRM may be created. The increasing economic and political integration of the European Union (EU) countries, for example, may cause a convergence, within Europe, towards a distinct European model of HRM. In Europe, 27 states, currently, are engaged in a historically unique experiment: they have agreed to subordinate national legislative decision making to European-level legislation. These developments have indirect effects on the way people are managed as a result of political and economic integration and direct effects through the EU's adoption of a distinct social sphere of activity. The Social Charter and its associated Social Action Programme are having an increasing legislative influence on HRM. Twenty-seven countries (plus some of the surrounding countries that have agreed to take account of EU legislation in the employment area or are candidate countries for EU membership) now share similar basic legislation on working hours, holidays, discrimination, health and safety, consultation with the workforce, and a host of other detailed legislative requirements. The advent of the European Union, providing institutional arrangements at the supranational level may, through such developments, support an institutional branch of convergence theory (Gooderham and Brewster 2003).

There is also a third theoretical possibility: that organizations are so locked into their respective national institutional settings that no common model is likely to emerge for the foreseeable future. Since HR systems reflect national institutional contexts and cultures and these do not respond readily to the imperatives of technology or the market, each country will continue to be distinctive (DiMaggio and Powell 1983). The literature often refers to divergence theories, but what is usually meant is 'non-convergence': no one is arguing that countries are becoming even more dissimilar – just that they remain distinctive in the way that they manage their HRM. Managers in each country operate within a national institutional context and a shared set of cultural assumptions. Neither institutions nor cultures change quickly and rarely in ways that are the same as other counties. It follows that managers within one country behave in a way that is noticeably different from managers in other countries. More importantly, change is path dependent. In other words, even when change does occur it can be understood only in relation to the specific social context in which it occurs (Maurice et al. 1986). Even superficially universal principles ('profit', 'efficiency'), may be interpreted differently in different countries (Hofstede et al. 2002).

Locke et al. (1995: 159) described the issue of convergence as an 'old debate': however, it is not a concept that has been used consistently. Attempts have been made to develop a more nuanced theory of convergence (Brewster et al. 2004; Mayrhofer et al. 2002). These authors develop a distinction between *directional* convergence (whether countries share the same trend) and *final* convergence (whether they are becoming more alike). In the literature, evidence of similarity in HRM between countries, or similar trends, has sometimes been taken as evidence of convergence: but convergence can only be shown over time – and if countries start, as they do, from different positions even similar trends (directional convergence) may not lead to increasing similarity between countries.

The evidence produced by the Mayrhofer and Brewster teams shows that in Europe many aspects of HRM show directional convergence – i.e. the trends *are* the same. This is not always the case: the ratio of HR specialists to the rest of the organization, or the size of the HR department, varies considerably with, mainly, country, but also with the size of the organization (Brewster et al. 2006) but does not show any clear directional trends. Neither does training and development, which is given high priority in many countries but seems to remain the first area for cuts when finances become tight. Despite the similarities in trends, however, there is very little evidence of countries becoming more alike in the way that they manage their human resources. The evidence is summarized as follows: 'From a directional convergence point of view, there seems to be a positive indication of convergence. However, when one looks at the question from a final convergence point of view, the answer is no longer a clear positive. None of the HR practices converge' (Brewster et al. 2004: 434)

Cultural and institutional explanations of differences in HRM

Comparative HRM, according to at least one authority, should attempt explanation as well as description (Boxall 1995). So if there are differences in the way that countries conceive of and practice HRM, what are the reasons for those differences? In broad terms, there are two competing sets of explanators: the cultural and the institutional. Are these differences 'sustained because people find it repulsive, unethical or unappealing to do otherwise ... [or] ... because a wider formal system of laws, agreements, standards and codes exist?' (Sorge 2004: 119).

Exploring the cultural explanators is not easy, because 'culture is one of those terms that defy a single all-purpose definition and there are almost as many meanings of culture as people using the term' (Ajiferuke and Boddewyn 1970: 154). Authorities like Fukuyama (1995) and Sako (1998) accord particular prominence to the possibility that organizations represent 'cultural communities' of rational utility-maximizing individuals. Variations in practices will be in line with different cultural contexts. Typically, these will reflect national boundaries, but this is by no means always the case. Thus, countries like Belgium, Spain and Switzerland contain communities speaking different languages, with different religions and different legislation: seeming, at least to the citizens there, sharply different in their approach to life. Cultural groups in the Middle East and Africa were divided by the colonial map makers and may have more in common with groups in countries across the national border than they do with other citizens of their own country. In many countries, however, especially the longer established ones and those within coherent geographical boundaries, such as islands, culture equates to country – and that is certainly the case in the research into workplace values (see, e.g. Hofstede 2001; House et al. 2004; Schwarz 1992, 1994; Spony 2003).

While the 'culturalist' school is an extremely broad one, what most of these approaches have in common is that they treat culture as a given; while it may be possible for a society to enhance its 'social capital', it is not possible to develop social trust deliberately and systematically, or radically depart from established rules and norms (Fukuyama 1995; Lane 1989). Culture is seen as shared by individuals as a means of conferring meaning, and adding sense, to social interactions. Even if the nature of that culture may be relatively fluid and subjective, it provides a persistent boundary, horizon or 'segment' to the lifeworld of individuals and clusters thereof.

A range of researchers have found geographically based, usually national, differences in deep-seated values about what is good or bad, honest or dishonest, fair or unfair, etc. (see, e.g. Hofstede 2001; House et al. 2004). These perceptions affect the way people in a country, especially here, perhaps, managers, view the world. Schwartz (1994), Schwartz and Sagiv (1995) and, more recently, Spony (2003) point to the interrelation between cultural-level and individual-level values: each individual will be different but the aggregation of their approaches makes what is acceptable and desirable in one country different from what is acceptable or desirable in another. Since human resource management is concerned with interactions between people at different hierarchical levels within an organization, these cultural differences will inevitably be reflected in differences in the way people are managed.

The institutional perspective, by contrast, sees the institutions of a society as being the environmental structures that keep them distinctive. Social arrangements in a nation are always distinct and many of the institutions are likely to shape the social construction of an organization. Thus, the general and vocational education system, the way labour markets work, employment legislation and the industrial relations system will all impact on the way that HRM can be conducted in particular states. HRM will be a function of the country's particular institutional arrangements – the 'societal effect' (Maurice et al. 1986). As with the culture effects, there seems to be a kind of societal recipe that it is possible to go against, or ignore, but only at a cost. Most people, or most organizations, do not do so.

The recognition of institutional differences is not new (Rosenzweig and Singh 1991). In particular, patterns of ownership vary (Brewster 2004). Public ownership has decreased to some extent in many European countries in recent years, but it is still far more widespread than in the USA. And private sector ownership may not mean the same thing. In many of the southern European countries particularly, ownership of even major companies remains in the hands of single families. In Germany, as a different example, most major companies are owned by a tight network of a small number of substantial banks. Their interlocking shareholdings and ownerships and close involvement in the management of these corporations mean less pressure to produce short-term profits and a positive disincentive to drive competitors out of the marketplace (Randlesome 1994).

While proponents of these two streams of thought generally give no more than a passing nod to the other view, it seems that neither an exclusively culturalist nor an exclusively institutional approach can be satisfactory. Many of the 'cultural' writers see institutions as being key artifacts of culture reflecting deep underlying variations in the values that they see between societies; many 'institutional' writers include culture as one of the institutional elements explaining differences. Giddens (1986) put forward the concept of structuration theory: individual behaviour and social structures are reciprocally constituted. Thus, institutions cannot survive without legitimacy, but individual perspectives are partially created and sustained by the institutional context. Arguably, the two explanations simply explore the same factors from different points of view (Brewster 2004; Sorge 2004).

The general management discussion is beginning to be reflected in the specific field of comparative HRM (Boxall 1995; Hollinshead and Leat 1995). In this respect, HRM is catching up with another aspect of the study of employment relationships, the study of industrial relations, which has long recognized the importance of international differences. Human resource management is increasingly acknowledged to be one of the areas where organizations are most likely to maintain a 'national flavour' (Rosenzweig and Nohria 1994) and is the point at which business and national cultures have the sharpest interface. This is shown in the next section.

HRM differences in practice

Reasons of space mean that it is impossible here to examine all the international variations in HR, so this chapter gives just three: two different HR practices (flexible working patterns and communications) and a brief discussion about the nature of the HR department.

Flexibility in labour patterns is now widely accepted as a critical issue in HRM. This is an area bedevilled with terminological problems. The term 'flexibility' is the one most commonly used in Europe. The European Commission prefers the term 'atypical working' and some trade unionists talk about 'vulnerable work'. Certain aspects of this subject are referred to as 'contingent working' in the USA. Arguably, all of these terms are to a degree inaccurate and certainly all the terms come with their own metaphorical baggage. Whatever the terminology, the assumption has been made that, with the amount of employment legislation and the embeddedness of the trade unions in the EU, the European workforce is highly inflexible and that this is linked to high levels of unemployment in some European states (see European Commission 1995). The evidence shows that this is wrong. Research conducted by the Cranet network, comparing organizations at national level across Europe (Tregaskis and Brewster 2006) is consistent with the national labour market statistics (European Commission various dates), and workplace-level data (Kersley et al. 2006) in showing extensive use of flexible working across Europe. Furthermore, some of these forms of flexibility (temporary employment and self-employment) are more widespread in Europe than in the USA, and in others (part-time work) the USA has about a median position on a ranking with the European countries (Standing 1997). Japan has a different pattern of flexible working to either of these territories, with considerable part-time working and temporary working, though less evidence of increases in these forms than elsewhere.

> Overall, organizations [in Europe] have tended to increase their use of contingent employment contracts from 1991 to 2000. This finding could be seen as indicative of regional isomorphic pressures for convergence, which have given rise to 'directional' convergence. However, the data also show that the divergence between the countries in evidence during the early 1990s remains a decade later. There is no evidence that either the regional institutional pressures coming from the European Commission or regional or global competitive pressures are creating 'final' convergence in organizational practice . . . [T]hese findings support the divergence (or at least the non-convergence or stasis) thesis that the role of national institutional systems is a powerful force for shaping local organizational responses with respect to the use of contingent employment contracts (Whitley, 2000; Hall and Soskice, 2001).
>
> Tregaskis and Brewster 2006

The Cranet data show that despite differences within countries between sectors, particularly, flexible working practices are growing in both extent and coverage almost everywhere. This is so in nearly all countries in Europe, in Japan and Australasia, in all sectors, in organizations both large and small, and whatever the form or origin of ownership. 'Atypical' work patterns or contracts, such as temporary, casual, fixed-term, home-based and annual hours contracts, are spreading, despite differing legal, cultural and labour traditions.

Rather than making use of a full range of the potential flexible working arrangements, most organizations still rely mainly on part-time or temporary employment. Throughout the last decade, at least four out of 10 organizations in Europe increased part-time or temporary employment. Fixed-term employment, much more a public sector practice, has also become more widespread. However, organizations where these forms of flexibility cover a majority of workers continue to be in a clear minority. Furthermore, the increase in the use of flexible contracts tends to be significantly higher among those organizations already making comparatively high use of such contracts.

The overall effect is to change the nature of the work relationship. There is now only just around a half of the European working population, for example, with standard (permanent, full-time, etc.) employment contracts. So many people now work part time, or on a temporary contract, or as self-employed, or on myriad other forms of work pattern, that the change in extent is developing into a change in kind. This will have extensive effects, also, beyond the world of work in areas such as finance and the housing market (mortgages and bank loans are not easy to come by for those on these flexible contracts); tax (many people are working but not earning enough to pay taxes); and demands on government resources.

Changes in the labour market that increase the amount of short-term and variable employment packages, or even the forms of getting work done through non-employment options such as subcontracting or consultancy, are arguably at least moving the situation in the developed countries back towards the practices of the past – and of the current undeveloped world. However, you cannot step into the same river twice: and flexible working practices now operate in a very different environment from those of the past.

The trends may be common, but practice is not. Between countries, and between organizations within countries, there are clear preferences for different kinds of flexibility (see Figures 11.1 and 11.2 for examples). No country or organization makes extensive use of the full range of flexible working patterns and contracts. Flexibility is dependent on a complex, interlocking web of national culture, history, institutions, trade union approaches and strength, governmental approaches (including legislation) and managerial tradition (Tregaskis and Brewster 2006). Despite the hopes of some European politicians, there is no simple correlation between flexibility and employment levels or training provision. The data do suggest that flexible workers get less training, but it does not appear to be linked with job creation; some kinds of flexibility in some countries can be linked to employment creation or diminution, but there is no overall pattern.

Thus, in Spain there is a high level of short-term employment with low levels of part-time work. Countries such as Austria, the Netherlands, Sweden and the UK have one-third or more of organizations with over 5% of the workforce on temporary contracts. Most of the other countries in Europe have far fewer. By contrast, the Netherlands, Sweden and the UK all have more than one-quarter of their working population having part-time jobs. These differences correlate with differences in the institutional environment of these countries (DeGrip et al. 1997; Ruiz-Quintanilla and Claes 1996; Tregaskis and Brewster 2006). Similarly, analyses of the extent of flexible working in Japan need to take into account the Japanese practice of restricting employment for women of above 'marriageable' age. Overall, although the trends are similar, there are still very different situations, assumptions and practices occurring in the different countries.

Effective communication is a requirement for all organizations and vital for those looking for commitment from workers to the objectives of the enterprise. It could be

| Figure 11.1 | **Proportion of organizations with more than one-fifth of employees fixed term or temp/casual, 2003/4** |

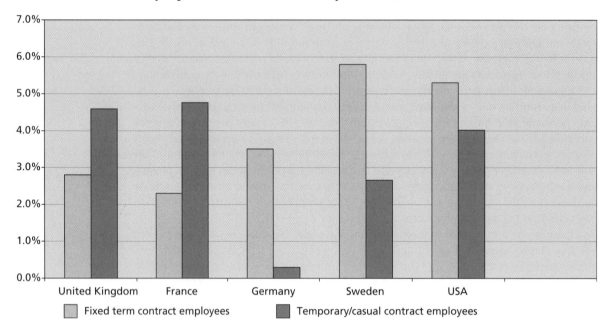

| Figure 11.2 | **Proportion of organizations with more than half of all employees part time, 2003/4** |

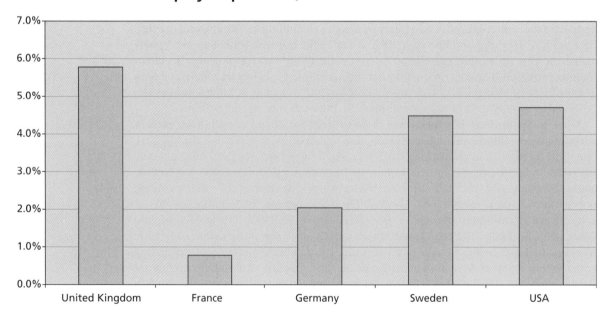

argued that at the organization level, effective communication is at the heart of effective human resource management. Yet there is less clarity about the most effective form and content of communication for these purposes: and whether that varies by country. The US Department of Labor (1993) approach, as we have seen, emphasizes individual communication as the key; while the European approach has tended to emphasize collective communication. Much of the literature associates the concept of HRM with the individualization of communication and a move away from, or even antagonism towards, the concept of industrial relations (IR) – communication and consultation which is collective and particularly that which is trade-union based.

This non-union implication sits uneasily with the history and circumstances of Europe (Brewster 2004) and of other countries around the world. Trade unionism in these countries remains widespread and important and has extensive, legally backed systems of employee communication. In Europe, for example, the establishment of workers' councils is required by law. These arrangements give considerable (legally backed) power to the employee representatives and, unlike consultation in the USA for example, they tend to supplement rather than supplant the union position (Brewster et al. 2006). In relatively highly unionized countries it is unsurprising that many of the representatives of the workforce are, in practice, trade union officials. In Germany, as one instance, four-fifths of them are union representatives. The balance between individual and collective communication is a matter for empirical investigation.

In fact, there have been increases in all forms of communication: through representative bodies (trade unions or works councils), as well as through direct verbal and written communication (Brewster et al. 2004). The latter two channels have expanded considerably. To a degree, increases in direct communication to employees can be explained by the development of technology: word processors and mail-merge systems have opened up the possibility of sending 'individual' letters to all employees. Electronic and computerized mail is now firmly part of the canon of downward communication, expanding enormously in the last three years of the twentieth century and continuing to do so. In the case of communications through representative organizations, most countries are still increasing their use – the proportion decreasing communications through this channel, where they exist, are still generally below one in 10, with the exceptions of Sweden (12%); some of the transformation economies of central Europe; and Australia, which is the only country where organizations decreasing their use of the representative communications channel is higher than the proportion increasing their use.

When upward communication is examined, the two most common means, by a considerable margin, are through immediate line management and through the trade union or works council channel. The evidence tends to support the analyses of those (Hollingsworth and Boyer 1997) who focus on the presence or absence within countries of communitarian infrastructures that manifest themselves in the form of strong social bonds, trust, reciprocity and cooperation among economic actors. There are clear differences between countries, with more communication being apparent in, broadly, the richer countries and less in, for example, the southern European countries. In addition, increases in communication, both up and down, appear to be larger in the countries where most communication goes on (Mayrhofer et al. 2000).

Access to financial and strategic information is clearly hierarchical. The higher your position in the organization the more likely you are to be regularly briefed about the financial performance of the organization or its strategic plans. While the hierarchy still persists, the information gap appears to have narrowed during the 1990s as an increasing number of organizations make sure that their administrative staff know about the organization's plans and performance. Unionized organizations are more likely than non-union ones to provide such information. There are noticeable differences in average 'slopes' in the distribution of this information: lower level employees in the Nordic countries, for example, receive considerably more information than those elsewhere.

The role of the HR function unsurprisingly, given these differences in areas such as the deployment of workers and communications, also varies considerably across countries. Most commentators argue that human resource management has become more important to organizations in the last decades. Since human resources and the knowledge and skills they incorporate are difficult to replicate, they offer the opportunity of obtaining sustained competitive advantage for the organization, at a time when traditional ways of obtaining competitive advantage become ever easier to copy. Based on this argument we might have expected to see the influence of the human resource function on corporate decision making increasing over time. Arguably, where the human resource function is represented at the key decision-making forums of the organization and closely involved in strategic decision making, awareness of the problems or opportunities that effective HRM might provide will be raised. The decision making in increasingly knowledge-reliant organizations will be improved. Evidence on three issues is instructive. These are: the position of HRM in relation to the decision makers within the organization; the role of line management; and the extent of outsourcing of HRM.

In terms of the HR department's influence with decision makers, one perceptive commentator has made the point that the rhetoric of the integration of the HR specialist function at the board level and its position of influence has outpaced the reality (Legge 1995). In terms of membership of the board, the Cranet research data (Brewster et al. 1999) show considerable stability over time, and considerable variation between

| Figure 11.3 | **HR on main board, 2003/4** |

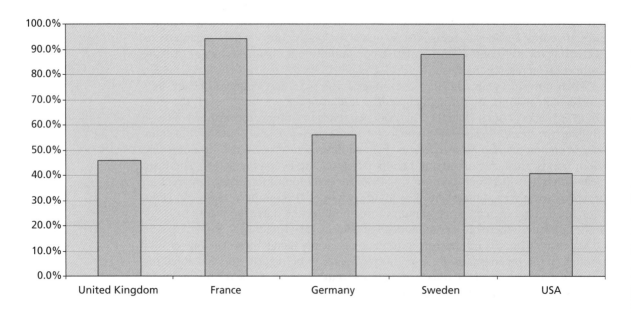

countries (see Figure 11.3). France, Spain, Sweden and Japan, for example, consistently report seven or eight out of 10 organizations having an HR director on the board (or equivalent), while in the central and eastern European countries and Israel the figures are much lower. Many other European countries, including the UK and Germany, and also Australia show a little less than half of the organizations with HR departments being directly represented at the top decision-making level. The position of the Netherlands and Germany is interesting. These are countries where employees have rights to have representatives at the supervisory board level: presumably the employee representatives ensure that the HR implications of corporate strategy decisions are taken into account. Germany is a particularly interesting case, as one of the few countries where HR representation on the board has increased notably over the rounds of the study, as human resources become more critical for these organizations and the function itself becomes less administrative. For the UK, although the WERS surveys in the UK are not addressed to senior HR specialists at the organizational level, the estimates from the workplaces indicate a similar pattern (Kersley et al. 2006). When it becomes a question – perhaps the key question – of HR influence on the corporate strategy, there is more uniformity: in most countries the personnel departments are involved from the outset in strategy formulation in around half the organizations.

The role of line managers in strategic (and indeed in operational) HRM has been seen as a touchstone of HRM (Storey 1992, 1995). In Europe, the trend is to give line managers more responsibility for the management of their staff and to reduce the extent to which human resources departments control or restrict line management autonomy in this area (Brewster et al. 1999). This has created problems, with both personnel specialists and line managers unhappy about the way things are moving. Here too, though, despite a common trend there are significant differences in practice. The subject of the line management role has been the topic of more discussion in the UK than anywhere else in Europe. In fact, however, Britain is one of the countries where senior personnel specialists consistently report that primary responsibility for a range of personnel issues is least likely to be given to or shared with line managers. On a range of personnel issues it is the Italians who are most likely to lodge responsibility with the personnel department; the British come next. This stands in sharp contrast to the Danes, for example, who, on all issues, tend to give much greater responsibility to line managers. These differences persist over time.

Organizations have become smaller over a decade of downsizing; new technology has been introduced; and 'overhead' departments have been under pressure to prove themselves. All this might imply that human resource departments would become smaller. However, the size of the HR departments relative to the total size of the organization has hardly changed in the last decade. Moreover, the differences between the countries in Europe in the size of HR departments remains (Brewster et al. 2006).

Conclusion

Similarities and differences in HRM

The evidence takes us back to the issues with which the chapter started. This chapter has been written from the contextual paradigm. A key question in comparative HRM is that of convergence: are there differences between countries, are these being reduced as the pressures to conform become stronger and, if so, what are they converging towards? The answers are, inevitably, complex. And those looking to defend one position or another can easily find evidence to support their case. Thus, there do seem to be trends (an increase in flexibility; a greater role for individualized communication; more line management responsibility for HRM) that are widespread, even if they do not seem to be diminishing the differences between the countries in the way they manage their HRM.

There are clear regional differences between, say, the patterns of contingent employment, anti-unionism and the role of the HR department in the USA, Europe and Japan. And, going back to the focus-pulling analogy, within Europe different sub-regional patterns can be distinguished, reflecting the wider discussion about business systems and varieties of capitalism (see, e.g., Amable 2003; Hall and Soskice 2001). This discussion of sub-regional developments in HRM should not pass without a small but significant detour to mention the 'test-bed' situation of the former Communist states of central and eastern Europe (CEE). Research indicates that while all of them have moved significantly away from the old models, the rate of change has been very different: the greater explanatory power of the contextual paradigm in such cases at least is manifest.

Below the sub-regional level there is clearly in existence a set of broad, relatively inert distinctions between the various national contexts of personnel management that makes any universalistic models of HRM problematic. The idiosyncratic national institutional settings are so variable that no common model is likely to emerge for the foreseeable future.

Our discussion of the issues of convergence and divergence in national patterns of HRM is, therefore, equivocal and perhaps needs more careful nuance than has been the case in much of the writing about HRM. Human resource management varies by country, sector and size of organization; by subjects within the generic topic of HRM; and by the nature of the organization (life stage; governance; market, etc.). There is a related need to examine the balance between the extent to which foreign organizations bring new practices into a country compared to the extent to which they adjust to local practices (Ferner and Quintanilla 2001). And we need to separate out policy from practice. Overall, however, the internationally comparative dimension of HRM is one that is demanding ever more attention from practitioners as they strive to cope with globalization: researchers are increasingly paying comparative HRM the same attention.

References

Ajiferuke, M. and J. Boddewyn (1970). '"Culture" and other explanatory variables in comparative management studies', *Academy of Management Journal* 13: 153–63.

Albert, F. J. (1989). *Les Ressources Humaines, Atout Strategique*. Paris, Editions L'harmattan. 75.

Amable, B. (2003). *The Diversity of Modern Capitalism*. Oxford, Oxford University Press.

Becker, B. and B. Gerhart (1996). 'The impact of human resource practices on organisational performance: progress and prospects', *Academy of Management Journal* 39: 779–801.

Beer, M., P. R. Lawrence, Q. N. Mills and R. E. Walton (1985). *Human Resource Management*. New York, Free Press.

Boxall, P. (1995). 'Building the theory of comparative HRM', *Human Resource Management Journal* 5(5): 5–17.

Brewster, C. (1999). 'Strategic human resource management: the value of different paradigms', *Management International Review* Special issue 1999/3(39): 45–64.

Brewster, C. (2004). 'European perspectives on human resource management', *Human Resource Management Review* 14(4): 365–82.

Brewster, C. and F. Bournois (1991). 'A European perspective on human resource management', *Personnel Review* 20 (6): 4-13.

Brewster, C., H. Larsen and W. Mayrhofer (1999). 'Human resource management: a strategic approach', in C. Brewster and H. Larsen, *Human Resource Management in Northern Europe*. Oxford, Blackwell.

Brewster, C., W. Mayrhofer and M. Morley (2004). *Human Resource Management in Europe: Evidence of Convergence?* London, Butterworth Heinemann.

Brewster, C., G. Wood, M. Brookes and J. van Ommeren (2006). 'What determines the size of the HR function? A cross-national analysis', *Human Resource Management* 45(1): 3-21.

DeGrip, A., J. Hoevenberg and E. Willems (1997). 'Atypical employment in the European Union', *International Labour Review* 136(1): 49-72.

Delery, J. and H. Doti (1996). 'Modes of theorising in strategic human resource management: tests of universalistic, contingency and configurational performance', *Academy of Management Journal* 39: 802-35.

DiMaggio, P. J. and W. W. Powell (1983). 'The iron cage revisited: institutional isomorphism and collective rationality in organizational fields', *American Sociological Review* 48: 147-60.

Drucker, P. (1950). *The New Society: The Anatomy of the Industrial Order*. New York, Harper.

Dyer, L. and T. Kochan (1995). 'Is there a new HRM? Contemporary evidence and future directions', in B. Downie, P. Kumar and M. L. Coates (eds) *Managing Human Resources in the 1990s and Beyond: Is the Workplace Being Transformed?* Kingston, Ontario, Industrial Relations Centre Press, Queen's University.

European Commission (1995). *Employment in Europe*. Luxembourg, Employment and Social Affairs Directorate.

Ferner, A. and J. Quintanilla (2001). 'Country-of-origin, host country effects and the management of HR in multinationals', *Journal of World Business* 36(2): 107-27.

Fombrun, C., N. Tichy and M. A. Devanna (1984). *Strategic Human Resource Management*. New York, Wiley.

Fukuyama, F. (1995). *Trust: The Social Virtues and the Creation of Prosperity*. New York, Free Press.

Gaugler, E. (1988). 'HR management: an international comparison', *Personnel* August: 24-30.

Giddens, A. (1986). *The Constitution of Society. Outline of the Theory of Structuration*. Cambridge, Polity Press.

Gooderham, P. and C. Brewster (2003). 'Convergence, statis or divergence? The case of personnel management in Europe', *Beta* 17(1): 6-18.

Guest, D. (1990). 'Human resource management and the American dream', *Journal of Management Studies* 27 (4): 377-97.

Hall, P. and D. Soskice (eds)(2001). *Varieties of Capitalism: The Institutional Foundations of Competitive Advantage*. Oxford, Oxford University Press.

Harbison, F. and C. A. Myers (1959). *Management in the Industrial World: An International Analysis*. New York, McGraw-Hill.

Hofstede, G. (2001). *Culture's Consequences*. 2nd edn. Thousand Oaks, CA, and London, Sage.

Hofstede, G., C. A. van Deusen, C. B. Mueller and T. A. Charles (2002). 'What goals do business leaders pursue? A study in fifteen countries', *Journal of International Business Studies* 33(4): 785-803.

Hollingsworth, I. R. and R. Boyer (1997). 'Coordination of economic actors and social systems of production', in I. R. Hollingsworth and R. Boyer (eds) *Contemporary Capitalism*. Cambridge, Cambridge University Press.

Hollinshead, G. and M. Leat (1995). *Human Resource Management: An International and Comparative Perspective*. London, Pitman.

House, R. J., P. J. Hanges, M. Javidan, P. W. Dorfman and V. Gupta. (2004). *Culture, Leadership and Organizations: The GLOBE study of 62 Societies*. New York, Sage.

Huselid, M. (1995). 'The impact of human resource management practices on turnover; productivity and corporate financial performance', *Academy of Management Journal* 38: 635-72.

Kersley, B., C. Alpin, J. Forth, A. Bryson, H. Bewley, G. Dix and S. Oxenbridge (2006). *Inside the Workplace: Findings from the 2004 Workplace Employment Relations Survey*. London, Routledge.

Kochan, T., H. Katz and R. McKersie (1986). *The Transformation of American Industrial Relations*. New York, Basic Books.

Kuhn, T. (1970). *The Structure of Scientific Revolutions*. Chicago, University of Chicago Press.

Lane, C. (1989). *Management and Labour in Europe*. Aldershot, Edward Elgar.

Legge, K. (1995). 'HRM: rhetoric, reality and hidden agendas', in J. Storey (ed.) *Human Resource Management: A Critical Text*, London, Routledge.

Lepak, D. and S. Snell (1999). 'The human resource architecture: toward a theory of human capital allocation and development', *Academy of Management Review* 24(1): 31-48.

Locke, R., M. Piore and T. Kochan (1995). 'Introduction', in R. Locke, T. Kochan and M. Piore (eds) *Employment Relations in a Changing World Economy*. Cambridge, MA, MIT Press.

Marchington, M. and I. Grugulis (2000). '"Best Practice" human resource management: perfect opportunity or dangerous illusion?', *International Journal of Human Resource Management* 11(6): 1104-24.

Maurice, M., F. Sellier and J. Silvestre (1986). *The Social Foundations of Industrial Power*. Cambridge, MA, MIT Press.

Mayrhofer, W., C. Brewster and M. Morley (2000). 'Communication, consultation and the HRM debate', in C. Brewster, W. Mayrhofer and M. Morley (eds) *New Challenges for European Human Resource Management*. Basingstoke, Macmillan.

Mayrhofer, W., M. Müller-Camen, J. Ledolter, G. Strunk and C. Erten (2002). 'The diffusion of management concepts in europe - conceptual considerations and longitudinal analysis', *Journal of Cross-Cultural Competence & Management* 3: 315-49.

Peltonen, T. (2006). 'The "newcomer" MNC and the re-organization of national industrial relations actor network: the case of the Finnish food-retailing sector', *International Journal of Human Resource Management* 17(9): 1591-1605.

Pieper, R. (ed.)(1990). *Human Resource Management: An International Comparison*. Berlin, Walter de Gruyter.

Purcell, J. and B. Ahlstrand (1994). *Human Resource Management in the Multi-Divisional Firm*. Oxford, Oxford University Press.

Randlesome, C. (1994). *The Business Culture in Germany*. Oxford, Butterworth Heinemann.

Rose, M. J. (1991). 'Comparing forms of comparative analysis', *Political Studies* 39: 446-62.

Rosenzweig, P. M. and N. Nohria (1994). 'Influences on human resource management practices in multinational corporations', *Journal of International Business Studies* 25(2): 229-52.

Rosenzweig, P. M. and J. I. Singh (1991). 'Organisational environments and the multinational enterprise', *Academy of Management Review* 16(2): 340-61.

Ruiz-Quintanilla, S. A. and R. Claes (1996). 'Determinants of underemployment of young adults: a multicountry study', *Industrial and Labour Relations Review* 49(3): 424-39.

Sako, M. (1998). 'Does trust improve business performance?', in C. Lane and R. Bachmann (eds) *Trust within and between Organizations*. Oxford, Oxford University Press.

Schwarz, S. H. (1992). 'Universals in the content and structure of values: theoretical advances and empirical tests in 20 countries', in M. P. Zanna (ed.) *Advances in Experimental Social Psychology*. New York, Academic Press.

Schwarz, S. H. (1994). 'Beyond individualism/collectivism, new cultural dimensions of values', in U. Kim, H. C. Triandis, C. Kagitcibasi, S. C. Choi and G. Yoon (eds) *Individualism and Collectivism*. London, Sage.

Schwarz, S. H. and L. Sagiv (1995). 'Identifying culture-specifics in the content and structure of values', *Journal of Cross-Cultural Psychology* 26: 92-116.

Smith, C. and P. Meiksins (1995). 'System, society and dominance effects in cross-national organisational analysis', *Work, Employment and Society* 9(2): 241-67.

Sorge, A. (2004). 'Cross-national differences in human resources and organization', in A. W. Harzing, and J. van Ruysseveldt (eds) *International Human Resource Management*. London, Sage: 117-40.

Sparrow, P. R., C. Brewster and H. Harris (2004). *Globalizing Human Resource Management*, London, Routledge.

Spony, G. (2003) 'The development of a work-value model assessing the cumulative impact of individual and cultural differences on managers' work-value systems: empirical evidence from French and British managers', *International Journal of Human Resource Management* 14(4): 658-79.

Standing, G. (1997). 'Globalisation, labour flexibility and insecurity: the era of market regulation', *European Journal of Industrial Relations* 3(1): 7-37.

Storey, J. (1992). *Developments in the Management of Human Resources*. Oxford, Blackwell.

Storey, J. (1995). *Human Resource Management: A Critical Text*. London, Routledge.

Tichy, N., C. J. Fombrun and M. A. Devanna (1982). 'Strategic human resource management', *Sloan Society Management Review* 23(2): 47-60.

Tregaskis, O. and C. Brewster (2006). 'Converging or diverging? A comparative analysis of trends in contingent employment practice in Europe over a decade', *Journal of International Business Studies* 37(1): 111-26.

Ulrich, D. (1989). 'Tie the corporate knot: Gaining complete customer commitment', *Sloan Management Review, World Economy* Summer: 19-28.

Ulrich, D. and N. Smallwood (2005). 'HR's new ROI: return on intangibles', *Human Resource Management* 44 (2): 137-42.

US Department of Labor (1993). *High Performance Work Practices and Firm Performance*. Washington, DC, US PMWright, Government Printing Office.

Whitley, R. (2000). 'The institutional structuring of innovation strategies: business systems, firm types and patterns of technical change in different market economies', *Organization Studies* 21(5): 855-86.

Williamson, O. (1985). *The Economic Institutions of Capitalism*. New York, Free Press.

Wright, P. M. and C. Brewster (2003). 'Editorial. Learning from diversity: HRTM is not Lycra', *International Journal of Human Resource Management* 14(8): 1299-1307.

Wright, P. M. and G. C. McMahan (1992). 'Theoretical perspectives for strategic human resource management', *Journal of Management* 18(2): 295-320.

Global staffing and the multinational enterprise

David G. Collings and Hugh Scullion

Introduction

The aim of this chapter is to explore the issue of global staffing which has been defined as 'the critical issues faced by multinational corporations with regard to the employment of home, host and third country nationals to fill key positions in their headquarter and subsidiary operations' (Scullion and Collings 2006b: 3). Global staffing is a key aspect of the management of human resource management in the international firm and it has been argued that it is increasingly seen as one of the primary HR practices used by MNCs to control and coordinate their spatially dispersed global operations, as managers increasingly realize the importance of HR practices in ensuring the profitability and viability of their international business operations (Dowling and Welch 2004). This chapter aims to critically examine some of the key themes that emerge in debates around global staffing. Specifically, it encompasses strategic and operational aspects of global staffing and has six main sections. The first section seeks to explain why global staffing has emerged as a key issue for MNCs. Section two addresses the issues of staffing foreign subsidiaries with an emphasis on the factors which influence the decision to staff foreign subsidiaries with parent country national (PCN) expatriates. Section three specifically examines motives for using expatriates. The role of the corporate HR function in staffing foreign subsidiaries is discussed in section four. Section five examines some issues in international talent management, with a recognition of the strategic constraints that aspects of international staffing can have on the implementation of international strategies. Finally, section six briefly considers the emergence of alternative forms of international assignment.

Emergence of global staffing as a key issue in international management

In exploring why global staffing has emerged as a key issue in international management we may highlight a number of significant trends.

1 There is growing recognition that the success of global business depends most critically on recruiting the required quality of senior management in multinational companies (Doz and Prahalad 1986; Schuler 2000; Scullion and Starkey 2000).

2 Staffing issues are different and more complex in the international environment due to the variety of cultural and institutional variations faced by multinational companies (Scullion and Collings 2006a; Torbiorn 1997).

3 The performance of expatriates continues to be problematic and the evidence suggests that the costs of poor performance in international assignments are often costly in human and financial terms (Dowling and Welch 2004; Thomas 1998).

4 International talent management has emerged as a key issue for MNCs (CIPD 2006b; Scullion and Collings 2006c). Indeed shortages of international managers are a growing concern for international firms and frequently constrain the implementation of global strategies (Scullion 1994).

5 Global staffing issues are becoming increasingly important in a far wider range of organizations partly due to the rapid growth of SME internationalization (Anderson and Boocock 2002).

6 Recent research highlights the growing importance of staffing strategies such as inpatriation, which reflect the growing need for MNCs to develop a multicultural international workforce (Harvey et al. 1999).

Indeed, the significance of staffing as a key HR concern in MNCs is unlikely to diminish in the future due to the rapid growth of emerging markets such as China and India (cf. PricewaterhouseCoopers 2005). These developments are leading to an increasing need for managers with the distinctive competences and the desire to manage in these culturally and economically distant countries. Also, there is the emergence of considerable competition between MNCs for those managers who possess the context specific knowledge of how to do business successfully in these markets (Björkman and Xiucheng 2002; Garten 1997). Further, global staffing is concerned with a much broader field than simply the deployment of parent country expatriates to foreign subsidiaries, a topic that has dominated the field of international human resource management for a number of decades. Global staffing, also considers issues related to the deployment of host and third country nationals in key positions within the multinational. We begin by looking at the factors that influence the configuration of staffing arrangements in multinational subsidiaries.

Staffing foreign subsidiaries

Having explored the emergence of global staffing as a key issue for MNCs, we now take a more strategic focus and look at the factors that influence the composition of senior staff in multinational subsidiaries. In this regard, Perlmutter's (1969: 11) seminal paper explored the multinationality of firms, through developing a typology of the multinationality of firms based on their orientation towards 'foreign people, ideas and resources' in the headquarters and foreign operations. He introduced a classification of multinationals that differentiated between firms based on their attitude toward the geographic sourcing of their management teams. Initially, four approaches to the staffing of MNCs were identified.

Ethnocentric organizations, where all key positions both in the headquarters and the subsidiary operations are filled by parent country nationals or citizens of the country where the HQ is located. In these organizations, home-based policy, practice and employees are viewed as superior and foreigners within the organization can be viewed as, and feel like, second-class citizens.

Polycentric organizations, where foreign subsidiaries have a large degree of autonomy and are primarily staffed by host country nationals (HCNs) or managers from the subsidiary location. Perlmutter (1969: 11) has compared these organizations to 'loosely connected group[s] with quasi-independent subsidiaries as centres'.

Geocentric organizations, where positions at both HQ and subsidiary level are filled with the 'best person for the job', regardless of nationality. Nationality and superiority are not related concepts in these firms and individual competence is more significant that nationality. Generally, these firms display quite complex organizational structures and require high levels of communication and integration across international borders.

Regiocentric organizations, where organizations are conceptualized and structured on a regional basis and managers are generally selected on the basis of the 'best in the region' with international transfers generally being restricted to within regions. Under this structure subsidiaries may have a relatively large degree of autonomy from the HQ (Heenan and Perlmutter 1979).

The implications for MNCs and their subsidiaries of pursuing these alternative staffing arrangements are beyond the scope of the current chapter but are explored in detail in Collings and Scullion (2006a: 18–31). Nonetheless, Perlmutter's work clearly provides a useful starting point to help understand staffing in foreign subsidiaries. Indeed, Schuler et al. (1993) posit that by managing the mix of PCN, HCNs and TCNs, MNCs may increase their ability to achieve learning, innovation and corporate integration. However, it is important to remember that this typology is primarily concerned with staffing policies for key positions within an MNC and thus its focus is on the top management team (TMT) positions at HQ and subsidiary locations (Harzing 2004; Torbiorn 1985). Further, the typology represents a number of ideal types of organization and it is unlikely that many MNCs will exactly fit any of the ideal types and indeed most organizations will display elements of more than one type. For example, based on a study of Chinese MNCs, Shen and Edwards (2004: 831) argue that the firms in their study adopted 'an ethnocentric approach, but with a strong polycentric tendency'. Thus, they argue, Chinese MNCs adopt firm-specific approaches, drawn from the four ideal types rather than any specific type (see also Bonache and Fernandez 1999). Harzing (2001b) also found that less than 10% of the companies in her study had a uniform staffing policy (only HCN or PCNs). The empirical work in this area suffers from a number of limitations however:

- Many studies fail to analyse the link between the expatriate policies pursued by the company and the international strategy of the company (Bonache et al. 2001; Sparrow et al. 2004).

- The literature has focused mainly on single aspects of the expatriate cycle and is quite fragmented in parts (Scullion and Brewster 2001).

- With a few notable exceptions (cf. Harzing 2001b) the studies in this field are limited due to their small sample sizes.

- The data in these studies are also generally self-report data and thus there have been calls for more rigorous research designs to control better for cultural biases (Schuler et al. 2002).

While acknowledging these limitations (cf. Thomas 1998 for a discussion in this regard), the literature highlights a range of factors which influence the composition of staffing arrangements in MNCs. However, while the evidence is not conclusive in a number of areas, a number of broadly consistent themes emerge in relation to staffing debates in MNCs.

First, the country of origin of the MNCs has an impact on staffing arrangements with Japanese MNCs most likely to utilize PCN expatriates in staffing key positions in foreign subsidiaries (Harzing 1999; Tung 1982). US MNCs represent the other extreme and they generally have lower levels of PCNs in subsidiaries than their Japanese and European counterparts (Harzing 1999; Tung 1982; Young et al. 1985). While it has been argued that the majority of European firms rely heavily on PCN presence (Mayrhofer and Brewster 1996; Scullion 2001) it is important to note that the European case is one of heterogeneity with empirical evidence suggesting that German firms are closer to the Japanese model while UK firms are more akin to their American counterparts (cf. Harzing 1999). It has also been argued that pragmatic rather than strategic considerations influence staffing patterns in European MNCs (Torbiorn 1994).

Second, alongside, the country of origin of the MNC, the host country also emerges as a significant moderating factor on the use of PCNs. This is particularly the case where the subsidiary is located in a developing country with a lack of suitably qualified HCNs (Boyacigiller 1990; Harzing 2001a) and lower levels of educational attainment (Gong 2003; Harzing 2004). In these situations, MNCs are more likely to deploy greater numbers of PCN expatriates to the subsidiary operations. It is important to note that in many instances these locations are not particularly appealing to PCN managers and staffing operations in locations considered less attractive to expatriate employees is emerging as a key strategic staffing issue for managers in multinational corporations.

Third, the cultural distance between these countries is also significant in explaining the number of PCNs in subsidiary operations (Boyacigiller 1990; Gong 2003) although, in a similar vein to an earlier point, cultural distance raises a number of issues with regard to the willingness of PCNs to accept assignments. In this regard it appears that where subsidiaries are located in countries that are culturally quite different from the country of the headquarter operation, MNCs tend to prefer to dispatch PCN managers to manage these subsidiaries.

Fourth, there is growing evidence to suggest that the age of the subsidiary impacts on the composition of staffing arrangements in foreign subsidiaries. In this regard, a growing body of more recent research suggests that the longer the subsidiary is established the lower presence of PCNs in key positions (Franko 1973; Gong 2003; Harzing 2001b). In explaining this trend, Welch (1994) argues that organizations' staffing requirements change to meet organizational needs as firms pass through different stages of the internationalization process (see also Adler and Ghadar 1990; Milliman et al. 1991). Hence, on balance it appears that the number of PCNs utilized by MNCs in the early stages of internationalization for control purposes is high, then levels off at a level necessary to ensure continuity in the international environment (Briscoe and Schuler 2004).

Finally, it has been argued that there can often be an ad hoc dimension to international staffing whereby decisions may be driven by necessity or pragmatism rather than for a particular strategic purpose (Collings and Scullion 2006b; Torbiorn 2004). In the following section we examine the reasons why companies deploy expatriates to manage their foreign operations and we consider both classic and recent contributions to our knowledge in this area.

Rationales for using expatriates

The reasons why MNCs use expatriate assignees to staff their foreign operations has been a central theme in the literature for many decades. For many centuries (since approximately 1900 BC) entrepreneurs have recognized the importance of physically relocating managers to foreign locations where business operations were based. Even in these historic times locals were viewed as inferior and restricted to lower level jobs while parent country national were afforded superior conditions, similar to modern day expatriates (Moore and Lewis 1999: 66–7). The rationale for deploying PCN expatriates to staff foreign subsidiaries is a key decision point in the international assignment cycle as recent research indicates that the reasons why expatriates are sent on assignment may impact on job performances, adjustment and roles performed (Shay and Baack 2004). However, it should be noted that there may be few 'pure' cases whereby assignments have a singular purpose, and many assignments generally have more than one rationale (Sparrow et al. 2004). In general terms though, Paik and Shon (2004: 63) argue that compared to their locally hired counterparts, expatriates are believed to have a better understanding of overall corporate priorities, an easier acceptance of headquarter-determined rules and a greater commitment to overall corporate goals. In exploring this debate we now consider two of the key theoretical contributions to the field.

Edström and Galbraith's study

The first key theoretical contribution to discussions on the motives for utilizing international transfers was Edström and Galbraith's (1977) seminal work, which identified three key motives for utilizing international transfers:

- *Position filling* when expatriates were deployed to fill key technical and managerial roles where qualified local country nationals were not available, particularly in developing countries.
- *Individual development* where organizations use international assignments as a means of developing individual employees. This type of assignment is aimed at developing the global competence of the individual manager and indeed organizations utilizing this type of assignee are likely to do so regardless of the competence of employees in the host environment.

- *Organizational development* where international assignments are utilized as a means of building global competence at an organizational level. Such assignments are primarily used to transfer knowledge between subsidiaries and to modify and sustain organizational structure and decision process (Edström and Galbraith 1977).

Harzing's typology

A further key classification of international assignments was Harzing's (2001c) study, which identifies three control specific roles of expatriates. This study is significant and merits discussion because it goes beyond the basic question of why MNCs use expatriates and sheds light on the more significant question of whether these roles are equally important in different situations. This stands in contrast to much of the North American literature, which often assumes universality despite the burgeoning literature substantiating the cultural diversity of values (cf. Hofstede 2001) and the diversity of business systems as a constraint on management behaviour (cf. Whitley 1999) and the impact of such diversity on organizational behaviour. Harzing (2001c) identified three forms of personal/cultural control that could be used by expatriate managers:

- First, managers can act as a means of replacing the centralization of decision making in the MNC and provide a direct means of surveillance over subsidiary operations. She labels assignees based around these purposes as *bears*, highlighting the degree of dominance these assignees have over subsidiary operations.

- Second, expatriates can be used to control subsidiaries through socialization of host employees and the development of informal communication networks. These assignees are termed *bumble bees*, which reflects the bees 'flying "from plant to plant" and create[ing] cross-pollination between the various offshoots' (Harzing 2001c: 369).

- Finally *spiders*, as the name suggests control through the weaving of informal communication networks within the MNC.

A significant contribution of Harzing's (2001c) study is the consideration of the applicability of the different roles of expatriate assignees in different circumstances. In this regard she argues that although expatriates generally appear to perform their role as *bears* regardless of the situation, the study suggests that their role as *spiders and bumble bees* tend to be more context specific. Specifically, the *bumble bee and spider* roles appeared to be more significant in longer established subsidiaries (longer than 50 years) while the *bumble bee* role also appeared to be important in newly established subsidiaries. Significantly the level of localization of subsidiary operations and lower levels of international integration (in that the subsidiary was not greatly reliant on the HQ for sales and purchases) were positively related to the likelihood of expatriates performing the *bumble bee and spider* roles. Perhaps unsurprisingly *bumble bees* and *spiders* were also more prevalent in greenfield than brownfield acquisitions.

We now turn to a theme often underexplored in discussions on global staffing, namely the role of the corporate HR function on staffing in MNCs. The corporate HR function can have a key role to play in global staffing and its orientation towards staffing will have significant implications for the configuration of staffing arrangements in the global firm.

Global staffing: the role of the corporate HR function

While considerable research has been undertaken on the roles and functions of corporate headquarters and its relationship with foreign subsidiaries (Goold and Campbell 1987; McKern and Naman 2003) the role of the corporate HR function in the international firm has been relatively neglected. In this regard, Hunt and Boxall (1998) examined the role of senior HR specialists as strategic partners and their findings suggested that HR specialists are not typically key players in the development of corporate strategy. However, studies in this area generally failed to consider the impact of the internationalization of business on corporate HR roles and the implications for global staffing. A notable exception was Scullion and Starkey's (2000), empirical study of 30 UK MNCs which examined the role of the corporate HR function specifically in the context of the international firm. They identified three distinctive groups of companies: *centralized* HR companies, *decentralized* HR companies and *transition* HR companies. The role of strategic staffing in each of these approaches will be discussed in turn.

The first group, *the centralized HR companies* comprised 10 companies with large corporate staffs operating in a large number of countries and were characterized by a high degree of coordination and integration of their foreign operations. These firms adopted a strategic approach to global staffing. Strong centralized control was maintained over the careers and mobility of senior management positions worldwide. In the global firms the greater degree of central support for staffing and management development reflected an increasingly strategic role for the corporate HR function (see also, CIPD 2005). International assignments were increasingly linked to the organizational and career development process and the management development function became increasingly important for developing high-potential HCN and TCN managers (Evans and Lorange 1989). In particular the practice of developing the latter two groups through developmental transfers to corporate HQ, i.e. inpatriation (Harvey et al. 1999) was becoming increasingly important in global firms.

The second group comprising 16 companies operated with a *decentralized approach* and reflected the trend towards a reduction in the size of corporate offices in many UK organizations (Goold and Campbell 1987; O'Donnell 2000). These companies tended to have a small number of corporate HR managers who undertook a more limited range of activities than their counterparts in the first group. However, a key finding of the research was that two-thirds of the decentralized companies reported an increased influence of corporate HR over global staffing and, in particular, over the management of top management and senior expatriates in the previous five years. The need for greater coordination and integration associated with globalization led to a shift away from the highly decentralized approach of the early 1990s (Storey et al. 1997) and this was reflected in significant moves to establish central control over the careers and mobility of expatriates. However, in practice the coordination of international transfers of managers in the highly decentralized businesses was more problematic due to greater tensions between the short-term needs of the operating companies and the long-term strategic management development needs of the business. Empirical research highlighted a number of staffing strategies and methods that were used to address this problem including job rotation, developing informal networks, forums to encourage cross-border transfer of knowledge and learning and finally, encouraging other informal communication channels (Paauwe and Deuwe 1995; Paauwe and Boselie 2003; Scullion and Starkey 2000).

The final group, the *transition HR companies*, comprised four highly internationalized companies that had grown mainly through acquisitions. They were transition HR companies in the sense that they were in the process of shifting away from the decentralized approach adopted in the first half of the 1990s. There was a greater degree of central control over global staffing including the management of expatriates than in the decentralized companies and strategic staffing had emerged as an important issue due to the growing importance of international acquisitions supporting recent findings that call into question the view that central control over staffing in the international firm has been abandoned (Arkin 1999).

In summary, in this section, we suggested that the more rapid pace of globalization has led to a more strategic role for HRM. With respect to global staffing strategies some MNCs operated a dual system where corporate HR manages a core of senior staff and key personnel while the rest of lower level management and staff are managed at the subsidiary level (Scullion and Starkey 2000). We also suggest that the role of the corporate HR function and the approach to staffing varies considerably in different types of international firms (Torbiorn 1997). Talent management in relation to high-potential HCN managers was identified as a critical HR issue for many MNCs and the growing importance of inpatriation as a development strategy was identified and we develop on this theme later (see also Brockbank and Ulrich 2002; CIPD 2006a).

International talent management

'The war for talent', reflecting the recognition that human capital represents a key source of sustainable competitive advantage for organizations has become a pervasive theme in the management literature in recent years (CIPD 2006a). Closely linked to this is the concept of international talent management, which can be defined as approaches to recruit, retain, develop and motivate a competent cohort of managerial talent with appropriate international experience in the global business environment. But is talent management something more than the latest HR 'fad'? (CIPD 2006a). This section discusses some of the major international talent management challenges and staffing constraints faced by international firms that seek to develop a pool of globally competent managers. It will highlight the strategic importance of these constraints in relation to the implementation of global strategies. These issues are becoming more significant as shortages of international management talent emerge as a critical strategic issue for many international firms and often constrain the implementation of global strategies.

In considering the talent management issue, there are a number of challenges that organizations face in staffing foreign positions with traditional PCN expatriates and that dominate the agendas of international HR managers in this area:

1 *Supply side issues*. Four key trends emerge in this regard – dual careers issues, the limited participation of women in international assignments, issues around repatriation and weaknesses of talent management systems at an international level.

2 *Demand side issues*. We point to the rapid growth of emerging markets in countries such as those in eastern Europe and India and China as important in explaining the growing demand for expatriate employees with the specific competences needed to manage in these markets. Further, the increasing demand for expatriate employees in a far wider range of organizations than the traditional large MNC partly due to the rapid growth of small and medium enterprise (SME) internationalization and international joint ventures (IJVs) is significant.

3 *Expatriate failure and associated controversies*. The long-established orthodoxy was that many expatriate assignments ended prematurely as a large percentage of employees returned home due to a failure to adjust to the host environment. Recent analyses, however, indicate that while expatriate performance remains a serious concern for many MNCs, high expatriate failure rates may not have been as widespread as originally believed (Harzing 1995) although the costs associated with failure in both financial and non-financial terms remain high.

4 *Performance evaluation*. The *performance* of expatriates continues to be problematic for MNCs, which is partly due to difficult challenges faced by expatriates between meeting the often conflicting demands of the HQ and subsidiary operations. Further, several other factors also impact on expatriate performance including adjustment, family adjustment, language competence etc., although the debate on adjustment and performance is still open (Thomas 1998).

5 *Costs*. Although, many firms do not have a true idea of the costs associated with expatriate assignments, it is generally estimated that the cost associated with the international assignment is between three and five times an assignee's home salary in a year. Given increasing cost pressures in many industries, cost issues represent a significant challenge for many MNCs in utilizing PCN expatriates.

Some of these issues (expatriate failure, costs and performance evaluation) have been debated for some time and can be considered *older challenges*, in that they have been associated with the field since the first academic studies emerged on the topic. Others however can be considered *newer challenges*, in that they have gained increasing significance in recent years; these include demand issues surrounding emerging markets and requirements for expatriates in a broader range of organizations; supply issues around career issues and specifically dual careers and the impact of 9/11 (see also Collings et al. 2007).

Managing the talent pipeline in the multinational corporation

Given the aforementioned issues, combined with the growing recognition of the significance of staffing arrangements in ensuring the success of global enterprises, one might expect to find sophisticated global talent management systems in many multinational enterprises. Research suggests however that, in practice, talent markets within MNCs tend to operate on a national or regional basis (Butler et al. 2006; Harris et al. 2003). In considering talent management at a national level, Lewis and Heckman (2006: 140) note 'a review of the literature focused on talent management reveals a disturbing lack of clarity regarding the definitions, scope and overall goals of talent management'. In considering talent management at a global level, Roehling et al. (2005: 213) similarly note 'when actually describing HR practices designed to develop leaders and construct an effective leadership pipeline in an organization, we know relatively little about what to do'. In this regard, talent management in the international context requires international HR managers to 'develop a much deeper level of understanding about the links between the business agenda and the capabilities of the most talented people in the organization, and also understand the potential for mobility around these people' (Sparrow et al. 2004: 121). This attempted 'calibration' of talent on a global basis often requires multinational employers to think about talent on a more global basis and also to think about 'who they are' and 'what they stand for' (Sparrow et al. 2004: 121).

In exploring some key factors that MNCs should consider in measuring the appropriateness of their talent management systems. Sparrow et al. (2004: 125) point to the following key indicators:

- added value per employee
- the proportion of talented recruits to total recruits in the recruitment process
- graduate retention: what percentage of graduates remain in the company for three years?
- the level of development provided to employees
- the proportion of vacancies filled through internal labour markets
- retention of key personnel.

In the context of the challenges faced by multinational organizations in staffing positions with PCN expatriates outlined already, organizations will be increasingly required to develop capabilities to manage talent on a global basis. One could argue that MNCs' success in developing appropriate global talent management will be key in explaining their success on a global basis. However, recent research suggests there is a wide variety of approaches to talent management and that no single 'blueprint' can be applied to all organizational contexts. All multinational companies will have different resourcing requirements for their current and future talent pipeline and these will primarily influence the talent management strategy that an organization develops (CIPD 2006a). HRM in Action 12.1 outlines an example of a sophisticated talent management system developed by Marriott, a global hospitality company operating in over 70 countries and employing in excess of 100,000 employees. This mini-case outlines a notable attempt to overcome the lack of effective integration of the key elements evident in many talent management systems. The system aims to develop a talent and succession system that provides line managers with the tools to ensure a continuous alignment of talent and organizational abilities with business priorities. It is an example of an integrated and sophisticated talent management system.

Given the challenges to the traditional PCN assignment identified earlier and the failure of many MNCs to harness global talent on an integrated basis, many global firms are seeking alternatives to the traditional expatriate assignment in staffing global positions, a topic to which we now turn.

HRM in Action 12.1 Marriott's human capital review

As we noted earlier, a major weakness of talent management systems is the lack of effective integration of the key elements of such systems. This mini-case outlines a notable attempt to overcome this weakness, namely the strategic human capital review introduced by Marriott, a leading worldwide hospitality company, headquartered in Washington, DC, and employing over 100,000 employees in 70 countries. The objective of the system was to develop a talent and succession system that provides line managers with the tools to ensure a continuous alignment of talent and organizational abilities with business priorities.

The case illustrates Marriott's shift from a static succession planning process towards a more holistic approach that involved moving towards a better 'joining up' system of HR practices and business strategy in relation to global staffing requirements. Marriott's human capital review involved four key stages and these are now outlined (for further detail see Scullion and Collings 2006c).

Step 1. The first step of Marriott's human capital review (HCR) involved expanding business leaders' focus to include aligning both talent and organizational capability with business priorities. This is shown in Figure 12.1.

Step 2. The second step involves enhancing talent assessment criteria through the introduction of Marriott's leadership talent development inventory (LTDI) which is a tool used to gather

Marriott's human capital review | Figure 12.1

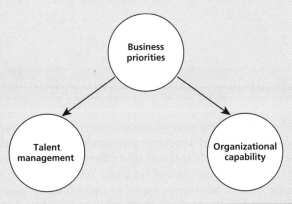

Human capital review	• Executive and key talent review • Leadership continuity planning	• Organizational capability assessment
Key questions addressed	Are we attracting, developing and retaining the best in the industry?	Have we established the right organizational circumstances to get maximum ROQ from our talent?
	Areas reviewed Talent acquisition Performance development Total compensation Work environment Retention management	Areas reviewed Organizational design (Structure, process, and job) Business culture alignment Change and learning management Performance measurement systems

critical information to improve discussions about talent development, performance and organizational impact. Under the LTDI approach executives and high-potential talent participate in a rigorous talent assessment which includes the following:

- in-depth accomplishments review
- detailed career history review
- multi-source assessment centres
- supervisor evaluation.

For each individual, the LTDI provides the following:

- performance overview
- strength and development areas
- development action items
- identification of possible next assignment
- readiness for next assignment.

Step 3. Marriott uses an organizational capability review (OCR) tool to help business unit managers assess the degree to which their organizational environment is supporting business priorities and utilizing talent. The OCR tool uses targeted questions to help focus managers' attentions on key OD and talent utilization issues. In addition, other questions encourage managers to think locally about the overall talent environment.

Step 4. Marriot's organizational capability department supports business leaders in the human capital review follow-up to better align their unit's talent and organization with business priorities. This requires the creation of an HR centre of excellence for organizational capability – the organizational capability department. And as we see in Figure 12.1, Marriott's expanded human capital review has created a more dynamic role for HR in the talent management process.

This provides an example of a sophisticated global talent management system as it operates in a highly successful MNC operating in a highly competitive sector.

Alternative forms of international assignment

The main focus of research on international assignments over the last 20 years has been on the traditional long-term assignment, which usually involves the relocation of the expatriate and their family to a different environment for a period of between one and five years (Scullion and Brewster 2001). Yet the evidence suggests the growing importance of alternative types of international assignment that have become increasingly prominent features of the pattern of global staffing (Fenwick 2004; Mayerhofer et al. 2004). These alternative or non-traditional assignments include short-term assignments (between three months and a year), international commuter assignments, frequent-flyer assignments, contractual assignments and virtual assignments. These alternative forms of assignment can be classified according to the length or duration of the assignment, which is usually determined by the purpose of the transfer and the nature of the task to be performed. (See Table 12.1.)

As already indicated, there are a number of factors that help to explain the trend toward alternative forms of international assignments, many of which are closely associated with the challenges to the traditional expatriate assignment. In specifically

Forms of international assignment	Table 12.1

Short-term assignments: between 3 months and one year	These are often temporary troubleshooting or project assignments and the aim is to fill a gap until a more permanent solution can be found.
Traditional expatriate assignments or Long-term assignments	The duration of the assignment may vary between one and four or five years and the expatriate has a clear role in the foreign subsidiary operation.
Rotational assignments	Staff commute from the parent country to a workplace in another country for a short period followed by a break in the home country. For example, this type of arrangement is very common on oil rigs.
International commuter assignments	This involves staff commuting from the home country to a workplace in another country, usually on a weekly or bi-weekly basis, while the family remains at home.
Frequent-flyer assignments	Staff undertake frequent international business trips but do not relocate.
Contractual assignments	These are common where staff with specific skills which are essential for completing international projects are assigned for a limited period of 6-12 months.
Virtual assignments	Under these arrangements staff do not relocate to a host location but have a responsibility to manage international staff from the home base.

Source: Scullion and Collings 2006d: 160: adapted from various sources

considering the growth of alternative forms of international assignments we point to four key factors:

- the shortage of managers willing to accept long-term international positions (see earlier)
- the high costs of expatriation
- the growing concerns regarding the balance between work and personal life among potential expatriate employees
- improved technology in communications and air transport have broadened the options for organizations (Mayerhofer et al. 2004).

While there has been a significant growth in the use of alternative forms of international assignments there is little evidence of a significant decline in the use of long-term assignments (as suggested by McComb 1999). There is a growing body of evidence to suggest that what is happening is the emergence of a portfolio of international assignments in MNCs (Collings et al. 2007; Fenwick 2004; Tahvanainen et al. 2005; Welch and Worm 2006). It is argued that alternative forms of international assignments provide more flexibility to MNCs in terms of global staffing, in contrast to the more inflexible contractual arrangements associated with traditional expatriate assignments. This research also highlighted that staff involved in alternative assignments play a proactive role in their own adjustment and use their networks to meet the challenges they face rather than depend on support from the HR department (Mayerhofer et al. 2004). Each of these alternative types of international assignments has a unique set of advantages and disadvantages, a discussion of which is beyond the scope of this chapter (see Collings et al. 2007). Further, they present a number of specific strategic and operational HR challenges for the international HR managers charged with their administration. However, as yet we do not have a comprehensive understanding of the nature and operation or the organization and individual challenges associated with these alternative forms of international assignments. Thus, the study of these alternative forms of international assignments is likely to represent a key research theme in the global staffing field in the future.

Conclusion

In this chapter, we argue that global staffing represents a key aspect of international HRM practice in the multinational firm, we chart the changing landscape of global staffing and discuss some of the key trends in the area. Indeed, most indications suggest that global staffing issues will grow in importance in the coming years due to a range of factors, including: a growing awareness of the significance of staffing issues in ensuring the success of the global enterprise; the continued growth of trade in a growing range of developing countries and regions, including China, India and eastern Europe; and the internationalization of a growing number of small and medium enterprises.

We have noted that MNCs have a number of options with regard to staffing their foreign subsidiaries. It is likely, however, that a firm may utilize a range of staffing options in different circumstances and we explored a rage of factors that influence decisions with regard to staffing options. Further, it should be apparent that each of these options presents specific opportunities and challenges and that no particular type represents a panacea for MNC's staffing challenges. As argued elsewhere (Collings et al. 2007) the key is that organizations are clear about the requirements and objectives of each senior position in their subsidiaries and choose a staffing option best suited to these requirements on a case-by-case basis. In this regard, international assignments generally have specific purposes, position filling, corporate development or individual development to use Edström and Galbraith's terminology and it is important that the objectives are reflected in the HR policies and practices put in place to support individual assignments. Further, as McNulty and Tharenou (2006) note MNCs should consider the key question of expatriate return on investment (ROI) in evaluating the utility of expatriate assignments. They posit that this is key, not just in determining the rate of return on the assignments, but also in understanding why rates of return increase and decrease and the influences on such shifts. It also allows MNCs to move beyond traditional historical cost analyses of expatriate assignments which do not provide a true reflection of the cost of such assignments or their relative benefits.

In a similar vein, it has become clear that the corporate HR function can play a key role in managing international assignments and, more specifically, the global talent pipeline in the global firm. Drawing on Scullion and Starkey's study we have illustrated that multinational companies display a number of different orientations with regard to how they choose to manage the talent pipeline in the global firm. It is becoming increasingly clear that the management of talent on a global basis is likely to represent a key HR challenge for the international HR function moving forward. In managing this talent pipeline, it is also clear that MNCs must increasingly look beyond traditional expatriate assignments in staffing their global operations. Specifically we pointed to a number of alternatives including short-term assignments (between three months and a year), international commuter assignments, frequent-flyer assignments, contractual assignments and virtual assignments. All these options offer specific advantage and disadvantages. The development of appropriate HR policies to support such assignments represents a key role for international HR professionals in the current international business climate. This is likely to emerge as a key theme in the international HR literature in the future.

References

Adler, N. J. and F. Ghadar (1990). 'Strategic human resource management: a global perspective', in R. Pieper (ed.) *Human Resource Management: An International Comparison*. Berlin, De Gruyter.

Anderson, V. and G. Boocock (2002). 'Small firms and internationalisation: learning to manage and managing to learn', *Human Resource Management Journal* 12(3): 5-24.

Arkin, A. (1999). 'Return to centre', *People Management*, 6 May: 34-41.

Björkman, I. and F. Xiucheng (2002). 'Human resource management and the performance of western firms in china', *International Journal of Human Resource Management* 13: 853-64.

Bonache, J. and Z. Fernandez (1999). 'Expatriate compensation and its link to the subsidiary strategic role: a theoretical analysis', *International Journal of Human Resource Management* 8: 457-75.

Bonache, J., V. Suutari and C. Brewster (2001). 'Expatriation: a developing research agenda', *Thunderbird International Business Review* 43: 3-20.

Boyacigiller, N. (1990). 'The role of expatriates in the management of interdependence, complexity and risk in multinational corporations', *Journal of International Business Studies* 21: 265-73.

Briscoe, D. R. and R. S. Schuler (2004). *International Human Resource Management*, 2nd edn. London, Routledge.

Brockbank, W. and D. Ulrich (2002). *The New HR Agenda: 2002 HRCS Executive Summary.* Michigan, University of Michigan Business School.

Butler, P., D. Collings, R. Peters and J. Quintanilla (2006). 'The management of managerial careers', in P. Almond and A. Ferner (eds) *American Multinationals in Europe: Managing Employment Relations across National Borders.* Oxford, Oxford University Press.

CIPD (2005). *International Management Development Guide.* London, Chartered Institute of Personnel and Development.

CIPD (2006a). *Reflections on Talent Management. Change Agenda.* London, Chartered Institute of Personnel and Development.

CIPD (2006b). *Learning and Development: Annual Survey Report.* London, Chartered Institute of Personnel and Development.

Collings, D. and H. Scullion (2006a). 'Global staffing', in G. K. Stahl and I. Bjorkman (eds) *Handbook of Research in International Human Resource Management.* Cheltenham, Edward Elgar.

Collings, D. G. and H. Scullion (2006b). 'Approaches to international staffing', in H. Scullion and D. G. Collings (eds) *Global Staffing.* London, Routledge.

Collings, D. G., H. Scullion and M. J. Morley (2007). 'Changing patterns of global staffing in the global firm', *Journal of World Business,* 42: 2, in press.

Dowling, P. and D. Welch (2004). *International Human Resource Management: Managing People in a Global Context,* 4th edn. London, Thomson.

Doz, Y. and C. K. Prahalad (1986). 'Controlled variety: a challenge for human resource management in the MNC', *Human Resource Management* 25: 55-71.

Edström, A. and J. R. Galbraith (1977). 'Transfer of managers as a coordination and control strategy in multinational organizations', *Administrative Science Quarterly* 22: 248-63.

Evans, P. and P. Lorange (1989). 'The two logics behind human resource management', in P. Evans, Y. Doz and A. Laurent (eds) *Human Resource Management in International Firms: Change, Globalization, Innovation.* London, Macmillan.

Fenwick, M. (2004). 'On international assignment: is expatriation the only way to go?', *Asia Pacific Journal of Human Resources* 42: 365-77.

Forster, N. (2000). 'The myth of the "international manager"', *International Journal of Human Resource Management* 11: 126-42.

Franko, L. (1973). 'Who manages multinational enterprises?', *Colombia Journal of World Business* 8: 30-42.

Garten, J. (1997). *The Big Ten: The Emerging Markets and How They Will Change Our Lives.* New York, Basic Books.

Gong, Y. (2003). 'Subsidiary staffing in multinational enterprises: agency, resources and performance', *Academy of Management Journal* 46: 728-39.

Goold, M. C. and A. Campbell (1987). *Strategies and Styles: The Role of the Centre in Managing Diversified Corporations.* Oxford, Blackwell.

Harris, H., C. Brewster and P. Sparrow (2003). *International Human Resource Management.* London, CIPD.

Harvey, M., C. Speier and M. M. Novicevic (1999). 'The role of inpatriation in global staffing', *International Journal of Human Resource Management* 10: 459-76.

Harzing, A. W. (1995). 'The persistent myth of high expatriate failure rates', *International Journal of Human Resource Management* 6: 457-75.

Harzing, A. W. (1999). *Managing the Multinationals: An International Study of Control Mechanisms.* Cheltenham, Edward Elgar.

Harzing, A. W. (2001a). 'An analysis of the functions of international transfer of managers in MNCs', *Employee Relations* 23: 581-98.

Harzing, A. W. (2001b). 'Who's in charge? An empirical study of executive staffing practices in foreign multinationals', *Human Resource Management* 40: 139-58.

Harzing, A. W. (2001c). 'Of bears bees and spiders: the role of expatriates in controlling foreign subsidiaries', *Journal of World Business* 26: 366-79.

Harzing, A. W. (2004). 'Composing an international staff', in A. W. Harzing and J. van Ruysseveldt (eds) *International Human Resource Management,* 2nd edn. London, Sage.

Heenan, D. A. and H. V. Perlmutter (1979). *Multinational Organizational Development.* Reading, MA, Addison-Wesley.

Hofstede, G. (2001). *Culture's Consequences,* 2nd edn. London, Sage.

Hunt, J. and P. Boxall (1998). 'Are top human resource specialists "strategic partners"? Self-perceptions of a corporate élite', *International Journal of Human Resource Management* 9(5): 767-81.

Lewis, R. E. and R. J. Heckman (2006). 'Talent management: a critical review', *Human Resource Management Review* 16: 139-54.

Mayrhofer, W. and C. Brewster (1996). 'In praise of ethnocentricity: expatriate policies in European MNCs', *International Executive* 38: 749-78.

Mayerhofer, H., L. C. Hartmann, G. Michelitsch-Riedl and I. Kollinger (2004). 'Flexpatriate assignments: a neglected issue in global staffing', *International Journal of Human Resource Management* 15(8): 1371-89.

McComb, R. (1999). 'China's human resource odyssey', *China Business Review* September-October: 30-33.

McKern, B. and J. Naman (2003). 'The role of the corporate centre in diversified international corporations', in B. McKern (ed.) *Managing the Global Network Corporation.* London and New York, Routledge.

McNulty, Y. M. and P. Tharenou (2006). 'Moving the research agenda forwards on expatriate return on investment', in M. J. Morley, N. Heraty and D. G. Collings (eds) *New Directions in Expatriate Research.* Basingstoke, Palgrave Macmillan.

Milliman, J., M. A. Von Glinow and M. Nathan (1991). 'Organizational life cycles and strategic international human resource management in multinational companies: implications for congruence theory', *Academy of Management Review* 16: 318-29.

Moore, K. and D. Lewis (1999). *Birth of the Multinational*. Copenhagen, Copenhagen Business Press.

O'Donnell, S. W. (2000). 'Managing foreign subsidiaries: agents of headquarters or an independent network?', *Strategic Management Journal* 21: 525–48.

Paauwe, J. and P. Boselie (2003). 'Challenging "strategic HRM" and the influence of the institutional setting', *Human Resource Management Journal* 13(3): 56–70.

Paauwe, J. and P. Deuwe (1995). 'Organizational structure of multinational corporations: theories and models', in A. W. Harzing and J. van Ruysseveldt (eds) *International Human Resource Management*. Thousands Oaks, Sage.

Paik, Y. and J. D. Shon (2004). 'Expatriate managers and MNC's ability to control international subsidiaries: the case of Japanese MNCs', *Journal of World Business* 39: 61–71.

Perlmutter, H. V. (1969). 'The tortuous evolution of the multinational corporation', *Columbia Journal of World Business* 4: 9–18.

PricewaterhouseCoopers (2005). *International Assignments: Global Policy and Practice, Key Trends 2005*. London, PricewaterhouseCoopers.

Roehling, M. V., W. R. Boswell, P. Caligiuri, D. Feldman, M. E. Graham, J. P. Guthrie, M. Morishima and J. W. Tansky (2005). 'The future of HR management: research needs and directions', *Human Resource Management* 44(2): 207–16.

Schuler, R. S. (2000). 'The internationalization of human resource management', *Journal of International Management* 6: 239–60.

Schuler, R. S., P. S. Budhwar and G. W. Florkowski (2002). 'International human resource management: review and critique', *International Journal of Management Reviews* 4: 41–70.

Schuler, R. S., P. J. Dowling and H. DeCieri (1993). 'An integrative framework of strategic international human resource management', *Journal of Management* 19: 419–59.

Scullion, H. (1994). 'Staffing policies and strategic control in British multinationals', *International Studies of Management and Organization* 4(3): 18–35.

Scullion, H. (2001). 'International human resource management', in J. Storey (ed.) *Human Resource Management*. London, Thompson.

Scullion, H. and C. Brewster (2001). 'Managing expatriates: messages from Europe', *Journal of World Business* 36: 346–65.

Scullion, H. and D. G. Collings (2006a). *Global Staffing*. London, Routledge.

Scullion, H. and D. G. Collings (2006b). 'Approaches to international staffing', in H. Scullion and D. G. Collings (eds) *Global Staffing*. London, Routledge.

Scullion, H. and D. G. Collings (2006c). 'International talent management', in H. Scullion and D. G. Collings (eds) *Global Staffing*. London, Routledge.

Scullion, H. and D. G. Collings (2006d). 'Alternative forms of international assignments', in H. Scullion and D. G. Collings (eds) *Global Staffing*. London, Routledge.

Scullion, H. and K. Starkey (2000). 'The changing role of the corporate human resource function in the international firm', *International Journal of Human Resource Management* 11: 1061–81.

Shay, J. P. and S. A. Baack (2004). 'Expatriate assignment, adjustment and effectiveness: an empirical examination of the big picture', *Journal of International Business Studies* 35: 216–32.

Shen, J. and V. Edwards (2004). 'Recruitment and selection in Chinese MNEs', *International Journal of Human Resource Management* 15: 814–35.

Sparrow, P., C. Brewster and H. Harris (2004). *Globalizing Human Resource Management*. London, Routledge.

Storey, J., P. Edwards and K. Sisson (1997). *Managers in the Making: Careers, Development and Control in Corporate Britain and Japan*. London, Sage.

Tahvanainen, M., D. Welch and V. Worm (2005). 'Implications of short-term international assignments', *European Management Journal*, 23: 663–73.

Thomas, D. C. (1998). 'The expatriate experience: a critical review and synthesis', *Advances in International and Comparative Management* 12: 237–73.

Torbiorn, I. (1985). 'The structure of managerial roles in cross-cultural settings', *International Studies of Management and Organization* 15(1): 52–74.

Torbiorn, I. (1994). 'Operative and strategic use of expatriates in new organizations and market structures', *International Studies of Management and Organization* 24(3): 5–17.

Torbiorn, I. (1997). 'Staffing for international operations', *Human Resource Management Journal* 7(3): 42–51.

Torbiorn, I. (2004). 'Staffing policies and practices in European MNCs: strategic sophistications, culture-bound policies or ad hoc reactivity?', in H. Scullion and M. Linehan (eds) *International Human Resource Management: A Critical Text*. Basingstoke, Palgrave Macmillan.

Tung, R. L. (1981). 'Selection and training of personnel for overseas assignments', *Colombia Journal of World Business* 23: 129–43.

Tung, R. L. (1982). 'Selection and training procedures of US, European and Japanese multinationals', *California Management Review* 25(1): 57–71.

Welch, D. E. (1994). 'Determinants of international human resource management approaches and activities: a suggested framework', *Journal of Management Studies* 31: 139–64.

Welch, D. E. and V. Worm (2006). 'International business travellers: a challenge for IHRM', in G. Stahl and I. Bjorkman (eds) *Handbook of Research in International Human Resource Management*. London, Edward Elgar.

Whitley, R. (1999). *Divergent Capitalisms: The Social Structuring and Change of Business Systems*. Oxford, Oxford University Press.

Young, S., N. Hood and J. Hamill (1985). 'Decision making in foreign owned multinational subsidiaries in the United Kingdom', ILO Working Paper No. 35. Genev, ILO.

Current developments and future prospects

In this final part, the book focuses on three areas of significance to HR – the use of technology in handling HR matters, the place of ethics and ethical dilemmas in HRM and the management of HR in dynamic organizations. The three chapters forming this part of the book are of fundamental importance. They do not simply round off the volume with some musings about future prospects; on the contrary, these chapters set the agenda for future research, debate and practice.

In Chapter 13 Emma Parry and Shaun Tyson investigate the world of human resource information systems (HRIS) or, it is often termed, 'e-HR'. Drawing on recent empirical research, the authors examine the changes prompted and allowed by the adoption of EHR. They also specifically assess whether HRIS enables certain senior players in HR to raise their game to strategic business partner level. The chapter includes data showing comparative practice across EU countries. Investment in, and deployment of, EHR allows web-based self-service and thus technically frees up HR specialists to undertake more strategic roles. Drawing on a variety of case studies Parry and Tyson reveal that while the step-up to strategic a role may not always be easy or straightforward, there are some significant instances where the idea has been realized – at least in part. Moreover, the finding that integrating HR systems under leading business software solutions such as SAP for example, means that reports and analyses are enabled which transcend functional boundaries. While in one sense this may be good news for HR professionals, in another sense, as raised by Keith Sisson in Chapter 5, there is the inherent potential for some of the functions of HR to be undertaken by other specialists and other specialisms.

In Chapter 14, David Bevan examines the role of ethics in the context of HRM. Drawing in part on his extensive practical experience in business, Bevan reports on the 'dishonesty and venality' that he encountered. He makes sense of these experiences through a close study of recent literature on organizational ethics and ethics in HRM. The analysis is illustrated through two vignettes based on real-life occurrences which have, for obvious reasons, been anonymized. The chapter builds a novel case for a shift from ethical theorizing to ethical action in HRM.

Finally, in Chapter 15, Lee Dyer and Jeff Ericksen undertake a pioneering investigation of the concept of 'organizational agility'. They use the extended case of Google to illustrate their thesis. As the business environment increasingly appears to be characterized by frequent and discontinuous change, a crucial skill for strategic HR managers is how to build a correspondingly dynamic organization. In a sense, this changes the whole agenda for HRM. This chapter helps meet the need of those managers seeking guidance about how to manage such dynamic organizations. Fluidity and scalability are two central constructs in this endeavour. But seeking to meet the needs of rapid response may challenge HR policies that give emphasis to consistency and equity. Managing under conditions of turbulence evidently presents HR with some special challenges. Those persons planning to spend some time managing HR in the future will find it useful to attend closely to the messages contained in this final chapter.

Technology in HRM: the means to become a strategic business partner?

Emma Parry and and Shaun Tyson

The revolution within human resource information systems (HRIS) has slowly but inevitably affected the whole conduct of human resource management. These influences can be seen in all working practices within the function, but only recently has the strategic significance of HRIS been demonstrated as a common feature of organizational life. In this chapter, we focus on three questions: what is the business case for HRIS, to what extent is the adoption of HRIS facilitating a move to a strategic role for HRM and what do these changes mean for the function as a whole?

Human resource information systems (HRIS) have developed from those largely used for administrative and transactional purposes, to the use of IT in processes such as recruitment and selection, flexible rewards systems and e-learning, integrated call centre technology, shared services and self-service systems. As technology improves, organizations can use information systems to manage a larger number of HR processes in an increasingly effective manner to contribute to the availability of strategically significant information and knowledge, therefore potentially improving competitive advantage.

We have recently explored a series of detailed case studies designed to investigate these questions. This research was of private and public sector organizations, within different industry sectors, which aimed to provide an in-depth analysis of the use and impact of technology. Extracts from these cases appear throughout the chapter.

Personnel management was one of the earliest users of automated record keeping for payroll, benefits administration and employee record processing. Recently, growth in a strategically focused HRM ethos has produced an increase in demand for useful information regarding human resources (Ball 2001). This has led to suggestions of a perceived increase in the strategic influence of HRM and continued devolution to the line therefore implying a central role for HRIS in supporting the HR function and increasing its value to the organization. However, despite the attention paid to the notion of the development of HR as a strategic business partner (Ulrich 1997) and the view that technology should facilitate this shift, there is little empirical evidence yet to support the argument. There seems to be an absence of a comprehensive examination of the impact of technology on HR policies and practices and on the HR function itself.

Use of technology in HR

The gap in the academic literature is perhaps particularly surprising given reports of the extensive use of modern technology in HRM. The use of technology within HR has certainly increased over recent years with 77% of organizations using some form of HRIS in 2005 (CIPD 2005). Research from Watson Wyatt (2002) showed that of the European companies surveyed, 70% used the internet or intranet to deliver HR services to employees with 25% of them planning to enhance substantially their e-HR capabilities over the two years after the survey. This suggests that the use of technology within HR will continue to grow. Recent research published by Cranfield School of Management (2005) found even higher levels of use, with 82% of UK organizations having some form of HRIS, although the nature of these systems varied considerably (see Figures 13.1 and 13.2).

Kettley and Reilly in their recent report on e-HR (2003), have noted the range of definitions of e-HR. According to Kettley and Reilly, most 'visionary' definitions describe a fully integrated, organization-wide electronic network of HR related data, information, services, databases, tools, applications and transactions that are generally accessible at any time by employees, managers and HR professionals. Alternatively, more 'basic interpretations' suggest that e-HR may be an organization's adoption of a new software package for payroll or the posting of company policies on

| Figure 13.1 | **Type of HR information system (EU countries)** |

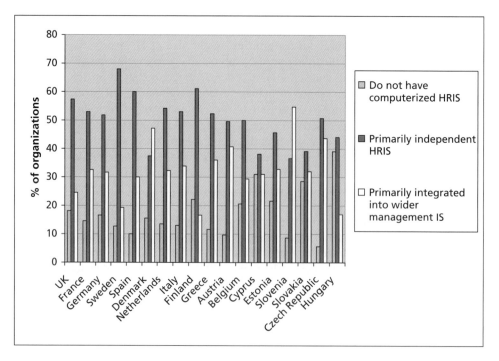

Source: Cranet Survey of Comparative Human Resource Management, International Executive Report 2005, Cranfield University

the intranet. For the purpose of this chapter, we will use Tannenbaum's (1990: 27) definition of HRIS as being used to 'acquire, store, manipulate, analyse, retrieve and distribute information about an organisation's human resources' and define technology in HR as any that is used to support these functions.

Technology can be used to support HR activity across the entire employment cycle from acquiring human resources (recruiting), to rewarding (performance management, pay and benefits), developing (training and development, career management), protecting (health and safety, employee relations) and to retaining human resources (retention strategies, work–life balance), (Ensher et al. 2002). In a similar fashion, Martinsons (1996) has divided the use of HRIS into 'unsophisticated' uses such as payroll and benefits administration, employee and absence records and 'sophisticated' uses such as recruitment and selection, training and development, HR planning and performance appraisal. The uses of technology within HR may be different across organizations. This is evidenced by a recent CIPD survey (2005) showing that the use of technology varied considerably with absence management being the most common function (85%), followed by training and development (75%), rewards (75%), managing diversity (57%) and recruitment and selection (51%).

One of the fastest growing trend in the delivery of HR information is 'employee self-service' (ESS) with 80% of large US companies delivering some information to employees via an ESS system by 2000 (Gueutal 2003). ESS applications can give employees the ability to access and maintain HR information about themselves via

Stage of EHRM web deployment (EU countries) | Figure 13.2

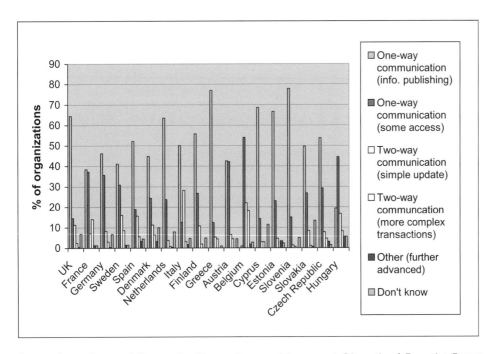

Source: Cranet Survey of Comparative Human Resource Management, International Executive Report 2005, Cranfield University

the web. ESS systems have even extended to the design of the employee's own pay package within the total value of the job, so that for example, at Nationwide Building Society employees can construct their own package of flexible benefits and can sacrifice varying proportions of their pay for higher pensions, improved holidays and the like as part of a total reward policy (Bissell 2004). Likewise, managerial self-service (MSS) provides a variety of HR tools and information for managers. These systems can provide managers with access to information about their subordinates and the ability to analyse information in order to improve managerial effectiveness, for example through pay modelling at salary review time.

Benefits of technology in HR – the 'business case'

The reasons behind an organization's decision to adopt technology within its human resource function may also be varied. Kettley and Reilly (2003) give the reasons for adopting e-HR as including cost cutting and aiding operational efficiency, the desire of the HR function to change the nature of its relationship with employees and line managers, the transformation of HR into a customer-focused and responsive function and the ability to produce comprehensive and consistent management information. Research from the Singaporean Ministry of Manpower (2003), divides the potential benefits of e-HR into 'hard' and 'soft' benefits (see Table 13.1).

Table 13.1	Potential benefits of e-HR

Hard $ benefits
Reducing service delivery costs by automating key HR business processes
Reducing correction costs by improving the accuracy of HR information
Eliminating costs with printing and distributing information to employees by making the information available online
Improving employee productivity by providing universal access on a 24/7 basis
Reducing data entry and search costs through employee and manager self-service
Enabling more cost-effective decision making through improved analysis of HR information
Minimizing IT infrastructure by moving to a common HR service platform
Soft $ benefits
Allowing instant processing of information – leading to reduction in cycle times
Increasing employee satisfaction by improving quality of HR service and providing access to information
Allowing HR function to become a strategic partner to the business as routine administrative work is minimized
e-HR can be used to signal a change towards an organizational culture that promotes initiative, self-reliance and improved internal service standards

Source: Singapore Ministry of Manpower 2003

The Kettley and Reilly report (2003) uses information from empirical research to divide the potential benefits of e-HR into three areas (see Figure 13.3).

According to this report 'operational efficiency' includes, for example, reducing overhead costs, enhancing the accuracy of data, eliminating the costs of printing and disseminating information, minimizing IT infrastructure costs by moving towards a common HR service platform and enhancing the ability to distribute HR information and services globally. 'Relational impact' is argued to change the nature of the relationship between HR, line managers and employees. 'Transformational impact' is thought to transform HR's role into that of a strategic business partner, adding greater value to the business by increasing HR's influence as customer focused consultants, enabling new, flexible and responsive methods for delivering HR services and expanding HR's reach as the experts of an organization's people processes and the developers of value propositions for different employee groups. Similarly, Shrivastava and Shaw (2004) discuss the impact of technology in HR in terms of (1) operational impact (alleviation of the administrative burden of HR and lowering of variable transaction costs and headcount); (2) relational impact (the improvement of the relationships HR has with its clients through improved response times and service levels and by providing decision support systems) and (3) transformational impact (redefining the scope of HR by enabling the function to concentrate more on strategic activities such as creating a learning environment, assisting in knowledge management and facilitating organizational transformation).

We might expect that the potential benefits just discussed provide the elements of any business case that an organization puts together to justify the implementation of technology within HR. Indeed, an examination of the business case for the introduction of an HRIS by the first of our case studies, Norwich Union, supports this suggestion. This business case was centred around four main drivers:

1 Enabling line management by encouraging a cultural shift so managers take responsibility for managing their people through being able to access and maintain records. This helps the company to build the functionality to cope with a flexible workforce.

Potential benefits of e-HR | Figure 13.3

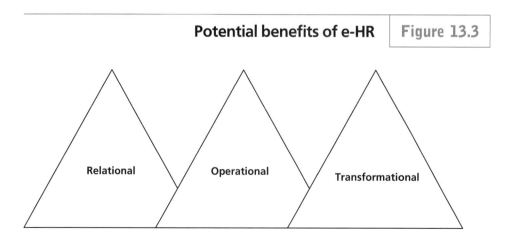

Source: Kettley and Reilly, *e-HR: An Introduction*, IES, 2003.

HRM in Action 13.1   Norwich Union

Norwich Union is the largest insurer in the UK and is part of the Aviva Insurance Group that has more than 60,000 employees. Human resources within Norwich Union are managed using a shared services model.

The company uses an Oracle HR information system (HRI) with an extensive system of manager self-service. Managers can use the system to inform fundamental changes with regard to their employees. These include: to change salary, cost centre and allowances, process leavers, update absences, produce reports, process overtime payments and compare salaries and performance ratings. The company also uses a degree of employee self-service with employees being able to: maintain personal details and emergency contact, provide information on their pay, request holidays, record absence, change bank account details and look at performance ratings and salary history. HR information is provided extensively on the intranet. The self-service system and HR intranet site is supported by two HR call centres, first, an employee services centre and, second, a managers' advice line. The system has been in place in some form since 2002.

HRM in Action 13.2   Cancer Research UK

Cancer Research UK is the world's leading independent organization dedicated to cancer research. Its objectives are to carry out world-class research, to develop effective treatments, to reduce the number of people affected by particular conditions and to provide authoritative information. The organization has 3500 employees, including over 3000 doctors, scientists and nurses in the UK and is managed by a HR team based in London. The organization has expanded considerably since its formation in 2002 and recruits to fill approximately 1000 vacancies per year. Recruitment is also managed by a single team, based in London.

The organization has adopted, or is in the process of adopting, three main technological systems:

1 An online recruitment system was recently introduced to manage the process for both internal and external recruitment from end to end.

2 The HR department has developed spreadsheets in order to perform a number of calculations that were previously problematic. These calculations currently fall into four main areas – redundancy payments, maternity pay, top-up payments for those workers who are funded by a different institution but are paid less and annual leave.

3 As regards self-service, an HRIS was initially introduced to perform basic HR record keeping and transactional payroll functions. This was followed by a wider range of functions, including vehicle management, expenses, occupational health, development and training and succession planning. Self-service will be introduced after a comprehensive change management programme.

2 Improving and simplifying core processes. As one manager put it, this is achieved by 'getting the basics right, by providing real time updates and immediate access for managers' simplification removes duplication of administration by supplying data entry at source. Improving the integrity of HR data and providing timely and accurate information enables the more effective and proactive management of people and increases online processing to drive the business towards standardization and economies of scale, it is argued.

3 Adding value through HR expertise is achieved by removing data-processing activity from HR without adding burdens to managers; supporting e-enablement of the business; allowing HR managers to move from transactional to performance management activity; facilitating the introduction of new HR activities online such as competencies and flexible benefits and encouraging individuals to take increased ownership of their own details and career management.

4 E-enablement of HR consists of: 'building the platform for tomorrow, today, to provide a progressive transactional HR system'; maximizing the use of this platform to improve administrative processes and to mirror business practice and expectations for a company of this size and status.

It can be seen then that Norwich Union's business case fits perfectly into the model proposed by Kettley and Reilly as it revolves around issues of operational efficiency, relational impact and transformational impact. A business case may not,

Success in meeting objectives: worldwide respondents reporting successful and somewhat succesful		Table 13.2

	North America (%)	Rest of world (%)
Improving data accuracy	92%	82%
HR staff acceptance	91%	100%
Employee acceptance	84%	88%
Manager acceptance	84%	82%
Employee services improvement	80%	88%
Meeting administrative cost savings goal	77%	59%
Enables HR to serve the organization more strategically	76%	81%
Align workforce with organizational objectives	70%	47%
Accountability	70%	63%
Enables your organization to recruit key talent	66%	41%
Enables employees and managers to make better decisions	67%	59%
Revenue growth	42%	59%

Source: CedarCrestone 2006 Workforce Technologies and Service Delivery Approaches Survey, 9th annual edition

however, cover all three of these areas as seen in Norwich Union. For instance, Cancer Research UK's introduction of an online recruitment system was based mainly around areas of operational efficiency such as the reduction of costs, faster and more efficient recruitment, increased accuracy of data entry and efficient management of speculative applications.

The potential benefits of using technology within HR are reasonably well documented and are apparent in the business cases put together by our case study organizations. However, less attention has been paid to whether these advantages are actually realized once the technology has been introduced.

Consultancy CedarCrestone in their recent survey of 324 organizations with more than 500 employees provided a rare analysis of organizations' success at meeting their objectives for using technology in HR (see Table 13.2).

Evidence from the CIPD survey (2005) showed that HRIS delivered slightly better against 'information criteria' such as reducing the administrative burden on the HR department and improving the quality, speed and flexibility of information, compared to 'economic criteria' such as reducing operational costs, improving productivity and profitability and reducing headcount.

The case studies thus far examined provide little evidence of how successful the technology had been at meeting its objectives. This should not, however, be taken as a criticism that the technology has failed to help HR functions to be successful, but that the organizations concerned have not yet measured the impact of the technology. Norwich Union reported that it has so far experienced cost savings of around £100,000 as a result of reduced headcount in HR and will also save around another £100,000 per annum once paper payslips have been phased out. Cancer Research UK has reduced its recruitment team by one and has also reduced the amount of paper used, although this has not been measured in monetary terms. Anecdotal evidence from such cases provides further suggestion that new technology is having an impact on operational efficiency at least. Interviewees in both organizations perceived an increase in the accuracy and efficiency of data entry, substantial time savings and reduced costs. Over time, the devolution of HR activity to the line can be expected to modify the relationship between line managers, employees and the HR function and to produce a shift in the type of work that HR will be required to perform. This will be discussed in more detail later.

Impact of technology on the role of the HR function

A number of authors have commented that the use of technology within HR not only makes HR activity more efficient, but may also facilitate a change in emphasis for HRM to become more strategic within the organization (Lawler and Mohrman 2003; Shrivastava and Shaw 2004). Recent literature has argued for the idea of HRM as a strategic business partner (Ulrich 1997) rather than in the administrative or transactional role that it has held historically. With the growth of information technology, much administration can be accomplished using self-service or automated systems, therefore the HR function can, and increasingly does make 'significant contributions to building an organisation that is staffed by the right human capital to carry out the work of the firm, and enable the accomplishment of business strategy' (Lawler and Mohrman 2003: 16). Snell et al. (2002) have observed that HR can meet the challenge of simultaneously becoming more strategic, flexible, cost efficient and customer oriented by leveraging information technology. IT can lower administrative costs, increase productivity, speed response times, improve decision making and enhance customer service all at the same time, according to this view.

Ensher et al. (2002) noted, through an analysis of the literature and interviews with HR professionals, five trends or impacts regarding the shift from HR to e-HR. These were:

1 substantial reductions in cost and time for many HR activities

2 transition of administrative activities from the HR department to the employees themselves

3 increase in information readily available to employees

4 need for integrating HR with other organizational systems, especially information systems

5 increased emphasis on HR as a strategic business partner.

The idea that technology can free up time that practitioners would traditionally have spent on administrative tasks, therefore allowing them to focus on strategic business issues, has been frequently observed in the literature (Lawler and Mohrman 2003; Ministry of Manpower 2003; Snell et al. 2002). Even 10 years ago, there was evidence that by automating as many processes as possible, HR was able significantly to reduce the time spent on routine administrative tasks, therefore allowing HR staff time to concentrate more on strategic aspects of the HR role and to be seen as partners to the line in the business (Groe et al. 1996).

Drawing on the resource-based view of organizations (Wright et al. 2001) Lawler and Mohrman go on to say that HR can play an important role in the formulation of strategy by making explicit the human capital resources required to support various strategies and strategic initiatives, by playing a leadership role in helping the organization to develop the necessary capabilities to enact the strategy and by playing a strong role in implementation and change management. Indeed, research by Watson Wyatt (2002) demonstrated that the most commonly recognized business benefit of e-HR is 'allowing HR to re-focus on becoming a strategic business partner' (2002: 11).

One of the most significant outcomes of the use of modern technology within HR appears to be the availability of accurate and detailed information. Kovach et al. (2002) note that as early as the mid-1990s HRIS began to be seen as an information resource and the data collected from HRIS can now provide management with a decision analysis tool as well as a robust database as they can provide detailed information in a variety of areas. Therefore, through the management of HR data, firms are now able to perform calculations that have effects on the business as a whole and can drive business decisions and strategies. Broderick and Boudreau (1992) also argued that a common payoff to using technology in HR is more efficient information management. Better HR information leads managers to ask more questions about how HR issues affect business performance. Bussler and Davies (2002) noted that information systems can transform HR data and add value by turning it into useable information. HR can then take this information and use it strategically to drive organizational decisions (Wilcox 1997). This implies HRIS can produce data-driven HR strategies and therefore encourage the shift from HRM being tactical and reactionary to instead playing a more strategic role.

Past literature has therefore proposed that technology may help facilitate a change in focus for the HR function from administrative and transactional work to strategic work. However, this hypothesis has seldom been investigated empirically.

Unfortunately, no one can really say what a more strategic function would be doing. According to Ulrich (1997) to be a business partner, you need to play all four roles, including change agent, admin expert and employee champion as well as strategist. In fact, there is little evidence that this shift towards being a strategic business partner has actually occurred in those organizations that use technology within HR. Yeung and Brockbank (1995) reported that although HR's stated intent was to focus on more strategic pursuits, in reality, 80% of its time was spent on transactional activities. Groe et al. (1996) noted at that time that the 'tremendous promise' that technology holds for the further development of the HR function as a business partner may not be realized as many organizations still used outdated hardware and software and only used HRIS for the most routine of functions.

Keebler and Rhodes (2002) reported that while two-thirds of survey respondents agreed that web self-service can speed HR's transformation into a more strategic player within the organization and free staff from the burden of administration to take on critical people management activity, only 37% actually felt that they were seeing a shift in HR's mission as a result of the move to the web. Lawler and Mohrman (2003) found that there was no increase in the amount of time that HR spent on being a strategic business partner between 1995 and 2001 (the figure remaining over time at around 20%) but they did see a significant increase (29% to 41%) in the proportion of HR managers who said they were a full partner in the business strategy process. Their research showed that while HR is most likely to be a full partner in the strategy process where they have a completely integrated HR system, having such a system does not of itself ensure that HR will be a strategic partner since in their study 46% of companies with a fully integrated HR system did not describe HR as a full strategic partner.

IBM is an example of an organization that has used technology extensively for people management for some time and as such can be used to illustrate the relational and

HRM in Action 13.3   IBM

IBM is the world's largest information technology company with revenues of $91 billion dollars in 2005. IBM UK employs approximately 20,000 employees of which around three-quarters work at least partly remotely, either at home or on customer sites. IBM uses a shared services HR model with an HR service centre in Budapest serving around 100,000 employees across Europe and HR Business Partners and HR Business Specialists aligned to parts of the business and specific HR processes respectively.

IBM UK uses an HR software package called HR Access, which covers both HR and payroll. There are also a number of standalone and specific tools available to employees and managers to facilitate a variety of HR functions. These systems involve a high degree of manager and employee self-service. Employees are provided with a laptop to facilitate mobile working and many have company broadband and telephony at home.

transformational impact of technology on HR. Within IBM, people management processes have been almost completely devolved to line managers and employees, so that HR practitioners are no longer required to perform administration or transactional work. This has facilitated a total change in HR structure with HR practitioners now adopting the roles of HR business partners who are indeed responsible for higher level HR tasks such as the design of new HR systems. Such a significant change in the role of HR cannot yet be seen within Norwich Union or Cancer Research UK, although more subtle effects are in evidence. Within Cancer Research UK, the automation of systems both in recruitment and in HR generally has meant that the HR team have more time to focus on other 'better value' issues so that they can add more value to the organization. The Head of Resourcing described how:

> The fact that they have more time has encouraged the resourcing team to be more proactive with their work and to take more responsibility for vacancies. Their role has shifted to one that is more customer-focused as they spend more time interacting with managers. Individuals who previously were responsible for data entry are now responsible for producing information for management . . . a more important and rewarding role.

A similar experience was reported by Norwich Union in that the system has removed much of the laborious transactional work out of HR so that people can work on more complex jobs which allows them the time to be more proactive. It is expected that in the future there will be hardly any administration staff, with managers doing this work themselves through the HRIS. The HR department would therefore consist of a core structure of people who would determine strategy in each process area.

The case of Cancer Research UK has also provided evidence of the impact of the availability of detailed and accurate information. The HRIS system means that the HR team can now produce statistics regarding a variety of HR processes, which can then be used as a basis for HR and managerial decision making. For instance, the system can produce reliable information showing the makeup of the current workforce with regard to age, gender and ethnicity. This information may be used as a basis for an examination and revision of recruitment and retention processes in order to improve the diversity of the workforce. The provision of reliable information has led to an increase in the perceived credibility of the HR function and this has led HR into an advisory role. HR advisors can now take information with them into discussions with managers and can provide remedies to problems as they have the necessary information at hand.

Nortel is also using the opportunity of the introduction of manager and employee self-service to reorganize the HR function and the way that it relates to and works with the manager population. Traditionally HR has had the responsibility for people transactions and processes but by empowering the managers to take more responsibility for these transactions the HR function can start to evolve and HR will concentrate on delivering added value to the business in other areas such as strategy and process design. In the past HR business partners have been quite heavily involved in facilitating the day-to-day people transactions whereas in the new model the HR business partners are predominately focused on strategic projects relevant to their specific line organization. Delivery teams have been introduced for all the key HR process areas such as performance management, pay delivery and recruitment. They are the experts that are consulted when the shared service centres are unable to answer questions and are responsible for process design and improvement. There is

HRM in Action 13.4   Nortel

Nortel is a recognized leader in delivering innovative technology solutions encompassing end-to-end broadband, voice over IP, multimedia services and applications and wireless broadband. Nortel has approximately 30,000 employees worldwide. The HR structure is based on the shared service model with centres in four locations globally.

From the early 1990s Nortel invested in building its own HR systems and produced some state-of-the-art HR tools. These included tools for organization structure management, manager self-service, salary planning and online recruitment. A decision was made in the late 1990s to combine all the core data onto a single instance SAP database in order to reduce the ongoing support cost of the HR systems. Since 2001, Nortel has reduced significantly in terms of size and as a result has had to look at the way it operates and how best to use its resources most efficiently. The earlier SAP implementation had resulted in more customization than had

originally been expected and less standardization than had originally been hoped for.

SAP modules were selected in order to support key manager and employee self-service activities. There were five modules selected together with the portal through which they were accessed. These were *personal administration* as the core foundation of the system that holds all the basic HR data allows a manager to view the functional information of their employees and, among other processes, change employee status, make salary, position and location of work changes; *organization management* that builds the organization structure and allows employees to be moved from one position to another in the system; *benefit administration*, a flexible benefits tool; *time and attendance*; and *performance and development* where key business and personal objectives together with the annual performance measurements are entered and maintained.

---

also a core HR strategy group that analyses information and designs the future people strategy using benchmarking and competitive intelligence exercises and works out the best ways to attract and retain staff. The new strategies that emerge from these teams will be passed on to the delivery teams to turn into workable HR processes involving the shared services team and the new self-service tools.

The transition from a transactional to a strategic role for HR may not be easy. The Ministry of Manpower report (2003) explained that the use of technology to change the role of HR is not without pain. HR practitioners need to reskill and add more value beyond administrative services. The HR teams within Cancer Research UK and Norwich Union have had to learn consultancy and communication skills so that they can work with their customers effectively. They have also had to develop skills in analysing and interpreting data so that they can make effective use of the information that is now available via the HRIS and have had to develop their strategic thinking and business writing skills.

Line managers also need to adapt to the increased responsibilities they have for HR issues. Indeed, it is for managers that the introduction of technology may cause the most difficulty through the devolution of large proportions of HR activity to the line. Stone et al. (2003) comment that the use of HR technology and the subsequent downsizing of the HR department has meant that managers take over control of many HR systems, therefore increasing their workload. Stone et al. also suggested that while technology may improve service to managers, managers actually prefer the assistance of a good HR professional. Line managers often baulk at being asked to perform what they view as basic HR work, therefore making the implementation of self-service systems and thus the changes to the HR function problematic (Groe et al. 1996).

Within Nortel, the role of the people manager now involves decision making in areas that they may not have experienced in the past. Managers are held accountable for people changes that impact their budgets and have an increased ability to make decisions that directly impact employees and the business. The objective of this system is to empower managers and to enable them actively to manage their people within the context of their business objectives, approved budgets, employee policies and procedures and laws. Managers are provided with information regarding policies and practices through a managers' website and processes have been structured and standardized to make their role less complex.

A similar system has been developed at Norwich Union. This has affected the way in which managers interact with HR, as managers now obtain their information directly from the intranet rather than from HR. The implementation of this system with managers within Norwich Union has not been without difficulty. Some managers do not use the system to its full capacity and still resent doing 'HR's work'. This may, however, be a reflection of the relatively short period of time that the system has been in place. Certainly, in IBM where manager self-service has been in use for some time, the managers appear to have no difficulties in using the system effectively without a second thought.

Conclusion

The business case for HRIS is argued with justifications from improved efficiencies, including headcount reduction and the opportunity to do more with the same resources, including redeployment to more 'strategic activity'. Developments in technology and the internet have brought complex and widespread applications into the realm of everyday work.

Although we have encountered few cases where there has been an economic evaluation of HRIS, this may be because the benefits achieved go beyond a simple ROI. For the generation brought up on their mother's laptop, not to use spreadsheets and new packages or not to apply for jobs online, seems absurdly old fashioned. After online banking, insurance, airline and hotel bookings have been routinely online for so many years, organizations that failed to use available and efficient technology-assisted processes in HRM would damage their employment brand in the eyes of current and future employees.

The business case has an efficiency and quality dimension. Companies are under pressure often to reduce 'indirect' labour costs. The scale and pace of work can be enhanced through HRIS and there is an increasing demand for accurate, timely information to inform decisions – whether at the work group level, for example in project management, or at the corporate level of e-learning, internet recruitment, absence control and the like. The increasing trend to integrate systems and to reduce the number of different systems is driven by a need to simplify and to leverage improvements.

Integrating HR systems under SAP for example gives opportunities for reports to come in formats that cross functional boundaries. Businesses thrive, survive and compete through a philosophy of continuous improvement, which necessarily includes HRM.

The evidence for HRM becoming more 'strategic' because the routine and standardized procedures are being automated is ambiguous. For those who see a need for HR to produce data-driven HR strategies, HRIS can be a boon. Leveraging new data sources to produce strategically valuable information means that HRM must be aware of what data are likely to affect performance in the long term. In some of our case study organizations there was a caucus of specialists in knowing how to find the data, the questions to ask and the likely sources, to whom HR strategists would refer. IT skills may not be yet well distributed in the HR function.

However, if it is argued that the reason HR has not yet come to be regarded as 'strategic' there are a number of questions to explore. For many years, commentators have forecast the impact of change forced by new technology. Snell et al. in 1995 quoted Parsons study of 1988:

> As IT changes operations within HR, it simultaneously recasts HR from solely an administrative function to one that is more oriented towards technical/professional expertise.
>
> (Snell et al. 1995: 162)

The quote shows that originally there was a belief that the release from routine work would allow HR to practise its specialism. Now we see this removal of routine, transactional work as providing time to become 'strategic business partners'. One problem with this argument is there is no consensus on what a 'business partner' in HR is at the strategic level. Many HR staff who have the business partner title are, in fact, firefighting as consultants to the line. But a major change to the HR function has occurred. In many organizations a three-part structure is in place. A shared service or call centre for all transactional work that has not yet gone to self-service, is supported by a group of 'business partner' HR consultants and a small group of HR policy makers. Sometimes that latter group has a strategic role as well or they may be the technical experts (for example in rewards, or development) while a small number of HR staff at the top provide strategic direction. Variants on this structure can be found in large dispersed organizations from IBM in Europe to Transport for London.

This shift to a consumer service approach to HR and the need for the reengineering of HR processes are one side of the changes. The other aspect is the impact on line manager relationships and the skills of HR staff themselves. The implications of this shift are still playing themselves out. One consequence is the formalization of routines or indeed the creation of routines where none existed. More information is collected, stored and manipulated in aggregate now, but that does not mean that HR staff know more than before about the people at work. Yet a different kind of engagement is now possible, through, for example, self-service, such as employees creating their own benefit packages online. The engagement of employees as customers gives the employee a new, more privileged and perhaps more adult-to-adult relationship with the employer instead of a paternalistic relationship.

As HR becomes more of a project management role, a call centre manager role and a consultancy manager role, so the commercial aspects of the senior HR roles are strengthened. Outsourcing solutions may be combined with these new roles, to give

HRM a general manager status. Detailed knowledge of the techniques in HRM may be useful in the consultancy sphere, but for HR in general the role is changing, pushed and pulled by technology and the need to do more with fewer people resources.

Acknowledgement

The authors wish to thank the CIPD for commissioning the research project which helps inform this chapter.

References

Ball, K. (2001). 'The use of human resource information systems: a survey', *Personnel Review* 30(5/6): 677-93.

Bissell, P. (2004). 'Total reward helps Nationwide become employer of choice', *IDS* October.

Broderick, R. and J. Boudreau (1992). 'Human resource management, information technology, and the competitive edge', *Academy of Management Executive* 6(2): 7-17.

Bussler, L. and E. Davies (2002). 'Information systems: the quiet revolution in human resource management', *Journal of Computer Information Systems* 42(2): 17-20.

CIPD (2005). *People Management and Technology: Progress and Potential*. London, CIPD.

Cranfield School of Management (2005). *Cranet Survey of International Comparative HRM*. Available at www.cranet.org.

Ensher, E., T. Nielson and E. Grant-Vallone (2002). 'Tales from the hiring line: effects of the internet and technology on HR processes', *Organizational Dynamics* 31(3): 224-44.

Groe, G., W. Pyle and J. Jamrog (1996). 'Information technology and HR', *Human Resource Planning* 19(1): 54-61.

Gueutal, H. (2003). 'The brave new world of e-HR', in *Advances in Human Performance and Cognitive Engineering Research, Vol. 3*. Amsterdam, Elsevier.

Keebler, T. and D. Rhodes (2002). 'e-HR: becoming the "path of least resistance"'. *Employment Relations Today* 29(2): 57-66.

Kettley, P. and P. Reilly (2003). *e-HR: An Introduction*. London, Institute of Employment Studies.

Kovach, K., A. Hughes, P. Fagan and P. Maggitti (2002). 'Administrative and strategic advantages of HRIS', *Employment Relations Today* 29(2): 43-8.

Lawler, E. and K. Mohrman (2003). 'HR as a strategic partner: what does it take to make it happen?', *Human Resource Planning* 26(3): 15-29.

Martinsons, M. (1996). 'Human resource management applications of knowledge based systems', *International Journal of Information Management* 17(1): 35-53.

Ministry of Manpower (2003). *e-HR: Leveraging Technology*. Case study series, 2/2003.

Parsons, C. K. (1988). 'Computer technology: implications for human resource management', in G. Ferris and K. Rowland (eds) *Research in Personnel and Human Resource Management, Vol. 6*. Stamford, CT, JAI Press.

Shrivastava, S. and J. Shaw (2004). 'Liberating HR through technology', *Human Resource Management* 42(3): 201-22.

Snell, S. A., P. R. Pedigo and G. M. Krawiec (1995). 'Managing the impact of information technology on human resource management', in G. Ferris, S. Rosen and D. Barnum (eds) *Handbook of Human Resource Management*. Oxford, Blackwell.

Snell, S., D. Stueber and D. Lepak (2002). 'Virtual HR departments: getting out of the middle', in R. Heneman and D. Greenberger (eds) *Human Resource Management in Virtual Organisations*. Greenwich, CT, Information Age Publishing.

Stone, D., E. Stone-Romero and K. Lukaszewski (2003). 'The functional and dysfunctional consequences of human resource information technology for organizations and their employees', in *Human Performance and Cognitive Engineering Research, Vol. 3*. Amsterdam, Elsevier Science.

Tannenbaum, S. (1990). 'HRIS: user group implications', *Journal of Systems Management* 41(1): 27-32.

Ulrich, D. (1997). *Human Resource Champions*. Boston, MA, Harvard Business School Press.

Watson Wyatt (2002). B2E/HER survey results 2002. Available at www.watsonwyatt.com.

Wilcox, J. (1997). 'The evolution of human resources technology', *Management Accounting* June: 3-5.

Wright, P. M., B. B. Dunford and S. A. Snell (2001). 'Human resource and the resource-based view of the firm', *Journal of Management* 27: 701-21.

Yeung, A. and W. Brockbank (1995). 'Re-engineering HR through information technology', *Human Resource Planning* 18(2): 24-37.

Ethics and HRM

David Bevan

After 30 years' practical experience in business I find I have an approach to ethics and management that is characterized by my colleagues as 'critical'. In academia the hegemonic project of commerce (Boltanski and Chiapello 2006) is naturalized as perfectly normal business (Chomsky 2004); Such quasi-normality contrasts starkly with what I witnessed. Dishonesty and venality seemed to animate the commercial world (see also Bataille 1991). HRM academics, over the past 10 years or so, have been unusual in offering a humanistically-inclined voice among the seductive dominant discourses of business as usual.

Previously

Reviewing the literature of ethics in HRM, Diana Winstanley and Jean Woodall (2000) detect the first signs of explicitly ethical interest in the work of Karen Legge (1995, 1998). She is among the commentators who apparently aspire at this (relatively late) date to critically question the consequences for HRM of the economic determinism of Milton Friedman (1962/2002). In the scope of this book (Winstanley and Woodall 2000), critical HRM becomes evident variously; through strands of Marxist capital/labour relations (Claydon 2000); through the constraints to ethics as a consequence of globalization (Legge 2000a); and through the adverse impacts of increasing competitiveness on the quality of life (Simpson 2000; Winstanley 2000). The volume closes with a call to individual integrity:

> [E]thical HRM is more than just setting standards of 'best practice', it is about knowing how to handle the tricky situations that depart from this. This is recognised by the ethics of care

which draws attention to the need to take account of the particular needs and circumstances of individuals and to involve them in moral deliberation.

(Woodall and Winstanley 2000: 285)

The book problematizes the ethics of HRM from a position of essentially modern ethical frameworks: Ethical egoism based in Hobbes which informs enlightened self-interest; notions of rights based in Kant – what is right for one is right for all, people may never be used as a means to an end; ethics based in notions of justice and the social contract from Rawls; utilitarian ethics based in Bentham and Mill that seeks an optimum solution for the greatest number of people; another version of the social contract known as stakeholder theory; a simplified version of discourse ethics that permits a talk about it approach to ethical decision making; the potentially oppressive ethics of care;[1] and virtue ethics based in Aristotle's concern with human intuition and empathy. Does any one of these frameworks inspire confidence? Are they authentic, workable guides to contemporary morality?

I suggest that it is precisely the reliance on these frameworks to which organizational ethical failures, such as they are, may be attributed. These frameworks are undoubtedly accurately summarized and historically interesting; but they are normative – they seek to assert moral facts. Of course, it is always wrong to kill and steal or lie; but there are circumstances in which most individuals will identify an alternate relative truth that can only be subjectively argued. When someone is threatening your life or the life of someone you love; when you are starving or in overwhelming need; when you desperately need to change the facts: none of these contexts makes an unlawful action right, but it may make the action a justifiable exception – in which case it can't always be wrong if there is a circumstance in which it would be not-wrong.

In respect of these ethical frameworks which position do you take: is any of these actually something on which we can all, or mostly, agree? If not, then they are practically useless (MacIntyre 2002b) – although they are great as an intellectual basis for domination (Foucault 1988). If yes – if you think utility is a good standard – how do you know what is best for the greatest number of people? Or will you settle for a cost-benefit analysis? I will leave these questions rhetorically open.

By its reliance on these enlightenment frameworks, and in the context of this present review, Winstanley and Woodall (2000) is a valedictory piece: a farewell to the failures or unachieved utopias of the enlightenment perhaps? From the perspective of 2007, Karen Legge's contemporary book (2000b) more accurately anticipates the gritty, critical future in which we seem to be operating and theorizing. The fragmented future is an epochalization, a metatheory, of life where changes occur so quickly that most of us live in a broken or unachieved version of the future we anticipated only a decade ago (Lincoln and Denzin 2005). Legge confronts the rhetoric of organizations with the realities of practitioner existence in a postmodern manner through critical evaluation and deconstruction – her conclusions are necessarily darker than those of the previously considered authors. She takes a neo-Nietzschian (Nietzsche 2003) perspective of the entrenched viciousness of organizational life, and closes, as though in passing acknowledgement to Winstanley and Woodall (2000), with a Bourdevine (Bourdieu 1998) notion: 'the "soft" normative model of HRM appears as a mirage, retreating into a receding horizon' (Legge 2000b: 339).

Currently

The objective–subjective (or positivist-emergent) polemic remains at the heart of this potential problem. There may be no objective ethical rules (MacIntyre 2002b; Nietzsche 2003; Williams 1987) and in contemporary globalized modernity with all its precariousness and uncertainty (Bauman 2000; Bauman 2004) we can either adopt the blatantly anachronistic, clockwork (i.e. Newtonian) morality, which promises certainties that we simultaneously know to be lies, or we attempt subjectively – as Winstanley and Woodall (2000) conclude – to emulate an individual level of integrity.

Unaffected by this potential paradigm incompatibility, the range of ethical and moral debate in HRM has continued to develop in recent years. As with all managerial projects, economic interest has prevailed and ethics are reduced to codes of governance or process that can be reduced further to key performance indicators – we know it makes sense. Beyond a generalized concern with treating employees fairly, there are a number of overlapping issues which may not be exclusively or intrinsically ethical. Yet, in these issues ethical interests may be considered to arise. These include, for example, the issues of health and safety, equal opportunity, privacy, diversity and discrimination, whistleblowing, compensation and pensions, downsizing and redundancy, career and personal development and work–life balance (Fisher and Lovell 2006; Hartman 2005). Nested within each is a complex range of issues in which the interests and rights of the individual will come into potential conflict with the interests of the organization. In respecting individual privacy for example, the security and reputational needs of the organization will have to be balanced, in matters such as testing for narcotics or child protection. Having considered the position achieved by the turn of the century or thereabout, the remainder of this chapter will consider aspects of current critical practice.

A subsequent, modernist approach to ethics possibly relevant to contemporary HRM is offered by DesJardins and McCall (2005), who suggest an analytic typology based on an overlapping array of varied and contingent rights. Along with the, perhaps, obvious category of *moral rights* (the entitlements that derive from moral rules or axioms on which ethical issues are generally decided) there are *legal rights* deriving from the regulation of a relevant jurisdiction and *contractual rights* which derive in some way from a relevant contract. So, an employee may be seen to have a moral right to choose employment according to his or her abilities, s/he will have a legal right to work only a certain number of hours each week and receive a minimum wage and a contractual right to certain benefits in respect of healthcare, life assurance and pension provision. There is a distinction between these three categories in a commercial context. While legal rights are enshrined in the law and generally inalienable and contractual rights may only be varied with the agreement of the contracting parties, there is no established code of moral rights. I cannot mediate this further. If the typology is useful for your practice, I encourage you to read the full text. I shall now leave modernism and normative frameworks to one side in favour of naturalism and practice.

The contemporary approach I wish to pursue here in contemplating ethics in HRM is more critically based. It is informed by interdisciplinary post-structuralist (hence postmodern in relation to the immediately preceding discussion) approaches to management, which articulates itself as critical management studies (CMS)[2] (Alvesson and Willmott 2003; Grey and Willmott 2005; Parker 2002); indeed it has become a special interest domain at the Academy of Management. To briefly encapsulate the opposition to CMS itself; its approaches are simultaneously characterized by practitioners as being *too Marxist* (Johnson 2004; Norberg 2002), and by academics as being *inadequately Marxist* (Callinicos 2006; Thompson 2005). As between these oppositions I shall not debate further here, rather I borrow from Richard Laughlin's (1995, 2004) notation of *research approach*, from which I interpret that theorization is a matter of *choice* and I choose to discuss ethics and HRM as informed by the interests of CMS.[3]

In common with other areas of management, questions have developed (for example) about the ethical basis of managerialism (Parker 2003) and the salience of ethics in business (Brenkert 2004), but there are not always answers to such questions. The performativity (Lyotard 1984) central to applied managerialism is not a goal outcome for CMS. Notwithstanding, ethically critical positions are not a priori anti-managerial, but rather genuinely grounded in an ethical deconstruction, or denaturalizing (Fournier and Grey 2000), of entrenched and questionable managerial practices. Such deconstruction challenges the status quo on the basis of a poststructuralist diagnosis of a contemporary failure of morality, based for example, in Nietzsche and Foucault (Bauman 1993, 2000, 2004; Bourdieu 1998, 2005; MacIntyre 2002a, 2006; O'Leary 2002; Williams 1987). Mutually contingent with CMS, a variant genealogy of critique may be traced from the concepts of *précarité* (qua precariousness) inherent in the conceptual confections of risk society (Beck 1992) and globalized modernity (Giddens 1990; Giddens 1999; Scholte 2005); an atomized fragmented future in which (I have suggested) the rational certainties of the enlightenment have been displaced and authority figures are no longer trusted by increasingly reflexive (self-questioning) individuals.

Action ethics

Having outlined the living context of ethics in the theory of precarious globalized modernity, I do not intend to spend further time here developing such theory, rather I shall now focus on action ethics or the ethics as practice (de George 2006). Instead of situating the production of ethical behaviour in a reflective deliberation of the moral subject, action ethics originates outside the individual. Action ethics is pre-emptive and imperious. It situates morality in the relationship that each of us subjectively entertains with the beings of other moral subjects, whether close or distant. This involves that action ethics does not proceed from any attribution of praise or blame for something that might be rationalized. In presenting action ethics, I shall rely on interpolating the phenomenological ethics of Emmanuel Lévinas. Instead of providing detailed principle(s), rule(s), code(s) or any other form of guidance likely to distinguish between good and evil in our actions, Lévinas presents ethics based in the perhaps confusing absolute relativism [sic] of always considering the needs of the other person and the congruency of any (re)action.

The chapter proceeds through a bricolage (Lévi-Strauss 1966) mediating reality with complementary theorizations. Two real-life case examples from the natural world of organizational HRM follow. Each is followed by a discussion of these contrasting scenarios. Action ethics relies on contingent subjectivity and this chapter provides material for reflection, there are no didactic conclusions. My experiences of the commercial world and teaching business ethics have persuaded me that the best – the most ethical – outcome for my practice is to awaken and develop ethical sensitivity in those who participate in my practice. I invite you, the reader, to reflect on what is written in the context of your personal experience, allowing these vignettes to create a unique, ethical learning experience.

HRM in Action 14.1 **Ethics in action 1**

RD is an experienced project manager in the field of information technology. He is a white British male in his late 40s, educated to postgraduate level, and with a professional qualification. He is divorced and lives in central London. Having successfully completed a five-year project related to the millennium bug, ending in 2001, he is offered a project director position in the same multinational firm. He will be responsible for the 'assessment and career development' of 500 IT project managers across the region of Europe, Middle East and Africa (EMEA) at the beginning of 2002; it is a 30-month project. He reports to the vice-president of human resources (VPHR) in the worldwide head office; he has been told he has been selected for the job because of his personal qualities of leadership and achievement. RD is given a spacious office in the corporate headquarters building, his name is painted on the door. The job initially (months 1/30-3/30) involves gregariously travelling around these (14) regional offices and meeting all the project managers face to face, while preparing an outsourced call for proposals for the design and supply of an assessment centre. In the first three months he meets the personnel involved and reviews the process of designing the assessment centre with a number of consultant suppliers. In refining the objectives for the daylong assessment centres, the parameters begin to change. The assessment centres initially were for the assessment of potential and recent hires, but the terms are changed subtly in a meeting (beginning of month 4/30) with the HR director. He

learns that it would be surely a good idea if all existing staff were to be assessed and then their future training needs could be elicited. The communication, which was originated in person with RD, is now conducted through email. The assessment centres are duly convened (overall budget £2,100,000) and deployed, beginning in month 6/30. Coincidentally with the assessment centres being deployed, RD is told that he will go to all the events and supervise the proceedings, he is also told he will no longer be required to attend the office but rather to work from the hot desk area or from home/travelling. Meanwhile, at the assessment centres, potential and recent hires are initially processed and RD circulates a memo to the full cohort announcing that they will all 'have the chance to develop their careers by attending the assessment centre at which they will be given a certificate of competence and a capability rating with suggestions for future training by a professional project management validation process'. RD encounters some resistance from a cadre of the managers in the French office who apparently suspect that everything may not be as innocent as it seems. Indeed, the French cohort generally refuses 'to submit to effective reselection' (their words) for a job they already hold (7/30). RD discusses these and other ripples of dissent in an exchange of phone calls with the VPHR (8/30). He is reassured that this might have been anticipated and is told that VPHR will sort things out. RD then receives a cc mail from VPHR addressed to all senior project managers in which the senior managers are directed to attend in order to 'give exemplary confidence in the assessment process to the line managers and below'. RD notes that since the original meeting at which he was appointed, he has only seen the VPHR once; at the meeting in month 4/30 and after month 9/30 he is never to meet with or speak to this individual again. Meanwhile, by the end of month 11/30, 60 assessment centres have been deployed across the region by the consulting firm and all consenting employees have attended. The career development stage is now due to begin beginning month 12/30.

In month 12/30 RD receives a cc mail from the finance director to VPHR concerning necessary economies following a shrinking of the market and asking for suggestions as to how such economies might be achieved at a starting level of £18,000,000 per annum. Later the same month RD receives a mail asking for details of all assessment centre data. At the beginning of month 14/30 RD turns on his phone and email to discover a welter of messages. It dawns on him during the course of some irate conversations that a mail has been circulated in his name issuing redundancy notices to 360 of the 500 project managers. RD attempts to speak to VPHR without success. He attempts to escalate the issue in the EMEA region, again without any success. The following day he receives a phone call from the counsel general's office requesting a meeting that same day at an office address in central London. RD arrives at the address to find that he is at a firm of a leading lawyers and, in the course of a brief meeting, he is advised that his contract has been summarily terminated, he receives 18 months' salary and in return for his signature on a mutual 'hold harmless' letter of

discharge he is paid a bonus of a further 30 months' salary.

In the course of his interview with the researcher – conducted under the terms of the Chatham House Agreement – RD claims to feel abused by this process. However, he shrugs his shoulders and says 'it's just business'. In the period of 12 months he has been paid £300,000 in salary and bonuses. He further discloses having profited 'rather nicely' to the sum of £210,000 from the business affairs partner at the consulting firm which obtained the winning bid for the assessment centres and to whom he had 'perhaps indiscreetly' unofficially indicated the level of the competing bids.

Reflection 1

This vignette involves professional managers – the fiduciary agents of shareholders – in a major quoted company and a partner in a city name consulting firm. One valid means of explicating an ethical theory would be to sample fully this dataset to establish a grounded theory of management ethics and the ethics of HRM (Glaser 1998; Glaser 2004; Glaser and Strauss 1967), such an ethics would be fully compliant with the liberal ethics of economics previously invoked:

> (T)here is one and only one social responsibility of business – to use its resources and engage in activities designed to increase its profits so long as it stays within the rules of the game. (Friedman 1962/2002: 133)

The rules of the game, both implicit and explicit for the players in vignette 1, being (the somewhat ambiguous) 'just business'.

Certainly in such contexts, widely popularized in the apparent and gross venality of the affairs of Enron, Parmalat, Hollinger International among others, it is possible to understand how a deconstructive, critical tendency in HRM may be linked to the emergence of characteristically reflexive, (non-)performative and denaturalizing questions as 'Is HRM ethical? Can HRM be ethical?' (Legge 1998) and 'Is HRM a hologram?' (Keenoy 1999). In order to determine (without limitation) alternate conceptual responses I adduce for consideration here the corporate nominalist[4] argument suggests. This suggests that corporations themselves should not be expected to have ethical agency – and therefore HRM ethics are at best unlikely. This position is also derived from *logical* arguments which suggest that corporations (and other organizational forms) having no pathology[5] (i.e. neither flesh nor blood) therefore have no moral agency; because only individuals have ethical agency. I rely on the entrenched nominalist position of economists who exclude the possibility and indeed question the benefits of confusing business with ethics (Friedman and Miles 2002; Henderson 2001) and philosophers who articulate a categorically corporate nominalist position as a starting point towards enjoining a new ethical pluralism (Werhane 1985). As for asserting that personal responsibility is the only possible means of ethical engagement, this has been discussed elsewhere, based in analyses of Lévinas (Bevan and Corvellec 2007) and Sartre (Ashman and Winstanley 2006), but I do not assert that this makes Lévinas and Sartre corporate nominalists in any sense. I assert that merely anthropocentric ethics is supported from the reading of these authors.

One response to such deconstructively inclined rhetoric would be to consider on what basis might I analyse an ethical nature for HRM? One commentator suggests a grammatical explication: the ethics of HRM (or capitalism itself) might be located by reference to questions such as 'Did you go into HRM to help the human race, or reduce the unemployment queues?' (Comte-Sponville 2004). Because, he asserts, if it was not for a specifically ethical purpose, why do you imagine that HRM will be ethical? Surely it's just what you do to make a living? The stark simplicity of this approach is potentially supported by arguments about the logical possibility of terms from Michael Jensen (2002). Jensen's argument would take us in a slightly different direction: in talking about HRM which of the potential compound indications is being maximized – the HR or the M? In HRM does the practitioner maximize his/her duty of care to the individual employee or to the interests of the employer? Jensen's point is that such questions are not susceptible to logical mediation. Either the HRM practitioner is enforcing the writ of the employer (i.e. for the benefit of the shareholder) or supporting the interests of employee: so (are you) maximizing the interests of your employer, or maximizing the interests of the employee? This is a serious rather than a trivial point. Jensen points out:

> It is logically impossible to maximize in more than one dimension at the same time, unless the dimensions are monotone transformations of one another.
>
> (Jensen 2002: 237)

In Jensen's theorem social welfare and survival are a severe constraint on the range of choices available, and thus (he suggests) they will be overlooked. Reverting briefly to the naturalistic world, Jensen's maximizing theorem is enacted in the earlier vignette; in such circumstances what is the value of a theory of ethics in HRM, what agency or choice is there for an ethical HRM?

John Roberts (2001) appears to suggest that I should dismiss the pessimistic and stark assumptions of this agency-centred paradigm, entraining an apparently endless polemical speculation on whether human nature is essentially trustworthy or not, in favour of considering trust and distrust as an outcome of the processes of accountability. For Roberts, accountability is not just a necessary constraint, a Foucaultian corrective reaction to the reckless or self-interested actions of the powerful. He prefers a structural relationship (Giddens 1991) in which the practices and processes of accountability produce, and reproduce, both the objective consequentialism of

HRM in Action 14.2   Ethics in action 2

JB is a white female in her mid 40s, educated to postgraduate level and a member of a professional institution. She is the human resources director of a FTSE 1000 firm where she has worked since leaving university at the age of 21. She is responsible for a significant employee cadre (a six-figure number on a global basis). In the course of our meetings, my main concern has been to discover how she considers her relationship with stakeholders. Over a period of three years I have spent more than 50 hours in her company – I mention this to establish our rapport. She is aware of my interest in ethics and she has confided in me that the joy she once had in her job is much reduced. Through an iterative prioritizing dialogue process, I establish that the main difference in the past 10 years (five of which she has been in this post) relates to the way in which communication has changed. From a time when she worked in a busy office with many assistants and endless phone calls and meetings, she now feels alienated by the decentralization of staff and the increasing (almost total) reliance on email as a means of communication over any other means: 'People used to drop in all the time, or at least the phone was always ringing – it was lively, alive. Now it is like a tomb in here. Just the blinking of my Blackberry and the regular bleeping of the incoming email alert on my desktop and traffic moving silently in the distance – I feel like a ghost.'

I reflect on this and at a subsequent meeting I discuss with her a range of the issues she deals with by email which are generally quite serious. I suggest to her that she has simply witnessed a necessary but predictable managerialist reduction of personal relationships. By physically distancing personal relations and simultaneously foregrounding notions of individuality and freedom management policies (of which she might equally and unintentionally be a contributing author) have made her remote from her cohort. This type of instrumental impersonalization is an ethical failure in Lévinasian terms because it robs her of the face-to-face intercourse which human subjectivity requires (in a phenomenological paradigm). In the course of a dialogue, I suggest that that she might try, despite any current fashion, facing (i.e. physically seeing, confronting) some of the people who she deals with as an experiment. We sit at her desk and identify from her incoming email five people whom she can see relatively easily, three of whom she knows and two she has not met and all of whom have small issues which do not demand (as such) a face-to-face meeting, but where also it would not be inappropriate.

Three weeks later, I meet her again as I am leaving another meeting. I imagine I am seeing an old friend who has fallen in love; she is, apparently, a transformed woman. In fact, the coaching dialogue led to a good suggestion and she has been resocialized in her relations with other humans. It is for her to acknowledge the difference this implausibly simple suggestion seems to have entrained. The policy in her working group is now moving in the direction of increased socializing so that people communicate ideally in a face to face and if not in a voice to voice: 'It probably decreases efficiency', she volunteers, 'but it makes it all seem really much more human.'

Reflection 2

To reject as simplistic these small ethical steps is to completely miss the point of ethical action. It is not about revolutions and great changes that ethics is enacted but more in line with the tranformational notions of Gabriel Tarde; what happens in the innovative process is that 'great *constant* forces [. . .] are given direction by *small, accidental, new* forces, which, by being grafted on the first ones, set into motion a new kind of periodic reproduction' (Tarde quoted in Taymans

1950: 616). In such small gestures I believe Lévinas offers us an action ethics which is constitutive of innate empathy between humans observed in the trivial act and phrase when two people arrive at the same door simultaneously:

'(We) say, before an open door, 'After you, sir!' It is an original 'After you, sir!' that I have tried to describe.

(Lévinas 1985: 89)

It is that simple to act ethically. How you decide you must now transpose such behaviour to an organizational level is something I suggest is impossible for me to mediate further. The route of individual responsibility is simple but it is not necessarily easy. Conversely, the pragmatic ethics of the project of management are systemic, codified and easy to perform – have a nice day!

individualized profit maximization and the subjective and essentially pluralistic (socializing) which leads us to question motives, beliefs and values. While this theorization presents a valid and coherent account of the structure of accountability in respect of Giddens (1976), here we elect to move on from ethical theorizing in favour of ethical action; after all, friendly fire and hostile fire are alternate theorizations of a missile hitting someone on whose life the effect will be largely identical in practice.

Roberts's direction to subjectivity is, notwithstanding, central to the action ethics I am seeking to present. The subjectivity of the physical body in the work of Emmanuel Lévinas (1969/2005, 1981/2004) is a precondition – sine qua non – to the ethical engagement with the Other (the 'other than me' in the sense of all that I am not or may not know). Such a body-centred precondition completely precludes and excludes the ethical sensitivity of bloodless organizations that have no sense to which to appeal. Lévinasian ethics is an ethics of endless responsibility for the Other and for justice. Based on this, my first claim would be that ethical responsibility cannot be contemplated by a corporation. Corporations lack the bodily subjectivity essential to a Lévinasian approach to the Other. Only humans have the capacity to act ethically and since corporations are not humans, it is impossible to speak of corporate ethics: we can only contemplate managerial ethics. The corollary of this approach for the corporations is that, while they are essentially neither ethical nor unethical, they can be a mask for the unethical behaviour of individuals or groups. These unscrupulous or careless individuals stand to profit from the completely misplaced notions of corporate (ir)responsibility which, I suggest, a reading of Lévinas repudiates. In recognizing this, the second claim is that business ethics can only be the responsibility of individual actors of management (see also Bevan and Corvellec 2007).

Let this lead us into a positive example through a second vignette, which involves a short sequence of developmental coaching in action ethics.

Conclusion

This chapter has attempted to foreclose, if only briefly, an interminable normative monologue, notwithstanding it may be confidently anticipated that colleagues in the positivist realm will continue working on it for decades to come. I have rather indicated why I think that ethical theorizing in HRM is of less practical value than (admittedly a theorization of) ethical action. By reference to two empirical examples, I have identified degrees of self-interested behaviour. No generalizations in respect of gender are offered – I have reported two simple episodes of HRM in naturalistic terms. A subjective analysis of the actions of alienation in one compared to the actions of proximity in the second, are, I suggest, initial object lessons for the ethically inclined.

[This chapter is dedicated to Diana Winstanley, a mentor and friend who died in July 2006.]

Notes

1. The ethics of care is frequently and inaccurately subsumed into feminist ethics.
2. 'Eclectic by design, CMS has combined various schools of post-Marxism, post-structuralism and also contemporary feminist theory to provide something of a discernible approach to analysing management (see Fournier and Grey 2000); one that attempts systematically to interrogate its philosophical assumptions, and the imperatives and techniques associated with its practice (Alvesson and Willmott 1992; Hancock and Tyler 2004: 620).
3. The Critical Management Studies Interest Group is a forum within the Academy of Management that encourages the expression of views critical towards established management practices and the status quo. Its main premise suggests that identifiable structural features of contemporary society – the profit imperative, patriarchy, racial inequality and ecological irresponsibility – can be seen to transform organizations into instruments of domination and exploitation. Driven by the shared desire to change this situation, CMS research, teaching and practice aims to develop critical interpretations of management and society and explicate radical alternatives. Its critique aims to connect empirical shortcomings in management, and individual managers with the wider demands of a socially divisive and ecologically destructive system within which these managers work. Sample topics include: critical theories of the nature of managerial authority, resistance to managerial authority, identity, rationality and subjectivity; critiques of managerialist theories of management and organization; critical assessments of emerging alternative forms of organization; critiques of political economy; critical perspectives on business strategy, globalization, entrepreneurship, technological innovation, computerization and management consulting practices; critical analyses of discourses of management, development and progress; critical perspectives on class, gender and race; the profit imperative and the natural environment; critical epistemologies and methodologies (Alvesson and Willmott 2003; Clegg and Hardy 1999; Grey and Willmott 2005).
4. For an extensive discussion of corporate nominalism and corporate realism see Iwai (2006).
5. That is, contrary to Bakan (2004).

References

Alvesson, M. and H. C. Willmott (1992). *Critical Management Studies*. London, Sage.

Alvesson, M. and H. C. Willmott (eds) (2003). *Studying Management Critically*. London, Sage.

Ashman, I. and D. Winstanley (forthcoming). 'For or against corporate identity? Personification and the problem of moral agency', *Journal of Business Ethics*.

Bakan, J. (2004). *The Corporation: The Pathological Pursuit of Profit and Power*. New York, Free Press.

Bataille, G. (1991). *The Accursed Share: Volumes 2 and 3*. New York, Zone Books.

Bauman, Z. (1993). *Postmodern Ethics*. Oxford, Blackwell.

Bauman, Z. (2000). *Liquid Modernity*. Cambridge, Polity Press.

Bauman, Z. (2007). *Wasted Lives*. Cambridge, Polity Press.

Beck, U. (1992). *Risk Society: Towards a New Modernity*. London, Sage.

Bevan, D. and H. Corvellec (2007). 'The impossibility of corporate ethics', *Business Ethics: A European Review*, 16(3).

Boltanski, L. and E. Chiapello (2006). *The New Spirit of Capitalism*. London, Verso.

Bourdieu, P. (1998). 'Utopia of endless exploitation: the essence of neoliberalism', *Le Monde Diplomatique* Paris: 8.

Bourdieu, P. (2005). *The Social Structures of the Economy*. Cambridge, Polity Press.

Brenkert, G. G. (2004). *Corporate Integrity and Account-ability*. London, Sage.

Callinicos, A. (2006). *The Resources of Critique*. Cambridge, Polity Press.

Chomsky, N. (2004). *Hegemony or Survival: America's Quest for Global Dominance*. Harlow, Penguin.

Claydon, T. (2000). 'Employee participation and involve-ment', in D. Winstanley and J. Woodall, *Ethical issues in contemporary HRM*. Basingstoke, Palgrave.

Clegg, S. R. and C. Hardy (eds)(1999). *Studying Organiza-tion, Theory and Method*. London, Sage.

Comte-Sponville, A. (2004). *Le Capitalisme est-il moral?* Paris, Albin Michel.

de George, R. T. (2006). 'The relevance to philosophy to business ethics', *Business Ethics Quarterly* 16(3): 381-90.

DesJardins, J. R. and J. J. McCall (2005). *Contemporary Issues in Business Ethics*. London, Thompson Wadsworth.

Fisher, C. M. and A. Lovell (2006). *Business Ethics and Val-ues*. Harlow, FT Prentice-Hall.

Foucault, M. (1988). *Politics, Philosophy, Culture: Inter-views and other writings 1977-1984*. London, Rout-ledge.

Fournier, V. and C. Grey (2000). 'At the critical moment: con-ditions and prospects for critical management studies', *Human Relations* 53(1): 7-32.

Friedman, M. (1962/2002). *Capitalism and Freedom*. Lon-don and Chicago, University of Chicago Press.

Giddens, A. (1976). *New Rules of Sociological Method*. New York, Basic Books.

Giddens, A. (1990). *The Consequences of Modernity*. Cam-bridge, Polity Press.

Giddens, A. (1991). *Modernity and Self Identity: Self and Society in The Late Modern Age*. Cambridge, Polity Press.

Giddens, A. (1999). *Runaway World: How Globalisation is Shaping Our Lives*. London, Profile Books.

Glaser, B. (1998). *Doing Grounded Theory*. Mill Valley, CA, Sociology Press.

Glaser, B. (2004). 'Naturalist inquiry and grounded theory', *Forum: Qualitative Social Research* 5(1): 68.

Glaser, B. and A. Strauss (1967). *The Discovery of Grounded Theory*. Chicago, Aldine.

Grey, C. and H. C. Willmott (eds)(2005). *Critical Manage-ment Studies*. Oxford Management Readers. Oxford, Oxford University Press.

Hancock, P. and M. Tyler (2004). '"MOT your life": critical management studies and the management of everyday life', *Human Relations* 57(5): 619-45.

Hartman, L. P. (2005). *Perspectives in Business Ethics*. Bos-ton, MA, McGraw-Hill.

Henderson, D. (2001). *Misguided Virtue: False Notions of Corporate Social Responsibility*. London, Institute for Economic Affairs.

Iwai, K. (2006). 'What is a corporation? - the corporate per-sonality controversy and comparative corporate gover-nance', in F. Cafaggi, U. Pagano and A. Nicita, *Legal Orderings*. Abingdon, Routledge.

Jensen, M. (2002). 'Value maximization, stakeholder theory, and the corporate objective function', *Business Ethics Quarterly* 12(2): 235-56.

Johnson, L. (2004). 'Capitalism is a cure, not a curse', *Sun-day Telegraph* 29 September 2004.

Keenoy, T. (1999). 'HRM as hologram: a polemic', *Journal of Management Studies* 36(1): 1-24.

Laughlin, R. (1995). 'Empirical research in accounting: alter-native approaches and a case for "middle range" think-ing', *Accounting Auditing and Accountability Journal* 8 (1): 63-87.

Laughlin, R. (2004). 'Putting the record straight: a critique of methodology choices and the construction of facts: some implications from the sociology of knowledge', *Critical Perspectives on Accounting* 15(3): 261-77.

Legge, K. (1995). *HRM: Rhetorics and Realities*. London, Macmillan.

Legge, K. (1998). 'Is HRM ethical? Can HRM be ethical?', in M. Parker, *Ethics and Organizations*. London, Sage.

Legge, K. (2000a). 'The ethical context of HRM: the ethical organization in the boundaryless world', in D. Winstanley and J. Woodall, *Ethical Issues in Contemporary HRM*. Basingstoke, Palgrave.

Legge, K. (2000b). *Human Resource Management - Rhetor-ics and Realities*. Basingstoke, Macmillan.

Lévi-Strauss, C. (1966). *The Savage Mind*. Oxford, Oxford University Press.

Lévinas, E. (1969/2005). *Totality and Infinity - An Essay on Exteriority*. Pittsburgh, PA, Duquesne University Press.

Lévinas, E. (1981/2004). *Otherwise than Being - or Beyond Essence*. Pittsburgh, PA, Duquesne University Press.

Lévinas, E. (1985). *Ethics and Infinity - Conversations with Philippe Nemo*. Pittsburgh, PA, Duquesne University Press.

Lincoln, Y. S. and N. K. Denzin (2005). 'The eighth and ninth moments - qualitative research in/and the fractured future', in N. K. Denzin and Y. S. Lincoln. *The Sage Hand-book of Qualitative Research*. London, Sage.

Lyotard, J.-F. (1984). *The Postmodern Condition: A Report on Knowledge*. Manchester, Manchester University Press.

MacIntyre, A. (2002a). *After Virtue*. London, Duckworth & Co.

MacIntyre, A. (2002b). *A Short History of Ethics*. London, Routledge Classics.

MacIntyre, A. (2006). 'Moral philosophy and contemporary social practice', in A. MacIntyre, *The Tasks of Philoso-phy: Selected Essays, Volume 1*. Cambridge, Cambridge University Press.

Nietzsche, F. (2003). *The Genealogy of Morals*. Mineola, NY, Dover Thrift Editions.

Norberg, J. (2002). *In Defence of Global Capitalism*. Stock-holm, Timbro.

O'Leary, T. (2002). *Foucault and the Art of Ethics*. London, Continuum.

Parker, M. (2002). *Against Management*. Cambridge, Polity Press.

Parker, M. (2003). 'Ethics, politics and organizing', *Organization* 10(2): 187–203.

Roberts, J. (2001). 'Trust and control in Anglo-American systems of corporate governance: the individualizing and socializing effects of processes of accountability', *Human Relations* 54(12): 1547–72.

Scholte, J. A. (2005). *Globalization: A Critical Introduction*. Basingstoke, Palgrave.

Simpson, R. (2000). 'Presenteeism and the impact of long hours on managers', in D. Winstanley and J. Woodall, *Ethical Issues in Contemporary HRM*. Basingstoke, Palgrave.

Taymans, A. C. (1950). 'Trade and Schumpeter: a similar vision', *Quarterly Journal of Economics* 64(4): 611–22.

Thompson, P. (2005). 'Brands, boundaries and bandwagons: a critical reflection of critical management studies', in C. Grey and H. C. Willmott, *Critical Management Studies*. Oxford, Oxford University Press.

Werhane, P. H. (1985). *Persons, Rights and Corporations*. Englewood Cliffs, NJ, Prentice-Hall.

Williams, B. (1987). *Ethics and the Limits of Philosophy*. London, Routledge.

Winstanley, D. (2000). 'Conditions of worth and the performance management paradox', in D. Winstanley and J. Woodall, *Ethical Issues in Contemporary HRM*. Basingstoke, Palgrave.

Winstanley, D. and J. Woodall (eds)(2000). *Ethical Issues in Contemporary Human Resource Management*. Basingstoke, Palgrave.

Woodall, J. and D. Winstanley (2000). 'Concluding comments: ethical frameworks for action', in D. Winstanley and J. Woodall, *Ethical Issues in Contemporary Human Resource Management*. Basingstoke, Palgrave.

Dynamic organizations: achieving marketplace agility through workforce scalability

Lee Dyer and Jeff Ericksen

Dynamic organizations (DOs) operate in business environments characterized by frequent and discontinuous change. For them, competitiveness is a moving target, a constant pursuit of proactivity and adaptability in the marketplace, preferably undertaken as a matter of course rather than with great travail. Imagine, as Hamel and Valikangas (2003) posit, a ratio in which the numerator is the number and salience of an organization's strategic manoeuvres and the denominator reflects the time, disruption and expense required to affect those manoeuvres. A DO's challenge is to enhance the numerator by constantly attacking the marketplace with a steady stream of customized client solutions, innovative products or services or creative ways of capitalizing on existing offerings (Brown and Eisenhardt 1997; D'Aveni 1994; Ilinitch et al. 1996; Roberts 1999), even as it concurrently drives down the denominator. As Hamel and Valikangas (2003: 54) put it:

> The goal is a strategy that is forever morphing, forever conforming itself to emerging opportunities and incipient trends. The goal is an organization that is constantly making its future rather than defending its past. The goal is a company where revolutionary change happens in lightning-quick, evolutionary steps – with no calamitous surprises, no convulsive reorganizations, no colossal write-offs, and no indiscriminate, across-the-board layoffs. In a truly [dynamic] organization, there is plenty of excitement, but no trauma.

Given these goals, it is not at all surprising that DOs tend to eschew traditional organizational forms and practices as excessively cumbersome and ossified and, alternatively, actively experiment with more nimble and flexible options (Gailbraith et al. 2002). This turn of events has opened up exciting new avenues of investigation for students of business strategy, organizational theory, leadership and the like (Peterson and Mannix 2003). So far, though, the field of strategic human resource management (SHRM) is lagging behind. Generally, the DO literature ignores or deals only superficially with people-related issues, while the SHRM literature has been slow to close the gap (Dyer and Shafer, 1999, 2003; Shafer et al. 2001; Wright and Snell 1998). This chapter represents a step toward filling the void. It delineates a process whereby a

DO might craft a human resource strategy to facilitate the attainment of a sustained competitive advantage. Our main purpose is to draw students of SHRM into the fray by providing a platform for further theoretical and empirical work. An ancillary aim is to provide tentative guidance for human resource strategists and students who are or soon will be wrestling with the realities of a dynamic world.

In a general sense, SHRM is concerned with the contributions that human resource strategies make to organizational effectiveness and the ways in which these contributions are achieved. Most, although clearly not all (e.g., Pfeffer 1998), of its adherents subscribe to a contingency perspective of the field, which basically rejects the notion of 'best practice', believing instead that superior results obtain when a firm's human resource strategy is tailored to fit its business strategy, as well as other important contextual features. The contingency view incorporates two fundamental assumptions: (1) various business strategies and contexts require different sets of workforce attributes and (2) different types of HR system (i.e., combinations of policies, programmes, and practices) are required to engender different sets of workforce attributes (Cappelli and Singh 1992; Schuler and Jackson 1987). The analytical process facing a theorist, researcher, or practitioner in any given situation, then, involves an analysis of context to identify essential workforce attributes and, then, to devise an HR system that will, if properly implemented, develop those attributes. This is the process followed here.

We begin by delineating the means by which a DO competes in its marketplace – an approach we call *marketplace agility* – and the organizational competencies it takes to make it work. Based on this analysis, we then propose a new way to conceptualize the notion of workforce attributes – dubbed *workforce scalability* – and show how it derives directly from the imperatives of marketplace agility and thus has the potential to be a source of sustained competitive advantage in dynamic situations. Following this, we identify nine broad principles that we believe would, when effectively operationalized, engender workforce scalability. Finally, we readily acknowledge the speculative nature of much of this analysis and suggest a number of questions for HR theorists, researchers, practitioners and students to ponder in the years ahead.

Marketplace agility

In turbulent markets competitive advantages are fleeting (D'Aveni 1994). This does not mean, however, that a DO has no hope of succeeding over time. Increasingly firms, as well as scholars, are beginning to explore ways in which a DO can gain a series of temporary competitive advantages that, while they ebb and flow, add up over time to a sustainable competitive advantage (Brown and Eisenhardt 1997; Ilinitch et al. 1996; Rindova and Kotha 2001). This requires marketplace agility; that is, the capacity to be better than actual or would-be competitors at continuously enhancing both dimensions of Hamel and Valikangas's (2003) ratio. We see this at work in consulting and other professional service firms that are particularly adept at the rapid delivery of highly customized client solutions at profitable prices. We see it at work at Google in the form of an endless stream of new business models (see box 15.1).

Marketplace agility is an umbrella business strategy. It describes in broad terms how a DO strives to attain competitive advantages, without delving into the nitty-gritty aspects of its ever-changing markets or business portfolios. Thus, somewhat paradoxically, it provides a stable base for the formation of a supporting human

---

HRM in Action 15.1   Google

Since its founding, it has repeatedly morphed its business model. Google 1.0 was a search engine that crawled the web but generated little revenue; which led to Google 2.0, a company that sold its search capacity to AOL/Netscape, Yahoo! and other major portals; which gave way to Google 3.0, an internet contrarian that rejected banner ads and instead sold simple text ads linked to search results; which spawned Google 4.0, an increasingly global entity that found a way to insert relevant ads into any and all web content, dramatically enlarging the online ad business; which mutated into Google 5.0, an innovation factory that produces a torrent of new web-based services, including Gmail … More than likely, 6.0 is around the corner (Hamel 2006: A16). Google has now announced that it is exploring the possibility of building its own high-powered servers and software.

---

resource strategy. But more is needed, namely the specification of the core meta-competence on which the strategy depends (see Hamel and Prahalad 1994: 223-33). A core meta-competence is a critical business capability that is formed by bundling or integrating a set of more specific contributing competencies (i.e., mini-processes consisting of particular skills and technologies). Logistics, for example is a core meta-competence for Federal Express, while scheduling and package tracking are two essential contributing competencies.

Essentially, a DO is an ever-changing portfolio of ventures. In pursuit of marketplace agility, the requisite core meta-competence, then, is the capacity to effectively and efficiently steer these ventures in and around a renewal cycle consisting of four contributing competencies: exploration, exploitation, adaptation and exit. Exploration involves the generation and testing of new ideas. Exploitation is how some of these ideas are transformed into solutions, products or services to be quickly delivered to the marketplace before competitors catch on and catch up. It is the point at which a DO capitalizes on its temporary competitive advantages to generate revenues. The exploration–exploitation dyad is always a challenge to manage (March 1991; Meilich 1997), but is made even more so in dynamic situations by the barrage of disruptive forces emanating from competitors and other sources. Thus the need for a third contributing competency: adaptation – the process of spotting emerging threats early and mounting immediate responses as necessary (Haeckel 1999; Lewin and Volberda 1999). Even a DO that is superb at adapting, however, knows that nothing is forever, so it must be not only willing, but also able to abandon unpromising ideas and even to cannibalize its own marketplace offerings on a timely basis without hesitancy or remorse (Foster and Kaplan 2001; Horn et al. 2006). This is the fourth contributing competency: exit.

Figure 15.1 shows a fictional DO that at Time 1 consisted of eight ventures spread around the renewal cycle. By time 2, this number had dropped to seven ventures, four survivors from Time 1 – all of which had transitioned to different places on the cycle – and three new ones. Snapshots taken at Times 3, 4, and so on would, of course, reveal very different patterns. Is this firm demonstrating the requisite core meta-competence? The answer is 'yes' if the portfolios of ventures that

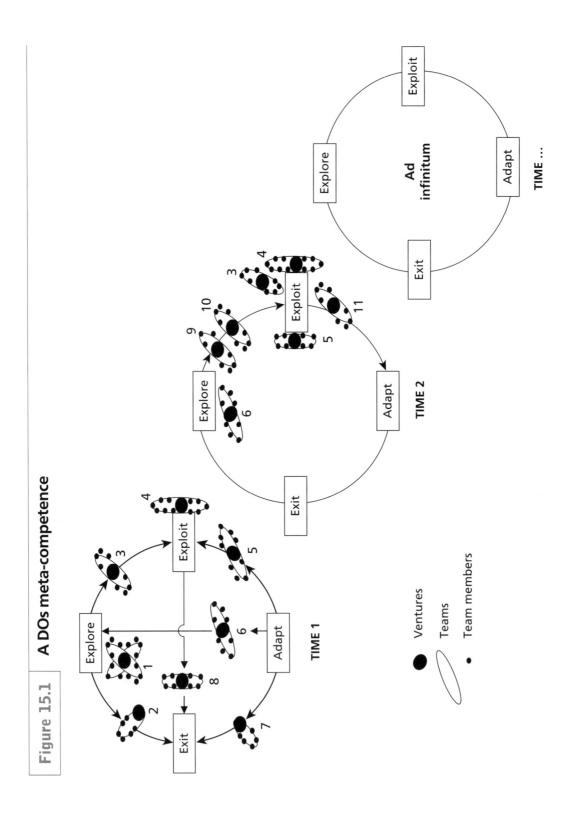

Figure 15.1 A DOs meta-competence

exist at various points in time are generating temporary competitive advantages and if the transitions from one portfolio to another are made smoothly and efficiently. The answer is 'no' if, for example, the firm fails to generate enough new ideas that can be exploited in the marketplace. Or if it does a bad job of exploiting its opportunities and fails to adapt or exit on a timely basis. Or if it gets blind-sided by its competitors too often and cannot sustain ventures long enough for them to pay off. And so on.

Google provides an example of a firm that appears to have mastered this core meta-competence. It constantly generates and experiments with innovative ideas, all of which are subjected to rigorous testing and a few of which (as noted earlier) actually see the light of day. Further, for an innovation machine, the company has thus far been surprisingly adept at exploiting its services (Vogelstein 2004). Its technology now powers over half of the web searches in the USA. and a host more worldwide. Less well known, perhaps, is the fact that the company currently captures about 20% of the $10 billion spent annually on online advertising. It also has a number of smaller ventures – the aforementioned Gmail, along with others such as Google News, Google Maps and Froogle – contending for market share.

Not that it has been all smooth sailing. The company has had to do its fair share of adapting over the years as new competitors emerged, technologies evolved and governments restricted its operations (e.g., in China). Currently, it is attempting to fend off the enervated efforts of two formidable competitors – Yahoo!, which is improving its capacity to tap into its extensive database of customers to provide highly personalized searches and advertising and Microsoft, which is integrating searches into Windows (Elgin 2004; Vogelstein 2004). Whether Google can outadapt and outexploit these much larger rivals over the long haul remains to be seen. If not, it could be forced to exit the search and related businesses. This is a company that is justifiably famous for its 'Darwinian environment in which every idea must compete on its merits, not on the grandeur of its sponsor's title' (Hamel 2006: A16), but whether this hard-nosed approach would prevail should the attacks on its core businesses begin to succeed in a big way is an interesting question indeed. What we can say is that thus far anyway Google has succeeded in generating a series of temporary competitive advantages, parlaying these into a sustained competitive advantage and making money. Its revenues have grown rapidly over the years and its operating margin currently exceeds 60%, higher even than Microsoft's in its prime (Hamel 2006).

As Figure 15.1 illustrates, operationalizing a DO's core meta-competence clearly involves endless reallocations of resources. The keys to success lie in resource alignment and resource fluidity. The former prevails when key resources are focused precisely on the ventures and activities that hold the greatest promise of success in the marketplace, while the latter means that resource transitions are being made quickly, easily and at a reasonable cost. Ongoing resource alignments enhance the numerator of Hamel and Valikangas's (2003) ratio, while resource fluidity facilitates (but does not guarantee) ongoing resource alignments, even as it also drives down the denominator of the ratio. In this formulation, a resource is any value-producing asset that a DO can bring to bear. Common examples include physical resources (e.g., favourable geographical locations and cutting-edge technologies), financial resources (e.g., ready cash and easy access to cheap credit), organizational resources (e.g., a unique design or salubrious culture) and the one of interest to us here: human resources.

Workforce scalability

Workforce scalability is the term we use to capture the capacity of an organization to keep its human resources aligned on an ongoing basis by constantly transitioning from one human resource configuration to another and another, ad infinitum, on a timely basis and in a seamless way (Dyer and Ericksen 2005). At this point, we expand on this definition and, using basic concepts from the resource-based view (Barney 1991), show how the construct helps to deliver a sustained competitive advantage in dynamic situations.

Workforce scalability defined

Workforce scalability indicates the evolution of human resource configurations on four dimensions: headcount, competence mix, deployment pattern and employee contributions. Headcount refers to full-time equivalents (FTEs). It is a function of number of employees (including regular and various types of contractual worker) times the number of hours these people work. Competence mix reflects how employees' knowledge and skills are distributed, while deployment pattern reflects their assignments across organizational and/or physical locations. Employee contributions relate to the organizational value of the tasks they are performing. Refer again to Figure 15.1. As this fictitious firm adds and subtracts ventures and shifts teams and team memberships over time, imagine the amount of change this entails in FTEs, competence requirements, assignments and the ways in which employees add value. Successfully meeting these ever-changing requirements is what workforce scalability is all about.

As the preceding discussion suggests, workforce scalability consists of two components: alignment and fluidity. In the SHRM literature, workforce alignment (or fit) exists when a firm's extant human resource configuration is in synch with the configuration required by its business strategy (e.g. Cappelli and Singh 1992; Schuler and Jackson 1987) or, put differently, when a firm has the right number of the right types of people in the right places at the right times doing the right things right (Dyer and Ericksen 2005; Dyer and Holder 1988). Notice that SHRM's notions of alignment and right correspond to the resource-based view's notion of valuable. Conceptually, they all refer to a workforce's capacity to contribute to the creation and implementation of successful strategic thrusts in the marketplace. But what makes the DO situation special is that for a DO, workforce alignment is a constantly moving target. Given ever-changing circumstances, a workforce configuration that is aligned at one point in time is unlikely to remain so for very long (refer again to Figure 15.1). This, of course, ups the ante on workforce alignment and makes workforce fluidity all the more crucial.

Workforce fluidity refers to the speed and ease with which transitions are made from one aligned human resource configuration to another and then another and another, ad infinitum. As suggested earlier, workforce fluidity helps a DO achieve workforce alignment (Wright and Snell 1998), even as it also serves to reduce the denominator in Hamel and Valikangas's (2003) ratio by minimizing the friction and pain otherwise associated with constant adjustments in headcounts, competence mixes, deployment patterns and employee contributions.

Workforce scalability and sustained competitive advantage

For a would-be DO, we propose, workforce scalability is a resource with the clear potential to help generate a series of temporary competitive advantages and, over time, a sustained competitive advantage. This is because, for any given firm, workforce scalability is likely to meet all four of the necessary and sufficient conditions postulated by the resource-based view of the firm (Barney 2001). The baseline requirement is that a resource be valuable, which by definition (and thus tautologically – see the Barney (1991) and Priem and Butler (2001) debate), workforce scalability is. But to generate even temporary competitive advantages a valuable resource also has to be rare. It would seem that workforce scalability is, although the available evidence is piecemeal and sparse. In a study of 196 small businesses, Ericksen (2006) found that, in general, workforce alignment was relatively rare, but that it was particularly so among firms operating in comparatively dynamic environments. Further, in a recent survey among 300 large US and European companies (alas, undifferentiated with respect to dynamism), respondents rated the fluidity of their firms on a scale of 1 (very flexible) to 5 (very rigid). The mean response was 3.38 and only 15% rated their firms 1 or 2 (Beatty 2005).

Even if workforce scalability is a valuable and rare resource, this is insufficient for it to produce a sustained competitive advantage. For this, it also must be inimitable and non-substitutable. Inimitability stems from a confluence of causal ambiguity and social complexity (Reed and DeFillippi 1990). The former makes it difficult for competitors to ascertain just how a DO achieved workplace scalability, while the latter, because of path dependence, makes it unlikely that an approach that works in one firm will work the same way in others. Logic, as well as the aforementioned data pertaining to rarity, suggests that workplace scalability is indeed difficult for competitors to copy, but we know of no evidence directly relating to this point. Further, some firms, such as IBM, are attempting to use technology to obviate the need for some elements of workforce scalability, especially geographic mobility, by bringing work to people rather than doing things the other way around (e.g. Hamm 2005). The extent to which this might negate the capacity of workplace scalability to generate sustained competitive advantage, however, remains to be determined.

There is a small amount of evidence to suggest that the components of workforce scalability are associated with firm performance, especially in dynamic situations. In the small business study noted earlier, Ericksen (2006) focused part of his analysis on firms that had attained aligned workforces and found that among those operating in relatively stable external environments the average annual increase in revenues was 18%, slightly above the sample average. Among those operating in volatile circumstances (where as noted above workforce alignment was rarer), the comparable sale growth figure was 25%. Other studies have documented how ineffectively many firms handle various aspects of workforce fluidity – e.g. the accession of new recruits (Penrose 1959), the internal allocation of employees (Henderson and Clark 1990; Tripsas 1997), and the release of non-performing and redundant employees (Cascio 2002) – and the resulting deleterious effects on organizational adaptation and change. A recent case study, summarized in Table 15.1, illustrates how Yahoo's! ability to achieve elements of workforce scalability contributed to its attainment of competitive advantage over Excite in the early years of the fast paced world of web-based search (Rindova and Kotha 2001).

Table 15.1	**Workforce scalability as a source of sustained competitive advantage**

Between 1994 and 1999, Yahoo! and Excite struggled for competitive advantage in the nascent web search business as it transforms from (1) pure search to (2) becoming an internet destination to (3) becoming an internet portal.

	Search engine: 1994–1996	*Internet destination site: 1996–1997*	*Internet portal: 1998–early 1999*
Competitive Advantage	Search capability	Search capability; Content creation; Brand	Search capability; Interactive services; Brand
Workforce alignment	Yahoo! builds staff of 80 'surfers' – to 50% of total staff Excite relies on technology and small editorial staff	Yahoo! adds 'surfers,' but percentage drops to 21% of total staff. 'Surfers' shift focus to content and partnering through 'producer teams'. Marketing and sales people constitute 50% of staff Excite lays off half its editorial staff – relies on partners for content. Adds business development personnel to manage partnerships	Yahoo! completes series of acquisitions to gain logistics capabilities Excite merges with @Home
Workforce Fluidity	Yahoo! puts effort into acquiring and developing a skilled pool of talent Excite buys its talent, almost as an afterthought	Yahoo!'s talented 'surfers' able to switch focus and activities. Company has capability to acquire and integrate marketing and sales staff Excite manages shift in focus, but only by hiring and firing	Yahoo! develops a successful process for integrating talent brought in through acquisitions Excite's best people mostly choose not to join @Home
Bottom Line	'[Excite was] very much trying to duplicate Yahoo! except that Yahoo! actually had a staff' (former employee)		

What remains to be done, however, is research that focuses on the full scope of workforce scalability. There is a need for studies that include both workforce alignment and workforce fluidity (all four dimensions) and examine not only the relationships between them, but also the issues of value, rarity, inimitability and non-substitutability directly. Then there is the 'so what?' issue. Do DOs that manage to attain relatively high levels of workforce scalability also realize temporary and/or sustained competitive advantages in the marketplace and achieve superior financial results?

Our analysis and the limited data available suggest that for any given DO, attaining a relatively high level of workforce scalability is likely to be a work in progress for some time to come. Currently, no one seems to know for sure how to do it and anyway, given the nature of the world today, the bar is likely to keep on rising. At this point, we use what is known or can reasonably be surmised to make some suggestions about how to get started.

Pursuing workforce scalability

An all-out assault on workforce scalability almost certainly requires the formation of a facilitative organizational context consisting of a highly adaptable organizational infrastructure and a stewardship approach to leadership, as well as a supportive HR system (Dyer and Shafer 2003). Given our focus (and space limitations), we bypass infrastructure and leadership issues to home in on the development of a supportive HR system. Specifically, we identify a set of key principles that can be used to guide the choice and design of various HR activities (staffing, training and development, work design, compensation, etc.) Focusing on a few key principles rather than a larger set of HR activities not only offers parsimony, but also allows for equifinality by leaving the door open for each DO to search for the specific package of activities that works best in its particular situation (Becker and Gerhart 1996).

We consider a principle 'key' if it meets three criteria. First, it has to be practical, meaning that managers and/or workforces have to be able to operationalize it. Second, there has to be a good reason to believe that, if successfully operationalized, it will significantly enhance workforce scalability (i.e., workforce alignment, workforce fluidity or both). Third, each principle should support complementarity; that is, its operationalization should increase the likelihood that positive payoffs will obtain from operationalizing the remaining principles in the set (Milgrom and Roberts 1995) – or in SHRM terms the principles should show the potential for horizontal fit or synergy (Delery and Shaw 2001; Wright and McMahan 1992).

Figure 15.2 maps the course to be followed. Attention is focused initially on workforce alignment, then on workforce fluidity and, ultimately, on tying the pieces together.

Pursuing workforce alignment

A DO's goal here, it will be recalled, is always to have the right numbers of the right types of people in the right places at the right times doing the right things right. The challenge, in the face of ever-changing business strategies and manoeuvres, is to avoid situations in which the organization has too few or too many employees or has other than minor competence mismatches, person–task misallocations and misdirected behaviours.

Guiding principles

In general, as Figure 15.2 shows, a DO can pursue this elusive goal in two ways – from the top down or from the bottom up.

From the top down: plan. The integration of HR planning with business planning is the classical approach to workforce alignment that has been talked about, albeit not necessarily practised, for many years (Bechet 2002; Dyer 1986). Unfortunately, it has its limitations for a DO because the unpredictability of the business environment makes it likely that most business plans will turn out to fall well short of prescient. The exercise can still be helpful as a learning experience and communication device and specific, short-range plans may well prove to be on the mark, but overall it is essential that a DO learn to treat formal business plans and their HR offshoots as at best suggestive, subject to change at a moments notice. In brief, for a DO the top-down approach, while perhaps helpful, is clearly insufficient to assure ongoing work-force alignment.

From the bottom up: instil a shared mindset. The complementary approach is to attack the issue from the bottom up. The key principle: instil a shared mindset. That is, do everything possible to assure that all employees are fully prepared to act and react as circumstances change – to quickly line up behind new strategic manoeuvres emanating from the top down or, even better, to sense environmental shifts early and initiate salient strategic moves on their own (Mintzberg and Waters 1985). This requires a shared mindset among employees (Ulrich and Lake 1990). For a DO, the challenge is to attain tacit coherence around the organization's purpose and

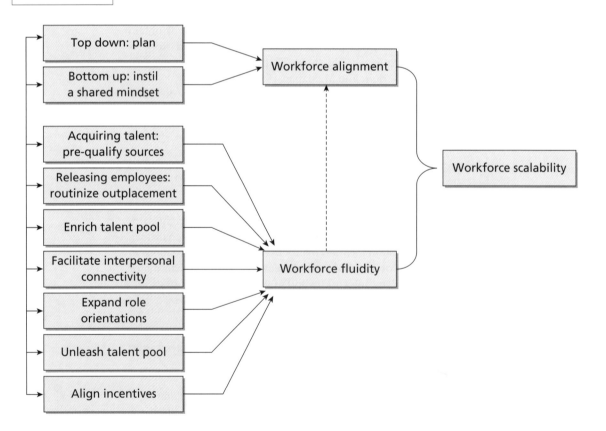

Figure 15.2 | **Pursuing workforce scalability: guiding principles**

processes in a way that actively encourages and facilitates ongoing workforce align-ment. The two key sub-principles are:

- create a common cause
- embed contextual clarity.

The creation of a common cause requires the articulation of an organizational vision or mission that is both aspirational and inspirational – as Google has done with its well-known mantra 'To organize the world's knowledge' – and then clearly com-municating it over and over in many different ways. The idea is to keep employees focused and fired up by making it perfectly clear what the firm exists to do and why this is a good thing for it, them and society. But employees also need to know where they fit in, which is why it is also essential to embed contextual clarity. This process begins with the articulation of the firm's business model(s) in a way that paints a com-plete picture of its environment, how it operates, what it takes for it to succeed and the crucial role that employees play in the grand scheme of things. It continues with efforts to assure that the business model is clearly understood and consensually inter-nalized by all employees (potential techniques include surround communication, open-book management and commitment management – see Dyer and Shafer 2003; Galbraith et al. 2002).

Driven by a common cause and informed with contextual clarity, a DO's employ-ees are well positioned to appreciate and understand the reasons behind sudden changes in business plans and to adapt accordingly. Equally important, they also have the wherewithal required to sniff out significant environmental changes on their own, to use this information to make timely and appropriate adjustments in business plans or to instigate new ones and to do whatever they need to do to assure they are realigned with the new business situation.

Pursuing workforce fluidity

The goal of workforce fluidity is to assure that all employee moves and behavioural adjustments, whether they involve a single individual or a group of employees, occur rapidly, seamlessly and efficiently. A step in the right direction, as Figure 15.2 shows, is to do a good job of operationalizing the foregoing principles. Flexible planning and a shared mindset grease the skids of workforce transitions. But there is more to it that this. Additional principles pertain to the facilitation of external staffing (i.e., the addi-tion and removal of people) and internal transitions.

Evidence suggests that firms often stumble when trying to use external staffing and internal transitions simultaneously (Anderson 2001; Brockner 1992; Charness and Levine 2002; Penrose 1959). In the small business study cited earlier this was indeed the case for firms operating in comparatively stable environments, but not for those operating in comparatively dynamic environments (Ericksen 2006). Among the latter, holding the effects of workforce alignment constant at high levels, firms that used both approaches concurrently increased their revenues by 34% annually, whereas those that shied away from this two-pronged approach had average annual revenue growth of about 20%. While hardly definitive, these data nonetheless suggest that for a DO the capacity to simultaneously employ external staffing and internal transitions provides essential complementarity or synergy (Dyer and Ericksen 2005). This is the premise on which the following analysis proceeds.

External staffing: guiding principles

External staffing is usually thought of as providing headcount flexibility (Cappelli and Neumark 2004). But it is also used to make adjustments in competence mixes, deployment patterns and even contributions (e.g., by systematically replacing low performers with high performers). In DOs, where constant adaptation is a way of life, it is essential that these transitions not only enhance workforce alignment, but also occur quickly and smoothly. To these ends, we suggest the following principles.

Acquiring talent: pre-qualify sources and individuals.
Organizations acquire talent in many different ways. First thoughts usually turn to the recruitment of regular employees. An increasingly popular alternative, however, is the use of contract employees of various types and a few firms even partner with other organizations to gain the temporary use of employees who have critical competences or are strategically located. Clearly, a great many considerations go into determining which source is best – that is, most likely to enhance workforce alignment – and when (Matusik and Hill 1998). At issue here, however, is fluidity, which means the speed and ease with which various sources can be tapped. This requires some up-front work. Consider, for example, the considerable effort that many firms put into maintaining effective relations with selected universities in attempts to streamline and improve the process of recruiting new college grads (Heneman and Judge 2005: 219–21). There is every reason to believe that a DO should apply the same principle when it comes to other sources of talent – especially since these sources usually have to be tapped more quickly and less regularly. The process is well known: pre-qualify those sources with the greatest potential for quickly producing highly qualified candidates and then do what it takes to establish long-term and close working relationships with them, partly to achieve priority in their queues and partly to assure that they know enough about the firm to do an effective job of pre-qualifying candidates before they are referred. For a DO, the process should extend beyond typical recruitment sources. Stories abound, for instance, of the ways in which the social networks formed in Silicon Valley are used to pre-identify and pre-qualify individuals with certain competences and the ease with which these people move around from company to company as their needs for talent ebb and flow (see, e.g., Finegold 1999).

Releasing employees: routinize outplacement.
The departure of employees is a tougher nut to crack (except, of course, in the case of temporary employees). There are two issues here. One involves the termination of employees whose competences have become obsolete or who otherwise are no longer doing the required job. The other involves layoffs of employees as circumstances change and they are no longer needed. Both require the routinization of the outplacement process, which involves a tough balancing act. A common tendency among employers is to delay termination and layoff decisions too long. To avoid this it is necessary to monitor employee performance and staffing patterns on an ongoing basis and to respond to red flags immediately. It is also necessary to establish a strong norm that says, on the one hand, the organization will take every reasonable step to avoid layoffs, but, on the other hand, there are no guarantees. None of this is likely to work though unless the firm

has a well-oiled outplacement process, probably in partnership with an external firm, that provides thorough counselling, extensive job search assistance and a generous severance package and does so in a way that employees perceive as fair and just. Studies suggest that the treatment received by laid off and terminated employees has a significant impact on survivors' willingness to adapt to future organizational changes and on their subsequent job performance (e.g., Brockner et al. 1994; Naumann et al. 1995).

Internal transitions: guiding principles

Theory and research suggest that internal transitions – whether self- or organizationally initiated – are more likely to occur when employees individually and collectively have the capability (C) required to make the moves and adjustments, as well as the unfettered opportunity (O) and desire or motivation (M) to do so. In a DO, we propose, C is enhanced by operationalizing two principles – enrich the talent pool and facilitate interpersonal connectivity – O is increased by operationalizing two principles – expand role orientations and unleash the talent pool – and M is facilitated by operationalizing a single principle – align incentives (in addition to the motivation provided by the firm's mission statement and the intrinsically motivating aspects of expanded opportunities).

Enrich the talent pool. A DO needs employees who possess broad competence profiles and behavioural repertoires (Wright and Snell 1998). The process of enriching the talent pool begins with the selection of employees for both diversity and fit. Diversity here refers not only to race and gender, but also to the backgrounds, experiences, knowledge and skills that new recruits bring to the firm. The search is for employees who, individually and collectively, bring a variety of perspectives, as well as foundational aptitudes on which they can build over time (Wright and Snell 1998). At the same time, somewhat paradoxically, a DO must screen for cultural fit to find employees whose personality traits and attitudes indicate a preference for change over stability and proactivity over passivity (Unsworth and Parker 2003). Consider Google's hiring process which has been described as 'grueling . . . akin to a Mensa test [that] values nonconformity nearly as highly as genius [and where] preference is given to candidates who have weird avocations and out-of-the-ordinary experiences' (Hamel 2006: A16). 'Googlers', the company's website (www.Google.com) says, 'range from former neurosurgeons, CEOs, and U.S. puzzle champions to alligator wrestlers and former marines . . . [who] . . . make for interesting cube mates.'

Once the right types of employee are on board, enriching the talent pool becomes a matter of fostering serial incompetence. 'In the face of change', Godin (2000) reminds us, 'the competent are helpless'. Competent employees are those who are an inch wide and a mile deep. They excel at applying sharply honed techniques over and over, but resist change because it threatens to destroy their identity. They are deadly in a DO. Serial incompetents, by the same token, are employees who could become competent in the usual sense, but instead regularly choose to experience temporary periods of incompetence, treating them as essential investments in staying one step ahead in an ever-changing world. A DO needs and needs to nurture serial incompetents. This involves making heavy investments in cutting-edge training and development, as well as providing unwavering support for employees who move from opportunity to opportunity in pursuit of smart risks that sometimes pay off in a big way, but always result in highly valuable future-oriented learning even when they fail (McGregor 2006; Pascale et al. 2000: 250-57). Google's website again: 'There are hundred of challenges yet to solve . . . creative ideas matter here and are worth exploring . . . [Googlers] . . . have the opportunity to develop innovative new products that millions of people will find useful.'

Facilitate interpersonal connectivity. Rapid redeployment and spontaneous collaboration with ever-evolving groups of colleagues require plenty of social grease. This comes from facilitating interpersonal connectivity to build social capital – the stock of meaningful relationships that foster and are fostered by high levels of trust and cooperation among employees (Nahapiet and Ghoshal 1998) – which makes it easy for them to openly share information about where and when talent is needed and who does and does not possess the requisite competences and work ethic, as well as to dispense with preliminaries and get right to work when new teams are formed. At Google, for example, there are hundreds of project teams, all with their own websites to provide up-to-date information on the status and prospects of various ventures (Hamel 2006).

Of course, there is nothing easy about facilitating interpersonal connectivity. Broadly, it involves (in addition to instilling a common mindset) breaking down barriers that inhibit communication in typical organizations, such as beliefs that knowledge is power (and thus should be hoarded) and the formation of subcultures and cliques, while building up infrastructures that facilitate communication, such as smaller units (see Gladwell 2000: Chapter 5), communities of practice, open-plan offices (Becker 2000; Conlin 2006) and state-of-the-art organizational intranets (Hyatt 2006). It also involves enhancing opportunities for small, rotating groups of employees to get together on a social basis (e.g., at off-site training programmes or even Friday afternoon 'beer busts' of the type popularized in Silicon Valley). Or as Google puts is, 'Work and play are not mutually exclusive. It is possible to code and pass the puck at the same time.'

Expand role orientations. Opportunity (O) in a DO stems in part from expanding role orientations so that few, if any assignments or tasks seem out of bounds. One way to do this is through discretionary-based work design (Dyer and Shafer 2003). In most organizations, jobs are defined in terms of a litany of tasks and responsibilities and the ubiquitous add-on 'other duties as assigned'. Discretionary-based work design is quite different. Instead of 'other duties as assigned', it emphasizes 'other duties as assumed'. That is, it specifies only a minimal core of required tasks and responsibilities and then opens up a maximally expansive zone of discretion within which employees are expected to take initiative in determining what needs to be done and then finding ways to get it done. Employees are thus encouraged to think broadly about the organization and their work and to be constantly on the lookout for new challenges, as well as new ways of accomplishing familiar tasks. There is synergy here; expanded role orientations help to enrich the talent pool even as an enriched talent pool (imbued with a shared mindset) is ideally suited to take full advantage of expanded role orientations.

Unleash the talent pool. Expanded role orientations focus primarily on making adjustments without employees changing roles. Unleashing the talent pool expands the realm of opportunity (O) further. It involves crushing the constraints that limit the free flow of talent from role to role or activity to activity. At Google, for example, all 1900 employees are expected to 'boldly go where no one has gone before' and all are strongly encouraged to spend up to 20% of their time working on off-budget, out-of-scope projects (Hamel 2006; Stross 2004). Unleashing the talent pool requires constant attention because most organizations are imbued with myriad factors that, while perhaps implemented for understandable reasons, have the unintended effect of creating turf battles over resources, including human resources. Common culprits include: centralized decision making, narrowly focused performance goals, rewards that are based on unit rather than organizational performance and budgets with no flexibility (see Ashkenas et al. 1995: Chapters 4 and 5). These, of course, have to go. In addition, though, to really attain a free flow of talent it is necessary to establish open auctions in which managers openly bid for the employees they need, while employees freely decide when and where to go (Hamel 2000). This has the effect of making talent an organizational rather than territorial resource.

Align incentives. Given plenty of capability (C) and opportunity (O), employees still need to be motivated (M) to make essential moves quickly and easily. This brings us to the issue of incentives. Baseline requirements for a DO, it would seem, are, first, to assure that the work is a rich and rewarding experience in and of itself and, second, to offer all employees (not just executives) well above prevailing market pay and benefits in hope of encouraging the attraction and retention of the very best talent. On its website, for example, Google touts its 'fun and inspiring workspace' and the opportunity to 'tackle the toughest problems in computer science and develop innovative products that make a positive difference in tens of millions of lives every day'. The company pays well (albeit without emphasizing it) and it offers a dazzling array of benefits: 'choice of medical programs, company-matched 401(k), maternity and paternity leave, an on-site doctor and dentist, massage and yoga, on-site day care, shoreline running trails, and even snacks and free lunches'. Further, a DO needs to base a significant part of pay on organization-wide results (e.g., stock options, which Google offers, or profit sharing) in an effort to keep employees focused on the big picture. Beyond these steps, it is wise to eschew rewards that discourage employee movements and adjustments, while emphasizing monetary and non-monetary returns that encourage these behaviours. In part, this means avoiding incentives that focus on narrow criteria such as team or unit performance, since these tend to encourage managers to hoard talent and employees to avoid taking even smart risks. It also means creating broad pay ranges that align with the notion of discretion-based work design and provide room for employees to enhance their pay without constantly fretting about getting promoted. Further, it means adopting some variation of skill-based pay to encourage the pursuit of serial incompetence. And finally, it means taking the radical step of utilizing peer evaluations as input into decisions about individual performance-based bonuses or non-cash awards and, if offered, individual merit pay. Generally, supervisors make such decisions without much, if any, peer input. This creates difficulty in DOs, however, because extensive employee movement limits supervisors' opportunities to observe the performance of their direct reports. Peers, contrariwise, know who among them move quickly and easily to new and appropriate assignments, readily assume multiple roles, rapidly ramp up to speed in new situations and make significant contributions to organizational results.

Where to from here?

A DO operates in a world where shift happens, so sustained competitive advantage is hard to come by. Success depends on the ability to attain and sustain marketplace agility by simultaneously attacking both the numerator and denominator of Hamel and Valikangas's (2003) ratio on an ongoing basis. This means continually besting competitors with a series of superior solutions (as some professional service firms do) or products, services, or business models (as Google has done), and doing so with an absolute minimum of organizational disruption and expense. To pull this off, we suggest, requires a DO to develop the capacity to juggle a constantly evolving portfolio of ventures each of which may traverse as many as four (not necessarily successive) contributing competency areas: exploration, exploitation, adaptation and exit. This, in turn, requires an unrelenting focus on both the alignment and fluidity of the firm's critical resources, including its human resources.

To this end, we suggest that a DO strive to attain workforce scalability – that is, workforce alignment coupled with workforce fluidity with respect to headcount, collective competences, deployment patterns and contributions. Workforce alignment is all about having the right number of the right types of people in the right places at the right times doing the right things right. Workforce fluidity prevails when every employee move and behavioural adjustment, whether involving a single individual or a group of employees, occurs rapidly, seamlessly and efficiently. To attain these goals we propose a set of nine principles that, when properly operationalized, should do the job. Pursuit of workforce alignment requires the implementation of formal HR planning, done with a degree of humility sufficient to encourage and facilitate ongoing adjustments as necessary by a workforce that shares a common mindset consisting of devotion to the firm's vision and a clear understanding of how the organization operates and what each member of the workforce can do to assure that it succeeds. Pursuit of workforce fluidity involves paying close attention to both external staffing and internal transitions. To enhance the fluidity of external staffing it is necessary on the input side to pre-qualify sources of applicants and even the applicants themselves and on the output side to routinize outplacement processes. The fluidity of internal transitions is promoted by simultaneously developing the capability (C), opportunity (O) and motivation (M) of employees to move and adapt as circumstances require. C is enhanced by enriching the talent pool and facilitating interpersonal connectivity, O by expanding role orientations and unleashing the talent pool, and M by aligning incentives.

Obviously, our analysis and prescriptions rest on a rather sparse empirical base, supplemented with a fairly large dose of interpretation. Our hope, though, is that the exercise is sufficient to pique the interest of SHRM theorists, researchers, practitioners and students to the point of constructive collaborations aimed at further clarifying both the process and content of HR strategy–making in DOs. The future research agenda should include, but not be limited to the following issues:

- Are dynamic organizations different enough from other organizations to justify attempts to design HR strategies just for them? Or, at the other end of the scale, is each such organization so unique that it is impossible to generalize across them when it comes to designing an HR strategy? In other words, is the concept of marketplace agility useful as a basis for forging HR strategy?

- Does the conception of DOs as bundles of ventures square with reality? If so, does this mean that the core meta-competence for a DO is really the capacity to successfully juggle these ventures as they move through the renewal cycle in varying sequences and at their own pace? If so, does it follow from this that a major operational imperative for a DO is to drill down on the issues of resource alignment and resource fluidity?

- Typically, SHRM theory and research depicts the 'black box' between business strategy and HR strategy in terms of employees' skills and on-the-job behaviours or performance. We have suggested that it makes more sense to use the concept of workforce scalability, especially when studying dynamic organizations – does this seem to make conceptual sense?

- SHRM theorists and researchers largely agree that the alignment of human resources with a firm's business strategy is a route to attaining sustained competitive advantage. But they are at odds as to whether the key lies in the alignment of the variables in the 'black box' – here workforce scalability – or of the components of the HR system. We align with the former view but future research will need to assess whether this is right.

- We propose nine principles to drive the formation of an HR system to keep a workforce constantly aligned and increasingly fluid. Are they all necessary? Collectively, are they sufficient to do the job? What different approaches, if any, could a dynamic organization try – and SHRM researchers therefore study?

This kind of research and practice agenda is likely to become more important in the future. The issues surrounding scalability go to the heart of strategic HR – the interface with business strategy, principles of consistency and fairness, and yet rapid response and adaptability to changing conditions.

References

Anderson, E. G. (2001). 'The nonstationary staff-planning problem with business cycle and learning effects', *Management Science* 47: 817–32.

Ashkenas, R., D. Ulrich, T. Jick and S. Kerr (1995). *The Boundaryless Organization*. San Francisco, Jossey-Bass.

Barney, J. (1991). 'Firm resources and sustained competitive advantage', *Journal of Management* 17: 99–120.

Barney, J. (2001). 'Is the resource based "view" a useful perspective for strategic management research? Yes', *Academy of Management Review* 26: 41–57.

Beatty, R. (2005). *Workforce Agility: The New Frontier for Competitive Advantage*. New York, PricewaterhouseCoopers LLP (White Paper).

Bechet, T. (2002). *Strategic Staffing*. New York, AMACOM.

Becker, F. (2000). 'Integrated portfolio strategies for dynamic organizations', *Facilities* 18: 411–20.

Becker, B. and B. Gerhart (1996). 'The impact of human resource management on organizational performance: progress and prospects', *Academy of Management Journal* 39: 779–801.

Brockner, J. (1992). 'Managing the effects of layoffs on survivors', *California Management Review* 24: 9–28.

Brockner, J., M. Konovsky, R. Cooper-Schneider, R. Folger, C. Martin and R. Bies (1994). 'Interactive effects of procedural justice and outcome negativity on victims and survivors of job loss', *Academy of Management Journal* 37: 397–409.

Brown, S. and K. Eisenhardt (1997). 'The art of continuous change: linking complexity theory and time-paced evolution in relentlessly shifting organizations', *Administrative Science Quarterly* 42: 1–35.

Cappelli, P. and D. Neumark (2004). 'External job churning and internal flexibility: evidence on the functional flexibility and core-periphery hypothesis', *Industrial Relations* 43: 148–82.

Cappelli, P. and H. Singh (1992). 'Integrating strategic human resources and strategic management', in D. Lewin, O. Mitchell and P. Sherer (eds) *Research Frontiers in Industrial Relations and Human Resources*. Madison, WI, Industrial Relations Research Association.

Cascio, W. (2002). 'Strategies for responsible restructuring', *Academy of Management Executive* 16: 80–92.

Charness, G. and D. Levine (2002). 'Changes in the employment contract: evidence from a quasi-experiment',

Journal of Economic Behavior and Organization 47: 391–406.

Conlin, M. (2006). 'Square feet. Oh, how square!', *Business Week* 3 July: 100–101.

D'Aveni, R. (1994). *Hypercompetition: Managing the Dynamics of Strategic Maneuvering*. New York, Free Press.

Delery, J. and J. Shaw (2001). 'The strategic management of people in work organizations: review, synthesis, and extension', in G. Ferris (ed.) *Research in Personnel and Human Resources Management,* Vol. 20. Oxford, Elsevier.

Dyer, L. (ed.) (1986). *Human Resource Planning: Tested Practices of Five Major U.S. and Canadian Companies*. New York, Random House and Human Resource Planning Society.

Dyer, L. and J. Ericksen (2005). 'In pursuit of marketplace agility: applying precepts of self-organizing systems to optimize human resource scalability', *Human Resource Managemen* 44: 183–8.

Dyer, L. and G. Holder (1988). 'Toward a strategic perspective of human resource management', in L. Dyer and G. Holder (eds) *Human Resource Management: Evolving Roles and Responsibilities*. Washington, DC, Bureau of National Affairs.

Dyer, L. and R. Shafer (1999). 'From human resource strategy to organizational effectiveness: lessons from research on agile organizations', in P. Wright, L. Dyer, J. Boudreau and G. Milkovich (eds) *Research in Personnel and Human Resources Management,* Supplement 4 (*Strategic Human Resource Management in the 21st Century*). Stamford, CT: JAI Press.

Dyer, L. and R. Shafer (2003). 'Dynamic organizations: achieving marketplace and organizational agility with people', in R. Peterson and E. Mannix (eds) *Leading and Managing People in the Dynamic Organization*. Mahwah, NJ, Lawrence Erlbaum.

Elgin, B. (2004). 'Why the world's hottest tech company struggles to keep its edge', *Business Week* 3 May: 82–90.

Ericksen, J. (2006). 'Workforce alignment, human resource scalability, and small business sales growth', unpublished PhD dissertation, Ithaca, Cornell University.

Finegold, D. (1999). 'Creating self-sustaining, high-skill eco-systems', *Oxford Review of Economic Policy* 4: 21–43.

Foster, R. and S. Kaplan (2001). *Creative Destruction: Why Companies that are Built to Last Underperform the Market and How to Transform Them*. New York, Currency.

Galbraith, J., D. Downey and A. Kates (2002). *Designing Dynamic Organizations*. New York, AMACOM.

Gladwell, M. (2000). *The Tipping Point*. Boston, MA, Little, Brown and Co.

Godin, S. (2000). 'In the face of change, the competent are helpless', *Fast Company* January–February: 230–34.

Haeckel, S. (1999). *Adaptive Enterprise: Creating and Leading Sense-and-Respond Organizations*. Boston, MA, Harvard Business School Press.

Hamel, G. (2000). *Leading the Revolution*. Boston, MA, Harvard Business School Press.

Hamel, G. (2006). 'Management à la Google', *Wall Street Journal* 26 August: A16.

Hamel, G. and C. K. Prahalad (1994). *Competing for the Future*. Boston, MA, Harvard Business School Press.

Hamel, G. and L. Valikangas (2003). 'The quest for resilience', *Harvard Business Review* September: 52–63.

Hamm, S. (2005). 'Beyond blue', *Business Week* 18 April: 68–76.

Henderson, R. and K. Clark (1990). 'Architectural innovation: the reconfiguration of existing product technologies and the failure of established firms', *Administrative Science Quarterly* 35: 9–31.

Heneman, H. and T. Judge (2005). *Staffing Organizations*. New York, McGraw-Hill.

Horn, J. T., D. P. Lovallo and S. P. Viguerie (2006). 'Learning to let go: making better exit decisions', *The McKinsey Quarterly* 2: 2–8.

Hyatt, J. (2006). 'The soul of a new team', *Fortune* 12 June: 134–41.

Ilinitch, A., R. D'Averi and A. Lewin (1996). 'New organizational forms and strategies for managing in hypercompetitive environments', *Organization Science* 7: 211–21.

Lewin, A. and H. Volberda (1999). 'Prolegomena on co-evolution: A framework for research on strategy and new organizational forms', *Organization Science* 10: 519–34.

March, J. (1991). 'Exploration and exploitation in organizational learning', *Organization Science* 2: 71–86.

Matusik, S. and C. Hill (1998). 'The utilization of contingent work, knowledge creation, and competitive advantage', *Academy of Management Review* 23: 680–97.

McGregor, J. (2006). 'How failure breeds success', *Business Week* 10 July: 42–52.

Meilich, O. (1997). 'The flexibility–efficiency debate: review and theoretical framework', paper presented at the 1997 Academy of Management Meeting, Boston, MA.

Milgrom, P. and J. Roberts (1995). 'Complementarities and fit: strategy, structure, and organizational change in manufacturing', *Journal of Accounting and Economics* 19: 179–208.

Mintzberg, H. and J. Waters (1985). 'Of strategies, deliberate and emergent', *Strategic Management Journal* 6: 257–72.

Nahapiet, J. and S. Ghoshal (1998). 'Social capital, intellectual capital, and the organizational advantage', *Academy of Management Review* 23: 243–66.

Naumann, S., R. Bies and C. Martin (1995). 'The roles of organizational support and justice during layoffs', *Academy of Management Journal* 38: 89–109.

Pascale, R., M. Millemann and L. Gioja (2000). *Surfing the Edge of Chaos*. New York, Crown Business.

Penrose, E. (1959). *The Growth Theory of the Firm*. Oxford, Oxford University Press.

Peterson, R. and E. Mannix (eds) (2003). *Leading and Managing People in the Dynamic Organization*. Mahwah, NJ, Lawrence Erlbaum.

Pfeffer, J. (1998). *The Human Equation: Building Profits by Putting People First*. Boston, MA, Harvard Business School Press.

Priem, R. and J. Butler (2001). 'Is the resource-based "view" a useful perspective for strategic management research?', *Academy of Management Review* 26: 22–40.

Reed, R. and R. DeFillippi (1990). 'Causal ambiguity, barriers to imitation, and sustainable competitive advantage', *Academy of Management Review* 15: 88–102.

Rindova, V. and S. Kotha (2001). 'Continuous "morphing": competing through dynamic capabilities, form, and function', *Academy of Management Journal* 44: 1263–81.

Roberts, P. (1999). 'Product innovation, product market competition, and persistent profitability in the U.S. pharmaceutical industry', *Strategic Management Journal* 20: 655–86.

Schuler, R. and S. Jackson (1987). 'Linking competitive strategies and human resource management practices', *Academy of Management Executive* 1: 207–19.

Shafer, R., L. Dyer, J. Kilty, J. Amos and J. Ericksen (2001). 'Crafting a human resource strategy to foster organizational agility', *Human Resource Management* 40: 197–211.

Stross, R. (2004). 'What is Google's secret weapon? An army of Ph.D.'s', *New York Times* (Business Section) 6 June: 3.

Tripsas, M. (1997). 'Unraveling the process of creative destruction: complementary assets and incumbent survival in the typesetter industry', *Strategic Management Journal* 18: 119–43.

Ulrich, D. and D. Lake (1990). *Organizational Capability: Competing from the Inside Out.* New York, Wiley.

Unsworth, K. and S. Parker (2003). 'Proactivity and innovation: promoting a new workforce for the new workplace', in D. Holman, T. Wall, C. Clegg, P. Sparrow and A. Howard (eds) *The New Workplace: A Guide to the Human Impact of Modern Working Practices.* Chichester, Wiley.

Vogelstein, F. (2004). 'Google @ $165: Are these guys for real?', *Fortune* 13 December: 98–110.

Wright, P. and G. McMahan (1992). 'Theoretical perspectives for strategic human resource management', *Journal of Management* 18: 295–320.

Wright, P. and S. Snell (1998). 'Toward a unifying framework for exploring fit and flexibility in strategic human resource management', *Academy of Management Review* 23: 756–72.

Index

THOMSON™

Introducing
Organizational Behaviour & Management

David Knights, *Keele University*
Hugh Willmott, *Cardiff Business School*

ISBN-10: 1844800350 • ISBN-13: 9781844800353 • Paperback
560pp • 2006

Introducing Organizational Behaviour & Management builds upon students' day-to-day experiences of work and organizations as they organize and manage their lives through work, study, and leisure. It uses examples drawn directly from everyday life to explain and explore the concepts that underpin organizational behaviour.

Uniquely, this book presents distinct and highly contrasting perspectives on organizational behaviour, mainstream and critical, to provide students with a comprehensive and multi-perspective view of the subject

TABLE OF CONTENTS

KEY FEATURES

Under the guiding hand of Knights and Willmott, some of the best names in contemporary organization studies introduce OB to students in a clear and accessible way

Students are introduced to the orthodox view of organizational behaviour and then guided through a more critical alternative view

Introduces an integrating framework based upon **6 core concepts** – power, identity, knowledge, freedom, inequality, and insecurity – from which to discuss all the topics.

Highlights the different academic disciplines OB draws on, including sociology, psychology, politics and economics, emphasizing the multi-disciplinary nature of the subject

Concentrates on the core OB topics. It adopts a selective rather than exhaustive approach to the field of organizational behaviour and management.

Centralizes students' own experiences of organizations (e.g. schools, universities, service providers, employers) to demonstrate how work relations and management activities are not so distant from students own everyday lives

Market-researched pedagogical features, a four-colour text design, and a supportive supplements package provide a stimulating teaching and learning environment for lecturers and students

For more information, please contact The Marketing Department, Thomson Learning EMEA Ltd, High Holborn House, 50-51 Bedford Row, London, WC1R 4LR Tel: +44 (0) 207 067 2500 Fax: +44 (0) 207 067 2600
Web: www.thomsonlearning.co.uk Email: info@thomsonlearning.co.uk